Practical Applications of Soft Computing in Engineering

Fuzzy Logic Systems Institute (FLSI) Soft Computing Series

Series Editor: Takeshi Yamakawa *(Fuzzy Logic Systems Institute, Japan)*

 Soft Computing Series — Volume 4

Practical Applications of Soft Computing in Engineering

Editor

Sung-Bae Cho
Yonsei University, Korea

Fuzzy Logic
Systems Institute
(FLSI)

 **World Scientific**
Singapore • New Jersey • London • Hong Kong

Published by

World Scientific Publishing Co. Pte. Ltd.

P O Box 128, Farrer Road, Singapore 912805

USA office: Suite 1B, 1060 Main Street, River Edge, NJ 07661

UK office: 57 Shelton Street, Covent Garden, London WC2H 9HE

British Library Cataloguing-in-Publication Data
A catalogue record for this book is available from the British Library.

PRACTICAL APPLICATIONS OF SOFT COMPUTING IN ENGINEERING
FLSI Soft Computing Series — Volume 4

ISBN 981-02-4523-8

Printed in Singapore by World Scientific Printers

To

Yoon-Bin and Joon-Hee

Series Editor's Preface

The IIZUKA conference originated from the Workshop on Fuzzy Systems Application in 1988 at a small city, which is located in the center of Fukuoka prefecture in the most southern island, Kyushu, of Japan, and was very famous for coal mining until forty years ago. Iizuka city is now renewed to be a science research park. The first IIZUKA conference was held in 1990 and from then onward this conference has been held every two years. The series of these conferences played important role in the modern artificial intelligence. The workshop in 1988 proposed the fusion of fuzzy concept and neuroscience and by this proposal the research on neuro-fuzzy systems and fuzzy neural systems has been encouraged to produce significant results. The conference in 1990 was dedicated to the special topics, chaos, and nonlinear dynamical systems came into the interests of researchers in the field of fuzzy systems. The fusion of fuzzy, neural and chaotic systems was familiar to the conference participants in 1992. This new paradigm of information processing including genetic algorithms and fractals is spread over to the world as "Soft Computing".

Fuzzy Logic Systems Institute (FLSI) was established, under the supervision of Ministry of Education, Science and Sports (MOMBUSHOU) and International Trade and Industry (MITI), in 1989 for the purpose of proposing brand-new technologies, collaborating with companies and universities, giving university students education of soft computing, etc.

FLSI is the major organization promoting so called IIZUKA Conference, so that this series of books edited from IIZUKA Conference is named as FLSI Soft Computing Series.

The Soft Computing Series covers a variety of topics in Soft Computing and will propose the emergence of a post-digital intelligent systems.

Takeshi Yamakawa, Ph.D.
Chairman, IIZUKA 2000
Chairman, Fuzzy Logic Systems Institute

Volume Editor's Preface

Since Prof. Lotfi Zadeh initiated, soft computing has been exploited in depth as a promising approach to achieving the goal of developing intelligent systems. The basic idea of soft computing is not in a single powerful methodology but in combination of several effective technologies. Among them fuzzy logic, neural networks, and evolutionary computation are the three major players in soft computing. This new approach is characterized by a degree of tolerance for uncertainty and imprecision that we used to face with in real-world problems.

Due to this nature, soft computing has been put forth not only with the theoretical developments but also with a large variety of realistic applications to consumer products and industrial systems. Application of soft computing has provided the opportunity to integrate human-like vagueness and real-life uncertainty to an otherwise hard computer program. This edited volume highlights some of the recent developments on practical applications of soft computing in engineering problems. All the chapters are sophisticatedly designed and revised by international experts to achieve the overall goal of giving the readers an in-depth knowledge about the engineering applications of soft computing.

This book consists of 16 chapters which can be divided by three parts. Chapters 1 through 7 focus on the engineering applications with one of the soft computing techniques, and chapters 8 through 13 deal with the combination of more than one techniques. Last three chapters present novel applications with general soft computing methodologies. It is hoped that this book is helpful for a wide audience ranging from industrial researchers to academic scholars.

Seoul, Korea
Sung-Bae Cho
Volume Editor
April 16, 2000

Contents

Chapter 1
Automatic Detection of Microcalcifications in Mammograms Using a Fuzzy Classifier

A. P. Drijarkara, G. Naghdy, F. Naghdy

School of Electrical, Computer and
Telecommunications Engineering
University of Wollongong, Australia

Abstract

Breast cancer is one of the most common forms of cancer found in Australian women, and it has a high mortality rate. With proper diagnosis and treatment methods, the high mortality rate could be reduced. The telltale sign in the mammograms which signals the development of tumour is microcalcifications, and this is where the attention should be focused on. The focus of this paper is on developing a fuzzy detection method of microcalcifications in a mammogram. A review of the previous work in the area of automatic detection of microcalcifications is conducted. The issue of uncertainty in medical imaging is discussed and appropriateness of fuzzy set theory for such applications is justified. The algorithm developed in this work to identify microcalcifications in a mammogram is described. The performance of this algorithm is finally demonstrated and some conclusions are drawn.

Keywords: breast cancer, mammogram, microcalcifications, fuzzy set theory, medical imageing, fuzzy image processing,

1.1 Introduction

Breast cancer is one of the most common forms of cancer found in Australian women, and it has a high mortality rate. Statistics from the National Breast Cancer Council reveal the following figures [1]:

- In 1990-1992, 7516 women on average were diagnosed with breast cancer annually;
- 2458 women on average died of the disease each year;
- the mortality rate between 1982 and 1992 was around 19 to 20 per 100000 woman-years.

With proper diagnosis and treatment methods, the high mortality rate could be reduced. This requires early detection of the tumours. The most effective method to date for early detection of breast cancer is mammography, or x-ray imaging, because it can detect non-palpable tumours. Currently, most breast screening centres still use photographic films to capture the x-ray image. In the examination process, the films are displayed on light boxes and examined visually by radiologists. The telltale sign in the mammograms which signals the development of tumour is microcalcifications, and this is where the attention should be focused on.

Microcalcifications are small deposits of calcium in the breast tissue. A significant proportion of carcinomas are found to have microcalcifications, which lead to the detection of these carcinomas in early stages [2].

Microcalcifications appear in mammograms as small spots which are brighter than the background. Generally it is relatively easy to detect them visually. However, in many cases they are not quite visible because of small size and low contrast. Their average size is only about 300μm, and most are smaller than 700μm. Some of the microcalcifications in their earliest stage have very low contrast against the background.

Another aspect which makes microcalcification detection difficult is the large number of images to be viewed, and the fact that the majority of mammographic images are normal. That is, only a small proportion of images might contain microcalcification. The screening process has become an overwhelming task for the limited number of radiologists available. Moreover, research suggests that the radiologist's sensitivity diminishes with the increasing number of images to be examined [3].

With the government promoting regular breast screening for every woman in the high-risk age group (50 years and older), it follows that in the near future the number of mammograms will increase significantly. Consequently, there is a need for a more efficient method for examining the mammograms.

Computer-aided diagnosis systems have been introduced to assist in the mammogram analysis process. Since only a small proportion of mammograms contain abnormalities, a significant portion of the radiologists' time is spent looking at normal images. An automated system can be designed to examine the images and draw the attention of the experts to the suspicious regions, allowing them to concentrate on these suspicious cases.

Most of the computer-aided diagnosis systems designed so far are not intended to replace the human expert altogether. This is partly because of the complexity of the problem, which cannot be completely defined and translated into mathematical equations which a computer can process.

Mammogram analysis is one of many applications of image processing. However, it has unique problems associated with the small size and low contrast of microcalcifications. The variability of the objects in terms of size and shape requires flexibility of the detection process.

An example of 'conventional' image processing methods which is not applicable for this application is the binary thresholding method. Binary thresholding is a basic image processing technique for separating objects from the background in digital images, according to the pixel intensity. In mammography application, some of the objects of interest may have lower intensity than the background in another part of the image. Therefore a global binary thresholding cannot be applied.

The focus of this paper is on fuzzy detection of microcalcifications in a mammogram. Initially a review of the previous work in the area of automatic detection of microcalcifications will be conducted. The issue of uncertainty in medical imaging will be discussed and appropriateness of fuzzy set theory for such applications will be justified. The algorithm developed in this work to identify microcalcifications in a mammogram will be then described. The performance of this algorithm will be finally demonstrated and some conclusions will be drawn.

1.2 Background Study

Research in the area of computer-assisted mammogram analysis has been carried out for more than a decade. An extensive review of the publications has been carried out by Astley *et al.* [4]. More recent publications in this area will be reviewed in this section. 45

Astley categorises mammographic abnormalities which can signal breast cancer into three groups: discrete abnormalities, diffuse spatial changes, and physical changes which occur over time [4]. Most of the research on mammographic image processing has been focussed on discrete abnormalities, which can be subdivided into calcifications and masses.

Microcalcification, in particular, has received more attention due to its significance in the early detection of breast cancer. It is one of the earliest non-palpable sign of breast cancer [4] and can be found in about 30 to 40% of tumours [2]. Currently, the only reliable method for detecting microcalcifications is mammography.

Most of the reported approaches to microcalcification analysis are carried out through three stages [5]:
- detection and segmentation of objects,
- extraction of object image parameters,
- classification of the objects.

The first stage is aimed at locating the lesions or abnormalities in the image. However, not all lesions are necessarily a cause for concern. Many of these lesions are perhaps just normal or benign changes in the breast tissue, or even noises or dirt which embed themselves during the filming process. In the later stages of the analysis process, these objects are classified according to their potential malignancy.

Most of the early work in this area has tended to 'binarise' the decision making process. This means that each stage or sub-process in the analysis chain determines whether or not a particular object should be passed on to the next stage according to a set of criteria or parameters. Such approach makes it difficult to deal with the 'grey area' objects: that is, objects whose parameters or quantities may not fully qualify for a particular criterion but may be quite significant. In other words, these objects have some degree of uncertainties in them. An ideal system should identify a grey-area object and give an estimate about the uncertainties associated with it. Some of the more recent work in this area has been applying fuzzy logic theory to address this issue.

1.2.1 Microcalcification detection methods

The majority of microcalcification detection methods can be divided into two groups: those that search for the microcalcifications by removing the background texture and/or enhancing the small objects, and those that perform segmentation on the image and extract the features of the segmented region to find the microcalcifications.

1.2.2 Background removal and object enhancement

In this approach the detection is performed in two stages. The background structures are removed from the image and small objects resembling microcalcifications are enhanced. Then the extracted objects are further processed and enhanced, to sort out false objects and noises.

This approach uses the signal-processing paradigm, in which the components of the image are defined in terms of signals with different frequencies. An image or an image object is said to have a high frequency if the pixel intensity changes rapidly in the spatial domain. Low-frequency images, on the opposite, are made of pixels whose values differs only a little. In the case of microcalcification detection, the object of interest, which is the microcalcification itself, is considered to be a high-frequency signal. On the other hand, the background, which is made up of the normal breast tissue, is considered to be a low-frequency signal.

In signal processing, it is common to use filters to separate the components of a signal which have different frequencies. The simplest forms of filters are the high-pass filter and the low-pass filter. As the name suggests, a high-pass filter preserves the high frequency components while suppressing the low frequency ones. The opposite applies for the low-pass filters. Image processing, as an extension of signal processing, also uses filters in the spatial domain to separate the components of an image. There are various theories and methods to implement frequency-based filters in the spatial domain.

1.2.3 High-frequency analysis

The background removal process is essentially a high-pass filtering process. In the spatial domain, there are various techniques and methods to implement filtering.

Nishikawa [6] uses a technique called the *difference-image*, which uses both high-pass and low-pass filters. The raw image is processed separately through each filter. The low-pass filter suppresses small objects, while the high-pass filter emphasises them. The low-pass filtered image is then subtracted from the high-pass filtered image, leaving the objects on a relatively plain background. For the high-pass filter, a fixed 3x3 kernel or filtering mask is used. The weakness of this method is that lesions larger than the kernel size will be diminished both in size and intensity.

Dengler [7] also uses the difference-image technique for separating the objects. For the high-pass filter, a Gaussian-based filter is used. This has an advantage over Nishikawa's kernel since the width of the filter is adjustable to suit objects with different sizes. Still, in each operation only one particular size of the filter can be used. If the sizes of the objects vary widely, objects much larger or much smaller than the filter size might be missed or significantly diminished.

Mascio [8] uses two filters for analysing the high-frequency signals: a round *high-emphasis* filter, which essentially is the same as the difference-image technique, and *texture gist* filter, which combines the erosion and dilation processes. The first filter emphasises objects with rather crisp boundaries and which are bigger than several pixels, while the second emphasises small and textured details in the image.

1.2.4 Texture analysis

Another way of distinguishing microcalcifications from the background is by analysing the textures. One way to analyse texture is by considering the local non-uniformity of the pixels, as done by Cheng [9]. It is postulated that microcalcification pixels can be distinguished from normal breast tissue pixels according to their local non-uniformities, which are calculated from their local variances (a statistical quantity of the neighbouring pixels). In Cheng's method, the pixels with low variances are removed, leaving some curvilinear background structures, which is further removed by calculating the length and elongation of the curves. The report does not explain how these quantities are determined.

Wavelet analysis is another, more effective method for analysing textures and has emerged lately as one of the popular methods for analysing mammograms [10], [11], [12], [13]. Full explanation of the wavelet theory is beyond the scope of this paper. For the purpose of background, it suffices to say that any signal has two characteristic components: frequency and time. In image processing, the time domain is analogous to the spatial domain. The wavelet transform is able to extract the frequency and time components from a particular signal, using a basis function which has two parameters: resolution (or scale) and translation [11]. The challenge is to find the correct values for these parameters in order to emphasise the objects whose parameters resemble those of a microcalcification.

The work reported by Yoshida [12] is an extension of the work reported in [6], discussed above. Basically the approach is the same as in their previous work, except that the wavelet transform replaces the high-pass filter. A supervised learning method is used to tune the wavelet to get the correct parameters. The wavelet transform method is reported to have a sensitivity of 95%, compared to 85% previously.

Naghdy *et al.* [13] uses two-tier Gabor wavelet and neural network environment to detect the microcalcifications. The Gabor wavelet is not only sensitive to frequency but also to orientations of signals in the spatial domain. The parameters of the Gabor wavelet are tuned using a fuzzy adaptive-resonance-theory neural-network classifier. Although the reported classification rate is about 93%, the author acknowledges that the classification method is not generic enough to classify all images.

1.2.5 Post-processing of background-removed images

Background removal processes do not yet produce the end result. Although most of the irrelevant background has been removed, some 'ghosts' of the background textures still remain. Also, there may be some other objects which resembles the real lesions and therefore pass through the high-pass filters, but are not of interest to the diagnosis. These might be objects (such as dirt or dust) which come in the way during the filming process, grains on the film screen, or electrostatic noises in the digitisation process. They are usually either very small or have high contrast relative to the background. Post-processing is required to remove the irrelevant objects.

Most of the post-processing methods use morphological operators to remove noises based on the size; for example, objects smaller than three pixels. The contrast of the objects relative to the background is another selection criteria.

Binary thresholding is almost always used at some stage of the post-processing. Because of this, the end result is binarised to zero and one, representing the background and the objects, respectively. Binarisation has one disadvantage: it removes the inherent uncertainties of the objects. For example, some objects have diffuse boundaries. From a medical point of view, the crispiness (or the fuzziness) of an object's boundary may have some significance in distinguishing benign from malignant lesions.

Another disadvantage of the background removal approach is that the image is altered at each stage of the process. Some information may be lost at any stage. This information, which contributes to the uncertainties of the object, may be of secondary significance, nevertheless, it may help to create a more accurate classification.

1.2.6 Contour analysis

An approach which does not involve background removal is proposed by Bankman [14]. To help explain this approach, the mammogram is considered as a topographic map where the height of the "landscape" is represented by the intensity values of the pixels. In this visualisation, microcalcifications will appear as hills or peaks protruding from a relatively flat background.

The "hills" can be detected by firstly drawing lines connecting adjacent pixels with the same intensities, commonly known as contours. The area around a peak will have several concentric contours. A microcalcification can be identified from the contours by evaluating the number of concentric contours and the size of the outermost contour.

To determine whether a set of concentric contours is a microcalcification, three features are evaluated: departure, prominence and steepness. Departure is a measure of the sharpness of the perceived edge of the object, which also marks the object's perimeter. Prominence reflects the relative brightness of the object compared to the background. Steepness is the gradient of the landscape, which gives a measure of whether the object has a sharp edge or a diffuse one.

This approach has the potential to extract the information about the image, in its original state.

1.3 Object classification

The objective of analysing microcalcifications is to classify the detected objects into one of the following categories [2]:

- highly suspicious for malignancy,
- definitely benign, or
- indeterminate.

In the reviewed microcalcification detection methods, the classification is usually based on the features extracted from the objects after the detection stage. Some of the reviewed work in this area, however, focuses solely on the classification methods without describing the detection and segmentation process and how the features are extracted.

1.3.1 Features used for classification

The features used for classification can be divided into two groups [15]. The first consists of features with direct correlation with the characteristic radiographic signs of malignancy known to radiologists. These include, for example, the number of microcalcifications in a cluster, the size and shape of individual microcalcification, and so on.

The second group of features are those which give good separation between distributions of malignant and benign cases. These are the features which may not be readily obvious or could not be perceived consciously by a radiologist.

Usually these features have to be calculated from the statistics of the numerical values of the pixel in the microcalcification area. The two parameters of the wavelet transform can be considered to fall into this group.

1.3.2 Classification methods

Classification can be done simply by determining whether the values of the features fall in the corresponding acceptance range, as done by Bankman [14]. The acceptance range is usually determined from the statistics of a number of samples or a training set. Bankman [14] reports that with this simple approach and using three features, the algorithm is able to detect the clusters and reject the other structures and artifacts with no false cluster. However, the test set consists only of two images. It is not certain how the system will perform with a larger number of test cases.

A follow-up of the above work is reported in [16], in which the classification is done by a feedforward neural network. The features, which are used as inputs for the neural network, are the same as in the previous work, plus four additional features: distinctness, compactness, mean slope and area of the base contour. The modified system is now tested on 18 test images. The result is a 93% sensitivity with 1.56 false cluster per image.

Neural network is also used by Jiang [15] in conjunction with the detection method similar to that reported in [6]. The inputs of the neural network are the following features: cluster area and circularity, number of microcalcifications per cluster, and per unit area, mean distance between microcalcifications, mean area and effective volume of microcalcifications, and the second highest irregularity measured for microcalcifications in a cluster. The system correctly classifies 38 out of 40 malignant clusters, and 34 out of 67 benign clusters.

Fuzzy logic and its variations have also been used, eg. [5], [17], [18]. Murshed et al. [17], [18] uses a fuzzy-ARTMAP based classification system for detecting cancerous cells in microscopic images. Although the object is different, the system probably can be modified for classifying mammographic images as well. The fuzzy ARTMAP system is actually a derivative of the neural network and not a 'real' fuzzy logic.

Bothorel et al. [5] is one of the first to implement a 'real' fuzzy segmentation and classification algorithm for analysing microcalcifications. The fuzzy segmentation method preserves the ambiguities of an object by extracting several possible contours which mark the border of the object. Each of the possible contours will have different membership value, denoting the probability of the contour of being the true border. Therefore, in the classification stage, the classification of one object is based not only on the features of a single contour, but also of all the possible contours.

1.4 Uncertainty in medical imaging and fuzzy set theory

Uncertainty and imprecision are closely associated with medical imaging. Consider for example, the boundaries of objects such as microcalcifications in mammograms. The brightness intensity of the pixels at the microcalcification's perceived boundary changes gradually, rather than undergoing a sudden change from dark to bright. This causes the object to be perceived as having fuzzy boundaries. This makes it difficult, for example, to measure the size of the object, since the location of the exact boundary is uncertain.

Uncertainties can also affect the classification of the objects. For example, microcalcifications are classified according to the shape and size. Elongated microcalcifications are suspicious of malignancy, while round ones are perhaps benign. Microcalcifications are small, but not too small. If a MC is too small, then it may just be noise.

The above examples illustrate how the characteristics of natural objects are described in *linguistic variables* such as *small* and *round*. Now, how small is small? If an object with three-pixel width is small, is a four-pixel wide object also small? A slightly oval object may be regarded as being round, since no natural object can be perfectly round. But to what extent can an oval object be considered round, before it becomes a linear object? Clearly, there are no exact limits for linguistic variables used to describe natural objects. In other words, the linguistic variables are *imprecise*.

Crisp logic handles imprecise variables by drawing a border line to separate the objects into two classes, eg. a class of *small* objects and a class of *not small* objects. Suppose we have several objects, measuring from 1μm to 500μm, and suppose a 'small' object is defined as being smaller than 200μm. Then all objects measuring less than 200μm are considered small. Say we have four objects labelled *a, b, c,* and *d*, each measuring 1μm, 198μm, 201μm, and 500μm respectively. Objects *a* and *b* will be considered small, while *c* and *d* are considered not small. The irony is that while *b* is only slightly smaller than *c*, they fall into the different classes. On the other hand, *a*, which is much smaller than *b*, is considered the same as *b*.

Fuzzy logic or fuzzy set theory avoids such irony by assigning a *degree of membership* to each object. Thus we can say that object *a* is small while object *b* is only slightly small. Formally, this will be denoted as: Object *a* belongs to the class of small object with high degree of membership, while object *b* belong to the same class, but with a lower degree of membership.

1.5 Applications of fuzzy theory in image understanding

Fuzzy logic has been widely (and chiefly) developed and applied in control systems. Many commercial electrical appliances have been designed with fuzzy logic control and are claimed to be more versatile than those designed with conventional logic. Fuzzy logic has also been studied for use in image processing and analysis as well, as reported in many publications.

One important reason for investigating the use of fuzzy logic in image processing is stated by Tizhoosh: "… fuzzy logic provides us with a mathematical framework for representation and processing of the expert knowledge" [19]. Thus fuzzy logic provides the means to bridge the gap between the imprecision of the linguistic variables and the numerical nature of the digital images. Tizhoosh further breaks down the area of fuzzy image processing into several fields. The fields which have been most widely studied and applied are *fuzzy clustering* and *rule-based systems*.

1.5.1 Fuzzy clustering

Fuzzy clustering is commonly applied for classification of data. Clustering is the process of grouping similar data. In image-processing applications, the pixels of an image can be regarded as individual data with their unique attributes, such as colour and location. Fuzzy clustering can be applied to perform segmentation of an image. The pixels can be clustered with respect to attributes such as colour and location, and the resulting clusters will represent the segments of the image. Segments can be clustered further with other segments to perform a higher level interpretation of the image. Examples of fuzzy clustering for image segmentation are reported in [20], [21], [22], and [23].

1.5.2 Rule-based systems

The rule-based systems consist of three basic components [24]: a set of rules, a data base and an inference engine. The rules are derived from expert's knowledge of the world and usually defined as a set of if-then rules, expressed in the form "if *condition* then *action*". The data base contains numerical data and provides the measures with which to assess the condition. The inference engine is the method with which the rules are assessed to produce the decision. While the first component (the rules) is common in any computerised system, the data base and the inference engine for fuzzy system are different from their 'conventional' counterparts. The difference is that the condition is measured in fuzzy, rather than crisp values, and the inference engine is able to incorporate this fuzziness in the decision-making.

A Rule-based system differs from clustering approach in the following way. Clustering system is basically an unsupervised learning system which creates its own rule by searching for a pattern in the data. In a rule-based system, on the other hand, the rules are derived from an expert knowledge.

The most common application of rule-based system is in the classification or recognition of objects or image segments, which can be considered as a high-level process. Usually the images are already segmented and the relevant features calculated. Examples of high-level fuzzy rule-based systems are [25] and [26].

The rule-based systems are also applied in low - and mid-level operations, which analyse the image at pixel level and the pixel neighbourhood. Examples of low-level fuzzy rule-based systems are reported in [27], [24], [28], [29], which include fuzzy edge detection, noise filtering and contrast enhancement.

1.5.3 Fuzzy logic in mammogram analysis

A few examples of the application of fuzzy logic in mammogram analysis were discussed in the previous section. Fuzzy methods have also been used to segment and detect other types of lesions, namely applications of fuzzy theory in image understanding of masses [30], [31]. All of these examples are mostly confined to the use of fuzzy in the high-level processes. In this work, fuzzy logic approach is applied to low-level operation in mammogram analysis, specifically for the detection of microcalcifications.

1.6 Fuzzy microcalcification detector

The system studied and developed in this work employs a rule-based system to detect and classify microcalcifications. At this stage, the work is more concentrated on the detection process. The rules are formulated based on the description of the expert of the microcalcifications. Fuzzy approach is used from the lowest level to the highest level of the image processing. The purpose of the study is to explore whether fuzzy logic theory can produce a more effective and less complex method for mammogram analysis.

Assumption in the formulation of the fuzzy rules is that if a microcalcification can be described specifically by an expert, it should be possible to recognise it using that description. A "specific" description means that all the distinguishing features are taken into account, although each feature may not have an exact measurement. For example, to distinguish a grape from a plum, it is sufficient to state that a grape is usually smaller than a plum, without specifying the exact size. In this work, the microcalcifications will be described in terms of their features commonly used by a radiologist to describe them.

1.7 Overview of the fuzzy method

The methodology developed in this study, is based on a number of concepts developed and validated in the previous work. One is Bankman's topographic approach, in which an object is visualised as a peak projecting prominently with respect to the local surround [14]. Using this concept a model of the object of interest can be developed. The fuzzy similarity analysis [32], is then applied to compare the detected object with the available models of a microcalcification. A high similarity score indicates that the detected object is a microcalcification. This concept is illustrated in Figure 1.

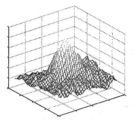

Figure 1. A typical microcalcification and its isometric plot.

A number of stages can be identified in the
- Locating the object. During this step the location of a potential object is defined in terms of the coordinates of one pixel from the object, ideally the one located in its centre. This step is achieved by applying *fuzzy peak detector*, which will be described later.
- Measuring the relevant features of the object.
- Performing classification based on the measured features. The classification process takes place in two stages. Initially, in a coarse selection procedure, the objects which are definitely not microcalcifications, are removed. In the second step the remaining objects' are graded according to the degree of their malignancy.

In developing the algorithm, the following characteristics of the microcalcifications have been used to distinguish them from other mammographic objects:
- **Brightness or pixel intensity.** The intensity at the centre of a microcalcification is much higher than the intensity of the pixels in the background surrounding the microcalcification.
- **Visible border.** The border of a microcalcification, though fuzzy in some cases, is still sharp enough to distinguish the object from the background. A border corresponds to a sudden change of intensity between the adjacent pixels. This is used to distinguish a microcalcification from some background structures, which, although resemble a peak in their topographic representation, do not have a visible border.
- **Distinction from noise and artifacts.** Noises and artifacts have the same semblance as microcalcifications, but they can be distinguished by size and contrast. Such objects usually are

smaller than microcalcifications and have much higher contrast. In other words, they are more "spiky".

1.8 Fuzzy detection

The core of the detection process is the Fuzzy Peak Detector, the purpose of which is to locate the peaks in the image. The peak detector is applied to a select group of candidate pixels. To eliminate peak-like objects other than genuine microcalcifications, a fuzzy edge detector is used to determine whether the objects have distinctive edges.

1.8.1 Fuzzy Peak Detector

The Fuzzy Peak Detector (FPD) developed in this work is a fuzzy-based neighbourhood operator which analyses a pixel in an image and determines whether it is part of microcalcification, based on the relationships between that pixel and the surrounding pixels. The generic term "peak detector" is used since the shape of a microcalcification resembles that of a peak. The FPD is designed in the similar fashion as a fuzzy edge detector [27], [28], [29], [30]. The fuzzy edge detector developed by Li *et al.* [29] is briefly explained below as a basis for the FPD.

Typically, a *neighbourhood operator* such as an edge detector determines whether a pixel in an image has a certain quality by evaluating the other pixels around that pixel within a window of observation. In general, the window of observation has a square shape with a size of N × N pixels, where N is usually an odd number. The pixel under consideration is located at the centre of the window. Unless otherwise stated, it will be labelled Q throughout this chapter. All the other pixels within the window are referred to as the *neighbour pixels* or just *neighbours*.

In the Li's edge detector algorithm, the size of the window is 3×3. The pixel under examination is marked Q and the neighbours are marked with numbers as in Figure 2.

3	4	5
2	Q	6
1	8	7

Figure 2. The window used by Li [29] for edge detection.

Fuzzy rules are then defined to describe the typical relationships between Q and the neighbours if Q were part of an edge. The relationship is defined in terms of the luminance or brightness difference between Q and the neighbours and is denoted *Dif_lum*, that is, *Dif_lum(i)* is equal to the luminance difference between *Q* and pixel *i*, for *i* = 1, ..., 8. *Dif_lum(i)* can be defined in two fuzzy labels: *NEG* and *POS*, where *NEG* means pixel *i* is much darker than *Q*, and *vice versa* for *POS*.

There are 8 rules for describing all the possible combinations of negative and positive luminances in a window containing an edge region. The first rule for detecting an edge is defined as Rule 1 below as an example. This rule represents the case when there is an edge running diagonally from the top-left corner to the bottom-right corner.

Rule 1:

If   *Dif_lum(1) is NEG and Dif_lum(2) is NEG and Dif_lum(8) is NEG and*

            Dif_lum(4) is POS and Dif_lum(5) is POS and Dif_lum(6) is POS
Then   *Lum(Q) is BLACK*

The outputs of Rule 1 and the other seven rules are defined in terms of *Lum(Q)* which determines the grey-level intensity of *Q* in the output image. *BLACK* is a fuzzy label denoting that *Q* has a low grey-level intensity. The truth of Rule 1 when applied to a particular image window is determined as follows. The membership function for *NEG* is applied to *Dif_lum(1)*, *Dif_lum(2)* and *Dif_lum(8)* and the resulting membership value is denoted $\mu_1(1)$, $\mu_1(2)$ and $\mu_1(8)$, respectively. Similarly, the membership function for *POS* is applied to *Dif_lum(4)*, *Dif_lum(5)*, and *Dif_lum(6)* and denoted $\mu_1(4)$, $\mu_1(5)$ and $\mu_1(6)$, respectively. The values of $\mu_1(1)$, $\mu_1(2)$, $\mu_1(8)$, $\mu_1(4)$, $\mu_1(5)$, and $\mu_1(6)$ represent the degree to which the respective neighbours satisfy Rule 1. These are averaged to give the weight *w(1)*, which is then defuzzified to give the value of *Lum(Q)*.

An example of images where *Lum(Q)* will have high membership value for *BLACK* is given in Figure 3. This image can also be considered as one of the templates or models for image regions containing edge pixels.

Figure 3. An image for which Rule 1 will give high membership value for BLACK.

Consider if the above fuzzy inference method is applied to microcalcification detection with some modification. Since the size of a microcalcification is usually several pixels wide, the window of observation need to be much bigger than the one used for edge detection. A hypothetical window for microcalcification detection and an arbitrary labelling of its pixels is depicted in Figure 4. Notice that the neighbours around the centre are labelled with prefix *b*, while the rest of the neighbours are labelled with prefix *a*.

a_1	a_2	a_3	a_4	a_5	a_6	a_7	a_8	a_9
a_{10}	a_{11}	a_{12}	a_{13}	a_{14}	a_{15}	a_{16}	a_{17}	a_{18}
a_{19}	a_{20}	a_{21}	a_{22}	a_{23}	a_{24}	a_{25}	a_{26}	a_{27}
a_{28}	a_{29}	a_{30}	b_1	b_2	b_3	a_{31}	a_{32}	a_{33}
a_{34}	a_{35}	a_{36}	b_4	Q	b_5	a_{37}	a_{38}	a_{39}
a_{40}	a_{41}	a_{42}	b_6	b_7	b_8	a_{43}	a_{44}	a_{45}
a_{46}	a_{47}	a_{48}	a_{49}	a_{50}	a_{51}	a_{52}	a_{53}	a_{54}
a_{55}	a_{56}	a_{57}	a_{58}	a_{59}	a_{60}	a_{61}	a_{62}	a_{63}
a_{64}	a_{65}	a_{66}	a_{67}	a_{68}	a_{69}	a_{70}	a_{71}	a_{72}

Figure 4. A hypothetical window for microcalcification detection.

Rule 1 will need to be modified as Rule 2 below.

Rule 2*: for the image illustrated in Figure 4:*
    IF   *pixel b_j is BRIGHT (for all j = 1 to 8), and*
               pixel a_k is DARK (for all k =1 to 72),
    THEN   *Q is a microcalcification.*

Figure 5 depicts an image window which matches Rule 2's description as a microcalcification.

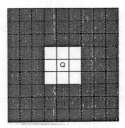

Figure 5. A hypothetical microcalcification image

In Figure 5, the white-coloured pixels represents the microcalcification which Rule 2 can detect, which means this rule can only detect a microcalcification with a square shape measuring 3 pixel wide and 3 pixel high. To detect a microcalcification with a different size or shape, another rule will be required. Since the size and shape of microcalcifications can vary greatly, this method will require a large number of rules to cover every possible variation. Each rule will specify to which neighbours the membership function *BRIGHT* is applied; and to which ones *DARK* is applied. Furthermore, the size of the window needs to be much larger if the image has a high resolution. The number of inputs in the rules is equal to the number of pixels in the window. For example, **Rule 2** will have 80 inputs in total. The large number of rules and the number of input in each rule make it impractical to apply this kind of rules for peak detecting purpose.

To simplify the computation, Rule 2 can be generalised as follows. Consider that in Rule 2, all pixels with the prefix *a* are those which are *far* from *Q*, and those with the *b* prefix are *near Q*. Then Rule 2 can be redefined as Rule 2a below.

Rule 2a:

IF   *the neighbour pixels which are NEAR Q are BRIGHT, and*
             the neighbour pixels which are FAR from Q are DARK,

THEN   *Q is a microcalcification.*

To determine the degree of truth of Rule 2a when it is applied to a particular image window, the following variables and labels need to be defined.

- Let p_n be the set of neighbour pixels in the window of observation of size N×N centred at pixel Q; and let p_i be a member of p_n; $i = 1, ..., M$; M = the number of neighbour pixels in the window.
- Let d_i be the spatial distance between p_i and Q, measured in pixel units.
- Let g_i be the relative grey-level intensity of p_i with respect to Q. If *Int(x)* denotes the grey level intensity of *x*, then $g_i = Int(p_i) / Int(Q)$. In other words, g_i is normalised to [0 1].
- Let *NEAR, FAR, DARK* and *BRIGHT* be the fuzzy linguistic variables to describe neighbour p_i with respect to Q. *NEAR* and *FAR* are functions of d_i, while *DARK* and *BRIGHT* are functions of g_i. The membership functions of these variables are shown in Figure 6. The fuzzy membership value $\mu_{NEAR}(p_i)$ will denote the degree to which neighbour p_i is *NEAR* (in everyday language, "how near p_i is"). Similarly, $\mu_{FAR}(p_i)$, $\mu_{DARK}(p_i)$ and $\mu_{BRIGHT}(p_i)$ are the membership values of the variables *FAR, DARK* and *BRIGHT* for neighbour p_i, respectively.

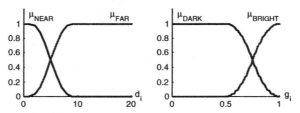

Figure 6. Membership functions for NEAR, FAR, DARK and BRIGHT.

Let $\mu_{MC}(Q)$ denote the degree of membership of pixel Q in the set of microcalcification pixels; and let $\mu(p_i)$ denote the degree to which neighbour p_i satisfies the antecedent part (the if-clause) of Rule 2a. Then Rule 2a can be written in fuzzy mathematical form as follows:

$$\mu_{MC}(Q) = \mu(p_1) \wedge \mu(p_2) \wedge \ldots \wedge \mu(p_M) \qquad (1)$$

where '$\wedge$' denotes the fuzzy-and operator. That is, pixel Q has a high membership degree in a microcalcification if all neighbours satisfy the condition of Rule 2a to high degrees.

The antecedent of Rule 2a requires that near neighbours to be bright, and far ones to be dark. This suggests that there are two groups of neighbours: *near* and *far*, to which different membership functions are to be applied: μ_{BRIGHT} to the *near* group, and μ_{DARK} to the *far* group. The value of $\mu(p_1)$ would be equal to $\mu_{BRIGHT}(p_1)$ if p_1 were near; otherwise, it would be equal to $\mu_{DARK}(p_1)$. However, it is not possible to determine which neighbours are near and which are far by separating them into two crisp groups (*near* and *far*), since crisp separation would violate the basic principle of fuzzy set theory.

In order to avoid crisp separation while still allowing the evaluation of μ_{BRIGHT} or μ_{DARK} on the appropriate group of neighbours, the linguistic variables for brightness and distance can be evaluated by combining the fuzzy membership functions using fuzzy logical operators.

To determine if a *near* neighbour is *bright*, let $\mu_{NB}(p_i)$ denote the degree of p_i being near and bright. That is, if p_i is *near* and is also *bright*, then $\mu_{NB}(p_i)$ is high. This is defined as

$$\mu_{NB}(p_i) = \mu_{BRIGHT}(p_i) \wedge \mu_{NEAR}(p_i) \qquad (2)$$

Conversely, let $\mu_{FD}(p_i)$ denote the degree of p_i being far and dark. If p_i is *far* and is also *dark*, then $\mu_{FD}(p_i)$ is high. This is defined as

$$\mu_{FD}(p_i) = \mu_{DARK}(p_i) \wedge \mu_{FAR}(p_i) \qquad (3)$$

Since $\mu_{NEAR}(p_i)$ and $\mu_{FAR}(p_i)$ are opposites, it follows that $\mu_{NB}(p_i)$ and $\mu_{FD}(p_i)$ cannot be both high at the same time (although they can be both low).

If either $\mu_{NB}(p_i)$ or $\mu_{FD}(p_i)$ is high, it infers that p_i belongs to one of these groups: the bright near neighbours, or the dark far neighbours. In either case, this means that p_i is one of the neighbours which satisfies the antecedent of Rule 2a. Therefore $\mu(p_i)$ in Eq. 1 can be defined as:

$$\mu(p_i) = \mu_{NB}(p_i) \vee \mu_{FD}(p_i) \qquad (4)$$

where '$\vee$' denotes the fuzzy-or operator; thus $\mu(p_i)$ denotes the degree to which p_i satisfies one of the antecedent of Rule 2a. Now the membership value of

$\mu_{MC}(Q)$ can be determined. The numerical value of $\mu_{MC}(Q)$ is obtained by averaging the values of $\mu(p_i)$ for all i:

$$\mu_{MC}(Q) = (\Sigma_i \mu(p_i)) / M \qquad (5)$$

Figure 7 illustrates the fuzzy inference process. Figure 7(a) represents the intensity profile (the intensities of the pixels along a line in the image) of a microcalcification. Figure 7(b) shows the image normalised to between zero and one. Figure 7(c) shows the degree of the pixels belonging to *BRIGHT* (solid line) and *DARK* (broken line). Figure 7(e) shows the degree of the pixels belonging to *NEAR* (solid line) and *FAR* (broken line). Figure 7(d) shows the and-combination of *BRIGHT* and *NEAR*, and Figure 7(f) shows the and-combination of *DARK* and *FAR*. Notice that if Figure 7(f) are combined with an 'or' or maximum operator, the result will have high values for most of the pixels.

Figure 8 illustrates the same process, applied on a non-microcalcification image. Notice that in this case, the or-combination image of Figure 8(d) and Figure 8 (f) will not have high values on the pixels which are far from the centre pixel.

In this application, the window size is 21×21 pixels. This is based on the average size of microcalcifications. Even if a microcalcification is actually wider than 21 pixels, the portion of the microcalcification which is covered by the window already has the characteristics of a peak which can be detected by the peak detector.

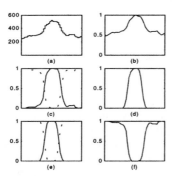

Figure 8. The fuzzy inference method applied to a microcalcification image.

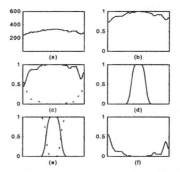

Figure 7. The same inference method applied to a non-microcalcification image.

1.8.2 Choosing candidate pixels

Candidate pixels are the image pixels to which the FPD is to be applied. Like many window-based image-processing operations, the FPD operates on a whole image by shifting the operator window to analyse every pixel in the image. However, only a small proportions of pixels in an image may have a high probability of being a microcalcification. To reduce the processing time, the peak detector is only applied to a select group of pixels called the candidate pixels.

The candidate pixels are the 'local peaks', which are pixels with higher intensity than the surrounding pixels. That is, if a window of size N×N is applied on a pixel x, and x has the highest intensity in that window, then x is a local peak. Every microcalcification has at least one pixel which is brighter than the surrounding pixels. Taking only local peaks as candidate pixels ensures that all potential microcalcifications are processed by the peak detector while reducing computation time.

1.8.3 Fuzzy membership functions

The basic membership functions for μ_{BRIGHT} and μ_{FAR} take the form of a S-function, while μ_{DARK} and μ_{NEAR} use the Z-function (the inverse of S-function) whose parameters are the break points as illustrated in Figure 9. These break points are determined in a fashion similar to the fuzzy C-means clustering approach [33].

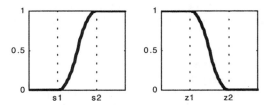

Figure 9. The S-function (left) and Z-function (right).
Points s1, s2 and z1, z2 are the parametric break points.

In the C-means clustering approach, the *support* of the fuzzy membership function for a class or cluster C, with respect to a variable X, is determined by the distribution of the data belonging to cluster C. The resulting membership function is a triangular function $f_\Delta(X)$ with its peak corresponding to the centre value of cluster C and the cut-off point determined by the variance of cluster C.

In our application, since most of the membership functions only need to distinguish between two classes or clusters of objects (for example, small vs. large), the membership functions are implemented by the S- and Z-functions, which can be considered as a fuzzy approach for binary thresholding.

Figure 10 illustrates the formation of a membership function. Suppose there are collections of objects which can be measured in terms of a variable x_l. Objects with small value of x_l are to be classified into Cluster 1, and those with large value of x_l into Cluster 2. To define the membership function for Cluster 1 based on the Z-function, the first cut-off points (z_1) is determined by member of Cluster 2 having the smallest value of x_l, while the second cut-off point (z_2) is determined by the member of Cluster 1 with the largest value of x_l.

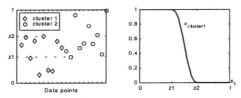

Figure 10. A membership function for Cluster 1 in terms of x_1.

The method of obtaining the fuzzy membership functions described here is used as a starting point only. In most cases, the values of the break points have to be refined by experiments to get the optimum separation between clusters.

1.8.4 Fuzzy edge detector

Many of the objects detected by the peak detector are normal background tissues which incidentally are brighter than the surrounding. As previously discussed, a real microcalcification can be distinguished from the normal tissue by the presence of a visible border. The border is extracted through the following steps:

- gradient extraction,
- ridge thinning,
- and fuzzy thresholding.

A gradient is the difference between the intensities of adjacent pixels. An edge can be observed when two adjacent pixels have significant intensity difference and therefore it corresponds to part of the image where the gradient is high. The gradient of an image can be extracted by numerical convolution using a gradient operator. Full explanation about convolution and gradient operators (such as the Sobel and Prewitt operators) can be found in many image-processing textbooks and will not be detailed here. The convolution masks used in this application are displayed in Figure 11.

0	0	0
1	0	-1
0	0	0

1/√2	0	0
0	0	0
0	0	-1/√2

0	1	0
0	0	0
0	-1	0

0	0	1/√2
0	0	0
-1/√2	0	0

Figure 11. The convolution masks used for gradient extraction.

Figure 12(a) shows an example of microcalcification. Figure 12(b) shows the result of a gradient extraction. It can be seen that the edges in Figure 12(a) correspond to the 'ridges' in Figure 12(b). The ridges are thinned to get a more accurate representation of the edges. Ridge thinning is performed by comparing every pixel in the gradient image with its neighbours in a 2×2 window. The pixel with the lowest intensity within the 2×2 window are assigned a new value of zero. This leaves the vertices or skeletons of the ridges, as shown in Figure 12(c).

(a) Original   (b) Gradient

(c) Thinned gradient   (d) Fuzzy thresholded

Figure 12. (a) Image of a microcalcification; (b) Gradient image; (c) Thinned gradient image, (d) Fuzzy-thresholded image, revealing the edges.

The thinned gradient image still contains residual ridges of the background image. These can be removed by thresholding the ridges at a certain level. It can be observed that the ridges which make the edges have significantly higher intensities than the background ridges. It can also be seen that the high-intensity ridges make up only a small proportion of the ridges in the image. The optimum threshold level appears to be related to the average value and the variance of the ridges. Figure 13 shows the histogram of the ridges, where point h_0 marks the value equal to the sum of the average and the standard deviation. Point h denotes the optimum threshold for this image and can be defined as follows:

$$h = m_r + k\, \sigma_r \qquad\qquad (6)$$

where m_r and σ_r denote the mean value and the standard deviation of the ridges, and k is a coefficient. The fuzzy membership function for edge pixels is then defined as an S-function with break points h_1 and h_2, each having the same relationships as in Eq. [6] with coefficients k_1 and k_2, respectively. The values of k_1 and k_2 are determined by c-means clustering from the values of k for other microcalcification samples. The result of the fuzzy thresholding is shown in Figure 12 (d).

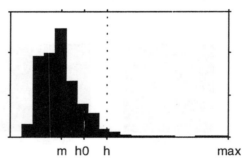

Figure 13. Histogram of the ridges in Figure 12 4(c).
m = mean; h_0 = mean + standard deviation; h = optimum threshold

The presence of border around an object can be determined quantitatively by counting the extracted edge pixels. The edge pixels are given weights which are the inverse of their spatial distance from the centre of the object. This weighing factor is necessary to normalise the edge-pixel counts of objects with different sizes. For example, suppose there were two circular objects with radii of r and $2r$, respectively. The perimeter of the larger object would be twice as long as the smaller one's, and therefore the edge-pixel count of the larger object would be twice as many as the other. By weighing the edge-pixel count by $1/r$ for the smaller object and by $1/2r$ for the larger object, the edge-pixel counts of both objects would be comparable.

Once again, c-means clustering is used to separate the true microcalcifications from the false objects based on the edge-pixel counts.

1.9 Validation of the fuzzy microcalcification detector

The proposed fuzzy microcalcification detector has been tested using a set of digitised mammogram from a database published by the Lawrence Livermore National Library in the US. This database contains 50 sets of mammogram images. Each set represents one patient and contains four images: the images of right and left breasts, each one viewed in two directions. The images are digitised from x-ray films at 35µm pixel size with 4096 grey levels (12 bits). Some of the images contain calcification, and a proportion of the calcifications are clustered. Each image with calcifications is accompanied by a truth file marking the individual calcifications. If the calcifications are clustered, there is another truth file marking the extent of the clusters. The database has one shortcoming: not all the individual calcifications are marked in the truth files.

The primary objective at this stage has been to identify the individual microcalcifications, regardless of whether they are malignant or benign.

1.10 Experimental results

The developed algorithm was applied to 40 images, all containing Microcalcifications. A number of images had clusters some which have been classified as malignant. The summary of results is illustrated in Table 1 and 2.

The results produced by the algorithm have been validated against the truth files provided by the mammogram library. The critical characteristics studied in this experiment are the sensitivity of the microcalcification detector. The algorithm has been applied only to the section of an image with tagged objects rather than the whole image. The objective has been to detect all the tagged microcalcifications and also to reduce the number of false objects.

1.10.1 Sensitivity analysis

The sensitivity of the system is measured by the number of objects missed missed, either in terms of individual microcalcifications or clusters. In most of the images, the false negative (FN) rates are very low compared to the true positive (TP). Hence an image with missed microcalcification would still be flagged as suspicious. The overall FN rate is summarised in Tables 3 and 4.

A number of images have a rather high false positive rates, which in some cases result in missing the cluster. A cluster is considered to be missed if less than 3 microcalcifications from that cluster are detected. The missed microcalcifications have a very small size and a low contrast. Individually, they are almost indistinguishable from noise. The peak detector and the edge detector have failed to detect them due to their characteristics being similar to the characteristics of noise or normal objects. These objects can only be recognised as microcalcifications when they are considered as part of a cluster.

1.10.2 Selectivity analysis

Selectivity is a measure of the detected false objects, often referred to as false positive (FP). The experiments carried out have identified some untagged objects in the truth files as microcalcifications. Since there are genuine microcalcifications not tagged by the truth files, not all of those identified objects are FP's. In such cases, we have used our own judgement to confirm whether a detected object is a true positive or a false positive. For some objects there is doubt about their status hence they are categorised as ambiguous.

The false positive rates are generally low compared to the true positive. In most cases, they may not cause false alarm. In the case of *bhrm* the false positive rate is too high due to isolation of the false objects from each other. In another case, *bolc*, the false objects are near the true objects, and the image would have been tagged as suspicious by the true objects anyway.

It should be also noted that the false positive rates reported here may be lower than actual, as the tests have not performed on the whole image, though a significant segment of 'normal' areas have been included.

1.11   Conclusions

This paper has demonstrated the feasibility of applying low-level fuzzy image processing to mammograms. The result obtained so far from the developed technology is quite promising, although there are some cases where the fuzzy rule-base fails. The sensitivity rate is quite high, considering the simplicity of the algorithm.

The images with which the system is validated have very high resolution, both in terms of pixel size and grey-level intensity. The higher information content enables the more subtle lesions to be revealed, but also presents more noise which resembles the subtle lesions.

The microcalcification detector fails to detect the fine and subtle microcalcifications which become part of clusters. To address this problem, the detection system needs to take into account the characteristics of the area surrounding the objects, which may include some form of textural analysis.

One of the drawback of the fuzzy system is the complexity of the computation, despite the simplicity of the rules which make up the fuzy system. The complexity is reflected on the amount of computing time required. This is largely due to the fact that conventional computers are designed for crisp logic systems, and therefore are not readily suitable for fuzzy logic systems.

Table 1. Result of microcalcification detection

Image	no. of tagged MC	MC missed	no. of tagged cluster	cluster with < 3 MC detected	False positive	Ambi-guous	Note
aklcc	6	0	0	0	1	1	
akrcc	8	0	3	0	0	4	
akrml	5	0	2	0	0	0	
allcc	8	1	0	0	2	8	
alrcc	11	0	2	0	0	0	
anlml	3	0	1	0	0	0	
anrml	4	0	0	0	2	0	
aprcc	3	0	2	1	0	0	i
aprml	4	1	1	1	0	0	i
aqlcc	3	3	1	1	0	0	i
aqlml	6	0	1	0	0	0	
aslcc	2	0	1	0	0	0	
aslml	3	0	1	0	0	0	
atrcc	9	4	0	0	0	0	
atrml	10	2	4	2	0	0	ii
aurcc	8	0	1	0	0	0	
awrcc	7	0	0	0	0	0	
awrml		0	0	0	0	0	
balcc	2	0	0	0	0	0	
balml	2	0	0	0	0	1	
bbrcc	2	0	1	0	0	0	
bbrml	3	0	1	0	0	0	
bflcc	2	0	0	0	1	3	
bglcc	9	4	2	0	0	0	
bglml	5	0	1	0	0	1	
bgrcc	5	0	1	0	0	2	
bhlcc	2	0	0	0	0	0	
bhlml	4	0	0	0	1	3	
bhrml	4	0	0	0	3	2	iii
bilcc	2	0	0	0	0	0	
bilml	3	0	0	0	1	1	
bircc	5	0	0	0	1	2	

i Missed cluster contains very fine microcalcifications.

ii 1 missed cluster is near enough to another one. 2nd missed cluster contains very fine microcalcifications.

iii FPs are isolated.

Table 2. Results of microcalcification detection

Image	no. of tagged MC	MC missed	no. of tagged cluster	cluster with < 3 MC detected	False positive	Ambi-guous	Note
birml	4	0	0	0	0	6	
bmrml	1	0	0	0	0	0	
bolcc	9	0	0	0	4	7	iv
bolml	6	0	0	0	1	3	
borcc	3	0	0	0	0	5	
borml	2	1	0	0	0	0	
bqlml	6	0	0	0	0	0	
bwrcc	3	0	1	0	0	0	

Table 3. False Negative rate for microcalcifications.

No. of MC	No. of missed MC	FN rate
185	12	93.5%

Table 4. False Negative rate for clusters.

No. of cluster	No. of missed cluster	FN rate
29	5	82.8%

References

[1] A. Kricker, P. Jelfs, "Breast cancer in Australian women 1921-1994: Summary", [online]   http://www.nbcc.org.au/pages/info/resource/nbccpubs/bc21-94/summary.htm, January 1999.

[2] P. Sylvia H. Heywang-Köbrunner, "Diagnostic breast imaging: mammography, sonography, magnetic resonance imaging, and interventional procedures", Stuttgart, Thieme, 1997.

[3] H. D. Li, M. Kallergi, L. P. Clarke, V. K. Jain, R. A. Clark, "Markov random field for tumor detection in digital mammography," IEEE Transactions on Medical Imaging, vol. 14, no. 3, p. 565-76, 1995.

[4] S. Astley, I. Hutt, S. Adamson, P. Miller, P. Rose, C. Boggis, C. Taylor, T. Valentine, J. Davies, and J. Armstrong, "Automation in mammography: computer vision and human perception," State of the art in digital mammographic image analysis, ed. K. W. Bowyer and S. Astley, World Scientific, Singapore, 1994.

---

iv FPs are near to TP.

[5]   S. Bothorel, B. B. Meunier, S. A. Muller, "Fuzzy logic based approach for semiological analysis of microcalcifications in mammographic images," International Journal of Intelligent Systems. 12(11-12):819-848, 1997 Nov-Dec.

[6]   R. M. Nishikawa, M. L. Giger, K. Doi, C. J. Vyborny, R. A. Schmidt, "Computer-aided detection of clustered microcalcifications on digital mammograms," Medical & Biological Engineering & Computing, no 33, pp 174-178, 1995.

[7]   J. Dengler, S. Behrens, and J. F. Desaga, "Segmentation of microcalcifications in mammograms," IEEE Transactions on Medical Imaging, vol. 12, no. 4, pp 634-642, 1993.

[8]   L. N. Mascio, J. M. Hernandez, C. M. Logan, "Automated analysis for microcalcifications in high resolution digital mammograms", [Online], http://www-dsed.llnl.gov/documents/imaging/jmhspie93.html, 7 January 1998.

[9]   H. D. Cheng, M. L. Yui, R. I. Freimanis, "A new approach to microcalcification detection in digital mammograms," 1996 IEEE Nuclear Science Symposium, 1996.

[10]   D. Nesbitt, F. Aghdasi, R. Ward, J. Morgan-Parkes, "Detection of microcalcifications in digitized mammogram film images using wavelet enhancement and local adaptive false positive suppression," IEEE Pacific Rim Conference on Communications, Computers, and Signal Processing. Proceedings, 1995.

[11]   G. G. Lee, C. H. Chen, "A multiresolution wavelet analysis and Gaussian Markov random field algorithm for breast cancer screening of digital mammography," 1996 IEEE Nuclear Science Symposium Conference Record, 1996.

[12]   H. Yoshida, Wei Zhang, W. Cai, K. Doi, R. M. Nishikawa, M. L. Giger, "Optimizing wavelet transform based on supervised learning for detection of microcalcifications in digital mammograms," Proceedings. International Conference on Image Processing, 1995 .

[13]   G. Naghdy, Yue Li, J. Wang, "Wavelet Based Adaptive Resonance Theory (ART) Neural Network for the Identification of Abnormalities in Mammograms," National Health Informatics Conference, HIC 97, Sydney, Australia. pp67. Paper 67 on CDROM publication.

[14]   I. N. Bankman, W. A. Christens-Barry, I. N. Weinberg, D. W. Kim, R. D. Semmel, W. R. Brody, "An algorithm for early breast cancer detection in mammograms," Proceedings. Fifth Annual IEEE Symposium on Computer-Based Medical Systems, 1992.

[15]   Yulei Jiang, R. M. Nishikawa, D. E. Wolverton, M. L. Giger, K. Doi; R. A. Schmidt, C. J. Vyborny, "Mammographic feature analysis of clustered microcalcifications for classification of breast cancer and benign breast diseases," Proceedings of the 16th Annual International Conference of the IEEE Engineering in Medicine and Biology Society. Engineering Advances: New Opportunities for Biomedical Engineers, 1994.

[16]   I. N. Bankman, J. Tsai, D. W. Kim, O. B. Gatewood, W. R. Brody, "Detection of microcalcification clusters using neural networks," Proceedings of the 16th Annual International Conference of the IEEE Engineering in Medicine and Biology Society. Engineering Advances: New Opportunities for Biomedical Engineers, 1994.

[17]   N. A. Murshed, F. Bortolozzi, R. Sabourin, "Classification of cancerous cells based on the one-class problem approach," Proc. SPIE Applications and Science of

Artificial Neural Networks II, Steven K. Rogers; Dennis W. Ruck; Eds. Vol. 2760, p. 487-494, 1996.

[18] N. A. Murshed, F. Bortolozzi, T. Sabourin, "A fuzzy ARTMAP-based classification system for detecting cancerous cells, based on the one-class problem approach," Proceedings of the 13th International Conference on Pattern Recognition, 1996.

[19] H. R. Tizhoosh, "Fuzzy Image Processing: Potentials and State of the Art", Methodologies for the Conception, Design and Application of Soft Computing; Proc. IIZUKA '98, pp. 321-324, 1998.

[20] A. L. Ralescu, J. G. Shanahan, "Fuzzy perceptual grouping in image understanding", Proc. IEEE Int. Conf. on Fuzzy Systems 1995. v.3 pp. 1267-1272, 1995.

[21] L. Khodja, L. Foulloy, E. Benoit, "Fuzzy Clustering for Color Recognition Application to Image Understanding", Proc. 5th IEEE Int. Conf. on Fuzzy Systems, v. 2 pp. 1407-1413, 1996.

[22] T. Sarkodie-Gyan, C-W. Lam, D. Hong, A. W. Campbell, "A Fuzzy Clustering Method for Efficient 2-D Object Recognition", Proc. 5th IEEE Int. Conf. on Fuzzy Systems, v. 2 pp. 1400-1406, 1996.

[23] H-S. Rhee, K-W. Oh, "A Validity Measure for Fuzzy Clustering and Its Use in Selecting Optimal Number of Clusters", Proc. 5th IEEE Int. Conf. on Fuzzy Systems, v. 2 pp. 1020- 1025, 1996.

[24] J. M. Keller, "Fuzzy Logic Rules in Low and Mid Level Computer Vision Tasks", Proceedings, 1996 Biennial Conference of the North American Fuzzy Information Processing Society, pp. 19-22, 1996.

[25] B-T. Chen, Y-S. Chen, W-H. Hsu, "Image Processing and Understanding based on the Fuzzy Inference Approach", Proc. 3rd IEEE Conf. on Fuzzy Systems, pp. 254-259, 1994.

[26] C. Demko, E. Zahzah, "Image understanding using fuzzy isomorphism of fuzzy structures," IEEE Int. Conf. on Fuzzy Systems. v 3 p 1665-1672, 1995.

[27] C. Bezdek, R. Chandrasekhar, Y. Attikiouzel, "New fuzzy model for edge detection," Proc. SPIE Applications of Fuzzy Logic Technology III, Bruno Bosacchi; James C. Bezdek; Eds. Vol. 2761, p. 11-28, 1996 .

[28] C-Y. Tyan, P. P. Wang, "Image processing-enhancement, filtering and edge detection using the fuzzy logic approach," Second IEEE International Conference on Fuzzy Systems, 1993.

[29] W. Li, G. Lu, Y. Wang, "Recognizing white line markings for vision-guided vehicle navigation by fuzzy reasoning", Pattern Recognition Letters, v. 18 pp. 771-780, 1997.

[30] M. Sameti, R. K. Ward, "A fuzzy segmentation algorithm for mammogram partitioning", Proc. 3rd Int. Workshop on Digital Mammography, 1996.

[31] B. Kovalerchuk, E. Triantaphyllou, J. F. Ruiz, J. Clayton, "Fuzzy logic in computer-aided breast cancer diagnosis - analysis of lobulation" Artificial Intelligence in Medicine, 11(1):75-85, 1997.

[32] K. H. L. Ho, N. Ohnishi, "FEDGE – Fuzzy Edge Detection by Fuzzy Categorization and Classification of Edges", [online] http://www.bmc.riken.go.jp/sensor/Ho/fedge/fedge.html, January 1999.

[33] Z. Chi, H. Yan, T. Pham, "Fuzzy algorithms: with applications to image processing and pattern recognition", World Scientific Publishing Co., 1996

Chapter 2

Software Deployability Control System: Application of Choquet Integral and Rough Sets

James F. Peters III[1] and Sheela Ramanna [1, 2]
[1]Department of Electrical and Computer Engineering,
University of Manitoba, Winnipeg, Manitoba R3T 2N2
Canada, jfpeters@ee.umanitoba.ca
[2]Department of Business Computing, University of Winnipeg,
Winnipeg, Manitoba R3T 2E9 Canada, s.ramanna@uwinnipeg.ca

Abstract

This paper introduces an application of a combination of approximate time windows, the Choquet integral, and rough sets in the design of a software deployability control system. A multi-criteria evaluation of coalitions of software development technologies is considered in approximate reasoning about the deployability of software products. Measurements with the Choquet integral are incorporated into a feedback system used to control software deployability. Decision rules capture dependencies between function points, project duration requirement, aggregation of granulations of multi-criteria evaluations of software development technologies with the Choquet integral, and magnitude of relative error in cost estimation. The method of rule derivation comes from rough sets. A fuzzy measure model of the importance of various coalitions of software technologies is introduced. The approximate character of the reasoning stems from the inherent imprecision of measurements of processing complexity. The approach is illustrated relative to software cost estimates for a collection of twenty-five software projects. The contribution of this paper is a formal description of an approximate time software deployability feedback control system based on an approximate reasoning approach to assessing software cost and software quality.

Keywords: approximate time, Choquet integral, control system, cost, decision rules, deployability, function points model, fuzzy measure, multi-criteria evaluation, software

2.1   Introduction

At each stage in the life cycle of a software system, evaluation of products of the software process hinge on three basic measurements: cost, reliability and quality

[1].   These measurements provide a basis for deciding whether to deploy or continue development of a software system.   For a number of reasons, these measurements are approximate.   The approximate character of software cost and quality measurements has been investigated in [2]-[4].   The issue of software deployability and frameworks for approximate real-time decision systems are investigated in [5]-[8].   Approximate time itself and approximate time windows have been investigated in [9]-[11].   A prevalent problem in software system cost estimation models is the assessment of the impact of interacting system components on the total work (a Man Month (MM) measurement) required to complete a project.   In the case of Albrecht's Function Points (FPs), for example, total MM estimates are based on assessing the impact of Technical Complexity Factors (TCFs) on the functionality of software.   TCFs are assumed to be independent of each other as well as independent of system size [2].   FP estimates of project MMs have been shown to have significant relative error, and to be sensitive to system size, particularly whenever the functionality of smaller projects is in the 50 to 100 MM range [2].   In addition, the TCFs used in FP analysis of a project fail to take into account the impact of coalitions of technologies such as integrated development environments, code generation, web browsers, applet viewers and concurrent engineering on MM project requirements.   The key point to notice in FP analysis is that it depends on subjective multicriteria evaluation, and that it fails to take into the relation between factors underlying estimates of the functionality of a program as well as the importance of various coalitions of software development technologies on the software process.   It has been shown that the fuzzy integral can serve as an aggregation operator in multicriteria decision making [12]-[14].   In particular, the Choquet integral has been used extensively in multicriteria evaluations [7]-[8], especially in software cost estimation in [2]-[4].

An approximate reasoning system for making software development decisions relative to the impact of applications of recent software development technologies and software cost estimates needs to be investigated.   Such a system is introduced in this paper. For simplicity, this approximate reasoning system has been limited to measurements of processing complexity (the basis for cost estimates in Albrecht [15]). In this paper, Albrecht's approach to assessing processing complexity has been refined. Rather than attempt to estimate software development cost, the approach taken in this paper is based on the design of a software process which has been "sensitized" relative to a planned software cost. This is accomplished in a number of ways. To begin, a feedback system model of the of the software cost estimation process is given. A simplified view of this feedback system model is given in Fig. 2.1.

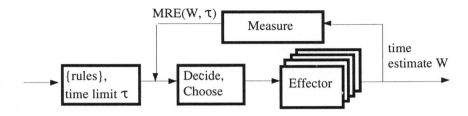

Fig. 2.1 Feedback System Model of Software Estimation Process

The approach to modeling the software cost estimation process introduced in this paper has been derived from Norbert Wiener's basic method of *control by information feedback* [16]. The estimation process is initialized with a reference duration, which is an upper bound on the time allowed to develop a product of a software process. The decider process in the feedback system model in Fig. 2.1 is governed by rules derived from decision tables which are part of a software process plan. The Choquet integral is used in a multicriteria evaluation of the impact of combinations of software development technologies on technical complexity as in [2]. Choquet integral values are granulated. The granulated Choquet integral values provide input to a roughly fuzzy Petri net relative to cut-off r and strength-of-connection w, which can be calibrated. A roughly fuzzy Petri net assimilates two technologies, fuzzy sets and rough sets, to facilitate description and analysis of decision systems and was introduced in [11]. This form of Petri net provides a high-level description of the construction of a decision table needed in the derivation of rules for the decider process. An approach to calibration of this form of Petri net is given in [9], which is based on a method described in [17]. An effector process in Fig. 2.1 represents a procedure designed to compute a result needed to continue the decision-making process.   The output of the effector processes in Fig. 2.1 is W, which is an estimate of the man-months required to develop a planned software product.   The measure process in Fig. 2.1 provides feedback to the decider.   Feedback consists in measurement of the magnitude of relative error (MRE) relative to a required software development time limit τ and W.   An unacceptable MRE value results in adjustments in the magnitude of usage of software development technologies used in arriving at an estimated man-month estimate for a project.   The contribution of this paper is the introduction of a feedback system for estimating and controlling software cost.

The paper is organized as follows.   In Section 2.2, a brief description of the methodology underlying the feedback system model for software cost estimation is given.   A high-level Petri net model of the system is presented in Section 2.3.   An application of the software cost estimation system is given in Section 2.4.

2.2   Basic Approach to Controlling Software Cost

The basic algorithm underlying the feedback system model for software cost estimation is given in Fig. 2.2.   We begin by explaining the inputs to the feedback system.   The functionality of a software system is assessed relative to what are known as Function Counts (FC) in [15].   Briefly, FC is a weighted sum of the form given in (1).

$$FC = \sum_{i=1}^{n} [(\text{itemCount}_i)(\text{complexityLevel}_i)] \tag{1}$$

Each itemCount_i equals the number of occurrences of an item in the behavioral (functional) description of software.   Item counts can be obtained from software descriptions (e.g., statecharts or Petri nets) during the early phases of a software process, which makes it possible to use Albrecht's function points method to derive preliminary software cost estimates.   A complexity level is assigned to each itemCount_i.   The influence of FC is moderated by a Technical Complexity Factor (TCF) in arriving at W (a MM estimate) as shown in (2).

W = 54(FC)(TCF) - 13,390 (2)

In Albrecht, TCF $\in$ [0.65, 1.35] , which represents an estimate of the cumulative effect of sources of processing complexity on a software development effort. The formula in (2) comes from Albrecht [15]. This is one among many approaches to estimating W due to Halstead [18]. Notice that the TCF estimate in Albrecht does not take into account the aggregative effect of newer software development technologies, which tend to mitigate "processing complexity" and which significantly influence software design, accelerate the coding phase thanks to code generation, and contribute to speedup due to parallel processing. Notice in Fig. 2.2 that TCF is replaced by an adjusted TCF (adjTCF), which takes into account the influence of recent software development technologies.

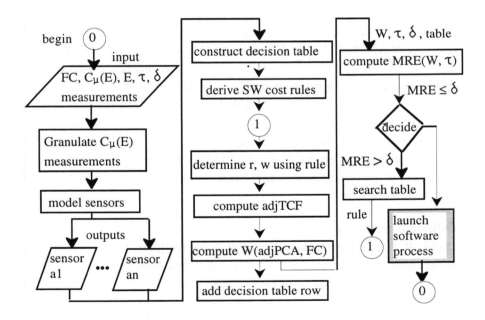

Fig. 2.2 Algorithm for Software Cost Estimation Based on Feedback

A multicriteria decision-making approach to assessing the impact of effort-reducing technologies is carried out using the Choquet integral, which we explain briefly in the next section.

2.2.1   Fuzzy Measures and the Choquet Integral

In an effort to provide an uncertainty measure of processing complexity in the context of more recent developments in software engineering, a subjective multicriteria evaluation methodology is introduced using the concept of fuzzy measure and the Choquet integral.   This effort is in keeping with the original application of the fuzzy integral by Sugeno [19], and the use of the fuzzy integral as an aggregation tool in multicriteria decision-making [12]-[14]. This approach offers a means of assessing the combined influence of more recent software development methodologies on software cost. It is assumed that a universe of discourse X specifies a finite space $\{x_1, ..., x_n\}$ and $\aleph$ is the set of all subsets of X, which is called a class.   A non-empty class F is called a σ-ring if, and only if (i) $\forall$ A, B $\in$ F, A - B $\in$ F , where A - B = $A \cap \overline{B}$ and (ii) $\forall$ A$_i$ $\in$ F, i = 1, 2, ..., $\cap_{i=1}^{\infty} A_i \in F$, i = 1, 2, ...   A σ-algebra is a σ-ring that contains X. A *fuzzy measure* μ is a mapping μ: X $\longrightarrow$ [0,1], where X is a universe of discourse in a measure space (X, $\aleph$) with $\aleph$ forming a σ-algebra over X such that (i) $\mu(\emptyset) = 0$, $\mu(X) = 1$, and (ii) A ß B $\Longrightarrow$ $\mu(A) \leq \mu(B)$ for each A, B ß $\aleph$. The triple (X, $\aleph$, μ) constitutes a fuzzy measure space.   Fuzzy integrals are aggregation operators on the hypercube $[0,1]^n$.   In developing a multicriteria evaluation of processing complexity, fuzzy integration is defined in terms of [0,1]-valued functions.

Definition (Choquet integral [20])
Let (X, $\aleph$, μ) be a fuzzy measure space, f: X $\longrightarrow$ [0,1], and let the indices of X be permuted so that 0 <= f(x$_{(1)}$) $\leq$...$\leq$ f(x$_{(n)}$) $\leq$ 1, and A$_{(i)}$ = $\{x_{(i)}, ..., x_{(n)}\}$, f(x$_{(0)}$) = 0.   The Choquet integral C$_\mu$ of f with respect to the fuzzy measure μ is defined by (3).

$$C_{\mu}(f(x_1),...,f(x_n)) = \sum_{i=1}^{n} (f(x_{(i)}) - f(x_{(i-1)}))\mu(A_{(i)}) \qquad (3)$$

Let $C_\mu()$ be a Choquet integral where μ is a fuzzy measure defined on subsets of criteria $X = \{x_1, ..., x_n\}$. The fuzzy measure μ specifies weights on the criteria, which can be either a weight $\mu(\{x_i\})$ on an individual criterion x_i or a weight $\mu(\{x_i, x_{i+1}, ...\})$ on any group of criteria $\{x_i, x_{i+1}, ...\}$. This is a key feature of a Choquet integral (and of fuzzy integrals in general), namely, the fuzzy measure makes it possible to express effects of the interaction of criteria within a universe of discourse X. In the context of the software cost estimation method given in Fig. 2.2, let X be a collection of software development technologies. In this context, a criterion is viewed as some mode of software development in the sense of a method or manner in which software is developed. Let e map $x \in X$ to $[0, 1]$ in estimating the per cent of reduction in effort resulting from the application of a new technology during software development. Let $C_\mu(e(x_1),...,e(x_n))$ be a Choquet integral value computed relative to the evaluation of various possible combinations of software development technologies. Values of $C_\mu()$ are granulated as a step toward arriving at an estimate of the adjusted TCF.

2.2 Granulating Choquet Integral Values

There is some justification for evaluating Choquet integral in the context of information granules, a clustering of measurements with vaguely defined boundaries. An information granule consists of a "clump" of similar values [21]-[22]. In the software cost estimation model investigated in this paper, Choquet integral values approximate the effect of software development technologies. By granulating Choquet integral values, we gain a means of interpreting integral values relative to the degree-of-membership of each value in selected granules. In Fig. 2.3, it is assumed that Choquet integral values for evolving software modules are approximately normally distributed. For example, the degree-of-membership of a Choquet integral value in a granule labeled low is computed relative to a particular Gaussian distribution of the form given in (4)

$$low[x] = exp\left[\frac{-(C_\mu(e(x_1),...,e(x_n)) - m_{low})^2}{s_{low}^2}\right] \quad (4)$$

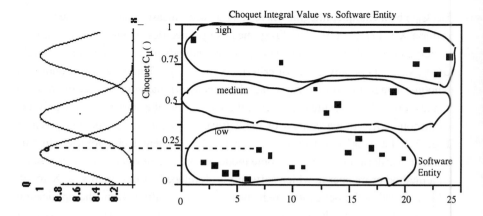

Fig. 2.3 Sample Granulation of Choquet Integral Values

The mean m_{low} and variance s_{low}^2 in (4) determine the modal point and spread in the graph of degrees of membership of Choquet integral values. The modal point m_{low} and spread s_{low} of the Gaussian distribution in (4) will vary depending on the distribution of the data in a granule.   For example, let $m_{low} = 20$, $m_{med} = 45$, $m_{high} = 85$ be the modal points for three granules (each with s = 15) named low, med, and high, respectively. The graphs of low, medium, and high are shown in Fig. 2.4.

Let $mC_\mu()$ be the degree-of-membership of $C_\mu()$ in the granule named med.   We make the simplifying assumption

$$TCF = 1 - m\ C_\mu()$$

This approach to computing TCF stems from the view that a value of 1 for TCF represents maximum, "complete" technical complexity.   Values less than 1 represent the beneficial influence of various combinations of software development technologies, which have the effect of decreasing technical complexity. In computing an adjusted TCF, we introduce a fuzzy computational approach   to   deriving   values   of   adjTCF   using adjTCF = ((TCF → r) s w)

where TCF → r is a fuzzy implication, which computes a value in [0, 1] by various means relative to a cut-off or reference point r. The value of TCF → r is aggregated relative to a strength-of-connection w using an s-norm operation. The advantage to this approach is that adjTCF can be calibrated relative to r, w, and some software project duration target value.

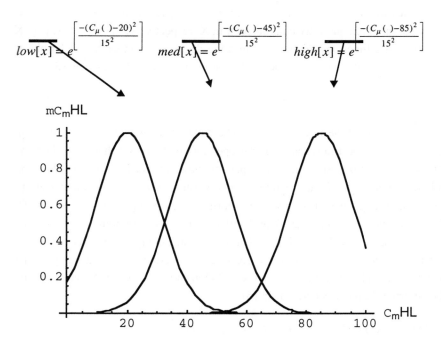

$$low[x] = e^{\left[\dfrac{-(C_\mu(\ )-20)^2}{15^2}\right]} \qquad med[x] = e^{\left[\dfrac{-(C_\mu(\ )-45)^2}{15^2}\right]} \qquad high[x] = e^{\left[\dfrac{-(C_\mu(\ )-85)^2}{15^2}\right]}$$

Fig. 2.4 Sample Choquet Integral Measurement Distributions

The intuition behind this approach to computing adjTCF is that each calibration represents either increased or decreased application of software technologies as a means of adjusting estimated development time relative project deadlines.

2.3 Fuzzy Sets: Basic Concepts

Fuzzy sets are distinguished from the classical notion of a set (also called a crisp set) by the fact that the boundary of a fuzzy set is not precise [23].   The characteristic function for a set X returns a value indicating the degree of membership of an element x in X.   For a crisp set, the characteristic function returns a value in $\{0, 1\}$. A fuzzy set is non-crisp, and was introduced by Zadeh [24].   By contrast with a crisp set, the characteristic function for a fuzzy set returns a value in $[0, 1]$.   Let U, X, $\tilde{A}$, x be a universe of objects, subset of U, fuzzy set in U, and an individual object x in X, respectively.   For a set X, $\mu_{\tilde{A}}$: X $\rightarrow$ [0, 1] is a function which determines the degree of membership of an object x in X.   A fuzzy set $\tilde{A}$ is then defined to be a set of ordered pairs as in (5).

$$\tilde{A} = \{ (x, \mu_{\tilde{A}}(x)) \mid x \in X \} \tag{5}$$

The set X is called the reference set.   The counterpart of intersection and union (crisp sets) are the t-norm and s-norm operators in fuzzy set theory.   For the intersection of fuzzy sets, the min operator was suggested by Zadeh [24], and belongs to a class of intersection operators (min, product, bold intersection) known as triangular or t-norms.   A t-norm is a mapping t : $[0,1]^2 \rightarrow [0, 1]$. The algebraic sum (also called probabilistic sum) is commonly used for the union of fuzzy sets [24].   The probabilistic sum belongs to a class of union operators called triangular co-norms (or s-norms).   An s-norm is a mapping s : $[0,1]^2 \rightarrow [0, 1]$.   For example, let x, y belong to a fuzzy set $\tilde{A}$, and compute the s-norm relative to x and y as in (6)

$$\mu_{\tilde{A}}(x) \ s \ \mu_{\tilde{A}}(y) = \mu_{\tilde{A}}(x) + \mu_{\tilde{A}}(y) - \mu_{\tilde{A}}(x)\mu_{\tilde{A}}(y) \tag{6}$$

In fuzzy set theory, the symbol "$\rightarrow$" denotes a multivalued implication operation.   Many forms of implication are possible [25]-[27].   For simplicity, the Lukasiewicz and Gaines forms of implication are compared in (7) and (8).

$$(r \rightarrow x)_{Lukasiewicz} = \begin{cases} 1 - r + x, & \text{if } r > x \\ 1, & \text{if } r \leq x \end{cases} \qquad (7)$$

$$(r \rightarrow x)_{Gaines} = \begin{cases} \dfrac{x}{r}, & \text{if } x < r \\ \min\left(1, \dfrac{x}{r}\right), & \text{otherwise} \end{cases} \qquad (8)$$

In the case of Gaines, $r_i \rightarrow x_i = x/r$ for values of $x < r$ (see Fig. 2.5). Otherwise, $r_i \rightarrow x_i = \min(1, \frac{x_i}{r_i})$, $r \leq x$, and the $\rightarrow$ is induced by the product operation. Hence, values of $r_i \rightarrow x_i$ rise smoothly along the r-axis to the 45° line. Notice, for example, that for $r = 0.5$ and $x = 0$, we have $r_i \rightarrow x_i = 0$. By contrast, the Lukasiewicz form of implication $r_i \rightarrow x_i = 1 - r_i + x_i$ for $r_i > x_i$ "ramps up" more rapidly than the Gaines form of implication (see Fig. 6). Otherwise for Lukasiewicz, $r_i \rightarrow x_i = 1$, $r \leq x$, the $\rightarrow$ has a constant value of 1. As a result, for $r = 0.5$ and $x = 0$, we have $r_i \rightarrow x_i = 0.5$.

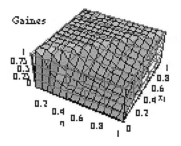

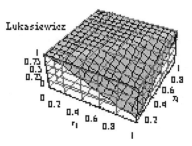

Fig. 2.5 $r_i \rightarrow x_i$ [Gaines]

Fig. 2.6 $r_i \rightarrow x_i$ [Lukasiewicz]

Returning to the algorithm, it should be mentioned that preliminary values of r and w reflect decisions made relative to FC, granulated Choquet integral values, adjTCF, project deadline τ, estimated project duration W, and magnitude of relative error (MRE).   These decisions are organized in decision tables constructed and analyzed with rough set theory.   From such decision tables, rules can be derived which guide the selection of appropriate values of r and w.

2.4   Rough Sets: Basic Concepts

Rough set theory offers a systematic approach to the conceptualization of decision systems and the derivation of rules useful in approximate reasoning [28]-[39].   To begin, let S = (U, A) be an information system with set U (universe of objects) and set A (attributes).   Then let R be a relation defined on U. For x, y ∈ U, let xRy indicate that x has relation R to y.   R is a tolerance relation, if xRx (reflexivity) for x ∈ U and for all x, y ∈ U, if xRy, then yRx (symmetry).   In the case where transitivity also holds, R is an equivalence relation over U.   The notation U/R (known as the quotient set) denotes the family of equivalence classes of R.   For x ∈ U, the notation $[x]_R$ identifies an equivalence class in U/R.   The equivalence class $[x]_R$ is called an elementary category or concept of R [28].   A subset X in U is called a reference set, which can be approximated with two other sets in (9) and (10).

$$\underline{R}X = \{x \in U \mid [x]_R \subseteq X\}, \; lower \; approximation \tag{9}$$

$$\overline{R}X = \{x \in U \mid [x]_R \cap X \neq \varnothing\}, \; upper \; approximation \tag{10}$$

The pair $(\underline{R}X, \overline{R}X)$ is a rough set with reference set X.   The vagueness of a set stems from its borderline region.   A measure of the accuracy of a set X ⊆ U is computed using $\alpha_R(X)$ (see (11)).

$$\alpha_R(X) = \frac{|\underline{R}X|}{|\overline{R}X|}, \; accuracy \; measure \tag{11}$$

The accuracy measure $\alpha_R(X)$ captures the degree of completeness of our knowledge represented by X.   The degree of incompleteness of our knowledge represented by a set X (its roughness) is computed using $\rho_R(x)$ given in (12)

$$\rho_R(X) = 1 - \alpha_R(X), \ R - roughness \ of \ X \tag{12}$$

Similarity among members of an equivalence class provides the basis for what is known as the indiscernability relation.   Let B be a subset of the set of attributes A, and let Ind(B) be the set of all elements of X that match each other relative to B (see (13)).

$$Ind(B) = \{(x,y) \mid \forall a \in B, a(x) = a(y)\} \tag{13}$$

The Ind(B) relation simplifies the investigation of a particular information system, where the representatives of U/Ind(B) are studied.   Knowledge reduction is possible using the method shown in [28],[31],[33],[38].   A minimal subset B $\subseteq$ A such that Ind(B) = Ind(A) is called a reduct of A. Any set of attributes has one or more reducts [39].   Let a $\in$ P in A. The attribute a is indispensable in P if Ind(P) $\neq$ Ind(P - {a}).   The set of all indispensable attributes in P is called the core of P (denoted CORE(P)), which can be considered the most important part of knowledge [28].   For an information system S, the set of all reducts in S is denoted RED(S) [37].

In deriving decision system rules, the discernability matrix and discernability function are essential [33].   Given an information system S = (U, A), the nxn matrix (c_{ij}) is called the discernability matrix of S (denoted M(S)) defined in (14).

$$c_{ij} = \{a \in A: a(x_i) \neq a(x_j)\}, \text{ for i, j} = 1, ..., n. \tag{14}$$

A discernability function fM(S) for information S is a boolean function of m boolean variables $a_1, ..., a_m$ corresponding to attributes a_1, ..., a_m respectively, and defined in (15).

$$f_{M(S)}(a_1^*, ..., a_m^*) =_{df} \wedge \{\vee c_{ij}^* \mid 1 \leq j < i \leq n, c_{ij} \neq \emptyset\}, c_{ij}^* = \{a^* \mid a \in c_{ij}\} \tag{15}$$

Precise conditions for decision rules can be extracted from a discernability matrix as in [31].   For the information system S = (U, A), let B $\subseteq$ A and let P (V_a) denote the power set of V_a, where V_a is the value set of a.   For every d $\in$ A - B, a decision function $d_d^B : U \longrightarrow P(V_a)$ is defined in (16).

$$d_d^B(u) = \left\{ v \in V_d \mid \exists u' \in U, (u', u) \in Ind_B.d(u') = v \right\} \tag{16}$$

In other words, $d_d^D(u)$ is the set of all elements of the decision column of S such that the corresponding object is a member of the same equivalence class as argument u. The next step is to determine a decision rule with a minimal number of descriptors on the left-hand side. Pairs (a, v), where a $\in$ A, v $\in$ V are called *descriptors*. A decision rule over the set of attributes A and values V is an expression of the form given in (17).

$$a_{i_1}(u_i) = v_{i_1} \wedge ... \wedge a_{i_j}(u_i) = v_{i_j} \wedge ... \wedge a_{i_r}(u_i) = v_{i_r} \underset{S}{\Rightarrow} d(u_i) = v \tag{17}$$

where $u_{i_j} \in U$, $v_{i_j} \in V_{a_{i_j}}$, $v \in V_d$, j = 1,...,r and r $\leq$ |A|.   Let $\parallel \tau \parallel_S$ denote the meaning of term τ.   A rule is true in system S if (18) holds.

$$\parallel (a_{i_1} = v_{i_1}) \wedge ... \wedge (a_{i_r} = v_{i_r}) \parallel \subseteq \parallel (a_p = v_p) \parallel \tag{18}$$

The fact that a rule is true is indicated by writing it in the form given in (19).

$$(a_{i_1} = v_{i_1}) \wedge ... \wedge (a_{i_r} = v_{i_r}) \underset{S}{\Rightarrow} (a_p = v_p) \tag{19}$$

Let R $\in$ RED(S) be a reduct in the set of all reducts in an information system S. For an information system S, the set of decision rules constructed with respect to a reduct R is denoted OPT(S, R) [36]-[37].   Then the set of all decision rules derivable from reducts in RED(S) is the set in (20).

$$OPT(S) = U\{ OPT(S, R) \mid R \in RED(S) \} \tag{20}$$

2.5   Petri Net Model of Cost Estimation Process

Considerable work has already been carried out in modeling decision system rules with Petri nets [31], [40]-[44]. This aim of the earlier as well as the current research has been to simplify the analysis of large information systems, and the transformation of such systems as well as derived rules into corresponding concurrent models. The motivation for introducing rough Petri nets stems from an effort to capture the understandings and operations from rough set theory, which have been used to construct both general-purpose as well as highly-specialized decision systems. An overview of the types of Petri nets and related set theories leading to a Petri net of model of the software cost estimation process, is given in Fig. 2.7.

In what follows, it is assumed that the reader is familiar with classical Petri nets [40],[41] as well as the basic structure of coloured Petri nets found in [42]-[44]. Rough Petri nets are derived from coloured and hierarchical Petri nets as well as from rough set theory[4]. The complete process of deriving rules for a decision system can be modeled with a rough Petri net at a sufficiently high level to facilitate an understanding of a particular rule-derivation process. In addition, the strengths of connections (weightings of attribute computations) in a rough Petri net can be calibrated. Fuzzy Petri nets are derived from classical Petri nets and fuzzy set theory [45]-[50]. Fuzzy Petri nets can also be defined in the context of coloured Petri nets to facilitate implementation as in [17]. Rough fuzzy Petri nets are derived from rough Petri nets and fuzzy Petri nets. This form of Petri net makes it possible to add learning capability to a decision-making rule-derivation process, which combines the use of fuzzy sets and rough sets in rule formulation.

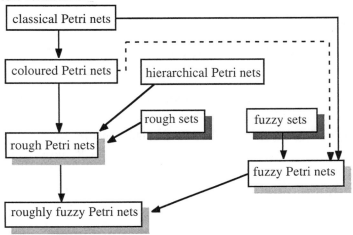

Fig. 2.7 Lineage of Petri Nets

2.5.1   Rough Petri Nets

A rough Petri net (rPn) is a structure $(\Sigma, P, T, A, N, C, E, I, W, \mathbb{R}, \rho)$ where Σ (data types), P (places), T (transitions), A (arcs), N (maps A to (PxT) $\cup$ (TxP)), C (maps P to Σ), E (maps A to expression E(a) of type C(p(a))), I (maps P to closed expressions p(a) of type C(p)) are as in a coloured Petri net (CPN). Strengths-of- connections (chosen from a finite set of weights W) are assigned to arcs with $\rho: A \longrightarrow W$. A *strength of connection* $w_i \in W$ specifies the relative importance of input to a sensor (a form of attribute in rough sets), and guarantees a certain magnitude of input to a transition.   Weights are restricted to values in the interval [0, 1].   Let X, S, ξ be a set of inputs, information system S, and reduct ξ belonging to set of all reducts RED(S) of S, respectively.   Let S = (U, A) be an information system and let R be an equivalence relation which forms the quotient set X/R, where $R \subseteq A$ and $X \subseteq U$.   Also, recall that the notation X/R (known as the quotient set) denotes the family of equivalence classes of R. The set $POS_R(X) = \underline{R}X$ is the set of all elements of U which can classified as elements of U - X.   Similarly, the set $NEG_R(X) = U - \overline{R}X$ is the set of those elements of U which can be classified as elements of X [22].   Further, let the set $\mathbb{R}$ consist of

$$\sigma_{X/R}, \, {}^{\rho}POS_R(X), \, {}^{\rho}NEG_R(X), \, {}^{\rho}\inf{}_A(X),$$
$$\rho_{dec_A}(X), \, {}^{\rho}M(S), \, {}^{\rho}RED(S), \, {}^{\rho}fM(RED(S)), \, {}^{\rho}OPT(S), \, {}^{\rho}OPT(R,S)$$

which identify distinguished procedures used to construct the quotient set X/R, set $POS_R(X)$ and set $NEG_R(X)$, as well as procedures to construct an information system table, decision system table, discernability matrix, set all rules for a decision system, and set of all rules relative to a reduct R, respectively.   The prescription of the elements of $\mathbb{R}$ is non-exhaustive. The arc expression function E has been specialized relative to a finite set of rough set operations $\mathbb{R}$ such that

E: A → ℝ. The operations in ℝ are used to describe processes which are the key components of an approximate reasoning system, namely, decision tables, discernability matrices and functions, reducts, and rules. Assume that each input x has a strength-of-connection w. Further, let S = ({x}, a ∪ {d}) be a decision system with a single input, attribute a, and decision d. An example of a rough Petri net with a single transition is given in Fig. 2.8.

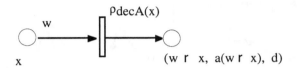

Fig. 2.8 Single-Transition Rough Petri Net

The output of the net in Fig. 2.8 is a tuple (w ☐ x, a(w ☐ x), d) representing a decision system table with a single row. The computation w ☐ a(x) aggregates w and x with the anonymous operation ☐: $[0,1]^2 →$ [0,1]. In the absence of a specific strength-of-connection, the default value of w is 0 and w ☐ x equals x. This is the case in Fig. 9. To construct a multi-transition rough Petri net, let a_1, a_2,...,a_i,...a_n, represent a collection of sensors A in a decision system S = (U, A ∪ {dec}). Also, let dM, df, ℰ, {rule} represent discernability matrix, discernability function, reduct ℰ in RED(S) for a decision system S, and set of rules derived from ℰ. The rough Petri net in Fig. 2.9 describes the process of constructing a set of rules derived from S.

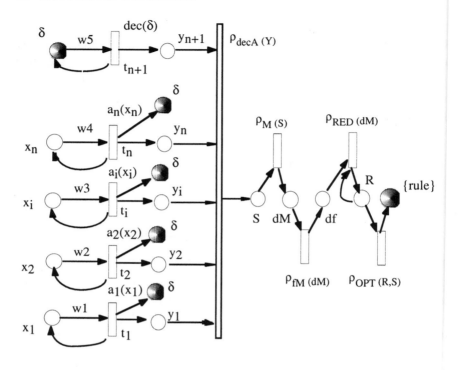

Fig. 2.9 Sample Decision System Model

To simplify the rough Petri net model in Fig. 2.9, aliasing of input place δ of transition t_{n+1} has been used.   Then the output place labeled δ of transitions t_1, t_2, ...,t_i, ..., t_n provides input to transition t_{n+1}. By allowing transitions in a rough Petri net to represent subnets, it is possible to model complex information systems concisely.   This is in fact what has been done in Fig. 2.9, where each of the transitions represents a subnet modeling a process needed to carry out necessary computations.   For example, the transition labeled $\rho_M(S)$ decomposes into a subnet designed to model the process which constructs a discernability matrix.

2.5.2 Fuzzy Petri Nets

Research concerning fuzzy Petri nets and their application is quite extensive [45]-[58]. Fuzzy Petri nets offer a concise means of modeling the interpretation of data points which have been granulated. In the case where the objects of a universe are granulated, sensors in a decision system aggregate weighted degree-of-membership computations. Further, a fuzzy Petri net makes it possible to model a form of neural processing where modulators and strengths-of-connections are calibrated [17], [40]-[51]. Such calibrations make it possible to express the intentions of system designers in assessing software quality, and to construct a variety of highly-specialized software quality measurement frameworks.

A Fuzzy Petri Net (FPN) is a structure $(\Sigma, P, T, A, N, C, E, I, M, W, Z, \varsigma, \rho)$ where $\Sigma, P, T, A, N, C, E, I$ are as in a CPN [43]. Annotations of arcs with strengths of connections chosen from a finite set of weights W are determined by $\rho: A \longrightarrow W$, and *modulators* (also called reference points) chosen from the finite set M are determined by $\varsigma: A \longrightarrow M$. A *strength of connection* $w_i \in W$ specifies the relative importance of input, and guarantees a certain magnitude of input to a transition. A *modulator* $r_i \in M$ prescribes a certain magnitude of the level of marking of a place which must be maintained. Weights and modulators are restricted to values in the interval [0, 1]. The arc expression function E has been specialized relative to a finite set Z such that $E:A \longrightarrow Z$. The expressions in Z make it possible to compute degrees of membership of values in a universe of discourse in fuzzy sets, to perform aggregations, and any other necessary operations for the functioning of a particular system. Minimally, Z has four operations consisting of what are known as a dominance AND {OR} as well as conjunctive {disjunctive} ways of aggregating weighted inputs to a transition (see (21)).

$$Z = \{ \overset{n}{\underset{i=1}{T}}((r_i \rightarrow x_i) \ s \ w_i) \qquad \text{--dominance AND operation,}$$

$$\overset{n}{\underset{i=1}{S}}((r_i \rightarrow x_i) \ t \ w_i), \qquad \text{--dominance OR operation,}$$

$$\overset{n}{\underset{i=1}{S}}(x_i \ t \ w_i) \qquad \text{--OR operation,}$$

$$\overset{n}{\underset{i=1}{T}}(x_i \ s \ w_i) \qquad \text{--AND operation} \} \qquad (21)$$

The operations in Z employ triangular norms s, t, as well as the implication operator $\rightarrow$ where r_i specifies a threshold level which modulates the strength of firing coming from the ith input place. Depending on the marking of the input places, a transition can fire. In contrast to two-valued Petri nets, the generalized version studied includes a gradual firing (strength of firing) of transitions together with level of marking of places. First, let us discuss a generic model of a transition represented in Fig. 2.10. An elementary FPN has a single multivalued (fuzzy) transition z_i with inputs x_i (input signal), r_i (reference point), w_i (weight), and single output place out_k.

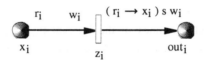

Fig. 2.10 Elementary fuzzy Petri net

Each input x_i is a fuzzy number (i.e., result of applying a membership function to an element of a universe of discourse which consists of real numbers). The results out_1, ..., out_n of elementary FPNs are aggregated. The level of firing of transition in a fuzzy Petri net is determined by (22).

$$Z = \overset{n}{\underset{i=1}{T}}[(r_i \rightarrow x_i) \ s \ w_i] \qquad (22)$$

For the computation (19) associated with transition Z, the limit "n" denotes the number of input places; x_i, a level of marking at the i-th place; r_i, a level of modulation of the input; and w_i, an associated degree of contribution of the x_i to the overall firing of the transition. Here "s" and "T" (or t) denote s- and t-norms. Similarly, " $\rightarrow$ " denotes a multivalued implication operation. Many forms of implication are possible. For simplicity, the Gaines form of implication has been used in aggregating granulated software quality measurements.

2.5.3 Roughly Fuzzy Petri Nets

Roughly fuzzy Petri nets were introduced in [9]. In this section, roughly fuzzy Petri nets are presented as a straightforward extension of rough Petri nets. This form of Petri net provides a methodology for concise description of the construction, analysis and calibration of approximate reasoning systems relative to software cost estimation (see Fig. 2.11). The introduction of roughly fuzzy Petri Nets (rfPNs) is motivated by the need to develop mathematical models of decision-making systems relative to aggregations of granulated inputs such that the models are capable of learning, and are designed to react to dynamic changes in the reduct set for different samples of decision tables. A roughly fuzzy Petri net (rfPn) is a structure given in (23)

$$(\Sigma, P, T, A, N, C, E, I, M, W, \mathbb{R} \cup Z, \varsigma, \rho) \qquad (23)$$

where Σ, P, T, A, N, C, E, I, W, $\mathbb{R}$, ρ are as in a rough Petri net. The set $\mathbb{R}$ is augmented with operations in Z from fuzzy Petri nets to handle aggregations of granulated inputs.

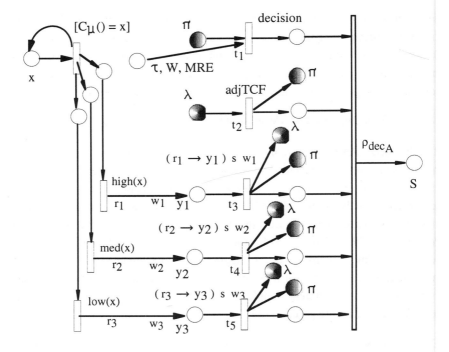

Fig. 2.11 Petri Net Model of Software Cost Decision System

The modulators (also called cut-offs or reference points) of operations in Z are in the set M.   The operation $\mathfrak{s}$ maps arcs to modulators (or "cut-offs") chosen from the finite set M.   In effect, a roughly fuzzy Petri net is an extension of the rough Petri net model, which provides a concise means of modeling the process of deriving rules for an approximate reasoning system for software cost estimation.

To simplify the roughly fuzzy Petri net model in Fig. 2.11, aliasing of input places λ and π of transitions t_1 and t_2 , respectively, has been used.   For example, the output place labeled λ of transitions t3, t4, t5 provides input to transition t2.   The rfPn in Fig. 2.11 models the operations of the sensors for a decision system S.   The place labeled S in Fig. 2.11 becomes input to the back end of the rough Petri net in Fig. 2.9. Observe that Choquet integral values are viewed relative to the extent that a multicriteria evaluation is a part of a granule, and this estimate of degree of membership initializes the roughly fuzzy Petri net in Fig. 2.10. In the case where cut-offs and strengths of connections are incorporated into a roughly fuzzy Petri net for processing software cost measurements, then learning is possible. Second, the outputs of sensors can be calibrated by a roughly fuzzy Petri net in providing inputs to a decision system table. In this case, appropriate values of r and w are computed off-line as a result of supervised learning relative to target values as in [17], [50]-[51].

2.6 Example Software Cost Estimation

The decider process in the feedback system in Fig. 2.1 implements a roughly fuzzy Petri net similar to the one in Fig. 2.11 with a number of enhancements. Rules are derived from a decision table based on rough set theory. Whenever the decider is stimulated by new input, it selects a rule which comes closest to satisfying the conditions for the selection of necessary r, w values. In each case where feedback of an MRE greater than some preset threshold δ, new r and w values are calibrated. This process continues until the MRE value is below δ. In estimating W (man months needed to complete a project), negative values are excluded in

$$W = |\; 54 \; (FC) \; (adjTCF) - 13,390 \;|$$

The Magnitude of Relative Error (MRE) value is computed relative to W and required project duration τ in

$$MRE = \frac{|\; (required \; time \; t) - W \;|}{W}$$

Table 2.1 Software Development Technologies

Technology	Description
ide	integrated development environment (usually includes editor, error checker, debugger, graphical user interface, ability to link files, compiler)
team	cooperating software engineering teams, e.g., cleanroom engineering model.
av	applet viewer for web browser applications
web	use of web to maintain software requirement descriptions
awt	abstract windowing toolkit in Java programming

A collection of 25 Java programs have provided a testbed for the multicriteria decision-making approach to software cost estimation.   A collection of five software development technologies been found to influence the TCF in a significant way. These technologies are briefly described in Table 2.1.   In effect, various combinations of these technologies are judged to have varying influence on a software development effort in saving time. Let X equal the set {ide, team, av, web, awt}.

The set X of five technologies in Table 2.1 results in a total of 2^5 coefficients of fuzzy measure relative to the power set of X.   The values of the coefficients reflect preferences or judgments about the worth of each combination of technologies. Let P(X) denote the power set (set of all subsets) of X. To begin, it is necessary that these coefficients of fuzzy measure satisfy the rule

$$A \subset B \Rightarrow \mu(A) \leq \mu(B), \text{ where A, } B \subseteq P(X)$$

It is helpful to carry out multicriteria evaluation of elements of P(X) relative to a lattice of coefficients of fuzzy measure.   In the case where X = {ide, team, av, web, awt}, we need to consider a lattice with 32 coefficients that will be used in Choquet integrations.   Such a lattice is given in Fig. 2.12.   Sample "scores" associated with coefficients are given in this lattice.   Consider, for example,

$$\{web\} \subset \{team, web\} \Rightarrow \mu(\{web\}) \leq \mu(\{team, web\})$$
$$0.28 \leq 0.43$$

$$\{team, \subset \{team, \Rightarrow \mu(\{team, \leq \mu(\{team,$$
$$web\} \quad av, \quad web\}) \quad av,$$
$$web\} \quad web\})$$
$$0.43 \leq 0.59$$

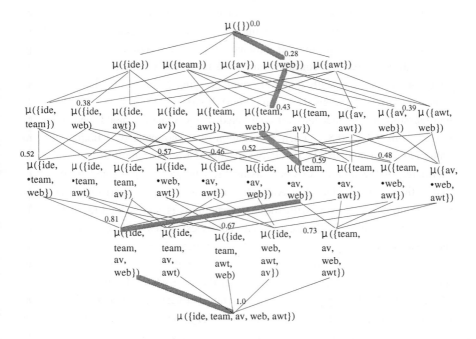

Fig. 2.12 Lattice of Fuzzy Measure Coefficients

To complete preparation for an application of the Choquet integral in software cost estimation, we introduce a function e used to estimate the per cent of usage of various combinations of technologies in a software project. That is,

e : X → [0,1], X ⊆ P(X)

In the context of software engineering, these scores reflect preferences concerning combinations of technologies. Notice that $\mu(\{ide, team, web\})$ equals 0.52 and $\mu(\{team, av, web\})$ equals 0.59, which suggests that combining an integrated development environment with an engineering team approach using the web is better than the combination of development methods $\{ide, team, web\}$. The heavier, shaded lines mark the paths in the lattice in Fig. 2.12 reflecting sample choices one can make in technology combinations relative to monotonically increasing coefficient values. The function e can be defined in a number of ways. For simplicity, assume that each value of e is computed relative to checklists serving as indicators of the per centage of project usage of each technology combination. Next we consider sample data from a collection of 25 Java development projects with function counts varying between 200 and 1300, and target durations between 1800 and 9600 hours. Values of the degree-of-membership of Choquet integral considered in the granule named med (medium) ranged from 0.3 to 0.8. Each aggregation of a "normalized" Choquet integral value led to an adjusted TCF relative to cut-off r and strength-of-connection w. Estimates of the number of hours using the Choquet integral tend to be lower than estimates computed with Albrecht's method. A comparison of TCF and project duration estimates with these two methods is shown in Fig. 2.13. The dashed line in Fig. 2.13 indicates Albrecht's estimates and, not surprisingly, these estimates are consistently higher than estimates (solid line) derived with the new method. The contrast between estimates with these two methods is seen more clearly in Fig. 2.14. For example, in the case where the function count is 750 in Fig. 2.14(a), project durations range between 2,800 and 27,000 hours relative to the adjusted TCF based on the fuzzy measure of the importance of various software development technologies. By contrast, using Albrecht's method of estimating the value of TCF and assuming FC equal to 750, project duration estimates range between 12, 935 and 41,285 hours.

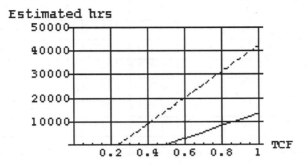

Fig. 2.13 Comparison of Project Duration Estimates
[dotted line = Choquet, solid line = Albrecht]

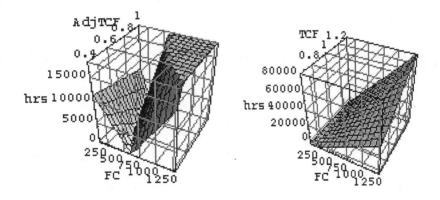

Fig. 2.14(a) Choquet-based Method   Fig. 2.14(b) Albrecht's Method

Sample TCF and adjTCF estimates relative to a sampler of software development projects is given in Table 2.2.

Table 2.2   Sample Software Cost Decision Table

FC	TCF	τ (hrs)	nC$_\mu$	adjTCF	W(C$_\mu$)	MRE	r	w
206	1.07	2960	0.4130	0.9354	2984.7	0.0083	0.64	0.22
228	1.04	2339	0.4130	0.8960	2357.9	0.0080	0.68	0.24
215	1.26	2026	0.4130	0.9737	2042.8	0.0082	0.61	0.4
281	1.35	2278	0.4130	0.7336	2257.9	0.0089	0.88	0.2
291	1.01	2110	0.4130	0.9853	2092.3	0.0085	0.6	0.32
351	1.15	2406	0.4130	0.8346	2428.7	0.0093	0.74	0.2
378	0.88	2182	0.4130	0.7620	2164.9	0.0079	0.84	0.21
400	0.98	1880	0.4130	0.5352	1882.9	0.0015	0.94	0.22
487	1.2	7350	0.7552	0.7802	7280.8	0.0095	0.32	0.09
479	1.25	7161	0.7552	0.7937	7140.9	0.0028	0.31	0.02
537	0.75	2780	0.3375	0.364	2834.7	0.0193	0.663	0.04
773	1.15	7650	0.7552	0.5045	7668.9	0.0025	0.49	0.01
1282	0.88	8500	0.7552	0.3167	8535.7	0.0042	0.79	0.01
1319	1.17	9650	0.7552	0.3247	9735.9	0.0088	0.77	0.01

A comparison of relative errors for a collection of 25 projects is given in Fig. 2.15.

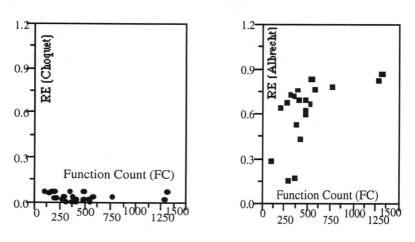

Fig. 2.15 Relative Errors with Two Methods

The relative error of cost estimates with Albrecht's method tends to increase as function count estimates increase, climbing to 0.9 for projects with function counts above 1200. By contrast, cost estimates based on considerations of the coalition of software technologies have low, fairly uniform relative error measurements (in most cases, RE < 0.2).

Table 2.2 instantiates a decision system for software cost estimation. Values in the columns with FC, TCF headings represent function counts and technical complexity for actual software projects using Albrecht's method. The TCF column is given to facilitate comparisons with the adjusted TCF (adjTCF), which is a function of nC_μ, r and w. MRE values in Table 2.2 result from a comparison of upper bound τ and computed duration W. The feedback system in Fig. 2.1 is implemented with rules derived from a decision system table and provide a basis for selecting r and w. Rules derived from real-valued sensors like those in Table 2.2 are discretized relative to interval rather than individual sensor values. This is made possible by the quantization of the real values of software cost estimation sensors so that sensor values are partitioned into intervals. Let $\mathbb{R}$ be the set of real numbers, and let $\mathbb{R}^k$ be a k-dimensional affine space. An object in a decision table is treated as a point in $\mathbb{R}^k$ where k is the number of conditional sensors $a \in A$ such $a \neq d$ in $S = (U, A \cup \{d\})$. Then the objects in decision table are partitioned into r decision classes using the method described by H.S. Nguyen in [59]-[60]. The important consequence of this classification scheme is that all objects belonging to the same class have the same decision. This result has the effect of reducing the number of rules that must be considered in approximate reasoning. To illustrate this approach to rule formation in the context of software cost estimation, let x[*, b) for values of a sensor x so that * $\leq$ x <b, where the lower bound * is indeterminate. Similarly, x[a, *) represents values of x in a $\leq$ x < * where the upper bound is left indeterminate. The notation x({a < x $\leq$ b}) asserts that sensor x is defined relative to the set

$\{(a, b) \mid a < x \leq b\}$

Further, let fc, tau, ncu, mre represent function count, time limit, granulated Choquet integral value, and magnitude of relative error, respectively. The notation fc([*, 400)), for example, specifies that * ≤ fc < 400.   Rules for selecting w have the form given in (x) and (y).

fc([*, 400.0)) AND tau([8500.0, *)) AND
ncu([*, 0.584)) AND mer({0.0025<mer≤0.0085}) ⟹ w(0.1) OR w(0.2)   (x)

fc([*, 400.0)) AND tau([*, 2100.0)) AND
ncu([*, 0.584)) AND mer({0.0025<mer≤0.0085}) ⟹ w(0.2) OR w(0.4)   (y)

In the case where selected columns of decision table 2 have been implemented in a feedback control system for software cost, rule (y) would result in the selection of trial values of w, either w = 0.2 or w = 0.4, in the case where project constraints have the form

FC	τ (hrs)	nC_μ	MRE	r	w
215	2026	0.4130	0.0082	?	?

Similarly, the decider in the feedback control system would make its selection of cut-off r values based on rules having a similar form.   It is a straightforward task to derive these rules using Rosetta [61].   After encoding such rules, the decider process is governed by some form of rule-firing algorithm.

Decider Rule Firing Algorithm

step 1.   Let {fc, tau, nC_μ, mer }, a_i, a_j, a_k, a_{mer}, v_{ai}, v_{aj}, v_{ak}, v_{amer} be experimental values for function counts, etc. observed during actual operation of a software cost feedback control system, sample decision system condition sensors for a sample control rule r ∈ D(S), and sensor values from decision system table (U, A ∪ {d}, V), respectively.   Let s be defined as a sum

$$s = (a_i(x) - v_{ai}) + (a_j(y) - v_{aj}) + (a_k(z) - v_{ak}) + (a_{mer}(zz) - v_{amer})$$

where x is an input value (x is the observed function count fc; y, the time limit tau; z, the degree of membership of Choquet integral value nC_μ in granule n; zz,

MRE value) evaluated with sensors a_i, a_j, a_k, a_{mer} in A (for example) to produce a particular value v_{ai}.

step 2.   Let n, m be the number of r, w rules, respectively. Let s_i, $1 \leq i \leq n$, s_j, $1 \leq j \leq m$ be sums of the form introduced in step 1 relative to n rules for r and m rules for w, respectively.   Then let m_r, m_w be functions defined as follows as follows:

$$m_r : s_1, ..., s_i, ..., s_n \longrightarrow i \text{ such that } s[i] = \min(s_1, ..., s_i, ..., s_n)$$
$$m_w : s_1, ..., s_j, ..., s_n \longrightarrow j \text{ such that } s[j] = \min(s_1, ..., s_j, ..., s_n)$$

In other words, m_{kp}, m_{kd} each finds the index of the smallest sum, which identifies the premise of a rule which is closest to the measured condition during the operation of a controller.

step 3.   Let $r := r[i]$, $w := w[j]$ be the new values of cut-off and strength-of-connection used to estimate project duration W.   Then compute W.

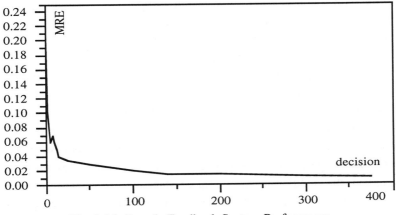

Fig. 2.16 Sample Feedback System Performance

In the case where experimental values lead to an unacceptably high relative error, a new row is added to the initial decision table relative to adjusted values of r and w.   Recalibration of r and w results in the introduction of new rules.   For a collection of similar software projects, the feedback system eventually stabilizes. Trial runs of the feedback system relative to the sample collection of software projects required between 400 and 1500 epochs to achieve a satisfactory relative error. For example, a trial run of the feedback system relative to one of the 25 Java projects required 400 epochs to achieve a relative error less than 0.01 based on FC = 537, τ (tau) = 2780, nC_μ = 0.449 (see Fig. 2.16).

2.7   Concluding Remarks

This paper presents a roughly fuzzy Petri net model of a real-time feedback control system useful in controlling the cost of products of a software process. Since the basic approach to software cost estimation suggested by Albrecht requires a knowledge of software functionality, it is possible to estimate the cost of software entities early in a software process (see, for example, [1]).   Hence, it is possible to study the feasibility of a timing-constraint on a description of a software entity relative to possible coalitions of software development technologies.   The heart of the feedback system introduced in this paper is a fuzzy measure which models the importance or strength of each form of coalition of software development technologies in arriving at decisions about combinations of such technologies deliver the most benefit in controlling software cost.   In this context, the coalition means union, combination or fusion where the fuzzy measure of a combination can be greater than the fuzzy measure of coalition individuals.   The not-so-obvious advantage to this approach is that the importance $\mu(\{t\})$ of an individual development technology t in a software process may be less than the fuzzy measure $\mu(A \cup \{t\})$ for a coalition of development technologies A combined with t. Adequate representations of fuzzy measures suitable for multicriteria decision-making have presented in [12].

Also, notice that the feedback system algorithm in Fig. 2.2 is based on a hard real-time system design. This stems from the fact that the feedback system enforces a timing constraint imposed on each software product. The estimated completion time W is measured relative to duration τ. The subtlety of this approach is that by introducing various values of τ, a software development team can measure the required contribution of coalitions of software development technologies needed to satisfy a project timing constraint. In practice, the functionality of software as well as the availability and feasibility of coalitions of software technologies evolves and continuously changes. The feedback system described in this paper suggests how one might cope with these changes by adjusting the extent of change needed in the technical complexity factor to develop a software product within a required time. Finally, the design and analysis of the proposed feedback system will be aided by rough Petri net and roughly fuzzy Petri net models of decision table-building and rule derivation processes as well as models of the cost estimation rules themselves similar to rule-modeling in [11].

Acknowledgements First, we thank Prof. Michel Grabisch, Thomson-CSF Laboratories, Orsay Cedex, France, Prof. Andrzej Skowron, Faculty of Mathematics, Computer Science and Mechanics, Warsaw University and Prof. Zbigniew Suraj, Institute of Mathematics, Rzeszow, members of the Institute of Mathematics at Warsaw University for discussions we have had related to this research. Second, we gratefully acknowledge the funding for this research provided by the Natural Sciences and Engineering Research Council of Canada (NSERC) operating funds for both authors, Canadian Space Agency, the University of Manitoba research grants committee, and the University of Winnipeg research grants committee.

References

[1]   J.F. Peters and W. Pedrycz, Software Engineering: An Engineering Approach. NY, John Wiley & Sons, Inc. 2000.

[2]   J.F. Peters and S. Ramanna: Application of Choquet Integral in Software Cost Estimation. IEEE Int. Conf. on Fuzzy Systems, New Orleans, 1996, 862-866.

[3]   W. Pedrycz, J.F. Peters, S. Ramanna, Design of a software quality decision system: A computational intelligence approach, CCECE'98, Waterloo, Ontario, May 1998, 513-516.

[4]   J.F. Peters and S. Ramanna: A rough sets approach to assessing software quality: Concepts and rough Petri net models. In: Rough Fuzzy Hybridization. A new Trend in Decision –Making, edited by S.K. Pal and A. Skowron. Singapore, Springer-Verlag 349-380.

[5]   J.F.Peters and S. Ramanna, Time-constrained software cost control system: concepts and roughly fuzzy Petri net model. In: Computational Intelligence in Software Engineering, W. Pedrycz, J.F. Peters (Eds.). Singapore, World Scientific Publishing Co., Pte. Ltd., 1998, 339-370.

[6]   J.F.Peters and S. Ramanna, Software Deployability Decision System Framework: A Rough Sets Approach, Proceedings IPMU'98, Paris, France, June, 1998, 1539-1545.

[7]   J.F. Peters, S. Ramanna, Application of the Choquet integral in a software deployability control system, Proc. of the 5th Int. Conf. on Soft Computing and Information/Intelligent Systems, Iizuka, Fuduoka Japan, 16-20 October 1998, vol. 1, 386-389.

[8]   J.F. Peters, L. Han, S. Ramanna, The Choquet integral in a rough software cost estimation system. In: M. Grabisch, T. Murofushi, M. Sugeno (Eds.), Fuzzy Measures and Integrals: Theory and Applications. Heidelberg, Germany, Springer-Verlag, 1999.

[9]   J.F. Peters, Time and clock information systems: Concepts and roughly fuzzy Petri net models. In: Rough Sets in Knowledge Discovery edited by L. Polkowski and A. Skowron. Physica Verlag, a division of Springer Verlag, vol. 2, 1998, 385-418.

[10] J.F. Peters, L. Han, S. Ramanna, Approximate Time Rough Software Cost Decision System: Multicriteria Decision-Making Approach. In: Lecture Notes in Artificial Intelligence 1609. Berlin: Springer Verlag, 1999, 556-564.

[11] J.F. Peters, S. Skowron, Z. Suraj, W. Pedrycz, S. Ramanna, Approximate real-time decision-making: Concepts and roughly fuzzy Petri net model, International Journal of Intelligent Systems, vol. 14, no. 4, 1999, 4-37.

[12] M. Grabisch: Alternative representations of discrete fuzzy measures for decision making. Int. J. of Uncertainty, Fuzziness and Knowledge-Based Systems 0, 0, 1997, 1-21.

[13] M. Grabisch, Fuzzy integral in multicriteria decision making. *Fuzzy Sets and Systems*, 69: 279-298, 1995.

[14] M. Grabisch, H.T. Nguyen, E.A. Walker: Fundamentals of Uncertainty Calculi with Applications to Fuzzy Inference. Boston, Kluwer Academic Publishers, 1995.

[15] A. Albrecht and J.E. Gaffney: Software Function, Source Lines of Code, and Development Effort Prediction: A Software Science Validation. IEEE Trans. on Software Engineering, SE-9, 6 (1983) 639-647.

[16] N. Wiener, Cybernetics: Or Control and Communication in the Animal and the Machine. Cambridge, MA, MIT Press, 1961.

[17] W. Pedrycz, J.F. Peters, Learning in fuzzy Petri nets. In: Fuzzy Petri Nets, Cardoso, J., Sandri, S. (Eds.). Berlin, Physica Verlag [in press].

[18] M.H.Halstead, Elements of Software Science, North Holland, New York, 1977.

[19] M. Sugeno: Theory of fuzzy integrals and its applications. Ph.D. Thesis, Tokyo Institute of Technology, 1974.

[20] G. Choquet, Theory of capacities. Annales de l'Institut Fourier, 5, 1953, 131-295.

[21] L.A. Zadeh, Fuzzy logic = computing with words. IEEE Trans. on Fuzzy Systems 4/2 (1996) 103-111.

[22] L.A. Zadeh, Toward a theory of fuzzy information granulation and its certainty in human reasoning and fuzzy logic. Fuzzy Sets and Systems 90/ 2 (1997) 111-128.

[23] G.J. Klir, M.J. Wierman, Uncertainty-Based Information: Elements of Generalized Information Theory. Report, Center for Research in Fuzzy Mathematics and Computer Science, Creighton University, Omaha, Nebraska 63178, U.S.A., 1997.

[24] L.A. Zadeh, Fuzzy sets, Information and Control 8 (1965) 338-353.

[25] B.R. Gaines, Multivalued logics and fuzzy reasoning. BCS AISB Summer School, Cambridge, 1975.

[26] J. Lukasiewicz, Logic and the problem of the foundations of mathematics. In: Jan Lukasiewicz, Borkowski, L. (Ed.), Amsterdam, North-Holland Pub. Co., 1970, 278-294.

[27] D. Ruan, A critical study of widely used fuzzy implication operators and their influence on the inference rules in fuzzy expert systems. Ph.D. thesis, Gent, 1990.

[28] Z. Pawlak, Rough Sets: Theoretical Aspects of Reasoning About Data. Boston, MA, Kluwer Academic Publishers, 1991.

[29] Z. Pawlak, Rough sets: present state and future prospects. ICS Research Report 32/95, Institute of Computer Science, Warsaw Institute of Technology, 1995.

[30] Z. Pawlak, Grzymala-Busse, J.W., Slowinski, R., Ziarko, W.: Rough Sets. Communications of the ACM 38 (1995) 88-95.

[31] A. Skowron, Extracting laws from decision tables: a rough set approach. Computational Intelligence 11/2 (1995) 371-388.

[32] A. Skowron, L. Polkowski, Rough mereology: A new paradigm for approximate reasoning. Journ. of Approximate Reasoning 15/4 (1996) 333-365.

[33] A. Skowron, C. Rauszer, The discernability matrices and functions in information systems. In: Intelligent Decision Support, Handbook of Applications and Advances of the Rough Sets Theory, Slowinski, R. (Ed.), Dordrecht, Kluwer Academic Publishers, 1992, 331-362.

[34] A. Skowron, Z. Suraj, A rough set approach to real-time state identification. Bulletin EATCS 50 (1993) 264-275.

[35] A. Skowron, Z. Suraj, Synthesis of concurrent systems specified by information systems. ICS Research Report 39/94, Institute of Computer Science, Warsaw Institute of Technology, 1994.

[36] A. Skowron, Z. Suraj, Discovery of concurrent data models from experimental data tables: a rough set approach. Institute of Computer Science Research Report 15/95, Warsaw Institute of Technology, 1995.

[37] A. Skowron, Z. Suraj, A parallel algorithm for real-time decision making: a rough set approach. Journal of Intelligent Information Systems 7 (1996) 5-28

[38] A. Skowron, Z. Suraj, A rough set approach to real-time state identification for decision making. Institute of Computer Science Research Report 18/93, Warsaw University of Technology, 1993.

[39] J. Sienkiewicz, Rough sets for boolean functions minimization. Research Report, Warsaw Institute of Technology, 1995.

[40] T. Murata, Petri nets: properties, analysis and applications. Proceedings of the IEEE **77/4** (1989) 541-580.

[41] C.A. Petri, Kommunikation mit Automaten. Schriften des IIM Nr. 3, Institut für Instrumentelle Mathematik, Bonn, West Germany. See, also, Communication with Automata (in English). Griffiss Air Force Base, New York Technical Report RADC-Tr-65-377, **1**, Suppl. 1, 1962.

[42] K. Jensen, Coloured Petri nets. In: Advances in Petri Nets 254 (1986) 288-299.

[43] K. Jensen, Coloured Petri Nets--Basic Concepts, Analysis Methods and Practical Use **1**. Berlin, Springer-Verlag, 1992.

[44] P. Huber, K. Jensen, R.M. Shapiro, Hierarchies in coloured Petri nets. Proc. Int. Conf. Science on Application and Theory of Petri Nets. In: Rozenberg, G. (Ed.), Lecture Notes in Computer Science 483 (1986) 261-292.

[45] W. Pedrycz, F. Gomide, A generalized fuzzy Petri net model. IEEE Trans. on Fuzzy Systems 2/4 (1994) 295-301.

[46] P. Scrinivan, D. Gracarin, Approximate reasoning with fuzzy Petri nets. Proc. IEEE Int. Conf. on Fuzzy Systems, San Francisco, CA (1993) 396-401.

[47] H. Scarpelli, F. Gomide, Relational calculus in designing fuzzy Petri nets. In: W. Pedrycz (Ed.), Fuzzy Modelling: Paradigms and Practice. Boston, MA, Kluwer Academic Publishers, 1996, 70-89.

[48] H. Scarpelli, F. Gomide, Fuzzy reasoning and high level fuzzy Petri nets. In: Proc. First European Congress on Fuzzy and Intelligent Technologies, Aachen, Germany (1993) 600-605.

[49] H. Scarpelli, F. Gomide, R. Yager, A reasoning algorithm for high-level fuzzy Petri nets. IEEE Trans. on Fuzzy Systems 4/3 (1996) 282-295.

[50] W. Pedrycz, J.F. Peters, S. Ramanna, T. Furuhashi, From data to fuzzy Petri nets: generalized model and calibration abilities. Proc. of Seventh Int. Fuzzy Systems Association World Congress (IFSA'97) III (1997) 294-299.

[51] W. Pedrycz, J.F. Peters, Information Granularity Uncertainty Principle: Contingency Tables and Petri Net Representations. Proc. Proc. North American Fuzzy Information Processing Society NAFIPS'97, Syracuse, NY, (1997) 222-226.

[52] M.L. Garg, S.I. Ahson, P.V. Gupta, A fuzzy Petri net for knowledge representation and reasoning. Information Processing Letters **39** (1991) 165-171.

[53] H.S. Son, P.H. Seong, A safety analysis method using fuzzy Petri nets. Proc. North American Fuzzy Information Processing Society (NAFIPS'97), Syracuse, NY (1997) 412-417.

[54] R. Gudwin, F. Gomide, Object networks--A modeling tool. Proc. IEEE World Congress on Computational Intelligence (WCCI'98), Anchorage, Alaska, 4-9 May 1998.

[55] J. Cardoso, G. Bittencourt, L.L. Caimi, A frame-based representation for fuzzy Petri nets. Proc. IEEE World Congress on Computational Intelligence (WCCI'98), Anchorage, Alaska, 4-9 May 1998.

[56] S. Sandri, J. Cardoso, Possibilistic timed safe Petri nets. Proc. IEEE World Congress on Computational Intelligence (WCCI'98), Anchorage, Alaska, 4-9 May 1998.

[57] T. Furuhashi, J.F. Peters, W. Pedrycz, A stability analysis of fuzzy control systems using a generalized fuzzy Petri net model. Proc. IEEE World Congress on Computational Intelligence (WCCI'98), Anchorage, Alaska, 4-9 May 1998.

[58] H. Ammar, L. Yu, A comparison of two analysis algorithms for fuzzy marking Petri nets. Proc. IEEE World Congress on Computational Intelligence (WCCI'98), Anchorage, Alaska, 4-9 May 1998.

[59] H.SNguyen: Discretization of real-valued attributes: Boolean reasoning approach. Doctoral Thesis, Faculty of Mathematics, Computer Science and Mechanics, Warsaw University, 1997.

[60] H.S. Nguyen, Rule induction from continuous data: New discretization concepts. Proc. of the Third Joint Conf. on Information Sciences, Raleigh, N.C., 1-5 March 1997.

[61] Rosetta Software System, http://www.id.ntnu.no/~aleks/rosetta/

Chapter 3
Predictive Fuzzy Model for Control of an Artificial Muscle

Petar B. Petrović

Faculty of Mechanical Enginering,
Belgrade University

Abstract

Modeling and control of a special type of the pneumatic actuator, called the Artificial Pneumatic Muscle (APM), is considered here. APM is able to exhibit many of the properties found in the real biological muscle. Contrary to its simple design, the control of APM is very complex due to its nonlinearity, compressibility of air, time varying properties, and difficulties in analytical modeling. In particular, the hysteretic behavior, which originates mainly from the extensive friction between different APM layers, is difficult to model. In order to overcome this problem, we propose a simple adaptive control law based on the APM predictive fuzzy dynamic model, which is able to cope with the inherent hysteresis of APM. Structure and parameters of the APM predictive fuzzy model are described through the fuzzy clustering of experimental data. The proposed predictive fuzzy model and its control law are verified through computer simulation.

Keywords : robotics, pneumatic actuator, predictive fuzzy model, model identification, fuzzy clustering, adaptive control

3.1 Introduction

An artificial pneumatic muscle (APM) was first developed for use in artificial limbs in the 1950's and, more recently, was commercialized in the 1980's by Bridgestone Rubber Company of Japan for robotic applications [1]. No moving parts, large force output per unit weight, intrinsic compliance, extremely simple design and easy maintenance, make it ideal for a number of robotic applications, such as robotic assembly, robotic painting, manipulation, human-robot interactions or walking robots.

APM consists of an expandable internal bladder (a rubber tube) surrounded by a braided shell. When the internal bladder is pressurized,

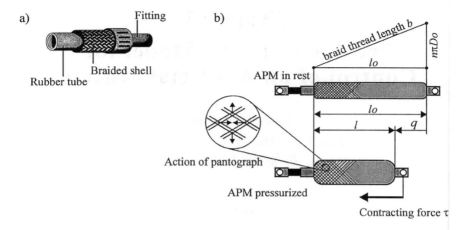

Fig. 3.1 Basic design of the Artificial Pneumatic Muscle (a)
and its functioning principle (b).

APM expands in a balloon-like manner against the braided shell. The braided shell acts to constrain the expansion in order to maintain a cylindrical shape. As the volume of the internal bladder increases due to the increase in pressure, the actuator shortens and/or produces tension if coupled to a mechanical load (shown in Fig. 3.1).

Unfortunately, accurate control and stabilization of the APM present a challenging problem. This is due to both the highly nonlinear functioning principle and the compressibility of air. Further complications arise from the nonlinear characteristic of airflow through a variable surface area orifice, dynamic characteristics of the servo-valve that meters the airflow and from the assumption that the air pressure changes uniformly in the actuator chamber. The actual air pressure response occurs during the time it takes an acoustic wave to travel the length of the actuator, so a specific dynamical phenomenon is present in the system, which is difficult to model. Finally, the actuator exhibits hysteretic behavior, because the pressure-position relationship is not the same within a single expansion/compression cycle. The wide hysteretic loop is a very serious problem from the aspect of the precision position control of the APM actuator. Effectively, the common problem of the actuator hardware complexity is transferred here into the control domain.

3.2 APM Analytical Model and Control Law synthesis

APM is a pneumatic actuator that converts pneumatic energy into mechanical. To find the relationship of the actuating force, length, and pressure, several quasi-static and dynamic experiments are performed. Starting from a basic mechanical functioning principle, a simplified quasi-static model may be derived using the energy conservation principle [2]. This model is further extended by the introduction of dynamic terms - inertial forces and friction forces. The obtained dynamic model is used to develop an accurate model-based control for the APM actuator.

3.2.1 *Analytical model*

The input work of the pressurized gas, which expands the inner bladder, is given by the following equation:

$$dW_{in} = pdLdS = pdV \qquad (1)$$

where: p is the difference between internal air pressure and environmental pressure, dS is the area vector, dL is the inner surface displacement and dV is the change in actuator volume. If is neglected, the friction between inner bladder and braided shell, and deformation work of inner bladder, the output work is defined as:

$$dW_{out} = -\tau dl \qquad (2)$$

where: τ is the actuating force i.e., axial tension, and dl is the change in actuator length. Applying the energy conservation principle, the input work should be equal to the output work, if no energy storage is present. Accordingly, combining (1) and (2), we obtain an approximate equation that links all basic physical variables of APM:

$$dW_{out} = dW_{in} \rightarrow \tau = -p\frac{dV}{dl} \qquad (3)$$

The stored work in the elastic structure of the bladder (strain energy) and the work needed to overcome frictional effects are not considered in the simplified quasi-static model (3).

Further, it may be assumed that the actuator volume depends only on its length, which is true in an approximation. This is because the extensibility of the braided shell threads is relatively low and the actuator barrel is an ideal cylinder. The last assumption is acceptable for long actuators, where the end effects are negligible, but unacceptable for short actuators. On the

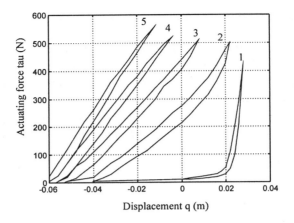

Fig. 3.2 An example plot of quasi-static experiments (the APM parameters are: $lo = 0.160$ m, $Do = 0.0127$ m, number of the braid thread turns $n = 1.46$, internal bladder material – silicone rubber 50 Shore, braided shell material - polyester).

basis of the assumptions introduced and by applying basic mechanical relations to the functioning of the APM braided shell, equation (3) may be transformed into:

$$\tau = -p\frac{dV}{dl} = \frac{b^2}{4\pi n^2}(1-3\frac{l^2}{b^2})p \tag{4}$$

By n and b are denoted design parameters of the actuator, see Fig. 3.1. Introducing the actuator generalized coordinate defined as $q = l_0 - l$, equation (4) becomes:

$$\tau = (D_1 + D_2q + D_3q^2)p = f(q)p \tag{5}$$

where D_1, D_2 and, D_3 are the APM synthesized design parameters. The simplified quasi-static model shows that the actuating force is a linear function of the relative internal air pressure, p, and a nonlinear function of the actuator displacement, q. This kind of behavior is evident in experimental plots, shown in Fig. 3.2. The sloped loops represent the actuating force-displacement dependence (CW hysteresis direction) for different values of working pressure (isobaric experiments). The working pressure is indicated above each particular curve. The difference between the analytical model (2) and the measured quasi-static behavior originates from the adopted approximations. Elimination of friction in the actuator was the most important approximation.

By means of equation (5), APM is modeled as a gas spring with nonlinear stiffness characteristic. Besides friction, the functioning of a real APM is governed by its inertial characteristics. After introducing friction and inertial terms into the quasi-static model (5), dynamic behavior of the APM may be written as follows:

$$M\ddot{q} + F^w(q,\dot{q},p) + f(q)p = \tau \tag{6}$$

where: M is the equivalent mass of the actuator moving part, $F^w(q,\dot{q},p)$ is the nonlinear function which describes the friction forces arising inside of APM (friction inside the rubber tube material, friction inside the braided shell structure, friction between the rubber tube and the braided shell, and friction of pressurized gas).

Further, it may be assumed that the friction term in (6) is a linear function of the working pressure, p. Then, the APM dynamic model (6) may be expressed as an explicit function of the working pressure:

$$M\ddot{q} + \mu(q,\dot{q})p + f(q)p = \tau \tag{7}$$

The nonlinear function $\mu(q,\dot{q})$ denotes the lumped model of friction forces coming from different sources in the APM structure. Dynamics of a pneumatic servo valve is not considered. The control law will be developed on the basis of the APM dynamic model only. An extension of the dynamic model (7) is possible by introduction of pneumatic flow equations, as given in [3].

3.2.2 *Control law synthesis*

According to the nonlinear approaches used in control systems of robotic manipulators, the basic scheme for the displacement control of APM should be based on partitioning of the control law into two parts. The first part of the control law is model-based, which allows the application of the supposed knowledge of the particular system under control. The model-based portion has to be set up so that it reduces the system, which then resembles a unit mass system. The second part is error-based. The error-based creates error signals by differencing desired and actual control variables and, then, multiplying these errors by appropriate gains. The model-based portion is defined as:

$$\tau = \alpha\tau' + \beta \tag{8}$$

where α and β are the functions defined by the dynamical model of the object to be controlled, and τ' is the new input into the system. In order to make the APM system, given by the dynamic model (7), appear as a unit mass from the input τ', functions α and β should be chosen as:

$$\alpha = M \tag{9}$$
$$\beta = [\mu(q,\dot{q}) + f(q)]p \tag{10}$$

and combining it with a servo portion for the unit mass system, the control law becomes:

$$\tau = \alpha[\ddot{q}_p + k_v(\dot{q}_p - \dot{q}) + k_p(q_p - q)] + \beta =$$

$$= M[\ddot{q}_p + k_v\dot{e} + k_pe] + [\mu(q,\dot{q}) + f(q)]p \tag{11}$$

where $e = q_p - q$ is an error function and subscript p denotes programmed values. A block diagram of the decoupled and linearized position control law, given by (11), is shown in Fig. 3.3.

Stability and precision control of AMP actuator are very important considering its applications in robotic manipulators. The proposed control law (11) may serve as a good basis for improving them, but only in cases where an accurate model of APM is known in advance. The knowledge of α and β functions defined in accordance with (9) and (10) is essential. A possible solution to the problem of identification of these functions is considered further.

3.3 APM Predictive Fuzzy Model

In our previous work [4] we have used usual way to represent non-linear mappings in control systems by means of fuzzy dynamic formal structures, based on context sensitive architecture. Mechanical behavior of the APM has been modeled as a simple mapping between its input and output variables, using measured I/O data. On that way important information regarding connection between past and current states in functioning of an APM (process development) are not preserved. Ambiguity in I/O mapping which exists as a consequence of APM hysteretic behavior (hysteresis loop shown in Fig. 3.2) may not be solved without past output data. The next output value of tension, τ, produced by APM should be *predicted* not only by information of changing in APM input variables, but by information of past values of tension too.

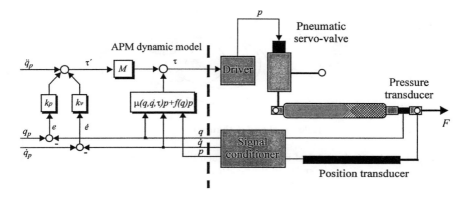

Fig. 3.3 Block diagram of the model-based APM control law.

3.3.1 *Predictive Fuzzy Model*

In general, prediction is the process of generating information for the possible future development of a process from data about its past and its present development. By prediction is possible to find a global underlying structures, models, and formulas, which can explain the behavior of the process in the long run as well as for understanding the past.

Prediction may be based on two types of data: (1)*time-series* data and (2)*stationary* (time independent) data. For control of dynamic systems, prediction of time-series events is of special interest.

When prediction is done on the basis of only one independent variable it is called a *univariate prediction*, otherwise, it is called a *multivariate prediction* [5]. A general form of a heuristic rule for time-series prediction is (graphical presentation is given in Fig. 3.4):

> **if** (previous time-moment values for the predicted variable(s) from solutions space are *si*)
>
> **and** (values for the features from the input domain are *dj*)
>
> **then** (next time-moment values for the predicted variable(s) will be *sk*)

Predicted value of an output variable *s* in a future time moment is based on *k* previous values. In this case, *k* is a lag of prediction. If exists a time

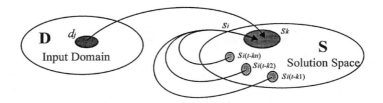

Rule: (**if** *si* **and** *dj* **than** *sk*)

Fig. 3.4   A general model of mapping between the input domain into the solution space in time-series prediction.

series of the variable s for the moments from 1 to t, that is $s(1)$, $s(2)$, ..., $s(t)$, it is possible to predict $s(t+1)$ and also the next time interval values $s(t+2)$, ..., $q(t+m)$ using the previous time-moment values of the same variable.

According to the previous considerations, it is possible to build up various predictive models for the APM mechanical behavior using a time series of I/O data.   Some of these models for β function, which is given by the equation (10), are shown in Fig. 3.5.

The first model, shown in Fig. 3.5a, is based on univariate prediction.   In this model, the next-time value of β function is determined by the k previous values of the same function.   No inputs from the input domain are provided to the control system.

Fuzzy model shown in Fig. 3.5b is a multivariate model.   In addition to k previous values of the β function, the next-time value of the β function is determined by the additional input into the system coming from the input domain i.e., current value of the generalized coordinate q.

The third predictive fuzzy model, shown in Fig. 3.5c, is multivariate again, but in this case, next-time value of the β function is determined by k previous values of the β function and m previous values of the generalized coordinate q.   In this model, a part of history from the input domain is introduced.

Finally, the predictive fuzzy model shown in Fig. 3.5d is a multivariate predictive model, which is similar to the model shown in Fig. 3.5c.   But in this case, it has an additional input variable from the input domain i.e., pressure p (only the current value is used).   This variable is introduced to improve the information available to the system about the real physical input variables.

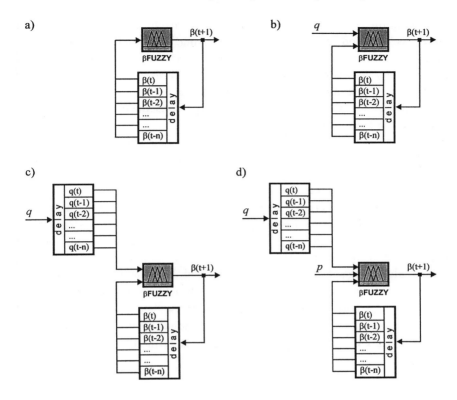

Fig. 3.5 Different prediction models for prediction next-step values of β function (10) which contains a hysteretic behavior of partitioned APM dynamic model.

Starting from the simplest model shown in Fig. 3.5a, the representation capability of the proposed predictive fuzzy model increases with the increase in its complexity. Better representative capability, i.e., more accurate prediction of the next-time value, is achieved at the expense of increased dimensionality of the predictive fuzzy model. Simultaneously, the robustness of the predictive fuzzy model is improved.

3.3.2 *Fuzzy model identification*

At the opposite to the 'subjective' methods for fuzzy model identification, where expert knowledge is used for I/O space partition and structure identification (fuzzy rule base of inference machine), we have adopted 'objective' method, based on fuzzy clustering. This method is 'objective' because in fuzzy model identification we use only I/O numerical data obtained by measuring real behavior of APM actuator. Features or properties of the measured data allow us to recognize or discover the structure of fuzzy model on formally consequent way, applying nonheuristic analytical tools.

At the first, we have to identify data clusters and after that, we have to transfer them into the appropriate set of fuzzy rules. This is the structure identification of the APM fuzzy model. The parameter set identification is considered in the separate subsection.

As an extension of crisp clustering, *fuzzy c-means* clustering is a data clustering technique for grouping similar data into categorically homogenous subsets called *clusters*, where each data point belongs to any one cluster to a degree specified by a membership function. Fuzzy c-means clustering of data points is defined by *variance criterion* [6]. Variance criterion measures the dissimilarity between the data points in a cluster and its cluster center by the Euclidean distance. In particular, for given data set $X = \{x_1, ..., x_n\}$ in p - dimensional vector space, and set of cluster centers $C = \{v_1, ..., v_c\}$, this distance is defined as:

$$d_{ik} = d_{ik}(x_k, v_i) = \|x_k - v_i\| = \left[\sum_{j=1}^{p}(x_{kj} - v_{ij})^2\right]^{1/2} \tag{11}$$

The data points belonging to any one of the clusters should be similar and the data points of different clusters as similar as possible. Specifying the number of clusters, c, as *a priori* data, it is possible to partition data set through satisfying the following objective function:

$$\min J(\widetilde{U}, v) = \min \sum_{i=1}^{c}\sum_{k=1}^{n}(\mu_{ik})^w \|x_k - v_i\|^2 \tag{12}$$

where $\widetilde{U} = [\mu_{ik}] \in R^{c \times n}$ is the fuzzy partition matrix, μ_{ik} is the membership degree of data point x_k to the i-th cluster and, w is the exponential weight factor that shapes fuzzy partition matrix (the larger w, the fuzzier partition matrix; no theoretically justified procedure exist for choosing w; usually is chosen $w = 2$). Cluster centers are determined by:

$$v_i = \frac{1}{\sum_{k=1}^{n}(\mu_{ik})^w}\sum_{k=1}^{n}(\mu_{ik})^w x_k, \quad w > 1, \quad i = 1, ..., c \tag{13}$$

and the membership degree of each data point is:

$$\mu_{ki} = \sum_{j=1}^{c} \left(\frac{\|x_k - v_i\|}{\|x_k - v_j\|} \right)^{-2/(w-1)} , \quad i = 1, \ldots, c, \quad k = 1, \ldots, n. \tag{14}$$

The nonlinear optimization problem described by equations (13) and (14) cannot be solved analytically. There exist iterative algorithms [6], which approximate the minimum of objective function (12), starting from a given initial position of the cluster centers. The quality of the solution depends strongly on the choice of the number of fuzzy clusters, c, and its initial positions, both as *a priori* data.

Instead of using an *a priori* number of fuzzy clusters c, the partitioning may be optimized by introduction additional criteria (searching for the optimal c). In [6] is proposed approach based on partition coefficient. The partition coefficient is defined as:

$$F(\tilde{U}, c) = \frac{1}{n} \min \sum_{k=1}^{n} \sum_{i=1}^{c} (\mu_{ik})^2 \tag{15}$$

Heuristic optimization criteria is further connected to the extreme of partition coefficient:

$$\max_{c} \left\{ \max_{\tilde{U} \in \Omega_c} F(\tilde{U}, c) \right\}, \quad c = 2, \ldots, n-1 \tag{16}$$

where Ω_c is the set of all optimal solutions for given c. In general, practical implementation of this approach is limited by monotonicity of partition coefficient (15).

An alternative approach is presented in [7], where is introduced a data fluctuation between clusters:

$$\sum_{i=1}^{c} \sum_{k=1}^{n} (\mu_{ik})^w \|v_i - x_s\|^2, \quad x_s = \sum_{k=1}^{n} (x_k) \tag{17}$$

Optimal partition is defined by global minimum of objective function:

$$J(\tilde{U}, c, v) = \min \sum_{i=1}^{c} \sum_{k=1}^{n} (\mu_{ik})^w \left\{ \|x_k - v_i\|^2 - \|v_i - x_s\|^2 \right\} \tag{18}$$

In general, a global minimum of (18) exists.

A third approach is based on specification of cluster radius as *a priori* data. A cluster radius is defined as:

$$\text{rad}\tilde{U}_i = \sup_{x_k \in U_i} d_{ik}(x_k, v_i) \tag{19}$$

Utilizing the cluster radius, a *subtractive clustering* algorithm is developed as extension of fuzzy c-means clustering [8]. This is fast, one-pass algorithm, dedicated for estimating the number of fuzzy clusters and the cluster centers in the given set of data points. The subtractive clustering is briefly described in Appendix A.

Each cluster center may be used as the basis of the rule that describes local behavior of the APM actuator. On that way we can build fuzzy model based on scattered partition instead of usually used uniform grid partition. Scattered partition always leads to the simple fuzzy model with only few fuzzy rules i.e., the number of fuzzy rules is equal to the number of identified fuzzy clusters. The minimum number of fuzzy rules has a high importance for real-time applications.

Coordinates of each data point vector x_k are further divided into two parts. First of them, $y = [y_1, ..., y_m]^T$, represents the input coordinates of the system, while the second, $z = [z_1, ..., z_l]^T$, represents the output coordinates. Here must be satisfied $m + l = p$. As it is proposed in [8], we have used first order Sugeno-Takagi fuzzy inference in the form:

$$R_j: \qquad \textbf{if } (y_1 \textbf{ is } \tilde{A}_j) \textbf{ and ... and}(y_m \textbf{ is } \tilde{A}_j) \textbf{ then}$$

$$z_q(y) = a_{j0} + a_{j1} * y_1 + ... + a_{jm} * y_m \qquad (20)$$

where: $\tilde{A}_j, j = (1,...,c)$ are the fuzzy sets of antecedents and $a_{ji}, i = (0,...,m)$ are the consequent parameters. Consequents are fuzzy singleton sets whose singleton output spikes may walk around the output space, as a linear function of the crisp input values. Each fuzzy rule represents one of the fuzzy clusters. Fuzzy rules are connected together by 'and' logical operator. Transferring of fuzzy clusters into Sugeno-Takagi fuzzy rules is described in Appendix B.

3.3.3   *Parameter Set Identification*

Adaptive fuzzy network ANFIS, proposed in [9], is used for parameter set identification of the APM fuzzy model (20). This fuzzy network is of feedforward type and consists of two types of nodes, placed in five layers. Parametric nodes are adaptive multipliers, while fixed nodes perform basic logical and arithmetic operations, required by adopted first order Sugeno-Takagi fuzzy inference. Links between nodes only indicate the flow direction of the signals. Parameter set may be updated using the set of data points X and appropriate batch learning algorithm (off-line learning) details are given in [9].

3.4 Computer Simulation

In order to verify the proposed APM predictive fuzzy model and control concept, a computer simulation was performed based on experimental training data. By the time this article was written only quasi-static measurements were performed. Thus, the simulations presented here relate only to the quasi-static part of the APM model. The lack of dynamic data is not important for the results obtained, because the hysteretic behavior comes mainly from the quasi-static domain.

Fig. 3.6 presents the simulation results obtained by a non-predictive fuzzy model presented in our previous work [4]. This is useful for comparison of advantages of the proposed predictive models. Obviously, this fuzzy model is not able to follow the hysteric type of nonlinearity. Instead of hysteresis loops, which exist in measured plots, only mean values are produced as the fuzzy output.

Simulation results for predictive models shown in Fig. 3.5a and Fig. 3.5b are shown in Fig. 3.7 and Fig. 3.8, respectively. Both proposed predictive models could follow hysteretic loops with acceptable quality of approximation.

a)   b)

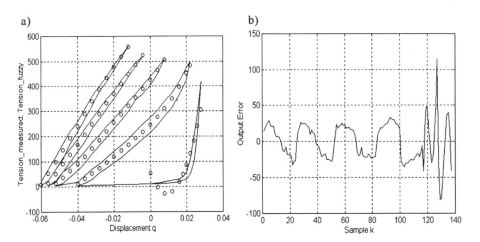

Fig. 3.6 Non predictive APM fuzzy model: a)measured (continuos line) and learned (circles) quasi-static part of APM dynamic model represented by β function (experimental data used for training are the same as those shown in Fig. 3.3); b)corresponding error graph, RMSE = 26.5342.

The univariate predictive fuzzy model is adopted in the form:

$$\beta(t+1) = \beta[\beta(t), \beta(t-6), \beta(t-12), \beta(t-18)] \tag{21}$$

where four previous time values of the β function are used for prediction of the next step value, $\beta(t+1)$. Accordingly, this predictive model has four inputs and one output. The previous time values of the β function input are chosen with time lag of 6 sampling units, starting from $\beta(t)$ and including $\beta(t-18)$.

a)

b)

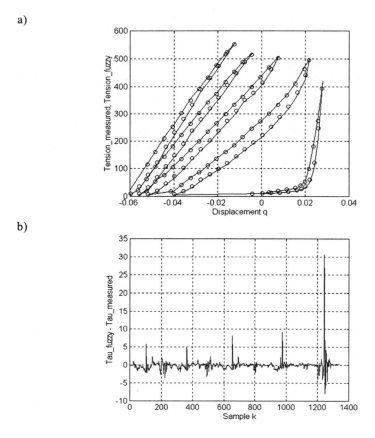

Fig. 3.7   Univariate predictive APM fuzzy model: a)measured (continuos line) and learned (circles) quasi-static part of APM dynamic model represented by β function (experimental data used for training are the same as those shown in Fig. 3.3); b)corresponding error graph, RMSE = 1.5527.

Introducing a generalized coordinate q as an additional input in the univariate model (21), a new multivariate predictive fuzzy model is obtained. The analytical formulation of this model is:

$$\beta(t+1) = \beta[q, \beta(t), \beta(t-6), \beta(t-12), \beta(t-18)] \qquad (22)$$

This predictive fuzzy model (the case b in Fig. 3.5) has five inputs and one output.

a)

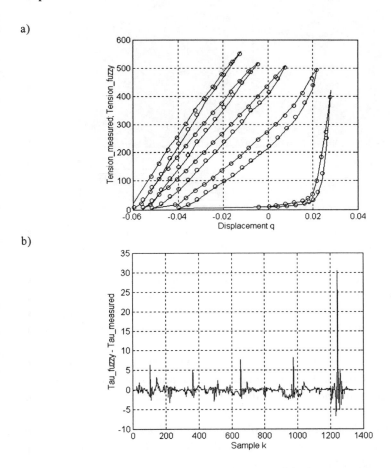

b)

Fig. 3.8   Multivariate predictive APM fuzzy model: a)measured (continuos line) and learned (circles) quasi-static part of APM dynamic model represented by β function (experimental data used for training are the same as those shown in Fig. 3.3); b)corresponding error graph, RMSE = 1.4941.

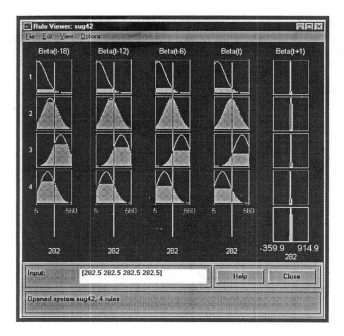

Fig. 3.9   Sugeno-Takagi inference for univariate predictive fuzzy model for quasi-static part of the APM dynamic model represented by β function.

The multivariate predictive fuzzy model has slightly better representative capabilities than the univariate one. Furthermore, the univariate model has a lower order. Considering the difference between corresponding RMSE values, it may be concluded that the univariate predictive model is more appropriate for the problem at hand.

Identification of the predictive fuzzy models were performed using a set of measured I/O data (I/O vector length is 1341 points) and the subtractive fuzzy clustering method. For scatter I/O space partitioning, cluster radius $r = 0.5$ and a bell shaped membership functions for antecedent variables were adopted. The output variable was modeled as a linear function of antecedent variables, as it was requested by the first order Sugeno-Takagi fuzzy inference (shown in Fig. 3.9).

As shown in Fig. 3.9, the quasi-static part of an APM dynamic model is expressed by four first order Sugeno-Takagi rules only:

R_1:   **if** $(\beta(t\text{-}18)$ **is** *Small*) **and** $(\beta(t\text{-}12)$ **is** *Small*)
      and $(\beta(t\text{-}6)$ **is** *Small*) **and** $(\beta(t)$ **is** *Small*)
      then $\beta(t\text{+}1) = a_{10} + a_{11}\beta(t\text{-}18) + a_{12}\beta(t\text{-}12) + a_{13}\beta(t\text{-}6) + a_{14}\beta(t)$

R_2:   **if** $(\beta(t\text{-}18)$ **is** *MediumLeft*) **and** $(\beta(t\text{-}12)$ **is** *MediumLeft*)
      and $(\beta(t\text{-}6)$ **is** *MediumLeft*) **and** $(\beta(t)$ **is** *MediumLeft*)
      then $\beta(t\text{+}1) = a_{20} + a_{21}\beta(t\text{-}18) + a_{22}\beta(t\text{-}12) + a_{23}\beta(t\text{-}6) + a_{24}\beta(t)$

R_3:   **if** $(\beta(t\text{-}18)$ **is** *MediumRight*) **and** $(\beta(t\text{-}12)$ **is** *MediumRight*)
      and $(\beta(t\text{-}6)$ **is** *MediumRight*) **and** $(\beta(t)$ **is** *MediumRight*)
      then $\beta(t\text{+}1) = a_{30} + a_{31}\beta(t\text{-}18) + a_{32}\beta(t\text{-}12) + a_{33}\beta(t\text{-}6) + a_{34}\beta(t)$

R_4:   **if** $(\beta(t\text{-}18)$ **is** *Large*) **and** $(\beta(t\text{-}12)$ **is** *Large*)
      and $(\beta(t\text{-}6)$ **is** *Large*) **and** $(\beta(t)$ **is** *Large*)
      then $\beta(t\text{+}1) = a_{40} + a_{41}\beta(t\text{-}18) + a_{42}\beta(t\text{-}12) + a_{43}\beta(t\text{-}6) + a_{44}\beta(t)$

Each fuzzy input variable is expressed by four linguistic values i.e., the term set is $L(\beta(t\text{-}k)) = \{Small, MediumLeft, MediumRight, Large\}$. This input space discretization is a result of the data clustering process performed. Thus, this is data driven discretization.

It is important to emphasize that using scatter partition of the I/O space, only four fuzzy rules were identified despite the fact that each of antecedent fuzzy variables had four fuzzy values. In the case of uniform grid partition of I/O space, which is common in applications of Sugeno-Takagi inference, antecedent fuzzy variables with four fuzzy values lead to the system of 256 rules. This figure by itself does not require any additional comment.

For the best fitting, the initial fuzzy model is further optimized by ANFIS (Adaptive Network-based Fuzzy Inference System) which is described in details in reference [9]. The univariate model identified has 32 parameters for the antecedent variables (two for each fuzzy value) and 20 parameters for the consequent variables). The parameter set of the adaptive network is updated after the whole training data set has been presented, i.e., only after each *training epoch*. The learning algorithm is based on a *batch learning paradigm* (on-line learning). Hybrid back propagation gradient decent and the least-squares method are used as a learning rule [9]. For example, Fig. 3.10 shows optimized membership functions for antecedent variable $\beta(t\text{-}6)$.   An example of learned partial mapping surfaces for the best fitting univariate predictive fuzzy model is shown in Fig. 3.11.

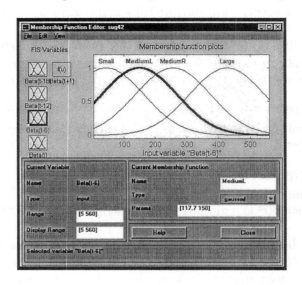

Fig. 3.10   Optimized fuzzy values of the antecedent fuzzy variable $\beta(t\text{-}6)$.

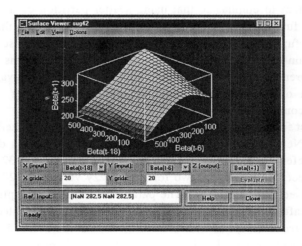

Fig. 3.11   An example of learned partial mapping surfaces
$\beta(t+1) = \beta\,'[\beta(t\text{-}6),\ \beta(t\text{-}18)]$ for a best fitting univariate predictive fuzzy model.

3.5 Conclusions

In this article, we have proposed a fuzzy system to control the artificial pneumatic muscle (APM). Contrary to the usual black-box architectures, the basic architecture of the fuzzy control system was determined using *a priory* knowledge expressed in the form of an approximate APM analytical model (context sensitive approach). In order to improve accuracy of the model, hysteretic behavior of APM was modeled by a predictive fuzzy model, using previous time output values as inputs as well as other input data. The problem of the dimensionality of the system was solved using scatter partition of the I/O space, based on application of subtractive fuzzy clustering. Fuzzy clustering is performed only by specifying cluster radius as input data. As a result, the number of rules required for accurate mapping is small, despite relatively high model dimensionality. After expressing the predictive fuzzy system in the form of an adaptive network, parameter set optimization was performed by a fast hybrid learning method. Future work is expected to address the extension of the quasi-static data by using data of the APM dynamic behavior.

References

[1] Inoue, K., "Rubbertuators and Applications for Robots", *Robotics Research: The 4th International Symposium*, Cambridge, MA, MIT Press, pp: 57-63 (1988).

[2] Chou, C.P. and Hannaford, B., "Measurement and Modeling of McKibben Pneumatic Artificial Muscles", *IEEE Transactions on Robotics and Automation*, Vol. 12, No. 1, pp: 90-102 (1996).

[3] Bobrow, J.E. and Jabbari, F., "Adaptive Pneumatic Actuation and Position Control", *Trans. ASME J. Dyn. Systems Measur. and Control.* (113) pp: 267-272 (1991).

[4] Petrovic, P.B. and Milacic, V.R., "A Fuzzy Dynamic Model and Control of an Artificial Pneumatic Muscle", *The 5th Int. Conf. on Soft Computing IIZUKA'98,* Iizuka, Fukuoka, JAPAN, pp:801-804 (1998).

[5] Kasabov, N.K., "Foundations of Neural Networks, Fuzzy Systems, and Knowledge Engineering", A Bradford Book, The MIT Press, Cambridge Massachusetts, London, England (1996).

[6] Bezdek, J.C., "Pattern Recognition with Fuzzy Objective Function Algorithms", *Plenum Press*, USA, (1981).

[7] Nakanishi, H., Turksen, I.B. and Sugeno, M., "A Review and Comparison of Six Reasoning Methods", *Fuzzy sets and systems* (**57**). pp: 257-294 (1993).

[8] Chiu, S.L., "Fuzzy Model Identification Based on Cluster Estimation", *J. of Intelligent & Fuzzy Systems*, Vol. **2** No. **3**, pp: 267-278 (1994).

[9] Jang, J.S.R., "ANFIS: Adaptive-Network-based-Fuzzy-Inference-Systems", *IEEE Trans. on Syst., Man, and Cybernetics*, Vol. **23**, No 3, pp: 665-685 (1993).

Appendix A

Fuzzy Clustering of I/O Data Points

Suppose the given data set:

$$X = \begin{bmatrix} x_{11} & \cdots & x_{1n} \\ \vdots & \vdots & \vdots \\ x_{p1} & \cdots & x_{pn} \end{bmatrix} \qquad (A\text{-}1)$$

is normalized i.e., fitted into a unit p-dimensional hypercube. According to [8] each data point is considered as a potential cluster center (this is a major limitation of the clustering method). Potential of data point is used as a dissimilarity measure for identifying cluster centers, as given by the following equation:

$$P_i^1 = \sum_{j=1}^{n} \exp\left[-\alpha \sum_{k=1}^{p} (x_{ik} - x_{jk})^2\right], \quad i = 1, \ldots, n \qquad (A\text{-}2)$$

Parameter α shapes the potential function in order to define the neighborhood of the fuzzy cluster to be identified. This parameter is defined by:

$$\alpha = 4/r_a^2 \qquad (A\text{-}3)$$

where r_a denotes so called cluster radius. Data points lying outside of the cluster radius have little influence on the potential function of the point x_i, given by (A-2). Cluster radius is defined as an *a priori* constant ranging from 0 to 1 (typically, r_a is in the range 0.25 to 0.5).

Data point with the highest potential is selected as a first cluster center:

$$v_1 = x_m, \quad x_m : \max\left\{P_1^1, \ldots, P_n^1\right\} \qquad (A\text{-}4)$$

In order to reduce the potential of data points close to the selected cluster center we apply the following formula:

$$P_i^2 = P_i^1 - P_{v1}^1 \exp\left[-\beta \sum_{k=1}^{p} (x_{ik} - v_{1k})^2\right], \quad i = 1, \ldots, n \qquad (A\text{-}5).$$

β denotes a constant which, in the same way as the constant α, influences the potential of each data point.   The value of the β constant may be defined by the following relationship $\beta = (1.5 \div 2)\ \alpha$.

The next cluster center is determined by the following equation:

$$v_2 = x_q, \quad x_q : \max\{P_1^2, ..., P_n^2\} \tag{A-6}$$

The further procedure is the same as for the first cluster center.   We have proposed a new criterion for ending the clustering process, i.e., the criterion which determines the number of fuzzy clusters c.   The clustering process is halted after the following condition is satisfied:

$$d_{ik} \geq 0.25 \frac{r_a^2}{\ln f} \tag{A-7}$$

d_{ik} denotes the distance between two cluster centers and f denotes the overlapping factor.   The overlapping factor f is an *a priori* constant ranging form 0 to 1 (typically, f is selected in the range 0.5 to 0.75).   As the overlapping constant is high, too many clusters will be generated.   The proposed criterion solves the problem of overfitting, which is a consequence of too many clusters generated.   Also, this criterion gives maximum freedom, enabling the clustering process to be data driven to the maximum extent.

Appendix B

Transferring Clustered I/O Data Points into the Fuzzy Model

We consider each cluster as one fuzzy relation of interval-valued variables in a multi dimensional I/O space. For each fuzzy cluster we define a compositional rule of inference in the form of a *generalized modus ponens*:

$$Z = Y \circ F \qquad (B\text{-}1)$$

where Y denotes the inputs, Z denotes the outputs, and F is the fuzzy relation roughly determined by one of identified fuzzy clusters.

First, we separate a coordinates of the data point set representing the centers of generated fuzzy clusters into two physical subsets, each of them referring to the input coordinates, Y_v, and output coordinates, Z_v, of the object to be modeled:

$$X^v = Y^v \cup Z^v = \begin{bmatrix} y_{11}^v & \cdots & y_{1c}^v \\ \vdots & \vdots & \vdots \\ y_{m1}^v & \cdots & y_{mc}^v \\ z_{11}^v & \cdots & z_{1c}^v \\ \vdots & \vdots & \vdots \\ z_{(p-m)1}^v & \cdots & y_{(p-m)c}^v \end{bmatrix} \qquad (B\text{-}2)$$

Membership functions representing the fuzzy values of the composite fuzzy variable in the m-dimensional input space are defined as:

$$\widetilde{Y}_i : \quad \mu_i^y = \exp\left[-\alpha_i^a \sum_{k=1}^m (y_k - y_{ik}^v)^2\right], \quad i = 1, \ldots, c \qquad (B\text{-}3)$$

In the same manner, fuzzy values of the composite fuzzy variable in the $(p - m)$-dimensional output space are defined by:

$$\tilde{Z}_i : \quad \mu_i^z = \exp\left[-\alpha_i^c \sum_{k=1}^{p-m}(z_k - z_{ik}^v)^2\right], \quad i = 1, \ldots, c \qquad \text{(B-4)}$$

Using (B-3) and (B-4) it is possible to build up fuzzy inference defined by (B-1) in the Mamdani-Assilian form:

R₁: if $(y_1$ is $\tilde{Y}_1)$ and $(y_2$ is $\tilde{Y}_1)$ and ... and $(y_m$ is $\tilde{Y}_1)$

then $(z_1$ is $\tilde{Z}_1)$ and $(z_2$ is $\tilde{Z}_2)$ and ... and $(z_{(p-m)}$ is $\tilde{Z}_2)$

.
.
.

Rc: if $(y_1$ is $\tilde{Y}_c)$ and $(y_2$ is $\tilde{Y}_c)$ and ... and $(y_m$ is $\tilde{Y}_c)$

then $(z_1$ is $\tilde{Z}_c)$ and $(z_2$ is $\tilde{Z}_c)$ and ... and $(z_{(p-m)}$ is $\tilde{Z}_c)$

or in the Sugeno-Takagi form with first order consequent:

R1:   if $(y_1$ is $\tilde{Y}_1)$ and $(y_2$ is $\tilde{Y}_1)$ and ... and $(y_m$ is $\tilde{Y}_1)$

$z_1(y) = a_{10}^1 + a_{11}^1 * y_1 + \ldots + a_{1m}^1 * y_m$ and ...

and ... $z_{(p-m)}(y) = a_{10}^{(p-m)} + a_{11}^{(p-m)} * y_1 + \ldots + a_{1m}^{(p-m)} * y_m$

.
.
.

Rc: if $(y_1$ is $\tilde{Y}_c)$ and $(y_2$ is $\tilde{Y}_c)$ and ... and $(y_m$ is $\tilde{Y}_c)$

$z_1(y) = a_{c0}^1 + a_{c1}^1 * y_1 + \ldots + a_{cm}^1 * y_m$ and ...

and ... $z_{(p-m)}(y) = a_{c0}^{(p-m)} + a_{c1}^{(p-m)} * y_1 + \ldots + a_{cm}^{(p-m)} * y_m$.

Final definition of the fuzzy relation F requires adjusting of the parameter set, applying nonlinear optimization methods.

Chapter 4

Fuzzy Supervisory Control with Fuzzy-PID Controller and Its Application to Petroleum Plants

Tetsuji Tani[1], Hiroaki Kobayashi[2], and Takeshi Furuhashi[3]

[1] Manufacturing Dept., Idemitsu Kosan Co., Ltd.
[2] Hokkaido Refinery, Idemitsu Kosan Co., Ltd.
[3] Dept. of Information Electronics, Nagoya University

Abstract

This chapter presents a new practical control system that can apply conventional PID controllers to nonlinear field by using fuzzy reasoning. The proposed system is a hierarchical one consisting of two components: (a) a Fuzzy-PID controller, and (b) a supervisor for setting the control target of this controller. The fuzzy controller in the Fuzzy-PID controller compensates the output error of the conventional PID controller. The supervisor calculates the control target by fuzzy reasoning. This hierarchical control system is applied to the temperature control in a petroleum plant. The parameters in fuzzy controller are tuned on-line in the actual plant and the system can control the temperature effectively in the transient state, such as feed property changing or operation mode changing, as well as in the steady state

Keywords : hybrid control system, practical control system, fuzzy controller, PID controller, Fuzzy-PID Controller, supervisory control, petroleum plant, transient state, temperature control, parameter tuning, feed property changing, operation mode changing, naphtha desulfurizing plant

1.1 Introduction

From the early stage of its emergence, automatic control schemes have been implemented in the refining industry. In most cases automatic control schemes have been relying on conventional regulatory controllers because of their easy-to-tune functionality. However, due to their poor response to a large time-delay, non-linearity, and disturbance, it has been very difficult to realize fully automatic control of all the process units in a refinery.

Well-experienced operators, working for refineries of the authors' company, control their plant with a lot of time-delays and interferences fairly well by manipulating the set points of regulatory controllers. Every refining company wishes to utilize its assets, no matter whether they are tangible or not, such as its control schemes, its operators' experience, and expertise, in order to maximize profit.

Conventional PID controller is still most popular in industrial applications, because it is easily adjustable and applicable to field use. There are many PID controllers in petroleum plants. However, the controllers cannot deal effectively with nonlinear and/or time-varying processes. In transient state of feed oil switching and changes in operation mode, for example, the plant is time-varying, and the nonlinear responses occur. The present system, therefore, needs well-experienced operators for compensating the outputs of the PID controller or for giving a suitable control target to the PID controllers in such states. Fuzzy controller and/or combinations of fuzzy and PID controller are useful for controlling complex systems within a certain control target [1-5]. In such a transient state, however, the control target must be modified.

This chapter presents a practical hierarchical control system consisting of two components: (a) a Fuzzy-PID controller, and (b) a supervisor for setting the control target of this controller. The fuzzy controller in the Fuzzy-PID controller compensates the output error of the conventional PID controller. The supervisor calculates the control target by fuzzy reasoning [6-9]. This chapter also presents a practical parameter-tuning scheme for the fuzzy controller.

The proposed hierarchical control system is applied to a temperature-control in the naphtha desulfurizing plant. This process has: (1) a nonlinear response, (2) a long dead time between the manipulated and control variables, and (3) little exact observation of phenomena due to a lack of effective sensor devices. The system controls the temperature effectively in the transient state, such as feed property changing or operation mode changing, as well as in the steady state.

1.2 Process Description and Control Problems

1.2.1 *Process Description*

The process of a naphtha desulfurizing plant is shown in Figure 1. This plant desulfurizes feed oil containing sour naphtha and sour liquefied petroleum gas (sour LPG) to produce naphtha and product LPG.

The feed oil is mixed with the hydrogen gas to promote the chemical reaction in the plant and is pumped to the heater to be heated up to a reaction temperature. The hot feed oil and hydrogen gas mixture is then fed to the reactor for desulfurization. The outlet mixture from the reactor is separated into sour gas and oil (naphtha and LPG) in the separator. The oil (naphtha and LPG) is then fed to the stripper to be separated into the product naphtha and the product LPG. The product LPG is extracted from the top of the stripper, and the product naphtha from the bottom.

To keep the quality of the product high, we have to control the tower-top temperature suitably at a certain value. We have two ways for controlling the tower-top temperature: one is to change the reboiler temperature, and the other is to change the reflux flow amount. There is a strong interaction between the reboiler temperature and the reflux flow amount. Setting of the suitable reboiler temperature can lead to the minimum amount of the reflux flow. This saves the reboiler heating energy. Therefore, the main manipulated variable (MV) is the reboiler temperature, and the controlled variable (CV) is the tower-top temperature.

The reflux flow amount is controlled by a conventional PID controller. The reboiler temperature is controlled by the fuel gas using a conventional PID controller. This paper discusses the control system for the tower-top temperature by controlling the reboiler temperature.

This plant has the following constraints to make the product quality meet the specifications: When the tower-top temperature of the stripper is too high, the product LPG becomes out of the specification, because pentane (C_5) is mixed to the product LPG. When the temperature is too low, the product naphtha goes out of quality because the remaining butane (C_4) makes the Vapor Pressure (VP) in the product naphtha too high. The VP is a measure of the surface pressure at the time of product naphtha being vaporizing. Motor gasoline with excessively high

VP causes vapor lock in the engine and that with too low VP causes difficulties in starting the engine .

Two kinds of product naphtha, which have different VPs, are produced. One is petrochemical plant-feed oil with a low VP (**operation mode A**), and the other is motor gasoline with a high VP (**operation mode B**). The tower-top temperature of the stripper must be changed to adapt to these two VP-specifications.

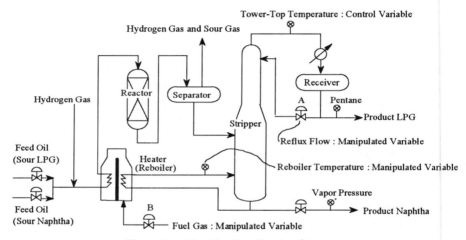

Figure 1.   Naphtha Desulfurzing Plant.

1.2.2   *Difficulties in Process Control*

We have the following difficulties in controlling the process:
(1) The behavior of the tower-top temperature by the reboiler has a nonlinear response with a long dead time.
(2) The feed amount and the mixture rate of feed oils, sour LPG and sour naphtha, usually vary every moment, especially vary greatly when the feed oil is switched. We cannot exactly observe the phenomena due to a lack of effective sensor devices.
(3) There is a disturbance in the heater. We use a center-wall type heater. The center-wall type heater is separated into two parts by a wall. One part is used for the reactor heater, and the other for the stripper heater (reboiler). The heating and cooling for the reactor make a large disturbance for the reboiler

temperature control, and vice versa.

(4) It is difficult to determine the reboiler temperature because it takes too much time to sense the VP of product naphtha.

1.3 Proposed Hierarchical Control System

The conventional PID controller could not control the tower-top temperature effectively. However well-experienced operators have controlled the tower-top temperature fairly well. We observed the procedures of well-experienced operators, and found that

(1) in the steady state, the operators compensated the output of the PID-controller to keep the tower-top temperature within a certain range, and

(2) in the transient state, the operators changed the control target to satisfy the Vapor Pressure specifications of product naphtha.

These operations gave the operators a heavy burden. The proposed hierarchical control system to replace the experienced operator is shown in Figure 2. This control system consists of two components: (a) a Fuzzy-PID controller, and (b) a supervisor for setting the control target of this controller. The fuzzy controller in the Fuzzy-PID controller compensates the output error of the conventional PID controller. The supervisor calculates the control target by fuzzy reasoning. This control system keeps the product quality within the specifications.

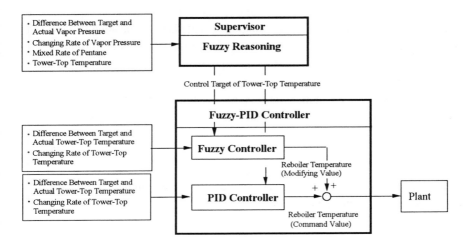

Figure 2.   Proposed Hierarchical Control System.

1.3.1 *Fuzzy-PID controller*

(a)   *Structure of Fuzzy-PID controller*

The Fuzzy-PID controller in Figure 2 has two components: the conventional PID controller and the fuzzy controller. These two controllers are constructed hierarchically. The function of the conventional PID controller is to give the command of the reboiler temperature to the plant. The fuzzy controller modifies the error in the command.

The command value of the reboiler temperature $u(t)$ is calculated by the conventional PID control, based on the closed-loop error $e(t)=T(t)-y(t)$, where $T(t)$ is the actual value of the tower-top temperature and $y(t)$ is a prescribed target of tower-top temperature at time t. This PID controller has the following standard form:

$$u(t) = K_c[e(t) + T_d \frac{de(t)}{dt} + \frac{1}{T_i}\int e(t)dt]$$

(1)

where K_c, T_d, T_i are the proportional gain, the derivative time, and the integral time of the controller, respectively.

The calculated command value $u(t)$ is modified by the output $c(t)$ of the fuzzy controller. Figure 3 shows the rules and the membership functions in the fuzzy controller for the modification. The rule table contains 15 rules. The input variables are $Te(t)$ and $\Delta T(t)$. $Te(t)$ means the difference between the target and the actual tower-top temperatures at time t, and $\Delta T(t)$ means the changing rate of tower-top temperature at time t. The output variable is compensating value for the PID output. We use the simplified fuzzy reasoning where the consequence of fuzzy rule is singleton [10-13]. Given the input values of $Te(t)$ and $\Delta T(t)$ at time t, the output of $c(t)$ is calculated by the rules.

Now, the tower-top temperature $v(t+\Delta t)$ at time $t+\Delta t$ is controlled by the Fuzzy-PID controller, which is calculated as:

$$v(t+\Delta t) = u(t) + c(t)$$

(2)

where Δt is decided as 30 seconds by the parameter tuning in Fuzzy-PID controller shown in the next section .

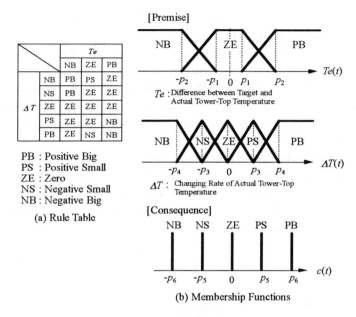

		T_e		
		NB	ZE	PB
	NB	PB	PS	ZE
	NS	PB	ZE	ZE
ΔT	ZE	ZE	ZE	ZE
	PS	ZE	ZE	NB
	PB	ZE	NS	NB

PB : Positive Big
PS : Positive Small
ZE : Zero
NS : Negative Small
NB : Negative Big

(a) Rule Table

(b) Membership Functions

Figure 3. Rules and Membership Functions of Fuzzy Controller.

(b) *Parameter Tuning in Fuzzy-PID controller*

Most applications of the fuzzy controller have difficulty in tuning membership functions of fuzzy rules. Some tuning methods for parameters of the membership functions have been proposed [14-16]. However, we cannot obtain proper tuning data because of noise in the process, interactions between variables, and a nonlinear response with a long delay time. The conventional tuning methods cannot be applied to the Fuzzy-PID controller. Therefore, we have tuned the Fuzzy-PID controller in the actual process manually as described below.

This subsection presents a simple and practical tuning method. The 15 control rules of the fuzzy controller contain 6 parameters ($p_1, p_2, ..., p_6$) which define membership functions as shown in Figure 3. The tuning process of the parameters is as follows:

Step 1 : We set the PID parameters to control the system in the steady state by a conventional method.

Step 2 : We set the cycle of fuzzy reasoning equal to that of an operator's compensation for the PID output.

Step 3 : We tune the parameters in the consequence of fuzzy rules. We check that the output of the fuzzy controller equals to that of well-experienced operators.

Step 4 : We start to control the process with the Fuzzy-PID controller and we tune the parameters of membership functions of the premise of fuzzy rules step-by-step. We narrow the supports of the membership functions as in the way shown in Figure 4, and stop changing them before the process becomes unstable. We tune the parameter of the *Te* first, then the parameters of *T* next. If we cannot achieve the requirement of control performance, go to Step 5, else stop.

Step 5 : We shorten the cycle of the fuzzy reasoning. This step corresponds to the increase in frequency of operator's intervention. Note that the more frequent the command value is modified, the smaller the value of output of the fuzzy rules is made. This reduction is set to be inversely proportional to the frequency. Go to Step 4.

Membership Function

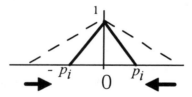

p_i : parameter of fuzzy rule

Figure 4.   Tuning of a Membership Function.

(c) Field-testing of Fuzzy-PID controller

We have done a field-testing of the Fuzzy-PID controller using an actual naphtha desulfurizing plant in the Idemitsu Hokkaido Refinery [17]. The purpose of the field-testing was to estimate the stability of the Fuzzy-PID controller. Table 1 shows the range of the tower-top temperature controlled by the conventional ones and proposed one. We used the PID controller and the manual operation as conventional methods.

Table 1.   Range of Controlled Tower-Top Temperature.

	Steady State	Feed Oil Switching
PID Controller	10 °C	Unstable
Manual Operation	0.7~11.5 °C	7.5 °C
Fuzzy-PID Controller	1.5 °C	3 °C

Figure 5 shows the corresponding results of control in the steady state by these methods. The horizontal axis is time, and the vertical axis is the tower-top temperature. The solid line is the result obtained by the PID controller. The thin broken line is that by the manual operation. The thick broken line is the temperature resulted from the proposed Fuzzy-PID controller. The requirement of the deviation from the target value of the tower-top temperature was within 4C. The conventional PID controller could not meet this requirement. The manual operation and the proposed controller could keep the temperature within this range. However, it was difficult for humans to be alert all the time, and the manual operation failed several times during the field-testing. At a time of this failure, the tower-top temperature deviated by 11.5C. The Fuzzy-PID controller could keep the deviation within ±1.5C throughout the field testing period in the steady state.

After the feed oil switching, the transient state lasted for several hours. The operator could not control the tower-top temperature stable as shown in Figure 6. The temperature deviated by −7.5C. The Fuzzy-PID controller could control it stable within 3C. These results show that the Fuzzy-PID controller can control the plant within the requirement in both the steady state and the transient state.

The Fuzzy-PID controller can control a process which involves a nonlinear response with a long dead-time and disturbance. The conventional PID controller cannot control such a process. The Fuzzy-PID Controller has the following features:

(1) With PID and fuzzy controllers, the process of nonlinear response can be controlled.

(2) The fuzzy reasoning modifies the PID controller output directly. Therefore, the control rules are simpler than those of the method of estimating the PID

parameters by fuzzy reasoning. We can easily tune the parameters of the membership functions.

(3) The fuzzy controller plays a role of a nonlinear controller by changing the gain of the PID controller. If necessary, we can add another input variables to the fuzzy control rules.

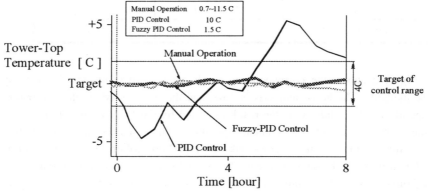

Figure 5.   Controlled Tower-Top Temperature in the Steady State.

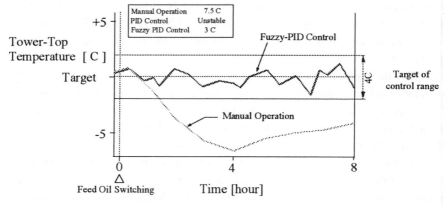

Figure 6.   Controlled Tower-Top Temperature in the Transient State .

1.3.2   *Fuzzy-PID Controller with Supervisor*

The Fuzzy-PID controller itself has shown its effectiveness while a suitable control target is set by well-experienced operators. However we must change the control target when the feed oil is switched. Furthermore the setting of the control target needs a lot of intervention by the operator, when the specifications of VP for the product is changed. This inconvenience has driven us to develop the supervisor in Figure 2, where we use fuzzy reasoning.

The function of the supervisor component is to modify the control target for the Fuzzy-PID controller in order not to mix pentane (C_5) with product LPG, and keep the VP within a certain value, in both the steady state and the transient state of feed oil switching. When the target of the VP of the product is changed, the supervisor changes the control target gradually, to adjust the VP without mixing pentane with the product LPG.

The rules for the fuzzy control in the supervisor component is shown in Figure 7. We use the simplified fuzzy reasoning.

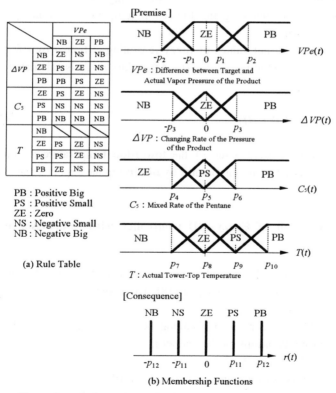

PB : Positive Big
PS : Positive Small
ZE : Zero
NS : Negative Small
NB : Negative Big

(a) Rule Table

(b) Membership Functions

Figure 7.   Rules and Membership Functions of Supervisor.

The output of fuzzy reasoning in the supervisor component is the additional value of the control target of the tower-top temperature from the present one. The rules for the fuzzy control are divided into three types depending on the inputs:

(R1) the difference between the target and the actual VP (*VPe*), and the change rate of the VP (ΔVP),

(R2) *VPe*, and the mixed rate of Pentane (C_5),

(R3) *VPe*, and the actual tower-top temperature (*T*).

The function of the first set of rules (R1) is to keep the product quality within the VP-specifications by observing the VP and the ΔVP. The second (R2) is to keep the product quality within the pentane-specifications by observing the VP and the mixed rate of Pentane (C_5). These rules are to reduce the tower-top temperature to exclude the excessive pentane. The third (R3) is to keep the tower-top temperature within a certain range by observing the VP and the actual tower-top temperature, by reducing the tower-top temperature for not going out of usual-operation value.

Denoting the output values of fuzzy reasoning at time *t* by *r(t)*, the control target of the tower-top temperature $y(t + \Delta t)$ at time $t + \Delta t$ is calculated as:

$$y(t + \Delta t) \quad = T(t) + r(t) \tag{3}$$

where $T(t)$ is the current value of the tower-top temperature at time *t*. We decided that Δt is set at fifteen minutes by observing the expert's operation.

1.4 Control Result of Fuzzy-PID Controller with Supervisor in Actual Plant

We applied the hierarchical control system to a naphtha-desulfurizing plant at Idemitsu Hokkaido Refinery in Japan [18]. The results of on-line testing showed that the system could:

(1) achieve automatic control in changing the VP for products, and reduce the number of interventions by the operator,

(2) control the VP effectively,

(3) reduce the reflux flow amount, and save the heating energy,

in both the steady state and the transient state such as in the feed oil switching.

Figure 8 shows the control results in the change from the low VP of the product (**operation mode A**) to the high VP of the product (**operation mode B**). The horizontal axis is time, and the vertical axes are the reboiler temperature and the VP of the product. The top figure shows the results of manual control. We needed interventions by the operator 34 times per six hours to lower the reboiler temperature. The bottom figure shows the results by the hierarchical control. The VP change was done automatically by the hierarchical control system. The reboiler temperature was controlled down smoothly. This indicated that the hierarchical control system could save man-hours.

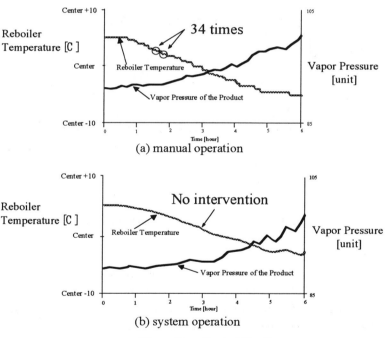

Figure 8. Control Results

Figure 9 shows the control results of the VP by manual operation and the proposed hierarchical control system for about one month. We had feed oil switching, which disturbed the VP control, every three or four days, also had the VP change every seven or eight days. In the operation for the low VP (**operation**

mode A), the range of the VP was 8.5 units by manual operation, while by the hierarchical control system, the range was 3.0 units. In the operation for the high VP (**operation mode B**), the VP range was 12.5 units by manual operation, while by the hierarchical control system, the range was 3.0 units. This shows that the hierarchical control system could control the VP more stable than by the manual operation.

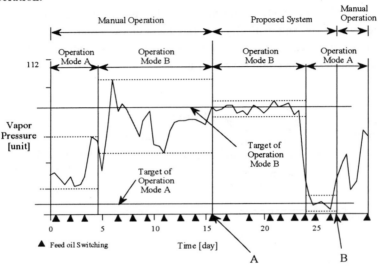

Figure 9.   Comparison with Manual Operation and Hierarchical
Control System in VP Control

The hierarchical control system reduced the average of the reflux flow amount by 0~400 kiloliters per day from that by the manual operation in the operation for the low VP (**operation mode A**). In the operation for the high VP (**operation mode B**), the reduction was 140 kiloliters per day. This shows that the hierarchical control system could save more energy than the manual operation (Table 2).

Table 2.   Comparison with Manual Operation and Hierarchical Control System in VP
and Reflux Flow

	Operation Mode A	Operation Mode B
< Manual Operation > Range of Vapor Pressure Average of Reflux Flow	8.5 [unit] Base A	12.5 [unit] Base B
< Proposed System > Range of Vapor Pressure Average of Reflux Flow	3.0 [unit] Base A $-(0\sim400)$ [kl/day]	3.0 [unit] Base B -140 [kl/day]

1.5 Conclusion

This chapter presented a practical hierarchical control system that consisted of
two components, the Fuzzy-PID controller and the supervisor by fuzzy reasoning.
A practical way of parameter-tuning of fuzzy controller was also presented.

The performance of the conventional PID controller was enhanced in
controlling a process that had: (1) a nonlinear response, (2) a long dead time
between the manipulated and controlled variables, and (3) little exact observation
of phenomena due to the lack of effective sensor devices. While a proper control
target is given, the Fuzzy-PID controller itself has shown its effectiveness in
controlling the process in both the steady state and the transient state. The
hierarchical control system has shown its effectiveness in; (1) automatic change
in the VP for the products, (2) controlling the quality of the products to meet the
specifications, and (3) reducing the energy of the heater in both the steady state
and the transient state.

References

[1] H. Ichihashi and H. Tanaka: PID and Fuzzy Hybrid Controller, 4th Fuzzy System
      Symposium, pp.97-102 (in Japanese) (1988)
[2] N. Matsunaga and S. Kawaji: Fuzzy Hybrid Control for DC Servomotor, Trans. IEE
      of Japan, Vol. 111- D, No. 3, pp.195-200 (in Japanese) (1991)

[3] A.Rueda and W.Pedrycz: A Design Method for a Class of Fuzzy Hierarchical Controllers, IEEE Int. Conf. on Fuzzy Systems (FUZZ-IEEE93), San Francisco, pp.196-199 (1993)

[4] S.H.He, S.H.Tan, F.Z.Xu and P.Z.Wang: PID Self-Tuning Control Using a Fuzzy Adaptive Mechanism, IEEE Int. Conf. on Fuzzy Systems (FUZZ-IEEE93), California, pp.708-713 (1993)

[5] A.Kraslawski: Chemical Engineering in Applications of Fuzzy Computation, pp.G7.1:1-13, Handbook of Fuzzy Computation, IOP Publishing Ltd., London (1998)

[6] H.Tseng, V.Hwanng, S.Lui: Fuzzy servo-controller: The hierarchical approach, IEEE Int. Conf. on Fuzzy Systems (FUZZ-IEEE92), San Diego, pp.196-199 (1992)

[7] S.Boverie, et al. Performance evaluation of fuzzy control through an international benchmark, Proc. IFSA'93 World Congress, Seoul, Korea, pp.941-944 (1993)

[8] D.Driankov, H.Hellendoorn, R.Palm Ed.,: Some Research Directions in Fuzzy Control, pp. 281-312, Theoretical Aspects of Fuzzy Control, H.T.Nguyen, M.Sugeno, R.Tong, R.R.Yanger Ed., John Wiley & Sons (1995)

[9] T.Kobayashi, T.Tani, N.Abe and S.Miyamoto: Comparison between Human Supervisory Control and Hierarchical Control System Based on Human's Knowledge in Petroleum Plant, IEEE Int. Conf. on Fuzzy Systems (FUZZ-IEEE98), Anchorage, Alaska, pp.200-204 (1998)

[10] M.Brrae and D.A.Rutherford: Fuzzy relations in a control setting, Kybernetes, No.7, pp.185- 188 (1978)

[11] H.Ichihashi and H.Tanaka: PID and Fuzzy Hybrid Controller, 4th Fuzzy System Symposium, pp.97-102 (1988) (in Japanese)

[12] M.Maeda and S.Murakami: Self-Tuning Fuzzy Controller, Trans. SICE of Japan, Vol.24, No.2, pp.191-197 (1988) (in Japanese)

[13] M.Mizumoto: Fuzzy Controls by Product-Sum-Gravity Method, Advancement of Fuzzy Theory and System in China and Japan (ed. by X.H.Liu and M.Mizumoto). International Academic Publishers, Vol.c1.1- 4 (1990)

[14] H. Nomura, I. Hayashi and N. Wakami: A Self-Tuning Method of Fuzzy Reasoning by Delta Rule and Its Application to a Moving Obstacle Avoidance, Journal of Japan Society for Fuzzy Theory and Systems, Vol.4- No.2, pp.379-388 (1992) (in Japanese)

[15] L. X. Wang and J. M. Mendel: Back-Propagation Fuzzy System as Nonlinear Dynamic System Identifiers, IEEE Int. Conf. on Fuzzy Systems (FUZZ-IEEE '92), San Diego, pp.1409-1416 (1992)

[16] L. Zheng: A Practical Computer-Aided Tuning Technique for Fuzzy Control, IEEE Int. Conf. on Fuzzy Systems (FUZZ-IEEE93), California, pp.702-707 (1993)

[17] T.Tani, M.Utashiro, M.Umano and K.Tanaka: Application of Practical Fuzzy-PID Hybrid Control System to Petrochemical Plant, IEEE Int. Conf. on Fuzzy Systems (FUZZ-IEEE'94), Orlando, Florida, pp.1211-1216 (1994)

[18] H.Kobyashi, H.Sugiyama, S.Kanazawa, T.Tani and T.Furuhashi: Fuzzy Supervisory Control with Fuzzy-PID Controller and Its Application to Petroleum Plants, IEEE Int. Conf. Soft Computing and Information/Intelligent Systems (IIZKA'98), Iizuka, Japan, pp.704-707 (1998)

Chapter 5

Genetic Algorithm-based Predictive Control for Nonlinear Processes

Seung C. Shin   and Zeungnam Bien
Korea Advanced Institute of Science and Technology

Abstract

GAs are known to be capable of finding an optimal value with better probability than the descent-based nonlinear programming methods for optimization problems. As such, a GA-based optimization technique is adopted in the paper to obtain optimal future control inputs for predictive control systems. For reliable future predictions of a process, we identify the underlying process with an NNARX model structure that consists of a regressor vector and a set of parameters containing all the weights of the neural network. To reduce the volume of neural network, we determine the elements of the regresssor vector based on the Lipschitz index and a criterion. The Gauss-Newton based Levenberg-Marquardt method is used to estimate the parameters because of its robustness and superlinear rate of convergence. Since most industrial processes are subject to their constraints, we deal with the input-output constraints by modifying some genetic operators and/or using a penalty strategy in the GA-based predictive control. Furthermore, we extend the control scheme to multi-input, multi-output nonlinear dynamical systems. Some computer simulations are given to show the effectiveness of the GA-based predictive control method compared with the adaptive GPC algorithm.

Keywords : genetic algorithm, NNARX model, Lipschitz index, training algorithm, predictive control, modified genetic operators, constraints, penalty function, adpative GPC, multi-input/multi-output

5.1 Introduction

Much progress has been made in the method of predictive control both in terms of theoretical understanding and practical applications since the concept of predictive control was introduced in the late seventies. In the early studies of predictive control, most of the control techniques have been investigated under the assumptions that the plant is linear and that the model is available *a priori* [1; 2; 3; 4]. Even though the linear model-based approach provides a satisfactory control in many process industries [5; 6; 7], it may not render a good control result when the controlled process is highly nonlinear.

Naturally, some nonlinear model-based design techniques have been developed to solve the limitation of the linear model approach. Since nonlinear models are so diverse, there are attempts to investigate specialized predictive control for a different class of nonlinear systems with special structures such as Hammerstein model [8] and bilinear model [9].

Besides, some kinds of learning network have been used to develop a predictive control method for general nonlinear processes. Specially, since it has been proved that the multilayer feedforward neural networks offer striking capability for modelling a nonlinear process without *a priori* knowledge [10], the neural networks have been adopted for a number of control applications as in identification of dynamic nonlinear processes and in constructing model-based control strategies [11; 12; 13]. Further, the neural networks are also used to provide future outputs of a process in the predictive control scheme and many related works are published in the literature (e.g. see [14; 15; 16; 17]).

Bhat and McAvoy [18] introduced the idea of neural network-based prediction model and used the model to control a chemical process. Saint-Donat *et al.* [14] derived an analytical expression for the gradient of the neural network model and used the expression in the sequential quadratic programming (SQP) to control a pH chemical stirred tank regulator (CSTR). Draeger *et al.* [15] designed a neural network to obtain future outputs of a laboratory-scale neutralization reactor and adopted extended dynamic matrix control (DMC) algorithm to handle the plant.

Norgaard *et al.* [16] proposed the instantaneous linearization method of the neural network around the current operating point and used the technique of generalized predictive control (GPC) to handle a pneumatic position servomechanism. Hu and Rose [17] proposed a prediction scheme with a radial basis function (RBF) learning netwrok and implemented the gradient projection method to optimize a criterion function iteratively in consideration of rate constraints on the controller output. Ahn and Kwon [19] proposed a predictive control method for a class of nonlinear process by using fuzzy learning networks.

Usually, the neural networks used in the methods of predictive control are trained to learn the structure of the underlying process and used to derive a control action. The nonlinearity of neural networks thus rendered is amenable to an optimization technique, which may lead to utilization of nonlinear programming methods. However, the local minimum problem of these methods is still outstanding and needs to be resolved by some new methodology such as genetic algorithm (GA).

In the paper, we adopt a GA-based optimization technique to obtain optimal future control inputs, noting that the GA-method is known to have better opportunity for finding an optimal value than a descent-based nonlinear programming method for optimization problems [20; 21]. The GA-based control problem has been formulated in [22], with an assumption that all signals possess unlimited bounds, but such an assumption is unrealistic because in practice all processes are subject to constraints. Therefore, we propose to deal with the input-output constraints of the processes by modifying genetic operators and/or using a penalty strategy. Moreover, we extend the GA-based predictive control scheme for single-input, single-output (SISO) plants to multi-input, multi-output (MIMO) processes in the frame of partitioned prediction models. Some simulations for nonlinear processes are given to show the superiority of the GA-based predictive control method to the adaptive GPC algorithm.

The paper is organized as follows. In Section 5.2, we describe the procedure of system identification using a neural network-based autoregressive with exogenous input (NNARX) model. In Section 5.3, we investigate the proposed unconstrained GA-based predictive control scheme on the basis of the NNARX prediction model. In Section 5.4, we present a couple of methodologies to treat the input-output constraints of a plant. In Section 5.5, we consider MIMO dynamical systems under the GA-based predictive control. Finally, some concluding remarks are given in Section 5.6.

5.2 System identification by using neural networks

In this section, we briefly describe the procedure of system identification for dynamical systems by using neural networks.

To identify the characteristics of a plant, we assume that experimental data describing the underlying system in its entire operating region has been obtained beforehand with a proper choice of sampling frequency;

specifically, let

$$Z^N = \{ [u(t), y(t)] \mid t = 1, 2, \cdots, N\} \tag{1}$$

denote an N input-output data set, where $\{u(t)\}$ is a set of control input signal, $\{y(t)\}$ represents a set of measured output signal, and t specifies a sampling instant number.

Using the available input-output data pairs, we construct an NNARX model to identify the relationship between input and output of the plant. The NNARX model consists of a regressor vector and a set of parameters containing all weights of the neural network, and is widely used for system identification of nonlinear dynamical systems because of its simplicity and fast convergence property during a training period [23; 24].

The regressor vector in the NNARX model can be described as follows:

$$\phi(t) = [y(t-1) \; \cdots \; y(t-n_a) \; u(t-n_k) \; \cdots \; u(t-n_k-n_b+1)]^T \tag{2}$$

and the predictor can be written as

$$\hat{y}(t|\theta) = \hat{y}(t|t-1, \theta) = g(\phi(t), \theta) \tag{3}$$

where θ is a vector of the set of parameters and g designates the function realized by the neural network. n_a and n_b denote the model order and n_k is the delay time of the system.

Fig.5.1 illustrates the structure of NNARX model where v_{ij} is the ij-th weight between the i-th hidden neuron and the j-th input node, w_i is the weight between the i-th hidden neuron and the output node, and v_{i0} and w_0 are the weights connected to the bais terms. The neurons marked with black circles in the hidden layer are nonlinear, whilst the neurons in the input and output layers are linear.

The quality of predictions in a model deeply depends on how to select the model order and the delay time in the regressor vector $\phi(t)$. The regressor vector with exact model order and delay time of the system can provide acceptable predictions with smaller size of network than those of the networks containing numerous arguments as their inputs, hence it is very important to choose them as accurately as possible.

To identify the exact model order, n_a and n_b, of a system, we examine the Lipschitz index [25] defined as follows. Generally, a nonlinear dynamical process can be formulated as

$$y = f(X) = f(x_1, x_2, \cdots, x_n), \tag{4}$$

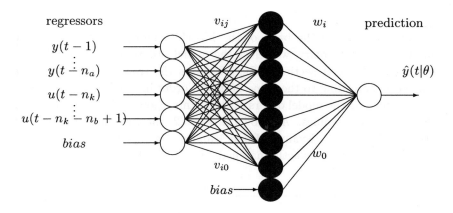

Fig. 5.1   NNARX model structure

where f is a continuous and smooth multivariable function over some region and its partial derivatives with respect to its arguments are assumed to be bounded. For the input-output formulation in (4), the following Lipschitz index is used to identify the optimal number of input variables

$$q^{(n)} = \left(\sum_{k=1}^{p} \sqrt{n} \cdot q^{(n)}(k) \right)^{1/p}, \tag{5}$$

where $q^{(n)}(k)$ is the k-th largest Lipschitz quotient among all $q_{ij}^{(n)}$ ($i \neq j, i, j = 1, 2, \cdots, N$) with the n input variables $(x_1, x_2, \cdots, x_n)$. Parameter p is a positive number (that is usually selected as $p = 0.01N \sim 0.02N$) and the Lipschitz quotient is defined as

$$q_{ij} = \frac{|y_i - y_j|}{|X_i - X_j|} \quad (i \neq j), \tag{6}$$

where $|X_i - X_j|$ is the difference of two points X_i and X_j in the input space and $|y_i - y_j|$ represents the difference of $f(X_i)$ and $f(X_j)$. Note that if one of the input variable x_n is not included in the reconstruction of the unknown function, the Lipschitz quotient $q_{ij}^{(n-1)}$ may be unbounded or extremely large. When a redundant input variable x_{n+1} is included, the Lipschitz quotient $q_{ij}^{(n+1)}$ changes only slightly but not significantly compared with

$q_{ij}^{(n)}$.

For example, on the basis of the Lipschitz index and by using 2,000 input-output data pairs, we select the model orders of Example Plants 1 and 2 (see the next section). Fig.5.2 shows the trend of Lipschitz index calculated according to the value of model order in both Example Plants.

By choosing the model orders at the turning points of the graph, we can obtain the exact values. As shown in Fig.5.2, the turning points indicate that $n_a=2$, $n_b=2$ for Example Plant 1 and $n_a=3$, $n_b=2$ for Example Plant 2, and the values are exactly matched with those of the systems.

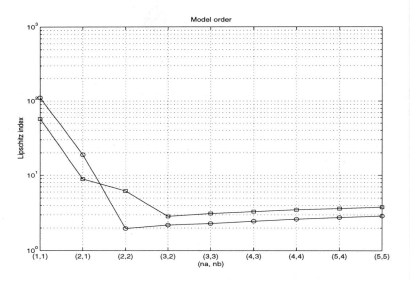

Fig. 5.2   Selection of model order for Example Plants 1($\circ$) and 2 ($\square$)

Although it is assumed that the delay time n_k is given or has been determined by other methods to determine the model order, the delay time must be chosen properly to generate good predictions of a system. To estimate the exact delay time by using only the data pairs allowed, we consider a simple low order model (e.g. $n_a=2$ and $n_b=2$) with variable delays and evaluate a criterion, such as mean square error (MSE) according to the value of delays. By observing a graph of the criterion, one may select the value of n_k which renders the best estimation. For instance, consider the above two Example Plants where we set $d = 0$ and $d = 4$ in Example Plants

1 and 2, respectively. As shown in Fig.5.3, we can choose the delay times of the models as $n_k=1$ and $n_k=5$ for Example Plants 1 and 2, respectively, by inspection of the delay times which give the lowest MSE values.

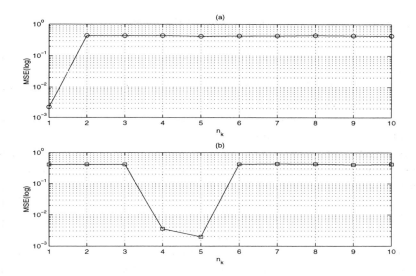

Fig. 5.3 Selection of delay time for (a) Example Plant 1 (b) Example Plant 2

On the other hand, we can also estimate the model order by choosing the order of a model that gives the best evaluation for a criterion function among models consisting of variable n_a and n_b with a fix delay time. However, this method is time-consumming and dependent on the model structure (e.g. number of hidden neurons or layers of the neural network) even though the method based on the Lipschitz index does not rely on the model structure.

Using the estimated model order and delay time, we build the regressor vector in (2), and then estimate the parameter vector θ in (3) by a prediction error approach minimizing the following MSE criterion:

$$V_N(\theta, Z^N) = \frac{1}{2N} \sum_{t=1}^{N} \left(y(t) - \hat{y}(t|\theta)\right)^T \left(y(t) - \hat{y}(t|\theta)\right). \tag{7}$$

Since the objective function (7) is related to θ nonlinearly, we find the estimate $\hat{\theta}$ such that

$$\hat{\theta} = arg \min_{\theta} V_N(\theta, Z^N) \tag{8}$$

by some iterative minimization scheme of the form [26]:

$$\theta_{k+1} = \theta_k + \mu_k d_k, \tag{9}$$

where θ_k specifies the parameter vector, d_k is the search direction, and μ_k is the step size at the k-th iteration. Because of its rapid convergence properties and robustness, we select the Gauss-Newton based Levenberg-Marquardt method [27] to find $\hat{\theta}$.

After estimating the parameters of the neural network, a validation process should be introduced for the model built. If a test set is available, the most common method of validation is to investigate the residuals (prediction errors) by cross-validations such as auto-correlation function of the residuals and cross-correlation function between controls and residuals on the test set. If a test set is not available (or although a test set is available), Akaike's final prediction error (FPE) estimate [26] offers some valuable insights. It reflects the prediction error variance that one will obtain, on the average, when the model is applied as a predictor for other data sets than those used for the identification.

If the constructed NNARX model satisfies given specifications, we then use it as a predictor in the control system. If not, we should repeat the previous steps to try another one.

5.3   Unconstrained GA-based predictive control

Based on the NNARX model describing the given plant precisely, we design a genetic algorithm-based predictive control system in this section. In addition, we compare the control results of the GA-based predictive control with those of adaptive GPC algorithm for several nonlinear plants.

5.3.1   *n-step-ahead predictions*

The block diagram in Fig.5.4 depicts a genetic algorithm-based predictive control system.

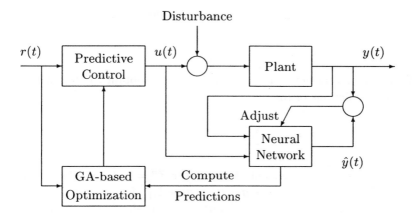

Fig. 5.4 Block diagram of the GA-based predictive control system

We assume that the plant can be described by a general discrete-time nonlinear dynamical system as follows:

$$y(t) = f\big(y(t-1), \cdots, y(t-n_a), u(t-n_k), \cdots, u(t-n_k-n_b+1)\big) \quad (10)$$

where $u \in R$ and $y \in R$ are the input and output of the plant respectively, $f : R^{n_a+n_b} \rightarrow R$ is an unknown continuous and smooth function, n_a and n_b represent the model order, and n_k denotes the delay time of the plant. It is assumed that sufficient input-output data pairs describing an operating point in question are available. For the plant in (10), we identify the nonlinear function f with an NNARX model and estimate the weights of the neural network with the Gauss-Newton based Levenberg-Marquardt method to minimize the cost function (7). By letting $bias = 1$, we can write the output of neural network in (7) as follows:

$$\hat{y}(t|\theta) = \sum_{i=1}^{h} w_i \sigma\Big(\sum_{j=1}^{m} v_{ij} z_j + v_{i0}\Big) + w_0, \quad (11)$$

where z_j is the j-th element of the input vector $Z = [y(t-1), \cdots, y(t-n_a), u(t-n_k), \cdots, u(t-n_k-n_b+1)]^T$, $m = n_a + n_b$ denotes the number of input nodes except the bias node, h is the number of hidden neurons, and

σ denotes a hyperbolic activation function defined by

$$\sigma(x) = \frac{1 - e^{-x}}{1 + e^{-x}} . \tag{12}$$

From the neural network-based identifier, we obtain the following n-step-ahead predictions of the plant:

$$\hat{y}(t + n) = \sum_{i=1}^{h} w_i \sigma \left(\sum_{j=1}^{m} v_{ij} z_j^n + v_{i0} \right) + w_0 \tag{13}$$

where z_j^n is the j-th element of the vector $Z^n = [\hat{y}(t + n - 1) \cdots \hat{y}(t + n - n_a)\, u(t + n - n_k) \cdots u(t + n - n_k - n_b + 1)]^T$ for $n \geq n_a$.

Note that once a predicted output is obtained, the value is used to provide further predictions by taking it as an element of an input vector. This prediction scheme has already been used in several literatures [14; 16]. Based on the future outputs of a plant provided with the neural network and reference signals, we obtain a future control sequence by using the genetic algorithm.

5.3.2   GA-based optimization

In the predictive control, the objective is to find the control action vector, $\underline{u} = [u(t) \cdots u(t + N_u - 1)]^T$, which minimizes the following quadratic cost function:

$$J(\underline{u}) = \sum_{n=N_1}^{N_2} \left(r(t + n) - \hat{y}(t + n) \right)^2 + \lambda \sum_{n=1}^{N_u} \Delta u(t + n - 1)^2 \tag{14}$$

where N_1 and N_2 are the minimum and maximum prediction horizon, respectively, N_u is the control horizon, λ is the control weighting factor, $\Delta u(t) = u(t) - u(t - 1)$, and $r(t)$ is the reference signal.

Since the objective function (14) shows strong nonlinearity caused by the neural network with respect to $\underline{u}$, we are led to adopt a nonlinear programming or other optimization techniques. In the paper, we use the genetic algorithm to find $\underline{u}$ through an evolutionary programming and feed the first element $u(t)$ to the plant.

We implement the genetic algorithm using real-valued string encoding because it is conceptually closer to the problem space and takes less search time than the binary string encoding. The population consists

Initialize first μ parents, $S(0) = \{s_1^0, \cdots, s_\mu^0\}$

Evaluate $S(0)$, calculate $F(s_i^0)$ based on $C(s_i^0)$

Repeat $k = 1, 2, \cdots$

      recombine $S(k)$ to yield offspring $S'(k)$

      evaluate $S'(k)$

      select $S(k+1)$ from $S(k)$ and $S'(k)$

EndRepeat (Until some stopping criteria are satisfied)

Fig. 5.5 Flowchart of the basic genetic algorithm

of a μ-tuple of candidate solutions, called chromosomes or individuals, $s_i \in \Omega (= R^{N_u}$, for unconstrained optimization), $i = 1, 2, \cdots, \mu$, where μ indicates the population size. Note that an individual solution s_i represents an arbitrary value of $\underline{u}$, say $\underline{u}^i$, to be optimized in the GA-based predictive control scheme.

Let $S(k) = \{s_1^k, \cdots, s_\mu^k\}$ be the population at generation k and $C : \Omega \to R$ be the real-valued objective function $J(\underline{u})$ in (14). The quality of an individual is measured by its evaluation function $F : \Omega \to R$. The value $F(s_i)$ is said to be the fitness of s_i, which is evaluated on the basis of the objective function C. The fitness $F(s_i)$ for a chromosome s_i in a minimization problem, for instance, can be calculated simply as

$$F(s_i) = \frac{1}{1 + C(s_i)}$$

or

$$F(s_i) = (C_{max} - C(s_i)) + C_{min},$$

where $C_{max} = \max_i C(s_i)$ and $C_{min} = \min_i C(s_i)$ for $i = 1, 2, \cdots, \mu$.

Fig.5.5 shows a flowchart of the basic genetic algorithm. The selection process is intended to choose a new population with respect to the probability distribution based on fitness values. With the assumption that individuals within a population are sorted according to their fitness values in descending order, several selection schemes for reproduction (generation of $S'(k)$ from $S(k)$) exist [28]. In most practices, a roulette wheel approach is adopted as the selection process. It belongs to the fitness-proportional selection where the selection probability p_i for a chromosome s_i is determined by

$$p_i = \frac{F(s_i)}{\sum_{i=1}^{\mu} F(s_i)} \quad \text{for } i = 1, 2, \cdots, \mu. \tag{15}$$

Typically crossover and mutation operators have been adopted to recombine the individuals in the population of solutions according to the probability of crossover (p_c) and the probability of mutation (p_m), respectively. Crossover used here is the one-cut-point method, which randomly selects one cut-point and exchanges the right parts of two parents to generate offsprings. Mutation alters one or more genes with a probability equal to the mutation rate.

Since the genetic algorithm searches a solution s_*^k which satisfies the condition

$$F(s_*^k) \leq F(s_i^k) \quad \forall\, i = 1, 2, \cdots, \mu \tag{16}$$

at each generation k, we can obtain the best solution s^* for all generations as follows: If $F(s_*^k) \leq F(s_*^{k+1})$, let $s^* = s_*^k$. Otherwise, let $s^* = s_*^{k+1}$. Increase k for one step and perform the procedure for all generations k. Actually, since the generation size (ρ) is limited, we select the chromosome s_*^ρ as the best solution in the GA-based optimization. Note that it is guaranteed that $F(s_*^\rho) \leq F(s_i^k)$ for all i and $k = 0, 1, \cdots, \rho$.

To show the control performance of the GA-based predictive control, we have performed computer simulations and have compared with an adaptive GPC for the following three kinds of plants.

(1) Example Plant 1: At first, we consider the following linear plant [2] expressed as

$$G(s) = \frac{Y(s)}{U(s)} = \frac{e^{-ds}}{1 + 10s + 40s^2},$$

where the sampling time is 1 second and $d = 3$. The corresponding discrete-time dynamic equation is

$$y(t) = 1.7570x_1 - 0.7788x_2 + 0.0115x_3 + 0.01058x_4$$

where $x_1 = y(t-1), x_2 = y(t-2), x_3 = u(t-d-1)$, and $x_4 = u(t-d-2)$.

(2) Example Plant 2: Next, we consider a nonlinear discrete-time process described by [11]

$$y(t) = \frac{x_1 x_2 x_3 x_5 (x_2 - 1) + x_4}{1 + x_2^2 + x_3^2}$$

where $x_1 = y(t-1), x_2 = y(t-2), x_3 = y(t-3), x_4 = u(t-d-1)$, and $x_5 = u(t-d-2)$. We set the time difference d to be 0.

(3) Example Plant 3: Thirdly, the following nonlinear discrete-time process expressed is considered:

$$y(t) = -0.3x_1 + 0.5\frac{x_2}{1 + x_1^2} + 2x_3 sin(\pi x_3),$$

where $x_1 = y(t-1), x_2 = y(t-2)$, and $x_3 = u(t-1)$.

To realize the adaptive GPC algorithm, we construct a linear ARX model by assigning the system order to be exactly the same as the model order and estimate the parameters of the model using the recursive least square (RLS) method with forgetting factor ($\gamma = 0.90$) online. We tune the control parameter λ to obtain good tracking performances with $N_1=1$, $N_2=10$, and $N_u=1$ for Example Plant 1 and $N_2=3$ for Example Plants 2 and 3, and set λ to be 1.0.

Table 5.1   Parameters in the GA-based predictive control for Example Plants 1,2, and 3

Plant	Identifier					Controller						
	n_a	n_b	n_k	h	N_u	N_1	N_2	λ	μ	ρ	p_m	p_c
1	2	2	4	8	1	1	10	1.0	20	20	0.25	0.12
2	3	2	1	8	1	1	3	1.0	50	20	0.25	0.12
3	2	1	1	8	1	1	3	1.0	50	20	0.25	0.12

In the GA-based predictive control, we use nonlinear NNARX models to identify the processes on the basis of the system identification discussed in Section 5.2. The parameters used in the NNARX prediction model and the GA-based controller are given in Table 5.1. The set point is updated every 20 samples from 0 to 1 and -1 repeatedly. In addition, we set the input space Ω in the genetic algorithm to be [-2.5, 2.5], [-2.0, 4.0], and [-1.5, 1.5] for Example Plants 1,2, and 3, respectively. Usually, the range between the minimum and maximum amplitudes of an input signal allowed in a plant can be regarded as the input space in the genetic algorithm.

Fig.5.6(a) and Fig.5.6(b) show the control results performed by both adaptive GPC and GA-based predictive control schemes for Example Plant 1. As shown in Fig.5.6(a), it seems that the control results are very similar except the beginning stage. Due to random initialization for the parameter vector in the adaptive GPC, big fluctuations occur in the early steps of the simulation. But the well-trained neural network provides good predictions and thus reduces the effect in the GA-based control system as shown in Fig.5.6(b).

Fig.5.7(a) and Fig.5.7(b) show the inputs and the responses produced by the two types of controller, respectively, for Example Plant 2. By comparing Fig.5.7(a) with Fig.5.7(b), we find that the GA-based control system yields a good tracking performance, whereas the adaptive GPC makes undesirable large fluctuations near $r(t) = \pm1$. The difference in the control outcomes is primarily related to the generalizing capability of the underlying prediction models. The linear model in the adaptive GPC algorithm does not provide good approximations for the given nonlinear process, and, consequently, the control system reveals distorted output responses.

For Example Plant 3, we can observe that the GA-based predictive control shows an excellent tracking efficiency for a class of nonlinear plants. Fig.5.8 and Fig.5.9 show the control responses generated by the two control methods with the initial value of $u(t) = 0.25$. As shown in the figures, the adaptive GPC method does not trace the reference trajectory well when the set point lies below zero, whereas the GA-based control method gives a tolerable tracking response. To examine the control results, we observe the system responses by changing the input values, which shows a large valley near origin $(u(t) = 0)$. If the initial value of $u(t)$ is set to be 0.25, the adaptive GPC algorithm can not escape the valley, and the consequences are shown in Fig.5.8. However, the GA-based control scheme searches for a solution in the entire input space simultaneously, so that it is less sensitive to the value of initial point and thus yields better solution than adaptive GPC as shown in Fig.5.9.

Although the GA-based predictive control method gives good tracking performance, the process time should be taken into account in the real applications. To illustrate some control performances of the GA-based predictive control system, we investigate the average process time per one step $(T_{p,ave})$, root mean square error (RMSE), and root mean square cost

(RMSC) for Example Plant 2. To contain the effect of tracking error and input variation, we define the RMSC as

$$RMSC = \sqrt{\frac{1}{P}\sum_{t=1}^{P} e(t)^2 + \lambda\frac{1}{P}\sum_{t=1}^{P}\Delta u(t)^2}, \tag{17}$$

where $e(t) = r(t) - y(t)$ and P denotes the period of the reference trajectory.

According to the population size (μ) and the maximum number of generation (ρ), we plot the three criteria in Fig.5.10 and Fig.5.11, respectively. Observe that the RMSE and RMSC decrease rapidly as μ and ρ increase, whereas the average process time increases almost linearly as μ and ρ increase. In addition, Table 5.2 shows the three control performances produced by the GA-based predictive control method for Example Plants 1, 2, and 3 with respect to $\mu = 20$ and $\mu = 50$. We perform the simulations with MATLAB Version 5.1.0 in a Pentium personal computer.

Table 5.2   Control performances of the GA-based control for Example Plants 1, 2, and 3

Plant	μ	$T_{p,ave}$ (sec)	RMSE	RMSC
1	20	0.5206	0.2206	0.2782
	50	0.7921	0.2190	0.2733
2	20	0.2491	0.1664	0.2610
	50	0.3806	0.1594	0.2538
3	20	0.2413	0.1855	0.2407
	50	0.3788	0.1678	0.1714

Fig.5.10, Fig.5.11, and Table 5.2 indicate that the tracking error and the process time should be cautiously chosen to satisfy a certain specification in GA-based predictive control systems.

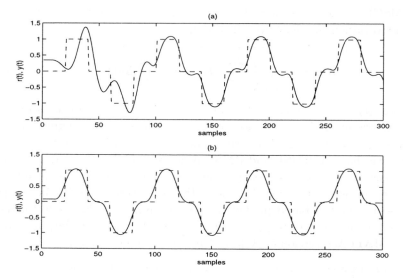

Fig. 5.6   Control results for Example Plant 1 (a) adaptive GPC (b) GA-based predictive controller

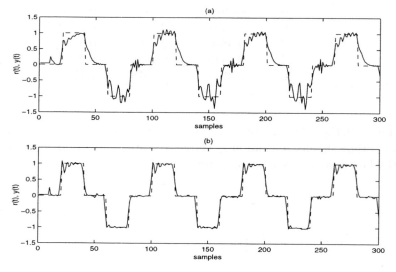

Fig. 5.7   Control results for Example Plant 2 (a) adaptive GPC (b) GA-based predictive controller

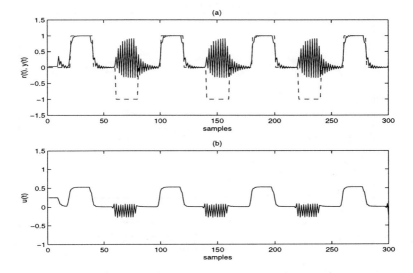

Fig. 5.8   adaptive GPC results for Example Plant 3

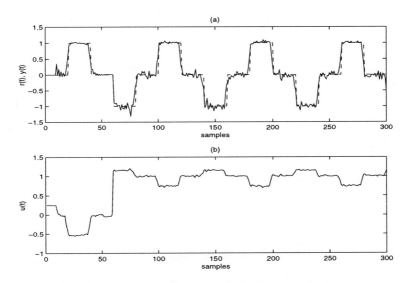

Fig. 5.9   GA-based predictive control results for Example Plant 3

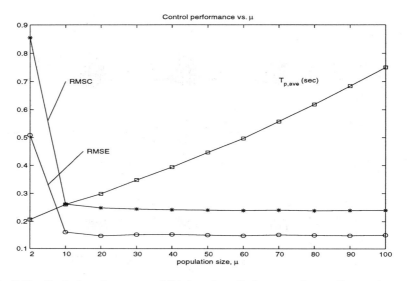

Fig. 5.10   Control performances of GA-based predictive control according to the population size μ for Example Plant 2 ($\rho = 20$)

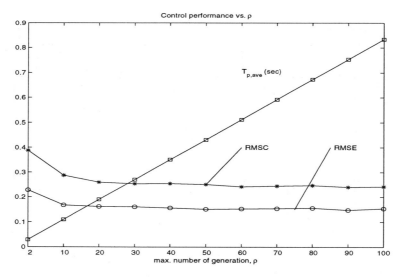

Fig. 5.11   Control performances of GA-based predictive control according to the maximum number of generation ρ for Example Plant 2 ($\mu = 10$)

5.4 Constrained GA-based predictive control

In the previous section, the control problem was formulated under the assumption that all the signals can be unbounded. However, such an assumption is not realistic because most practical processes are subject to constraints.

Including the amplitude limits of a control signal, slew rate limits of an actuator, and limits on an output signal, we may rewrite the optimization problem in (14) to be a problem of finding a control vector $\underline{u}$ minimizing the objective function of the form

$$J(\underline{u}) = (\underline{r} - \underline{\hat{y}})^T (\underline{r} - \underline{\hat{y}}) + \lambda \Delta \underline{u}^T \Delta \underline{u}, \tag{18}$$

subject to

$$
\begin{array}{ccccc}
u_L & \leq & u(t) & \leq & u_H & \forall\, t, \\
\Delta u_L & \leq & \Delta u(t) & \leq & \Delta u_H & \forall\, t, \\
y_L & \leq & y(t) & \leq & y_H & \forall\, t,
\end{array}
\tag{19}
$$

where $\underline{r} = [r(t+1) \cdots r(t+N)]^T$, $\underline{\hat{y}} = [\hat{y}(t+1) \cdots \hat{y}(t+N)]^T$, and $\Delta \underline{u} = [\Delta u(t) \cdots \Delta u(t + N_u - 1)]^T$. For simplicity in the derivation below, N_1 is set to be 1 and N_2 (prediction horizon) is to be N.

In addition to the above constraints, overshoots in manipulated variables can be considered as an unwanted aspect in some plants because, for example, an overshoot may produce a collision with the workspace in the case of robot manipulators. To deal with such overshoots, we add the following type of constraint to the control system:

$$y(t) \leq r(t) \quad \forall\, t. \tag{20}$$

From the viewpoint of predictive control, we can express the constraints as follows:

$$
\begin{array}{ccccc}
1_u \cdot u_L & \leq & \underline{u} & \leq & 1_u \cdot u_H, \\
1_u \cdot \Delta u_L & \leq & \Delta \underline{u} & \leq & 1_u \cdot \Delta u_L, \\
1_y \cdot y_L & \leq & \underline{\hat{y}} & \leq & 1_y \cdot y_H, \\
& & \underline{\hat{y}} & \leq & \underline{r},
\end{array}
\tag{21}
$$

where 1_u and 1_y denote vectors whose entries are all one with the size of $N_u \times 1$ and $N \times 1$, respectively. Note that, instead of the process output $\underline{y}$, the output of a model $\hat{y}$ is generally used to handle the constraints, since it represents the underlying plant accurately.

To deal with the constraints (21) in the GA-based predictive control, we modify some genetic operators and use a penalty strategy [21; 29] in the following.

5.4.1   *Modifying genetic operator strategy*

When all constraints are linear in the optimization problem, we can simply treat the constraints by using some specified genetic operators. The specific genetic operators guarantee that all parents and offsprings lie in a feasible solution space $\Omega \subset R^{N_u}$.

To satisfy the feasible condition of a population at an initial step, we select a subset of potential solutions from the space of whole feasible region randomly, and then fill the remaining subset of potential solutions with boundaries of the solution space. Based upon the initial selection, we recombine chromosomes to generate feasible offsprings by using some modified genetic operators such as uniform mutation, boundary mutation, non-uniform mutation, simple crossover, and arithmetical crossover.

To implement the uniform mutation, we select a random gene v_j (which represents $u(t+j-1)$ in $\underline{u}$) from a chromosome $s_v^k = < v_{ijl}^O \cdots v_j \cdots v_{N_u} >$ and change it as v_j' by assigning a random value within the amplitude bound $[v_L, v_H]$. Thereby we obtain the mutated chromosome $s_v^{k+1} = < v_{ijl}^O \cdots v_j' \cdots v_{N_u} >$ and can easily calculate the dynamic values v_L and v_H from the set of inequality constraints. By letting v_j' be v_L or v_H with equal probability, we achieve the boundary mutation.

To realize the non-uniform mutation, we change the random gene v_j as follows:

$$v_j' = \begin{cases} v_j + \Delta(k, v_L - v_j) & \text{if a random digit is 0,} \\ v_j - \Delta(k, v_j - v_H) & \text{if a random digit is 1,} \end{cases} \tag{22}$$

where $\Delta(k, \delta) = \delta \cdot (1 - a^{(1-k/\rho)})$ returns a value in the range $[0, \delta]$, $a \in [0, 1]$ is a random number, and ρ indicates the maximal generation number. Note that the selected gene v_j is changed by the amount of $\Delta(k, \delta)$ nonlinearly.

In the typical crossover operation, we select two random chromosomes $s_v^k = < v_{ijl}^O, \cdots, v_{N_u} >$ and $s_w^k = < w_{ij}^O, \cdots, w_{N_u} >$ in a population and cross the chromosomes after the j-th position. Thereby we obtain two new off-

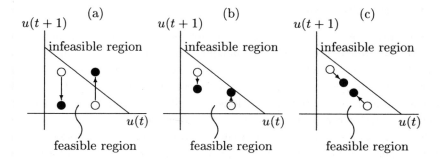

Fig. 5.12 Illustration of (a) typical crossover (b) simple crossover (c) arithmetical crossover (o: parent, •: offspring)

springs, $s_v^{k+1} = < v_{ijl}^O, \cdots, v_j, w_{j+1}, \cdots, w_{N_u} >$ and $s_w^{k+1} = < w_{ij}^O, \cdots, w_j, v_{j+1}, \cdots, v_{N_u} >$. But the typical form of crossover can produce offsprings outside of the feasible space Ω as shown in Fig.5.12(a).

To avoid this problem, at first, we carry out the simple crossover based on the properties of the convex space as follows:

$$s_v^{k+1} = < v_{ijl}^O, \cdots, v_j, \ w_{j+1}a + v_{j+1}(1-a), \cdots, w_{N_u}a + v_{N_u}(1-a) > \quad \in \Omega,$$
$$s_w^{k+1} = < w_{ij}^O, \cdots, w_j, \ v_{j+1}a + w_{j+1}(1-a), \cdots, v_{N_u}a + w_{N_u}(1-a) > \quad \in \Omega,$$

where $a \in [0, 1]$ is determined to satisfy the feasible condition.

Secondly, we perform the arithmetical crossover for the two chromosomes and obtain the offsprings as

$$s_v^k = a \cdot s_w^k + (1-a) \cdot s_v^k$$
$$s_w^k = a \cdot s_v^k + (1-a) \cdot s_w^k$$

where $a \in [0, 1]$. Note that the two crossover operations always guarantee closure in Ω.

The modified genetic operations are performed in the genetic algorithm according to the probabilities, p_{um}, p_{bm}, and p_{nm} for uniform, boundary, and non-uniform mutations, and p_{sc} and p_{ac} for simple and arithmetical crossovers, respectively. Fig.5.12 illustrates the operations of typical, simple, and arithmetical crossover for the two genes $u(t)$ and $u(t+1)$, in which the chromosome consists of $s^k = \{u(t), u(t+1)\}$ and $u(t+1)$ is crossed in the typical and simple crossover operations.

5.4.2   *Penalty strategy*

Essentially, the penalty technique transforms a constrained problem into an unconstrained problem by penalizing infeasible solutions, in which a penalty term is added to the objective function for any violation of the constraints. In genetic algorithms, the penalty technique is used to keep a certain amount of infeasible solutions in each generation so as to enforce genetic search toward an optimal solution from both sides of feasible and infeasible regions. Therefore, we do not simply reject infeasible solutions in each generation because they may provide much more useful information about an optimal solution than some feasible solutions do.

The main issue of penalty strategy is how to design the penalty function which can effectively guide genetic search toward the promising area of solution space. The relationship between infeasible chromosome and feasible part of the search space plays a significant role in penalizing infeasible chromosomes. The penalty value corresponds to the amount of its infeasibility under some measurement. However, there is no general guideline on designing a penalty function, and furthermore constructing an efficient penalty function is quite problem-dependent.

Considering the future predictions of a plant, we design a penalty function $P(\underline{u})$ and add it to the objective function (14) as follows:

$$J_C(\underline{u}) = J(\underline{u}) + P(\underline{u}). \tag{23}$$

The penalty function $P(\underline{u})$ is defined as

$$P(\underline{u}) = \sum_{i=1}^{N} \alpha^i(k) \sum_{j=1}^{M} d_{ij}^{\beta}(\underline{u}), \tag{24}$$

where $\alpha^i(k) = \alpha^i \times k$, k denotes the generation step, α and β are the parameters used to adjust the scale of penalty value,

$$d_{ij}(\underline{u}) = \begin{cases} 0 & \text{if } \underline{u} \text{ is feasible,} \\ |g_{ij}(\underline{u})| & \text{otherwise} \end{cases} \tag{25}$$

and g_{ij} denotes the j-th constraint of the i-step-ahead prediction, and M represents the number of constraints in one prediction output. Note that α penalizes the infeasibility of future predictions of the process by giving some weighting.

To show the validity of the constrained GA-based predictive control, we give some simulation results in the following example.

Table 5.3   Control parameters for the plant in Example 4.1

Example	μ	ρ	p_{um}	p_{bm}	p_{nm}	δ	r	p_{sc}	p_{ac}	a
4	50	20	0.12	0.15	0.20	0.5	0.9	0.25	0.25	0.7

■ EXAMPLE 4:   Consider a simple linear plant described by

$$G(s) = \frac{1}{1 + 10s} ,$$

where the sampling time is set to be 0.6 seconds.

To begin with, we handle the amplitude constraints of input signal by using the modified genetic operators. We set N_u=1, $N = 3$, λ=0.1, and all the parameters used in the constrained GA-based predictive control system are given in Table 5.3. Fig.5.13 shows the control results obtained. From the figures, we can observe that the introduction of the constraints on the manipulated variables has produced a slower closed loop response as expected.

Next, we apply a penalty technique to the plant to restrict overshoots of the process output. For the penalty function in (24), we let $\alpha^i(k) = \eta \cdot \alpha^i$ where η is a constant. Moreover, we can write $d_{ij}^\beta(\underline{u}) = d_i(\underline{u})$, since $M = 1$ and by setting $\beta = 1$. Therefore, $d_i(\underline{u})$ in the penalty function can be represented as

$$d_i(\underline{u}) = \begin{cases} 0 & \text{if } \hat{y}(t+i) < r(t+i), \\ |\hat{y}(t+i) - r(t+i)| & \text{otherwise} \end{cases}$$

where $\hat{y}(t+i)$, as a function of $\underline{u}$, is the i-step-ahead prediction of the process output at the current time t. We set the parameters as $\eta = 100$ and $\alpha = 0.9$. Note that the long-term prediction outputs have less penalties than the short-term predictions because $\alpha < 1$.

By applying an unconstrained GA-based predictive control with a prediction horizon 3, a control horizion 1, and the control weighting factor 0.1 to the plant, we obtain the control results as shown in Fig.5.14. As can be seen, the output shows a noticeable overshoot (solid line). However, the overshoot has been eliminated when the overshoot constraints are taken into account as shown in the same figure (dashed line).

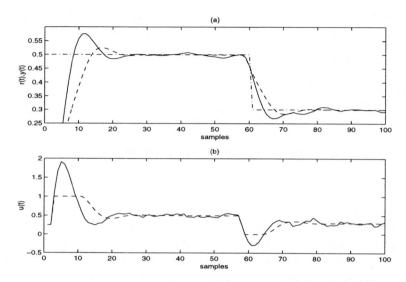

Fig. 5.13   GA-based control with input amplitude constraints; unconstrained case(solid line), constrained case(dashed line)

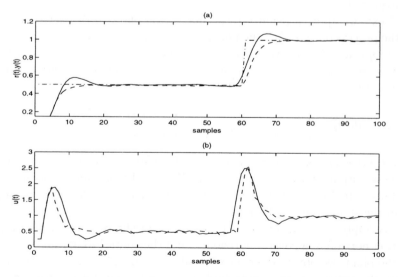

Fig. 5.14   GA-based control with overshoot constraints; unconstrained case(solid line), constrained case(dashed line)

5.5   GA-based predictive control for MIMO systems

In this section, we consider a nonlinear discrete-time MIMO process with p-input and q-output represented as

$$
\begin{aligned}
y_1(t) &= f_1\left(\phi_1^T(t-1)\right) \\
y_2(t) &= f_2\left(\phi_2^T(t-1)\right)
\end{aligned}
\tag{26}
$$

$$
\vdots
$$

$$
y_q(t) = f_q\left(\phi_q^T(t-1)\right),
$$

where f_is are unknown continuous and smooth functions, and

$$
\phi_j(t-1) = [\underline{y}_{1j}^T(t-1) \;\cdots\; \underline{y}_{qj}^T(t-1)\; \underline{u}_{1j}^T(t-1) \;\cdots\; \underline{u}_{pj}^T(t-1)]^T \tag{27}
$$

$$
\underline{y}_{ij}(t-1) = [y_i(t-1) \;\cdots\; y_i(t-n_{aij})]^T, \tag{28}
$$

$$
\underline{u}_{ij}(t-1) = [u_i(t-n_{kij}) \;\cdots\; u_i(t-n_{kij}-n_{bij}+1)]^T. \tag{29}
$$

n_{aij} and n_{bij} denote the number of elements of the i-th output variable and i-th input variable in $y_j(t)$, respectively, and n_{kij} denotes the delay time of the i-th input variable in $y_j(t)$.

For the plant in (26), we assume that sufficient input-output data pairs are available so that we can identify the nonlinear function f_is with NNARX models. To determine the model orders and delay times, we follow the procedure of system identification described in Section 5.2. To construct the neural network-based identifier, we may use any of the following two methodologies: (1) Use of a large volume of neural networks that all the neurons are connected with each other between two layers; (2) Use of q-partitioned neural networks for each output, in which each independent neural networks provide predictions of the corresponding process outputs with different model order and delay time. In the first approach, as implied in Section 5.2, the redundant input variables of a function f_i deteriorate the training efficiency by making an effect on the outputs that are not relevant to the original input variables. As such, we adopt the second approach to model the underlying MIMO plant.

To control MIMO processes, we change the objective function in (18) as follows:

$$
J_M(\underline{u}) = (\underline{r} - \hat{\underline{y}})^T Q(\underline{r} - \hat{\underline{y}}) + \Delta\underline{u}^T \Lambda \Delta\underline{u}, \tag{30}
$$

where

$$
\begin{aligned}
\underline{r} &= [r_1(t+1) \ \cdots \ r_1(t+N) \ \cdots \ r_q(t+1) \ \cdots \ r_q(t+N)]^T, \\
\underline{\hat{y}} &= [\hat{y}_1(t+1) \ \cdots \ \hat{y}_1(t+N) \ \cdots \ \hat{y}_q(t+1) \ \cdots \ \hat{y}_q(t+N)]^T, \\
\underline{\Delta u} &= [\Delta u_1(t) \ \cdots \ \Delta u_1(t+N_u-1) \ \cdots \ \Delta u_p(t) \ \cdots \ \Delta u_p(t+N_u-1)]^T.
\end{aligned}
$$

Q is a $(qN \times qN)$ weighting matrix for tracking errors, and Λ denotes a $(pN_u \times pN_u)$ control weighting matrix. By using partitioned neural networks, we obtain an n-step-ahead prediction of the l-th output as

$$
\hat{y}_l(t+n) = \sum_{i=1}^{h} w_i^l \sigma \Big(\sum_{j=1}^{m} v_{ij}^l z_j^{ln} + v_{i0}^l \Big) + w_0^l, \tag{31}
$$

where w^l and v^l denote the weights between input and output layers in the l-th partitioned neural network and z_j^{ln} is the j-th element of the input vector $Z^{ln} = [\underline{y}_{1l}^T(t+n-1) \cdots \underline{y}_{ql}^T(t+n-1) \ \underline{u}_{1l}^T(t+n-1) \cdots \underline{u}_{pl}^T(t+n-1)]^T = \phi_l(t+n-1)$. With the similar manner in the SISO case, we find $\underline{u} = [u_1(t) \ \cdots \ u_1(t+N_u-1) \ \cdots \ u_p(t) \ \cdots \ u_p(t+N_u-1)]^T$ which minimizes $J_M(\underline{u})$ by the genetic algorithm. However, the dimension of a chromosome increases from N_u to $(p \times N_u)$ in the case of MIMO systems.

A couple of two-input, two-output nonlinear processes are treated to illustrate the effectiveness of the GA-based predictive control.

Table 5.4   Control parameters for the plants in Example 5.1 and 5.2

EXAMPLE	N_u	N	Q	Λ	μ	ρ	p_m	p_c
5.1	1	3	$I_{2\times2}$	$0.1 \times I_{2\times2}$	100	20	0.25	0.012
5.2	1	3	$I_{2\times2}$	$1.0 \times I_{2\times2}$	200	20	0.25	0.001

■ EXAMPLE 5.1:   We consider a small signal model of a stirred tank reactor described by the following transfer matrix [7]

$$
\begin{bmatrix} Y_1(s) \\ Y_2(s) \end{bmatrix} = \begin{bmatrix} \dfrac{1}{1+0.1s} & \dfrac{5}{1+s} \\ \dfrac{1}{1+0.5s} & \dfrac{2}{1+0.4s} \end{bmatrix} \begin{bmatrix} U_1(s) \\ U_2(s) \end{bmatrix},
$$

where the manipulated variables $U_1(s)$ and $U_2(s)$ are the feed flowrate and the flow of coolant in the jacket, respectively. The controlled variables

$Y_1(s)$ and $Y_2(s)$ are the effluent concentration and the reactor temperature, respectively. The discrete-time model with a sampling time 0.01 minutes can be written as

$$\begin{bmatrix} y_1(t) \\ y_2(t) \end{bmatrix} = \begin{bmatrix} \dfrac{0.0952z^{-1}}{1 - 0.9048z^{-1}} & \dfrac{0.0498z^{-1}}{1 - 0.99z^{-1}} \\ \dfrac{0.0198z^{-1}}{1 - 0.9801z^{-1}} & \dfrac{0.0494z^{-1}}{1 - 0.9753z^{-1}} \end{bmatrix} \begin{bmatrix} u_1(t) \\ u_2(t) \end{bmatrix}.$$

For the output variables $y_1(t)$ and $y_2(t)$ of the plant, we design two partitioned neural networks and set the regressor vectors for each network as $\phi_1(t-1) = [y_1(t-1)\ y_1(t-2)\ u_1(t-1)\ u_1(t-2)\ u_2(t-1)\ u_2(t-2)]^T$ and $\phi_2(t-1) = [y_2(t-1)\ y_2(t-2)\ u_1(t-1)\ u_1(t-2)\ u_2(t-1)\ u_2(t-2)]^T$. The parameters used in the control system are given in Table 5.4 where $I_{2\times2}$ denotes (2×2) identity matrix. For two reference signals $r_1(t)$ and $r_2(t)$, we obtain the control results as shown in Fig.5.15. $r_1(t)$ changes from 0.5 to 0.4 at 0.6 minutes, whereas $r_2(t)$ maintains the value of 0.3. From the figures, we can find that the two process outputs trace the set points very well simultaneously possibly because the original process is linear.

■ EXAMPLE 5.2: Now, consider the following nonlinear dynamical process described by [24]

$$\begin{aligned} x_1(t+1) &= 0.9x_1(t)sin[x_2(t)] + \left(2 + 1.5\frac{x_1(t)u_1(t)}{1 + x_1^2(t)u_1^2(t)}\right)u_1(t) \\ &\quad + \left(x_1(t) + \frac{2x_1(t)}{1 + x_1^2(t)}\right)u_2(t), \\ x_2(t+1) &= x_3(t)\big(1 + sin[4x_3(t)]\big) + \frac{x_3(t)}{1 + x_3^2(t)}, \\ x_3(t+1) &= \big(3 + sin[2x_1(t)]\big)u_2(t), \end{aligned}$$

where $u_1(t)$ and $u_2(t)$ are the control inputs and the process outputs are $y_1(t) = x_1(t)$ and $y_2(t) = x_2(t)$.

To identify the relationships between inputs and outputs, we also design two partitioned NNARX models and then select the regressor vectors of the models as $\phi_1(t-1) = [y_1(t-1)\ y_2(t-1)\ u_1(t-1)\ u_2(t-1)]^T$ and $\phi_2(t-1) = [y_1(t-1)\ u_2(t-1)]^T$ for $y_1(t)$ and $y_2(t)$, respectively. The reference signals $r_1(t)$ and $r_2(t)$ vary from +0.5 to -0.5 and +0.2 to -0.2 at 60 samples, respectively.

Table 5.4 gives the parameters used in the control system and Fig.5.16 shows the control outcomes performed by GA-based predictive control method. Although the responses reveal some fluctuations near the set points, the effect can be diminished by increasing the number of populations and/or generations or by using a filter because it is originated from search operation in the genetic algorithm.

From the simulations, we find that the GA-based predictive control method gives a satisfactory control performance for nonlinear discrete-time MIMO processes.

5.6   Concluding remarks

In the paper, we have presented a predictive control scheme using the genetic algorithm to solve the problem of local minimum in the neural network-based control methods. To deal with the input-output constraints of a process in the GA-based predictive control, we have introduced some modified genetic operators and designed a penalty function. Moreover, we have extended the control scheme for SISO plants to MIMO plants in the frame of partitioned prediction models.

Some computer simulations were given to show the effectiveness of the GA-based predictive control in comparison with adaptive GPC algorithm. From our extensive simulation studies, it is found that the GA-based predictive control system gives better tracking performances than the adaptive GPC algorithm for a class of nonlinear processes, especially when the nonlinear plants have many local minima near an operating range. Hence, we may say that the GA-based control techniques can be utilized to handle complex processes that requires high quality control performances.

However, due to the inherent complexity of the genetic algorithm and the neural network-based prediction model, more process times are needed in the GA-based control system than the adaptive GPC. Thus the tracking error and process time should be carefully chosen to satisfy a certain specification in GA-based predictive control systems.

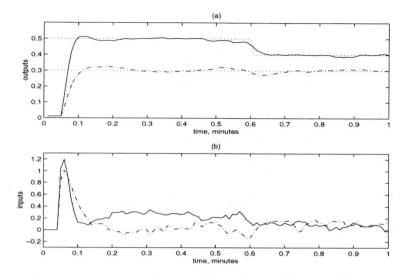

Fig. 5.15   GA-based predictive control results for the plant in Example 5.1 (a) $y_1(t)$ (solid line) and $y_2(t)$ (dashdot line) (b) $u_1(t)$ (solid line) and $u_2(t)$ (dashdot line)

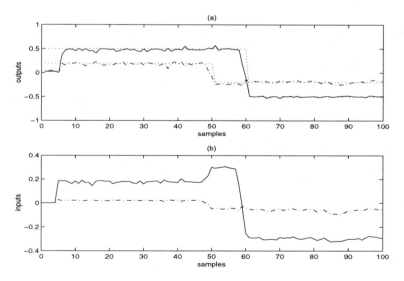

Fig. 5.16   GA-based predictive control results for the plant in Example 5.2 (a) $y_1(t)$ (solid line) and $y_2(t)$ (dashdot line) (b) $u_1(t)$ (solid line) and $u_2(t)$ (dashdot line)

References

[1] B.E. Ydstie. Extended horizon adaptive control. *Proc. 9th IFAC world congress*, pages 133–137, 1984.

[2] D.W. Clarke, C. Mohtadi, and P.S. Tuffs. Generalized predictive control - part I and II. *Automatica*, **23**:137–160, 1987.

[3] C.E. Garcia, D.M. Porett, and M. Morari. Model predictive control: theory and practice - a survey. *Automatica*, **25**:335–348, 1989.

[4] D.W. Clarke and R. Scattolini. Constrained receding horizon predictive control. *IEE Proc.*, **138**:347–354, 1991.

[5] J.A. Rossiter, B. Kouvaritakis, and R.M. Dunnett. Application of generalised predictive control to a boiler-turbine unit for electricity generation. *IEE Proc. Part-D*, **138**:59–67, 1991.

[6] J. Richalet. Industrial applications of model based predictive control. *Automatica*, **29**:1251–1274, 1993.

[7] E.F. Camacho and C. Bordons. *Model predictive control in the process industry*. Springer, 1995.

[8] Q.M. Zhu, K. Wanvick, and J.L. Douce. Adaptive general predictive controller for nonlinear systems. *IEE Proc.*, **138**:33–40, 1991.

[9] E.B. Feng, J.S. Yu, and W.S. Jiang. New method for predictive controller design for bilinear systems. *Int. J. Control*, **53**:97–111, 1991.

[10] K.C. Funahashi. On the approximate realization of continuous mappings by neural networks. *Neural networks*, **2**:183–192, 1989.

[11] K.S. Narendra and K. Parthasarathy. Identification and control of dynamical systems using neural networks. *IEEE Trans. on Neural Networks*, **1**:4–27, 1990.

[12] K.J. Hunt, D. Sbarbaro, and P.J. Gawthrop. Application of generalised predictive control to a boiler-turbine unit for electricity generation. *IEE Proc. Part D*, **138**:59–67, 1991.

[13] F.L. Lewis, K. Liu, and A. Yesildirek. Neural net robot controller with

guaranteed tracking performance. *IEEE Trans. on Neural Networks*, **6**:703–715, 1995.

[14] J. Saint-Donat, N. Bhat, and T.J McAvoy. Neural net based model predictive control. *Int. J. Control*, **54**:1453–1468, 1991.

[15] A. Draeger, S. Engell, and H. Ranke. Model predictive control using neural networks. *IEEE Control Systems*, **15**:61–66, 1995.

[16] M. Norgaard, P.H. Sorensen, and N.K. Poulsen. Intelligent predictive control of nonlinear processes using neural networks. *Proc. IEEE Int. Symp. Intelligent Control*, pages 301–306, 1996.

[17] J.Q. Hu and E. Rose. Generalized predictive control using a neuro-fuzzy model. *Proc. Asian Cont. Conf.*, pages 451–454, 1997.

[18] N. Bhat and T.J. McAvoy. Use of neural nets for dynamic modelling and control of chemical process systems. *Proc. American Cont. Conf.*, pages 1342–1347, 1989.

[19] S.C. Ahn, Y.H. Kim, and W.H. Kwon. A fuzzy generalized predictive control using affine fuzzy predictors for nonlinear systems. *J. of Intelligent and Fuzzy Systems*, **6**:185–207, 1998.

[20] A. Varsek, T. Urbancic, and B. Eilipic. Genetic algorithm in controller design and tuning. *IEEE Trans. on System, Man, and Cyber.*, **23**:1330–1339, 1993.

[21] Z. Michalewicz. *Genetic algorithms + data structures = evolution programmings*. Springer-Verlag, 1994.

[22] S.C. Shin and S.B. Park. GA-based predictive control for nonlinear processes. *Electronics Letters*, **34**:1980–1981, 1998.

[23] J. Sjoberg, H. Hjalmerson, and L. Ljung. Neural networks in system identification. *Proc. IFAC Symp. on SYSID*, **2**:49–71, 1994.

[24] M.M. Gupta and N.K. Sinha. *Intelligent control systems; theory and applications*. IEEE Press, 1996.

[25] X. He and H. Asada. A new method for identifying orders of i-o models for nonlinear dynamical systems. *Proc. American Cont. Conf.*, pages 2520–2523, 1993.

[26] L. Ljung. *System identification: theory for the user*. Prentice Hall, 1987.

[27] J.E. Dannis and J.J. More. Quasi-Newton methods, motivation and theory. *SIAM Review*, **19**:46–89, 1977.

[28] T. Back, R. Hoffmeister, and H.P. Schwefel. A survey of evolution strategies. *Proc. of Fourth Intl. Conf. of Genetic Algorithms*, pages 2–9, 1991.

[29] M. Gen and R. Cheng. *Genetic algorithms and engineering design*. John Wiley & Sons, 1997.

Chapter 6

Indirect Neuro-Control for Multivariable Nonlinear Systems with Application to 2-bar Load Systems

Jun Oh Jang[1] and Hee Tae Chung[2]

[1] Uiduk University
[2] Pusan University of Foreign Studies

Abstract

This paper represents identification and control designs using neural networks for a class of multivariable nonlinear systems. The proposed neuro-controller is a combination of linear controllers and a neural network controller, and is trained by indirect neuro-control scheme. The proposed neuro-controller is implemented and tested on IBM PC-based two 2-bar systems holding an object, and is applicable to many dc-motor-driven precision multivariable nonlinear systems. Also, we derive a practical bound on the tracking error using the Lyapunov function with the error dynamics and the weight training rules. The algorithm and experimental results are described. The experimental results are shown to be superior to be to those of conventional control.

Keywords : indirect neuro-control, neuro-controller, two 2-bar systems holding an object, tracking error bound

6.1 Introduction

In many engineering applications, a complete servomechanism often comprises multiple channels, or axes; for example, a multi-axis stabilized platform for line-of-sight targetting [1], or multi-axis machine tools [2]. The control of such multivariable nonlinear servomechanisms is, in general, not a simple problem as there exist crossing-couplings or interactions, between the different channels. In addition, such systems are usually required to maintain stable operation even when there are changes in the system dynamics.   Recently, advances in the area of neural networks have provided the potential for new approaches to the control of multivariable nonlinear systems through learning process.   Relevant features of the neural networks in the control context include among others their ability to model arbitrary differential nonlinear functions, and their intrinsic on-line adaptation and learning capabilities [3].   This fundamental link of the neural networks with nonlinear systems, together with the fact that reliable and inexpensive computing hardware is available, has resulted in a tremendous growth of research and development in this area.   Kawato et al. [4] used a hierarchical neural network model as an add-on component to the conventional linear controller in order to control the movement of a robot.   Lightbody and Irwin [5] propose a direct model reference adaptive control structure using a linear controller and a neural network in parallel in a chemical process and a missile control system.   Karakasoglu et al. [6] proposed a novel neural network structure and a training algorithm for the identification and decentralized adaptive control of complex dynamical systems characterized by an interconnection of several nonlinear dynamical subsystems.   However, due to the highly nonlinear functions and the existing coupling between the several subsystems, the neural network-based controller is not applicable to the complex dynamical systems can be modeled by an interconnection of several subsystems with multiple input and multiple output.   Cui et al. [7] proposed a direct control and coordination method using neural networks for multiple robot system. However, it is necessary to determine the direction matrix of the system for training the neural networks.

In this paper, we present the idea of controlling the multivariable nonlinear systems with a proposed controller. The proposed neuro-controller consists of two linear controllers and a neural network controller(NNC) for compensating the nonlinearity and interactions between the each system.   The NNC is trained through the neural network identifier(NNI) by an indirect learning scheme. By an example of two 2-bar systems holding an object, this paper gives an implementation of the idea of controlling a class of multivariable nonlinear systems using two PI controllers and two neural networks, which are employed as identifier and neural network controller.   The effectiveness of the proposed neuro-controller is demonstrated by experimental results of two 2-bar systems holding an object.

6.2 Two 2-bar systems holding an object

As an example of multivariable nonlinear systems, two 2-bar systems holding an object (Fig. 6.1) has been chosen for the experiment. Suppose two 2-bar systems have an identical mechanical configuration, then the dynamic equation of 2-bar system j is given by

$$T_j(t) = (J_e + J_m)\ddot{\theta}_{2j}(t) + B\dot{\theta}_{2j}(t) + G + T_c + T_d + F_j[\theta_{2j}(t),\dot{\theta}_{2j}(t)],$$
$$j = 1,2 \qquad (1)$$

where θ_{2j} is the angular position of the 2-bar system j, the coefficient terms J_e, J_m, B, and G represent the effective inertia term, the motor inertia term, the viscous term, and the gravity term, respectively [8]. T_j represent the motor torque, $F_j[\theta_{2j}(t),\dot{\theta}_{2j}(t)]$ includes coupled and unmodeled dynamics. T_C represent the Coulomb friction in the motor while T_d is the disturbance. The unmodeled dynamics include out-of-plane movement of the bar, wobbling, sensor dynamics, etc. The control is applied only to the second joint and the first joint is just a variable load in 2-bar systems, respectively.

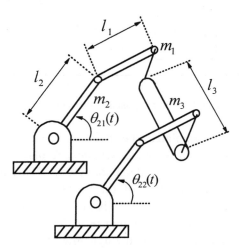

Fig. 6.1   Two 2-bar systems holding an object.

6.3   Indirect neuro-control of two 2-bar systems

The structure of the NNI and design techniques of the proposed neuro-controller are presented in this section for experimentally controlling the velocity of the 2-bar system, $\dot{\theta}_{2j}(t)$, $j=1,2$.   Fig. 6.2 shows the NNI and the proposed neuro-controller, which has two linear controllers and a NNC for compensating the nonlinearities and interactions between the each system.   Linear controllers are designed independently of, and separately, each other.

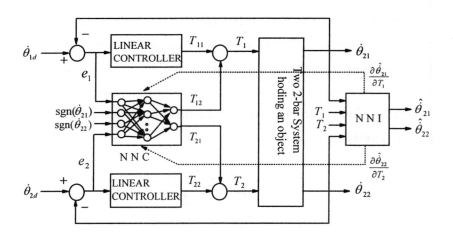

Fig. 6.2   The proposed neuro-control system.

The NNI, which emulates the dynamic behavior of the plant, is necessary for indirect neuro-control scheme and plays an important role in the update of the neuro-controller parameters.   This update is achieved by obtaining a better estimate of the gradient in the gradient descent technique using the trained NNI.   It is noted that the NNI is trained in a series-parallel mode [9], before being used for control.   The parameters of the NNI are updated to follow the dynamics of the plant in the reported research since this is found to increase accuracy.   The output of the NNI

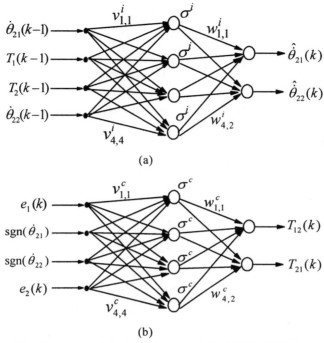

Fig. 6.3   Structure of the neural network (a) NNI (b) NNC.

in Fig. 6.3(a), with the number of nodes in successive layers 4-4-2, is given by

$$\hat{\theta}_{2j} = \sum_{m=1}^{4} [w_{mj}^{i} \cdot \sigma^{i} (\sum_{l=1}^{4} v_{lm}^{i} \cdot x_l^{i})], \quad j = 1,2 \tag{2}$$

with $\sigma^{i}(\cdot)$ the hyperbolic tangent function, v_{lm}^{i} the interconnection weights from first to second layer, w_{mj}^{i} the interconnection weights from second to third layer, and the superscript i implies NNI.   The inputs to the   NNI, $x^2 = [x_1^2, x_2^2, x_3^2, x_4^2]^T = [\dot{\theta}_{21}(k-1), T_1(k-1), T_2(k-1),$ $\dot{\theta}_{22}(k-1)]^T$, are composed of the control input and the plant output. The performance index for training the NNI is:

$$E_j^i(k) = \frac{1}{2}e_j^i(k)^2 = \frac{1}{2}[\dot{\theta}_{2j}(k) - \hat{\dot{\theta}}_{2j}(k)]^2, \quad j = 1,2 \qquad (3)$$

where $e_j^i(k)$ is defined as the error between the plant output, $\dot{\theta}_{2j}(k)$ and the output of the NNI, $\hat{\dot{\theta}}_{2j}(k)$. The second to third layer weights of the NNI, w_{mj}^i are updated by back propagating the error by the following equation:

$$
\begin{aligned}
w_{mj}^i(k+1) &= w_{mj}^i(k) - \eta \cdot \frac{\partial E_j^i(k)}{\partial w_{mj}^i(k)} \\
&= w_{mj}^i(k) + \eta \cdot \frac{\partial \hat{\dot{\theta}}_{2j}(k)}{\partial w_{mj}^i(k)} \cdot e_j^i(k) \qquad (4) \\
&= w_{mj}^i(k) + \eta \cdot \sigma^i (\sum_{l=1}^{4} v_{lm}^i(k) \cdot x_l^i(k)) \cdot e_j^i(k), \quad j = 1,2
\end{aligned}
$$

where η is the step size. Similarly, the first to second layer weights of the NNI, v_{lm}^i are updated by following equation:

$$
\begin{aligned}
v_{lm}^i(k+1) &= v_{lm}^i(k) - \eta \cdot \frac{\partial E_j^i(k)}{\partial v_{lm}^i(k)} \\
&= w_{lm}^i(k) + \eta \cdot \frac{\partial \hat{\dot{\theta}}_{2j}(k)}{\partial v_{lm}^i(k)} \cdot e_j^i(k) \qquad (5) \\
&= v_{lm}^i(k) + \eta \cdot x_l^i(k) \cdot \dot{\sigma}^i (\sum_{l=1}^{4} v_{lm}^i(k) \cdot x_l^i(k)) \cdot e_j^i(k),
\end{aligned}
$$

$$j = 1,2$$

where $\dot{\sigma}^i(\cdot)$ is the time derivative of $\sigma^i(\cdot)$.

Control input T_j to the plant is defined as:

$$T_j = T_{j1} + T_{j2}, \quad j = 1,2 \tag{6}$$

where T_{11} and T_{22} are the output of the linear controller 1 and 2, respectively. T_{12} and T_{21} are the output of the NNC. The outputs of the NNC in Fig. 6.3(b), T_{12} and T_{21}, with the number of nodes in successive layers 4-4-2, are given by

$$T_{12} = \sum_{q=1}^{4} [w_{q1}^c \cdot \sigma^c (\sum_{p=1}^{4} v_{pq}^c \cdot x_p^c)] \text{ and}$$

$$T_{21} = \sum_{q=1}^{4} [w_{q2}^c \cdot \sigma^c (\sum_{p=1}^{4} v_{pq}^c \cdot x_p^c)] \tag{7}$$

where v_{pq}^c are the interconnection weights from first to second layer, w_{qj}^c are the interconnection weights from second to third layer, and $x^c = [x_1^c, x_2^c, x_3^c, x_4^c]^T = [e_1(k), \text{sgn}(\dot{\theta}_{21}(k)), \text{sgn}(\dot{\theta}_{22}(k)), e_2(k)]$ are the inputs to the NNC. The inputs to the neural network controller, $e_j(k)$, are selected for compensation of nonlinearities in the plant since the PI controller is used for stabilization of plant dynamics. The signum function, $\text{sgn}(\cdot)$, is needed for Coulomb friction terms.

Since the NNC can not directly learn the nonlinearity of the plant, the interconnection weights of the NNC in Fig. 6.2 are updated by an indirect neuro-control scheme [10, 11] with the performance index:

$$\hat{E}_j^c(k) = \frac{1}{2} \hat{e}_j^c(k)^2 = \frac{1}{2} [\dot{\theta}_{jd}(k) - \hat{\dot{\theta}}_{2j}(k)]^2, \quad j = 1,2 \tag{8}$$

where $\hat{e}_j^c(k)$ is defined as the identified tracking error between the reference signal and the output of the NNI. The indirect neuro-control scheme of the NNC is as follows: the plant dynamics are identified by the NNI through a learning process, during which connection weights are updated in a direction to minimize the sum of squared errors between the plant output, $\dot{\theta}_{2j}(k)$ and the output of the NNI, $\hat{\dot{\theta}}_{2j}(k)$. Meanwhile, the partial derivative, $\dfrac{\partial \hat{\dot{\theta}}_{2j}}{\partial T_j}$, which is calculated by using the NNI and

the error signal, $\hat{e}_j^c(k)$, is used to update the weights of the NNC by employing the dynamic backpropagation scheme [9], which provides a

better estimate of gradients, $\dfrac{\partial \hat{\dot{\theta}}_{2j}}{\partial T_j}$. Therefore, the second to third layer

weights of the NNC, w_{qj}^c, are updated by back propagation of the identified tracking error, $\hat{e}_j^c(k)$, through the NNI by the following equation:

$$
\begin{aligned}
w_{qj}^c(k+1) &= w_{qj}^c(k) - \eta \cdot \frac{\partial \hat{E}_j^c(k)}{\partial w_{qj}^c(k)} \\
&= w_{qj}^c(k) + \eta \cdot \left(\frac{\partial T_{j2}(k)}{\partial w_{qj}^c(k)} + \frac{\partial T_{j1}(k)}{\partial w_{qj}^c(k)}\right) \cdot \frac{\partial \hat{\dot{\theta}}_{2j}(k)}{\partial T(k)} \cdot \hat{e}_j^c(k) \\
&= w_{qj}^c(k) + \eta \cdot \sigma^c(\sum_{p=1}^{4} v_{pq}^c(k) \cdot x_p^c(k)) \times \\
&\qquad \sum_{m=1}^{4}[v_{j+1m}^i(k) \cdot \dot{\sigma}^i(\sum_{l=1}^{4} v_{lm}^i(k) \cdot x_l^i(k)) \cdot w_{mj}^i(k)] \cdot \hat{e}_j^c(k),
\end{aligned}
\tag{9}
$$

$$j = 1,2$$

utilizing the facts that $\dfrac{\partial T_{11}(k)}{\partial w_{q1}^c(k)} = 0$, $\dfrac{\partial T_{12}(k)}{\partial w_{q1}^c(k)} = \sigma^c(\sum_{p=1}^{4} v_{pq}^c(k) \cdot x_p^c(k))$,

$\dfrac{\partial T_{21}(k)}{\partial w_{q2}^c(k)} = 0$, and $\dfrac{\partial T_{21}(k)}{\partial w_{q2}^c(k)} = \sigma^c(\sum_{p=1}^{4} v_{pq}^c(k) \cdot x_p^c(k))$ from (7). The first to second layer weights of the NNC, v_{pq}^c are similarly updated by the following equation:

$$v_{pq}^c(k+1) = v_{pq}^c(k) - \eta \cdot \frac{\partial \hat{E}_j^c(k)}{\partial v_{pq}^c(k)}$$

$$= v_{pq}^c(k) + \eta \cdot \frac{\partial T_{j2}(k)}{\partial v_{pq}^c(k)} \cdot \frac{\partial \hat{\dot{\theta}}_{2j}(k)}{\partial T_{j2}(k)} \cdot \hat{e}_j^c(k) \qquad (10)$$

$$= v_{pq}^c(k) + \eta \cdot x_p^c(k) \cdot \dot{\sigma}^c(\sum_{p=1}^4 v_{pq}^c(k) \cdot x_p^c(k)) \cdot w_{qj}^c(k) \times$$

$$\sum_{m=1}^4 [v_{j+1m}^i(k) \dot{\sigma}^i(\sum_{l=1}^4 v_{lm}^i(k) \cdot x_l^i(k)) \cdot w_{mj}^i(k)] \cdot \hat{e}_j^c(k),$$

$$j = 1 \text{ and similar for } j = 2.$$

The group of equation (4) through (10) describes the back propagation neural network training algorithm [12]. Neural network control of multivariable nonlinear plants using gradient methods suffers from the drawback that it is not possible to obtain reliable estimates of the derivative through the plant. This derivative estimation process is rendered easy by a NNI, which is an important advantage of indirect neuro-control scheme. It is noted that the control input generation and the weight updates of the NNC and the NNI are executed in one sampling time.

6.4 Analysis on error dynamics of the neuro-control system

In this section, the system error dynamics are analyzed and a bound on the tracking error is derived. The dynamics of the plant may be rewritten from (1) by :

$$T_j(t) = (J_e + J_m)\ddot{\theta}_{2j}(t) + B\dot{\theta}_{2j}(t)$$
$$+ G + T_c + T_d + F_j[\theta_{2j}(t), \dot{\theta}_{2j}(t)], j = 1,2 \qquad (11)$$

and for 2-bar system 1 :

$$T = J\dot{\omega} + B\omega + T_d + T_f \tag{12}$$

where $J(= J_e + J_m)$ is inertia term, $\omega(= \dot{\theta}_{2j})$ is the angular velocity, $T_f(= G + T_c + F_j[\cdot])$ is the nonlinear function, T_d is the bounded unknown disturbance, and T is the control input. It is assumed that $T_d < |\tau_d|$, with τ_d, a known positive constant. Given the reference signal ω_d, the tracking error is expressed by $e = \omega_d - \omega$. Differentiating tracking error and using (12), the dynamics of the plant may be written in terms of the tracking error as:

$$J\dot{e} = -Be - T + f + T_d \tag{13}$$

where the nonlinear plant function f is

$$f = J\dot{\omega}_r + B\omega + T_f. \tag{14}$$

Define now a control input as:

$$T = T_{11} + T_{12} = K_f e + T_{12} \tag{15}$$

where the linear controller gain K_f, and T_{12}, an estimate of f, will be provided later by some means not yet disclosed. Then, the closed loop system becomes

$$J\dot{e} = -(K_f + B)e + \tilde{f} + T_d \tag{16}$$

where the functional estimation error $\tilde{f}$ is given by:

$$\tilde{f} = f - T_2. \tag{17}$$

Equation (16) is an error system wherein the tracking error is driven by the functional estimation error. In the remainder of the paper we shall use (16) to focus on selecting the neural network training algorithm that the neural network approximates the nonlinear plant function f.

A three-layer neural network (NN), which is similar to that shown in Fig. 6.3, has a net output given by

$$y = \sum_{q=1}^{N_2} [w_{q1} \cdot \sigma(\sum_{p=1}^{N_1} v_{pq} \cdot x_p)] \tag{18}$$

with new notations: $\sigma(\cdot)$, the activation function, v_{pq}, the interconnection weights from first to second layer, w_{q1}, the interconnection weights from second to third layer, N_1, the number of neurons in the first layer, and N_2, the number of neurons in the second layer. The NN equation may be conveniently expressed in a vector format by defining $\mathbf{x} = [x_1, x_2, \cdots, x_{N_1}]^T$, $\hat{W} = [w_{1,1}, w_{1,2}, \cdots, x_{1,N_2}]^T$, $\sigma(\cdot) = [\sigma_1(\cdot), \sigma_2(\cdot), \cdots, \sigma_{N_2}(\cdot)]^T$, $\sigma_i(\cdot) = \sigma(\cdot), i = 1, 2, \cdots, N_2$, and a matrix format by defining $\hat{V}^T = [v_{pq}]^T$. Then,

$$y = \hat{W}^T \sigma(\hat{V}^T \mathbf{x}). \tag{19}$$

A general function f can be modeled by a neural network as:

$$f = W^T \sigma(V^T \mathbf{x}) + \varepsilon \tag{20}$$

where W and V are constant ideal weights of the current weights $\hat{W}$ and $\hat{V}$ so that ε is bounded by a known constant ε_N, and ε is reconstruction error due to the neural network structure [3]. For practical situations, we assume that the ideal weights are bounded by known positive values so that $\| W \| < W_M$, $\| V \| < V_M$, where $\| \cdot \|$ is a matrix norm. Define the weight deviation or the weight estimation error as:

$$\tilde{W} = W - \hat{W}, \quad \tilde{V} = V - \hat{V}, \tag{21}$$

and the second layer output error for a given $\mathbf{x}$ as:

$$\tilde{\sigma} = \sigma - \hat{\sigma} = \sigma(V^T \mathbf{x}) - \sigma(\hat{V}^T \mathbf{x}). \tag{22}$$

The Taylor series expansion of the second layer output for a given $\mathbf{x}$ may be written as:

$$\sigma(V^T \mathbf{x}) = \sigma(\hat{V}^T \mathbf{x}) - \dot{\sigma}(\hat{V}^T \mathbf{x})\tilde{V}^T \mathbf{x} + O(\tilde{V}^T \mathbf{x}) \tag{23}$$

with $\dot{\sigma}(\hat{z}) \equiv d\sigma(z)/d(z)/_{z=\hat{z}}$ and $O(\cdot)$ denoting sum of high order terms.

Denoting that $\dot{\hat{\sigma}} \equiv \dot{\sigma}(\hat{V}^T\mathbf{x})$, we have:

$$\tilde{\sigma} = \dot{\sigma}(\hat{V}^T\mathbf{x})\tilde{V}^T\mathbf{x} + O(\tilde{V}^T\mathbf{x}) = \dot{\hat{\sigma}}\,\tilde{V}^T\mathbf{x} + O(\tilde{V}^T\mathbf{x}) \qquad (24)$$

Now, define the neural network functional estimate of (20) by:

$$T_2 = \hat{W}^T\sigma(\hat{V}^T\mathbf{x}) \qquad (25)$$

with $\hat{V}, \hat{W}$ the current values of the ideal weights V and W as provided by the training algorithms subsequently to be discussed. Ignoring the actuator dynamics, select control input torque using (15) and (25) as:

$$T = K_f\,e + \hat{W}^T\sigma(\hat{V}^T\mathbf{x}) \qquad (26)$$

Using (20) and (26), the closed-loop error dynamics (16) become:

$$J\dot{e} = -(K_f + B)e + W^T\sigma(V^T\mathbf{x}) - \hat{W}^T\sigma(\hat{V}^T\mathbf{x}) + \varepsilon + T_d. \qquad (27)$$

Adding and subtracting $W^T\hat{\sigma}$ yields:

$$J\dot{e} = -(K_f + B)e + \tilde{W}^T\hat{\sigma} + W^T\tilde{\sigma} + \varepsilon + T_d. \qquad (28)$$

Adding and subtracting again $\hat{W}^T\tilde{\sigma}$ yields:

$$J\dot{e} = -(K_f + B)e + \tilde{W}^T\hat{\sigma} + \hat{W}^T\tilde{\sigma} + \tilde{W}^T\tilde{\sigma} + \varepsilon + T_d. \qquad (29)$$

Using the Taylor series approximation for $\tilde{\sigma}$, the closed-loop error system becomes

$$J\dot{e} = -(K_f + B)e + \tilde{W}^T\hat{\sigma} + \hat{W}^T\dot{\hat{\sigma}}\,\tilde{V}^T\mathbf{x} + \delta + \varepsilon + T_d \qquad (30)$$

where the disturbance terms δ is

$$\delta = \tilde{W}^T\dot{\hat{\sigma}}\,\tilde{V}^T\mathbf{x} + W^T O(\tilde{V}^T\mathbf{x}). \qquad (31)$$

The high order terms in the Taylor series, δ, is bounded by positive constant δ_N, i.e., $|\delta| < \delta_N$. It is important to note that the neural network reconstruction error ε, the plant disturbance T_d, and the high-order terms δ in the Taylor series expansion of f all have exactly the same influence as disturbances in the error system.

For the neural network training algorithm to improve the tracking performance of the closed loop system it is required to demonstrate that the tracking error, e is suitably small. Now, a bound on the tracking error is derived by the following theorem.

Theorem 1 : Let the reference signal be bounded. Take the control input (12) as (26). Let an NNC weight training algorithm be provided by (9) and (10). Then, the tracking error e evolves within a practical bound

$$|e| \le \frac{\delta_N + \varepsilon_N + \tau_d}{K_f + B}. \tag{32}$$

Proof : Define the Layapnov function candidate for the error dynamic (16) as :

$$L = \frac{1}{2}Je^2 + \frac{1}{2}(\tilde{W}^T \tilde{W}) + \frac{1}{2}tr(\tilde{V}^T \tilde{V}) \tag{33}$$

where $tr(\cdot)$ is trace. Differentiating yields:

$$\dot{L} = Je\dot{e} + \frac{1}{2}\dot{J}e^2 + (\tilde{W}^T \dot{\tilde{W}}) + tr(\tilde{V}^T \dot{\tilde{V}}) \tag{34}$$

whence substitution from (30) yields:

$$\dot{L} = -(K_f + B)e^2 + \frac{1}{2}\dot{J}e^2 + \tilde{W}^T(\dot{\tilde{W}} + \hat{\sigma}\, e) \\ + tr\tilde{V}^T(\dot{\tilde{V}} + \mathbf{x}e\hat{W}^T\dot{\hat{\sigma}}) + e(\delta + \varepsilon + T_d). \tag{35}$$

Since $\dot{\tilde{W}} = -\dot{\hat{W}}$ with W constant (and similarly for $\tilde{V}$) and if the dynamic of the plant are identified by the NNI, then $\hat{e}^c = e$. We can derive $\dot{\tilde{W}} = -\hat{\sigma}\, e$ and $\dot{\tilde{V}} = -\mathbf{x}(\dot{\hat{\sigma}}^T \hat{W}\, e)^T$ from the training rules and the assumption $|\dot{J}| = 0$ gives

$$\dot{L} = -(K_f + B)e^2 + e(\delta + \varepsilon + T_d). \tag{36}$$

and

$$\dot{L} \le -(K_f + B)|e|^2 + |e|(\delta_N + \varepsilon_N + \tau_d) \\ = -|e|[(K_f + B)|e| - (\delta_N + \varepsilon_N + \tau_d)]. \tag{37}$$

Thus $\dot{L}$ is negative as long as the term in brace is positive, which implies

$$| e | > \frac{\delta_N + \varepsilon_N + \tau_d}{K_f + B}. \tag{38}$$

According to the standard Lyapunov theorem, the tracking error decreases as long as the error is bigger than the right hand side of (38). This implies (32) gives a practical bound on the tracking error

$$| e | \leq \frac{\delta_N + \varepsilon_N + \tau_d}{K_f + B}. \tag{39}$$

The neural network reconstruction error ε, the bounded disturbance T_d, and the higher order Taylor series terms δ increase the bound on $| e |$. However, a small tracking error bound may be achieved by reducing δ_N by training the NNC and by decreasing the reconstruction error ε by properly selecting the structure of the NNC. Notice that since the linear controller gain K_f is determined according to the design of the linear controller, K_f can not be increased arbitrarily. However, large K_f may decrease the tracking error bound as long as the linear controller maintains the stability of the control system.

6.5   Experimental results

The effectiveness of the proposed neuro-controller by an experiment on the two 2-bar systems holding an object is presented in this section.   The experimental set up is shown in Fig. 6.4.   It consists of two 2-bar systems and an object.   The 2-bar system consists of a dc motor with a 2-bar, an encoder and a counter for output signal, a Digital-to-Analog (D/A) converter and a servo amplifier for control signal, and an IBM PC equipped with an Intel 8255 based interface card.   The voltage output from the computer is amplified using a pulse width modulated amplifier. An optical encoder with a quadrature decoder chip is used for angular position measurement.   Angular velocity is calculated from this position measurement by differentiation.   In the experimental set up, the proposed control scheme is implemented on the IBM PC with an Intel 486DX-66 microprocessor at a 100 Hz sampling rate.   The following values in the experiment were used.

$$m_1 = 0.5 \quad [Kg], \quad m_2 = 0.5 \quad [Kg], \quad m_3 = 1.0 \quad [Kg],$$

$$l_1 = 10 \quad [cm], \quad l_2 = 10 \quad [cm], \quad l_3 = 15 \quad [cm]. \tag{40}$$

Although the main thrust of this work is to discuss the neuro-controller in the 2-bar systems holding an object, it is necessary to add conventional linear controllers to evaluate the final results. A natural approach is to design the linear controllers in the neuro-controller. Therefore, we obtained the linearized models of the two 2-bar systems through the frequency response and the curve fitting method. The PI controllers based on the linearized models are tuned after obtaining the gains of the controller by the Ziegler-Nichols method [13]. For fairness of comparison, the gains of the PI controller are chosen to the identical gains of the PI part in the neuro-controller, i.e., $K_p = 5$ and $K_I = 2.5$. Fig. 6.5 shows the experimental response of the 2-bar system with rectangular reference signal by the PI controller.

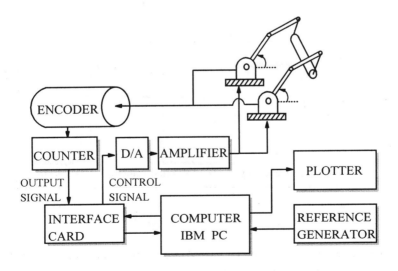

Fig. 6.4   Experimental setup.

Identification, which is essential for implementing the neuro-control strategies, is considered first. Subsequently, the neuro-control design results are discussed.   Randomly generated sinusoidal control inputs with

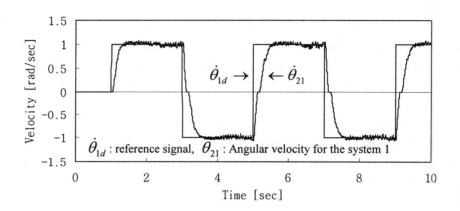

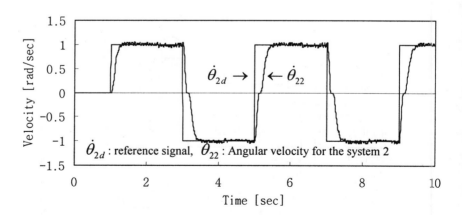

Fig. 6.5   Experimental results of the 2-bar system holding an object with the rectangular reference signal by the PI controller.

magnitude within ± 5 [v] and several frequencies up to 2 [Hz] are used as the training inputs after several tests using various signals. Fig.6.6 shows the neural network identification response obtained from the experimental

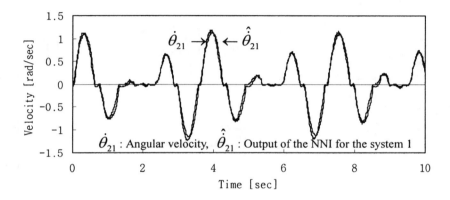

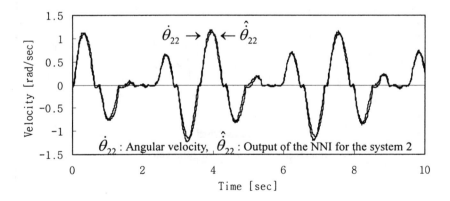

Fig. 6.6 Experimental results of the neural network identification with $T_j(t) = 1. + 2.5\sin 2\pi t + 3.5\sin 4\pi t$ [v], $j = 1,2$.

neural network identifier for the test signal $T_j(t) = 1. + 2.5\sin 2\pi t$ $+ 3.5\sin 4\pi t$ [v], $j = 1,2$. The NNI consistently gave very accurate outputs throughout the control phase of experiments also.   This observed

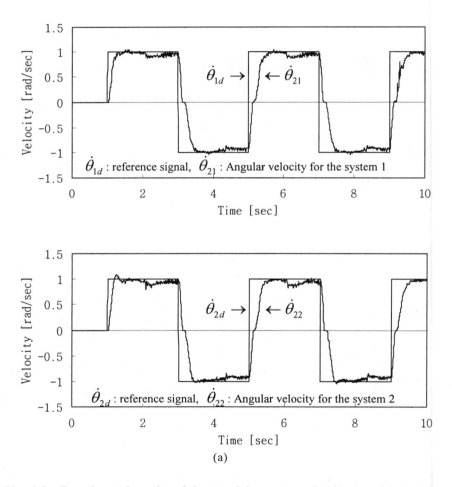

Fig. 6.7   Experimental results of the two 2-bar systems holding an object with the rectangular reference signal (a) by the PI controller and (b) by the neuro-controller.

capability of a NNI to model multivariable nonlinear systems in real-time so accurately is a significant result. Fig. 6.7 shows the experimental performance of the PI controller and the proposed neuro-controller for a rectan-

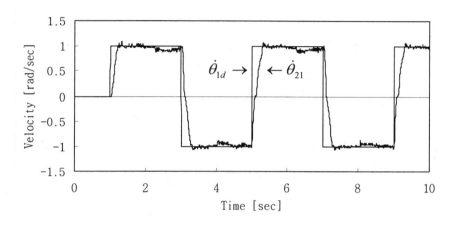

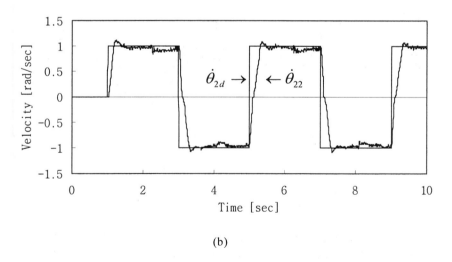

(b)

Fig. 6.7   (Continued.)

gular reference signal.   Since the bar moves in a vertical plane, the periodical characteristics of the 2-bar mechanism(oscillation) are shown in Fig. 6.7. The proposed neuro-controller is found to outperform the PI controller.

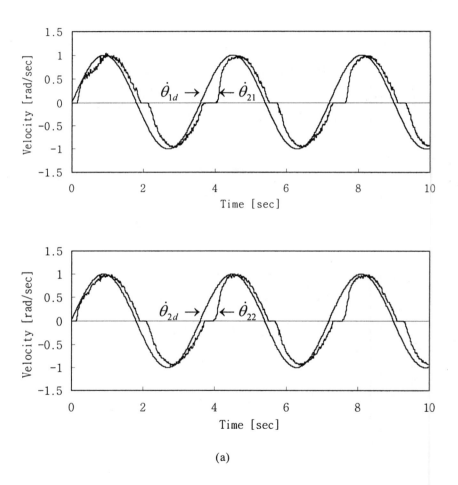

(a)

Fig. 6.8   Experimental results of the two 2-bar systems holding an object with the sinusoidal reference signal (a) by the PI controller and (b) by the neuro-controller.

For the sinusoidal reference signal, the deadzones in the vicinity of the zero velocity are observed in Fig. 6.8(a). This phenomena are related to the Coulomb friction, especially at low velocity. The proposed neuro-

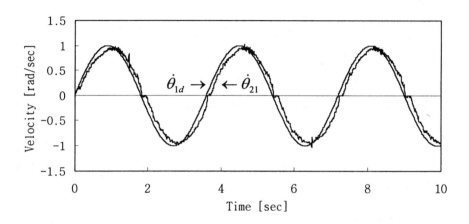

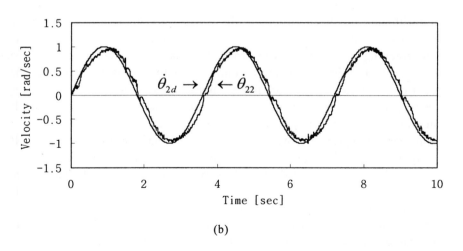

(b)

Fig. 6.8 (Continued.)

Table 6.1(a). Sum of square errors of the 2-bar system 1 in the experiment

Controller	Rectangular reference Signal	Sinusoidal reference Signal
PI controller	191.73	63.97
Neuro-controller	133.84	18.56

Table 6.1(b). Sum of square errors of the 2-bar system 2 in the experiment

Controller	Rectangular reference signal	Sinusoidal reference Signal
PI controller	184.80	53.58
Neuro-controller	146.28	12.26

controller outperforms the PI controller in Fig. 6.8(b).   Table 6.1 shows that the neuro-controller reduces the sum of square errors by about 20%-77% from those of the conventional controller.

6.6   Conclusions

The design method and implementation architectures for dynamic neural algorithms have been proposed for a class of multivariable nonlinear systems and successfully demonstrated experimentally. Also, a bound on the tracking error is derived from the analysis of the tracking error dynamics. The proposed neuro-controller outperforms the conventional controller for a rectangular and a sinusoidal reference signal.   A key feature of the neuro-controller is the usage of the NNC to compensate the nonlinear terms and interactions between the each system for a class of multivariable systems.   Also, it is noticeable that the update of the NNC weights is carried out effectively by the indirect neuro-control scheme.
Demonstration of the capability of neural networks to identify and control the experimental system in real-time is in itself significant, and shows the promising potential of such designs.   Although the two 2-bar systems holding an object is considered in the study, the proposed neuro-controller has applicability to a much larger class of multivariable nonlinear systems. It should be noted that the theoretical issues of convergence and stability

are not well understood for neural algorithms at present. However, since this can be said for most of the current control designs for nonlinear systems in general, neural networks can be viewed as viable alternatives for control of multivariable nonlinear systems.

References

[1] T. H. Lee, E. K. Koh, and M. K. Loh, "Stable adaptive control of multi variable servomechanisms, with application to a passive line-of-sight Stabilization system," *IEEE Trans. Ind. Electron.*, **43** (1), pp. 98-105, 1996.

[2] H. Y. Chuang, and C. H. Liu, "Techniques in cross-coupled digital adaptive feedrate control for multiaxes machine tools," *Control and Dynamic Systems*, **72**, pp. 265-301, 1996.

[3] K. Hornik, M. Stinchombe, and S. H. White, "Multilayer forward networks are universal approximator," *Neural Networks*, **2**, pp. 359-366, 1989.

[4] M. Kawato, Y. Uno, M. Isobe, and R. Suzuki, "A hierarchical model for voluntary movement and its application to robotics," *IEEE Contr. Syst. Mag.*, **8** (4), pp. 8-15, 1988.

[5] G. Lightbody, and G. W. Irwin, "Direct neural model reference adaptive control," *IEE Proc.-D*, **142**, pp. 31-43, 1995.

[6] A. Karakasoglu, S. I. Sudharsanan, and M. K. Sundareshan, "Identification and decentralized adaptive control using dynamical neural networks with application to robotic manipulator," *IEEE Trans. Neural Networks*, **4** (6), pp. 4-27, 1993.

[7] X. Cui and K. G. Shin, "Direct control and coordination using neural networks," *IEEE Trans. Systems, Man, and Cybernetics*, **23**, pp. 686-697, 1993.

[8] J. J. Craig, *Introduction to Robotics : Mechanics and Control*, Addison-Wesley, MA, 1986.

[9] K. S. Narendra and K. Parthasarathy, "Identification and control of dynamical systems using neural networks," *IEEE Trans. Neural Networks*, **1** (1), pp. 4-27, 1990.

[10] J. O. Jang, and G. J. Jeon, "A parallel neuro-controller for DC motors containing nonlinear friction," *Neurocomputing*, **30**, pp. 233-248, 2000.

[11] H. T. Chung, J. O. Jang, and W. C. Cho, "Indirect neuro-control of a class of multivariable nonlinear servomechanism," *Proc. of IIZUKA'98*, **2**, pp. 708-711, 1998.

[12] D. E. Rumelhart, G. E. Hinton, and G. E. Williams, "Learning internal

representations by error propagation," *Parallel Distributed Processing (edited by D. E. Rumelhart and J. McClelland)*, MIT Press, MA, 1986.

[13] J. G. Ziegler and N. B. Nichols, "Optimum settings for automatic controller," *Trans. ASME*, **64**, pp. 759-768, 1942.

Chapter 7

Evolutionary Computation for Information Retrieval based on User Preference

Hak-Gyoon Kim, Sung-Bae Cho

Department of Computer Science, Yonsei University

Abstract

Traditional agents based on index have limitation on large database, since they cannot cope with distributed dynamic environment. In order to overcome the limitation and search the information based on user's preference, this paper develops multiple distributed on-line web agents based on evolutionary computation to retrieve and search the information. The agents reproduce new one or disappear according to the relevancy of the document retrieved by the agent and the queries given by user. Moreover, the agents update the user profile according to the requested queries. Based on this mechanism, the whole system of agents evolves to reflect the user's preference appropriately. Therefore, the agents minimize access to less relevant documents, which increases the productivity of retrieving many relevant documents in a given period of time. Experimental results with several environments illustrate that the proposed agents produce better results than the conventional breadth first search and random search agents.

Keywords : Artificial life agents, Genetic algorithm, Information retrieval, User preferences, Relationship between hyperlinks

7.1   Introduction

Web has a large distributed collection of documents, which can be added, deleted or modified dynamically. Moreover, the document style is various. It takes much time and effort for users to search the Web environment like Fig. 7.1. This requires search agents making automatic decisions for users. Due to these reasons, several search agents have been developed and investigated.

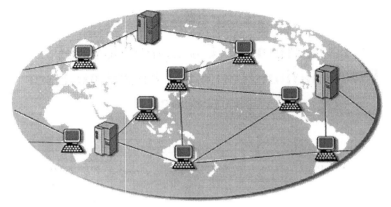

Fig. 7.1 Web environment

Usual search agents retrieving information on Web are mainly devised for static and non-distributed environments. With these agents, end user gives queries to the server that maintains index files to get the list of relevant documents [1]. User's requests are processed through the use of index files, which are made and updated by off-line robot agents that collect and analyze the documents (see Fig. 7.2). Because of its fast response time, these search agents are prevalent now. However, they have several limitations. First, they cannot cope with dynamic change of documents. Second, they can abstract away important data by incorrect indexing and missing relations between documents [2]. Third, they cannot reflect on the user's preferences or habits [3]. To overcome these limitations, a new method is required to replace the index-based robot agents.

This paper uses following properties. If a document is relevant to users, there is high probability that the links in this document are also relevant to users. Also, the links close to meaningful keywords are more probable than any other links. Fig. 7.3 shows the document relation with abstract environment. The documents in the same category are fully connected, but those among different categories are not. We can see that the documents in related topic have many hyperlinks, while the other topics have fewer hyperlinks.

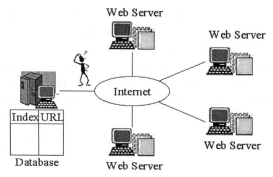

Fig. 7.2 Traditional search agents

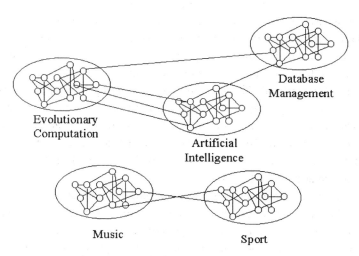

Fig. 7.3 Correlation between documents

This paper is inspired by Infospider that was originally proposed by F. Menczer [2]. Infospider has a population of on-line agents that search documents by deciding own actions locally. Each agent in population can reproduce the offspring or disappear according to the relevancy of the documents retrieved by the agent. The population of agents converges to optimal states through evolution. However, Infospider does not make use of user's preference. If we incorporate user's preference, we can provide more accurate information quickly and personalize the agents for user. To do this, this paper modifies the Infospider to utilize user profile. By updating the user profile at each query, it can reflect user's preferences. Artificial life agents maintain their competence by adapting to the user's preference that may change over time.

7.2   Backgrounds

7.2.1   *Information Retrieval*

Conventional information retrieval (IR) is very closely related to information filtering (IF) in that they both have the goal of retrieving information relevant to what a user wants. But there are three primary differences between information retrieval and information filtering [4]. First, user preferences (profiles) in information filtering typically represent long-term interests, while queries in IR tend to represent a short-term interest that can be satisfied by performing the retrieval. Second, information filtering is typically applied to streams of incoming data; in IR, changes to the database do not occur often, and retrieval is not limited to the new items in the database. Finally, a distinction can be made between the two, in that filtering involves the process of removing information from a stream, while IR involves the process of finding information in that stream.

Several methods have been proposed to retrieve more accurate information by using large, dynamic, distributed Web environment [5,6,8,9]. Autonomous agents or semi-intelligent agents manage large amount of information available online and estimate for user's shake with his or her preferences and habits [7]. With one's own preferences there are two approaches in information filtering.

In one approach, the system accepts information describing, the nature of an item, and based on a sample of the user's preferences, learns to predict which items the user will like [8,9]. This approach is called content-based filtering that is based on information retrieval and applies the weighted keyword vector representation [10]. Also, Several machine learning techniques have been suggested to produce the effective information agents, yielding for example agents that perform look-ahead searches and provide suggestions to the user on the basis of reinforcement learning [11]. Newt is a multiagent system that uses evolution and relevance feedback for information filtering [12]. In another approach, the user of the system provides ratings of some artifacts or items. The system makes informed guess about other items the user may like based on ratings other users have provided [13,14]. This is the framework for collaborative filtering.

7.2.2 *Genetic Algorithm*

Genetic algorithm is search algorithm based on the mechanics of natural selection and natural genetics. It combines survival of the fittest among string structures with a structured yet randomized information exchange to form a search algorithm with some of the innovative flair of human search. In every generation, a new set of artificial creatures (strings) is created using bits and pieces of the fittest of the old. An occasional new part is tried for good measure. Overall step of genetic algorithm is shown in Fig. 7.4. While randomized, genetic algorithm is no simple random walk. It efficiently exploits historical information to speculate on new search points with expected improvement. A genetic algorithm that yields good results in many practical problems is composed of three operations: reproduction, crossover and mutation [15].

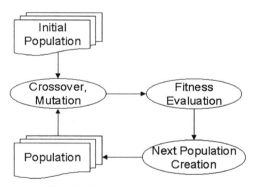

Fig. 7.4 Overall genetic algorithm

● Reproduction

This is a process in which individual strings are copied according to their objective function values, f (fitness function). Intuitively, the function f can be thought of as a measure of profit, utility, or goodness that we want to maximize. Copying strings according to their fitness values means that strings with higher value have higher probability of contributing one or more offspring in the next generation. This operator is an artificial version of natural selection, a Darwinian survival of the fittest among string creatures.

●   Crossover

Simple crossover may proceed in two steps. First, members of the newly reproduced strings in the mating pool are mated at random. Second, each pair of strings undergoes crossing over as follows: an integer position k along the string is selected uniformly at random between 1 and the string length minus one $[1, l-1]$. Two new strings are created by swapping all characters between position $k+1$ and l inclusively. Fig. 7.5 shows the simple crossover operator.

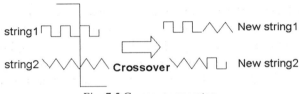

Fig. 7.5 Crossover operator

●   Mutation

It is needed because the individuals may become overzealous and lose some potentially useful genetic material occasionally. Even though reproduction and crossover effectively search and recombine extant notions in artificial genetic system, the mutation operator protects against such an irrecoverable loss. The frequency of mutation to obtain good results in empirical genetic algorithm studies is on the order of one mutation per thousand bit transfers. Mutation leads to conclusion that it is appropriately considered as a secondary mechanism of genetic algorithm adaptation. Fig. 7.6 shows the mutation operator.

Fig. 7.6 Mutation operator

Traditional genetic algorithms are based on selection schemes in which some global operation is applied to the individuals in the population to decide which individuals are to reproduce. In this environment, the population goes to optimum solution. This behavior is not the most appropriate in the information discovery domain, where as many relevant documents as possible need be retrieved, rather than just the most relevant one.

7.3 Artificial Life Agents

The authors of web document tend to classify the documents according to subjects and connect them in related topic. This tendency results in semantic topology. The semantic topology defines the co-relationship of documents. If some documents are relevant to users, there is high probability that the links in current document are also relevant to users. The proposed agents can reduce the search space by using this property.

```
Initialize agents;
Obtain queries from user;
While (there is an alive agent) {
    Get document D_a pointed by current agent;
    Pick an agent a randomly;
    Select a link and fetch selected document D_a';
    Compute the relevancy of document D_a';
    Update energy(E_a) according to the document relevancy;
    If (E_a > ε )
        Set parent and offspring's genotype appropriately;
        Mutate offspring's genotype;
    Else if (E_a < 0)
        Kill agent a;
}
Update user profile;
```

Table 7.1 Overall algorithm

The approach proposed here employs a genetic algorithm based on local selection. An agent's fitness is not compared with other members of the population. Rather, some measure of fitness is accumulated over time. Selection occurs in a distributed fashion, comparing energy with a fixed threshold. The result is the same type of non-converging behavior required for multimodal optimization, and therefore local selection is appropriate for the information discovery problem. It has a population of multiple information retrieval agents. The energy of each agent in population is increased or decreased according to the relevance of the document retrieved by agent itself. This method uses genetic algorithm based on local selection. The algorithm is shown in Table. 7.1.

7.3.1 *Initialization*

The agent's genotype is composed of confidence and energy. Confidence is the degree to which an agent trusts the descriptions that a document contains about its outgoing links, and energy represents agent's relevancy to the given queries. The energy is initialized to a constant threshold $\varepsilon/2$, and confidence is chosen randomly. As user profile is composed of the interesting links, each agent's starting point is initialized by user profile.

7.3.2 *Link Selection*

Relevancy of each link in document is estimated by computing physical distances between link and keywords matched to user queries. This estimation is based on the assumption that the majority of links close to keywords is more relevant to user's interest than others. For each link l in a document, the relevancy is calculated as follows.

$$\lambda_l = \sum_{k \in tokens} \frac{\text{match}(k,Q)}{\text{distance}(k,l)} \tag{1}$$

where k is tokens in document D_a, Q is a set of given queries, and distance(k, l) is the number of links separating k and l in the document. match(k, Q) gets to be 1 if k is in Q. Otherwise, it becomes 0.

To select a link to follow, we have used a stochastic selector to pick a link with probability distribution that is scaled up and normalized by agent's confidence. Confidence evolves by selection, reproduction, and mutation. Different confidence values can implement search strategies as different as best-first, random walk, or any middle course. With this distribution, an agent selects a link to follow.

7.3.3 *Update Energy*

After the agent fetches the document connected by selected link, it estimates the relevancy of a document that is proportional to the hit rate of the number of keywords to whole tokens in the document. Relevancy of the document is represented by

$$r(D_a) = \sqrt[4]{\frac{\sum match(k,Q)}{number(k,D_a)}} \qquad (2)$$

where $number(k, D_a)$ is the number of keywords in D_a.

An agent's energy is updated according to the relevancy of document. The use of network resource means the loss of the energy. If the document is already visited, the increase of energy is not expected.

$$E_A = E_A - expense + \begin{cases} r(D_a), & \text{if } D_a \text{ is new} \\ 0, & \text{otherwise} \end{cases} \qquad (3)$$

where $r(D_a)$ is the relevancy of document, and *expense* is the loss of energy.

7.3.4   *Reproduction*
Each agent can reproduce offspring or be killed by comparing the agent's energy with constant threshold ε. If the agent's energy exceeds the threshold, it reproduces offspring. The offspring's energy is fed by splitting the parent's energy, and the offspring is mutated to provide evolution with the necessary variation. The bound of confidence is determined by the current document relevancy. This mechanism can cause the population of agents to be biased to the regions where the relevant documents exist.

7.3.5   *Update User Profile*
User profile should coincide with user's interests. Since the agents learn about the user's interests by getting user's queries and feedback, it is important to update user profile after searching. The updated user profile is composed of relevant document URLs. With this property, user can personalize the agents as he gives queries repeatedly.

7.4   An Example

To get an idea of how each agent works, let us consider an example of agent's actions as shown in Fig. 7.7. Suppose that user gives query about 'sgml'. At initialization step, an agent a's confidence is given to 0.277 randomly, and energy is given to 0.2. It fetches a document in "*http://www.sil.org/sgml/sgml. html*" (see Fig. 7.7). This document contains 51 links in total, and each link's relevancy is estimated by Eq. (1).

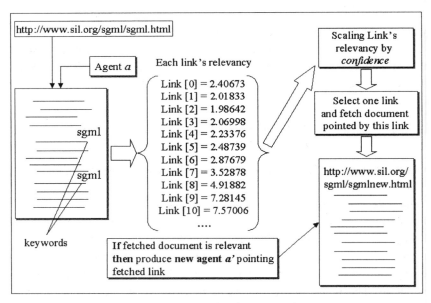

Fig. 7.7 An example of agent's action

Each link's relevancy is inversely proportional to the distance from keywords. Given link's relevancy, we scale up the link's relevancy with respect to agent's confidence. The result is shown in Table. 7.2.

Index	Link	Relevancy
10	www.sil.org/sgml/sgml.html	7.57
13	www.sil.org/sgml/bilio.html	7.56
14	www.sil.org/sgml/siteIndex.html	7.37
9	www.sil.org/sgml/sgml-tex.html	7.28
12	www.sil.org/sgml/sgmlnew.html	5.52

Table. 7.2 Top list of evaluated link

Next, the agent selects one link randomly according to the relevancy of the documents, and fetches the document pointed by this link. This means that if confidence value is low, the selection step is like random selection. Otherwise, the selection depends on the sequential order of the link's relevancy. The links that have high relevancy has more chance to be selected. In this example, the agent selects the document of "*http://www.sil.org/sgml/sgml-tex.html*".

Then, the document's relevancy is evaluated by Eq.(2). The relevancy of selected document relevancy becomes 0.426. Its energy is set to 0.526 by Eq.(3). If document's relevancy is greater than threshold ε, it reproduces a new agent pointing to the current document. Because the energy is higher than threshold ε=0.4, the offspring agent *a'* pointing to the document "*http://www.sil.org/sgml/sgml-tex.html*" is produced. The energy of the agent is updated as follows.

$$energy = \frac{current\ energy}{2} = \frac{0.526}{2} = 0.263 \qquad (4)$$

Mutation changes the offspring's confidence to some 0.299. By applying these steps over all agents, the population of the agents evolves. After these repetitions, the whole system sorts the documents by its relevancy. The final result is saved on the user profile.

7.5 Experimental Results

7.5.1 *Environment*

In order to provide a fair and consistent evaluation of the system's performance, we have restricted search space to a local machine, instead of real Web. We have collected a number of HTML pages with various topics, classified the pages according to the subjects, and put them in different directories. The initial user profile is composed of the top directories of local machine. The initial population size of agents depends on the number of URLs in user profile. We have compared the proposed agents with Breadth First Search (BFS) and Random Search agents. BFS searches every document exhaustively, while the proposed agents can search them selectively.

The initial population is composed of 10 agents. The population size has no limitation in run time. The constant threshold ε is set to 0.4. An agent whose energy is greater than ε can reproduce offspring. Initial agent's energy is set to ε/2. The agent uses the network resource, which means loss of energy. This loss of energy is called *expense*, and set to 0.1. The process is influenced by the *expense* value. If we increase the *expense* value, the agents have less chance to search further. Irrelevant agents may disappear quickly, and there is some possibility that even some relevant agents can disappear without searching the regions sufficiently. We select the *expense* value with trial and errors.

7.5.2   *Analysis of Result*
The energy increases as the agent searches relevant documents. Initially, 20% of population resides in the relevant regions. After some time passes, 90% of the population searches the regions where the relevant documents exist. The BFS and Random Search agents have the same initial condition, but later the distribution goes down to 30% and 25%, respectively. This result shows that the proposed agents can cut the agents irrelevant to the queries effectively.

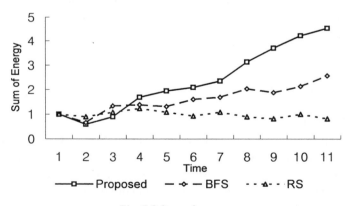

Fig. 7.8 Sum of energy

This feature can be proven with two experiments. Fig. 7.8 shows the sum of agents' energy. In the beginning, the majority of agents are not relevant but as time goes on the agents shift to the relevant ones. Since the relevant agent has high energy, we can conclude that if the sum of the energy is high, the majority of agents in population are appropriate for the queries. Fig. 7.9 shows the hit rate of relevant documents. In the beginning, the performance is not better than other search methods, but the performance of the proposed agents is improved rapidly. This result implies that each agent can cut irrelevant paths of documents effectively. The action of each agent goes toward relevant document paths gradually. By using this property, the proposed algorithm can reduce the access to irrelevant documents.

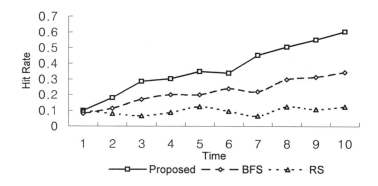

Fig. 7.9 Hit rate

We have tested the performance improvement in case the user gives queries in the same category. For each query, the user profile is updated according to document relevancy. And, the agents reflect the user's preference adaptively. As the user gives the queries in the same category, the proposed agents improve the response time according to the queries. Fig. 7.10 shows the results over the two tasks. In task 1, a sequence of queries is provided as computer, artificial intelligence, neural network, agent, evolution, user feedback, retrieval, and search. In task2, the sequence is like: computer, DSSSL, SGML, grove, property set, repository, and database. Initial response time is not good, but as the queries are given repeatedly, we can see the improvement of the response time for the two tasks.

7.6 Concluding Remarks

This paper has presented a new method that searches the relevant documents intelligently. This intelligence is based on the semantic topology that emphasizes the role of hyperlink in Web. The agents can reproduce or disappear by this property. The proposed agents system has following characteristics.

- The system utilizes the document structures to reduce search spaces.
- By not using the index and limiting the search space, the server load has been reduced.
- The use of user profile has resulted in implementing the concept of personalized search agent.

We can see that a population of agents that learn and evolve has a great potential to model user's preference and adapts well in Web.

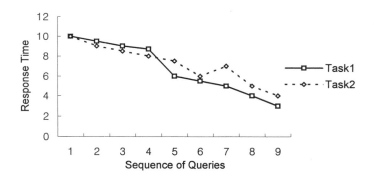

Fig. 7.10 Response time for the queries in the same category

References

[1] G. Salton and M. McGill, *Introduction to Modern Information Retrieval*, McGraw-Hill, Tokyo, 1983.
[2] F. Menczer, "ARACHNID: Adaptive retrieval agents choosing heuristic neighborhoods for information discovery," *International Conf. on Machine Learning*, 1997.
[3] H. Lieberman, "Letizia: An agent that assists Web browsing," *Proc. of the*

[4] *International Joint Conf. on Artificial Intelligence*, 1995.

[5] N.J. Belkin and W.B. Croft, "Information filtering and information retrieval :Two sides of the same coin," *Comm. of the ACM*, 35(12), pp.29-37, 1992.

[6] A. Moukas, "Amalthaea: Information discovery and filtering using a multiagent evolving ecosystem," *Applied Artificial Intelligence: An International Journal*, 11(5), pp.437-457, 1997.

[7] F. Menczer and R. Belew, "From complex environments to complex behaviors," *Adaptive Behavior* 4, 1996.

[8] P. Maes, "Agents that reduce work and information overload," *Comm. of ACM*, 37(7), pp. 31-40, 1994.

[9] M. Balabanovicand, and Y. Shoham, "Learning information retrieval agents: Experimental with automated web browsing," *AAAI SSS Info. Gathering from Heterogeneous, Distrib. Envst*, 1995.

[10]   M. Pazzani, J. Muramatsu, and D. billsus, "Syskill & Webert: Identifying interesting web sites," *Proc. of the Thirteenth National Conf. On Artificial Intelligence*, 1996.

[11] G. Salton and C. Buckley, "Term weighting approaches in automatic text retrieval," *Journal of Information Processing & Management*, 24(3), pp. 513-524, 1987.

[12] R. Armstrong, D. Freitag, T. joachims and T. Mitchell, "Webwatcher: A learning apprentice for the world wide web," *AAAI SSS Info. Gathering from Heterogeneous, Distrib. Envst*, 1995.

[13] B. Sheth and P. Maes, "Evolving agents for personalized information filtering," *Ninth Conf. of Artificial Intelligence for Application*, 1993.

[14] U. Shardanand and P. Maes, "Social information filtering: Algorithms for automating 'Word of Mouth'," *Proc. of the Computer-Human Interaction Conference*, 1995.

[15] J.A. Konstan, B. Miller, D. Maltz, J.L. Herlocker, L. Gordon, and J. Riedl, "GroupLens: Applying collaborative filtering to Usenet News," *Comm. of the ACM*, 40(3), pp. 77-87, 1997.

[16] D.E. Goldberg, *Genetic Algorithms*, Addison-Wesley, 1989.

Chapter 8

On-line tool condition monitoring based on a neurofuzzy intelligent signal feature classification procedure

Pan Fu, A. D. Hope and G. A. King
Systems Engineering Faculty
Southampton Institute, U.K

Abstract

Cutting tool condition is a major factor relating to the state of the machine tool. Monitoring tool condition by using an integrated system composed of multi-sensors, signal processing devices and intelligent decision making plans is a necessary requirement for modern automatic manufacturing processes. An intelligent tool wear monitoring system will be introduced in this paper. A unique fuzzy driven neural network based pattern recognition algorithm has been developed from this research. It can fuse the information from multiple sensors and has strong learning and noise suppression ability. This lead to successful tool wear classification under a range of machining conditions.

Keywords : condition monitoring, feature extraction, fuzzy logic, neural network, pattern recognition

1. Introduction

Modern advanced machining systems in the "unmanned" factory must possess the ability to automatically change tools that have been subjected to wear or damage. This can ensure machining accuracy and reduce the production costs. Coupling various transducers with intelligent data processing techniques to deliver improved information relating to tool condition makes optimization and control of the machining process possible.

Many kind of sensing techniques have been used to monitor tool condition. An approach was developed for in-process monitoring tool wear in milling using frequency signatures of the cutting force [1]. By processing the force signals, three characteristic parameters, the derivative of force wave form, power and coefficient of auto-correlation had been found to be relevant to tool wear [2]. Y. S. Liao found that the motor current increased nearly linearly from the beginning to the end of the tool's useful life if only one material was machined in turning [3].

Acoustic emission (AE) has been recognized as a promising means for on-line tool condition monitoring. The skew and kurtosis of the AE root mean square (RMS) were related with the increase of the tool flank wear [4][5]. The dominant frequency components of AE signal was considered generally below 500 kHz and in this range the spectra amplitudes were found to increase with the accumulation of tool wear [6]. The amount of tool wear in face milling was related to the change of the envelope (signal boundary) of the vibration signal [7]. Grieshaber et al used spectral density and spectral area of vibration signal to identify tool wear in milling [8].

Sensor fusion and intelligent signal processing are necessary tools for reliable tool condition monitoring. Artificial neural networks (ANNs) were proved to be suitable for integrating information from acoustic emission and cutting force sensors to predict tool wear in turning operation [9]. Choi et al [10] developed a neural network-based real-time tool wear monitoring system. P.G.Li et al. [11] used fuzzy pattern recognition algorithm to estimate drilling tool wear from fuzzy manipulation.

In this study, a fuzzy driven neural network was developed to accomplish multi-sensor information integration and tool wear state classification. By imitating the thinking and judging modes of human being, the network shows some remarkable characteristics. Multi-sensor signal features are combined while their specific importance are properly considered. The effects caused by experimental noise can also be decreased greatly. The established monitoring system provided accurate and reliable tool wear classification results over a range of cutting conditions.

2. Tool wear relevant features and the tool condition monitoring system

Most existing tool wear sensing methods can be classified into two major categories. In direct sensing, optical, radioactive and distance transducers are used to measure the actual tool wear directly. For indirect sensing, some parameters correlated with tool wear are measured by using transducers, e.g. force, AE, vibration, power, temperature and roughness. Direct measuring processes possess high accuracy while indirect methods are less complex and more practical for industrial applications.

In the milling process, the cutting operation is intermittent and the cutting tool is always rotating. Hence the signals are noisy and it is not convenient to mount sensors on the tool. The sensors selected must be able to suit these special circumstances and after carrying out a number of experiments, the four sensors chosen were load, force, acoustic emission and vibration.

The experiments were carried out on a Cincinnati Milacron Sabre 500 machining centre. As with many other modern machining systems, it delivers a motor current signal that corresponds to the actual power consumption. Fig.1 shows a typical load signal and the variation of it's mean value with different flank wear values (VB).

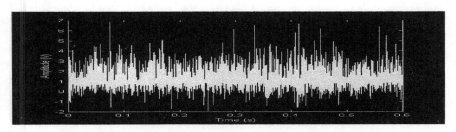

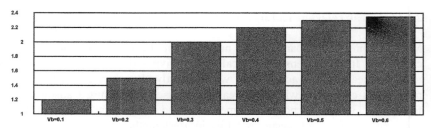

Fig.1 Power consumption of the spindle motor.

Tool wear causes an increase in the cutting force components. In this work a KISTLER 9257B force dynamometer was used to measure cutting forces in three mutually perpendicular directions. The dynamometer has a measuring range of 5000 N in each direction, linearity of 1%, stiffness of 350 N/μm in the Z direction and 1000 N/μm in the X and Y directions and a resonant frequency of 4kHz. Fig.2 shows a typical time domain force signal and FFT analysis results for both new and worn inserts.

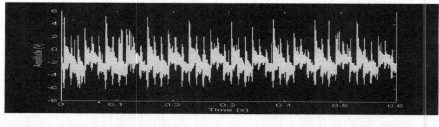

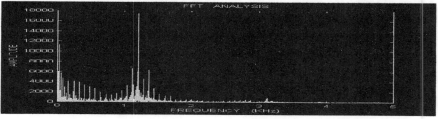

(a)   cutting force in X direction and the spectrum for new inserts

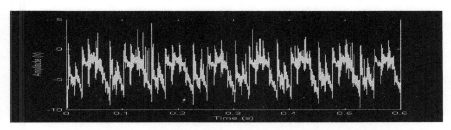

(b) cutting force in X direction and the spectrum for the worn inserts

Fig.2 Cutting force signal and spectral analysis results

The AE measuring apparatus includes an AE sensor and a signal processing device. The AE sensor has a measuring frequency range of 100 kHz - 2 MHz. The 60 dB pre-amplifier connects the AE sensor to the AE output instrument and has a 113 kHz - 1.1 MHz built-in filter. The analogue module receives the input from the pre-amplifier and provides the outputs for both amplified AE analogue signals and AE RMS signals. Fig.3 displays typical AE signal and power spectrum analysis results for both new and worn inserts.

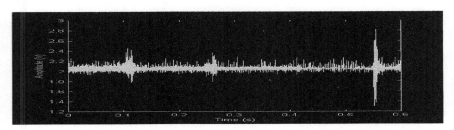

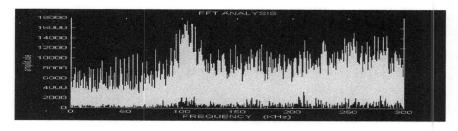

(a)   AE signal and spectrum of new inserts

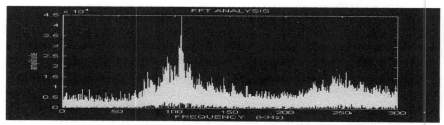

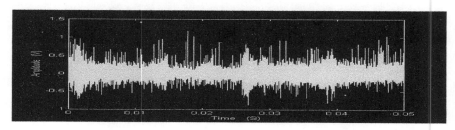

(b)   AE signal and spectrum of worn inserts

Fig.3 AE signal and power spectrum analysis results

An accelerometer was mounted in the feed direction. The sensor has the following specifications: charge sensitivity 13.15 pC/g, frequency response 5 - 33 kHz, mounted resonant frequency 50 kHz. Signals were passed through a charge amplifier and then recorded by the computer. A typical vibration signal and power spectrum analysis results for both new and worn inserts are shown in Fig.4.

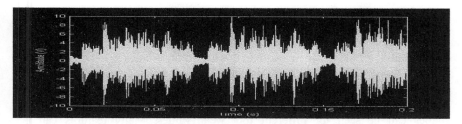

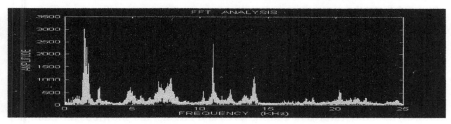

(a) vibration signal and spectrum for new inserts

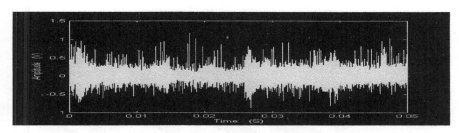

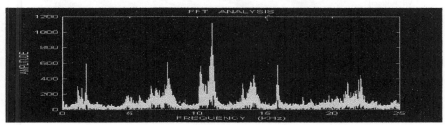

(b) vibration signal and spectrum for worn inserts

Fig.4 Vibration signal and power spectrum analysis results

It can be seen from the above pictures that the four sensors chosen can provide healthy signals to describe the tool condition in a milling operation. The current measurement is relatively simple and it's mean value can reflect tool wear reliably although when compared with other signals it is less sensitive. Cutting force, AE and vibration signals can provide more meaningful information. In the time domain, the entry and exit of the inserts relative to the workpiece can be clearly recognized and obvious changes in the wave form shapes can be seen for different tool wear values. Many features can be obtained from the time domain, such as mean value, wave form coefficients, root mean square, skew and kurtosis, etc. Frequency analysis seems even more promising. The signal energy in many frequency ranges varies considerably as the flank wear increases and as these sensors have different working frequencies, many features can be extracted from a very wide frequency range. All the features stated above characterize the tool wear status from different aspects and establish the foundation for further pattern recognition. . Most features, as some features of cutting force and AE signals shown as an example in Figure 5 (under cutting condition 1*), are found relevant with the development of tool wear values (VB).

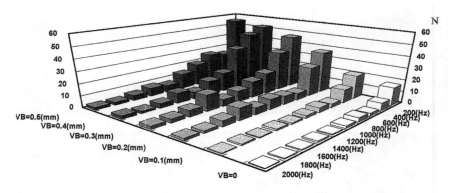

(a)   The spectra of cutting force (F_x) signal

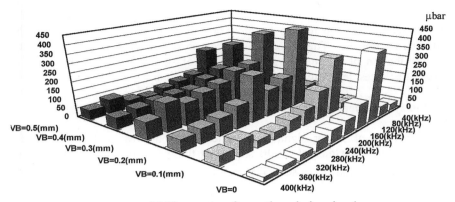

(b) The spectra of acoustic emission signal

Fig.5 The spectra of force and acoustic emission signal

As shown in Fig.6, the tool wear monitoring system is composed of four kinds of sensors, signal amplifying and collecting devices and the microcomputer. Features extracted from the time domain and frequency domain for future pattern recognition are as follows. Power consumption signal: mean value; AE-RMS signal: mean value, skew and kurtosis; Cutting force, AE and vibration: mean value, standard deviation and the mean power in 10 frequency ranges. Most features are found relevant with the development of tool wear values.

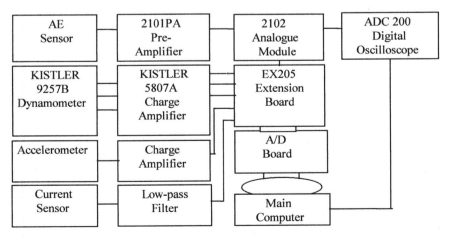

Fig.6 The tool condition monitoring system.

Tool condition monitoring is a pattern recognition process in which the characteristics of the tool to be monitored are compared with those of the standard models. The process is composed of the following parts: determination of the membership functions of signal features, calculation of fuzzy distances, learning and tool wear classification.

3. Fuzzy membership function

The features of sensor signals can reflect the tool wear states. Theoretical analysis and experimental results show that these features can be regarded as normal distribution fuzzy sets. The membership function of the fuzzy set A_i can be represented as:

$$A_i(x) = 1 - \frac{(x - a_i)^2}{2\sigma_i^2}, \quad a_i - \sqrt{2}\sigma_i \le x \le a_i + \sqrt{2}\sigma_i$$

$$= 0, \qquad \text{for all others} \tag{1}$$

where a is the mean value and σ is the standard deviation.

4. Fuzzy approaching degree

Fuzzy approaching degree is a quantitative index that represents the similarity of two fuzzy sets (A and B). Assume that $F(X)$ is the fuzzy power set of a universal set X and the map, $N{:}F(X) \times F(X) \to [0,1]$ satisfies:

(a). $\forall A \in F(X)$, $N(A,A) = 1$;

(b). $\forall A, B \in F(X)$, $N(A,B) = N(B,A)$;

(c). If $A, B, C \in F(X)$ satisfies:
$$|A(x) - C(x)| \ge |A(x) - B(x)| \ (\forall x \in X),$$
$$\text{then} \ \ N(A,C) \le N(A,B).$$

So the map N is the approaching degree in $F(X)$ and $N(A,B)$ is the approaching degree of fuzzy set A and B. Approaching degree can be calculated by using different methods. Here the inner and outer products are used.

Assume that $A, B \in F(X)$, so $A \bullet B = \vee\{A(x) \wedge B(x): x \in X\}$ is defined as the inner product of A and B and $A \oplus B = \wedge\{A(x) \vee B(x): x \in X\}$ is defined as the outer product of A and B. Finally, in the map $N: F(X) \times F(X) \rightarrow [0,1]$, $N(A, B)$ is the approaching degree of A and B:

$$N(A, B) = (A \bullet B) \wedge (A \oplus B)^c \tag{2}$$

5. Fuzzy driven neural network

Using the conventional fuzzy pattern recognition technique, the fuzzy distances (such as approaching degree) between corresponding features of the object to be recognized and the models are first calculated. Combining these distances can determine the fuzzy distances between the object and different models. The object should be classified to one of the models that has the shortest fuzzy distance (or highest approaching degree) with it. Fuzzy pattern recognition techniques are quite reliable and robust. They can be further improved by developing a method that can assign suitable weights to all the features to reflect the specific influences of different features in the pattern recognition process. For solving this problem, an advanced fuzzy driven neural network has been developed from this study.

Artificial neural networks (ANNs) have the ability to classify inputs. The weights between neurons are adjusted automatically in the learning process to minimize the difference between the desired and actual outputs. ANN can continuously classify and also update classifications. In this study, ANNs are connected with fuzzy logic techniques to establish a fuzzy driven neural network as shown in Fig. 7.

Here a back propagation ANN is used to carry out tool wear classification. The approaching degree results are the input of the ANN. The associated weights can be updated as:

$$w_i(new) = w_i(old) + \alpha \delta x_i \tag{3}$$

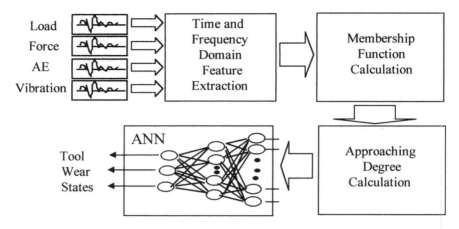

Fig.7 The fuzzy driven neural network

Here α , δ , x_i are learning constant, associated error measure and input to the i-th neuron. In this updating process, the ANN recognizes the patterns of the features corresponding to certain tool wear state. So in practical machining process, the feature pattern can be accurately classified. In fact the ANN assigns each feature a proper synthesized weight and the output of the ANN are weighted approaching degrees. This enables the tool wear classification process be more reliable. Fig. 8 shows the calculation process of tool wear states classification.

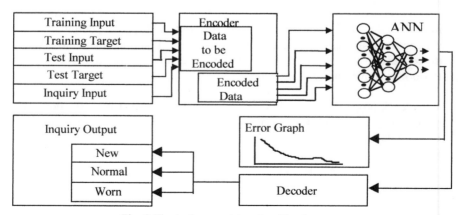

Fig. 8 The tool wear states classification process

6. Learning

Six standard tool wear values were selected as the models for the future pattern recognition, ranging from new to severe wear where the width of the flank wear area increased from 0 to 0.5 mm in steps of 0.1 mm. For each model with the standard wear value, the membership functions of all its features can be calculated and then stored in a library in the computer.

The training process of the ANNs is as the following: first, for every model (a cutting tool that has a standard wear value) , 10 groups of sensor signals are collected from the practical machining process. So 10 groups of membership functions of all the features for each model can be determined. These are called sub-membership functions. They can be considered as sub-models of each model having the same standard tool wear values. Then the approaching degree between the corresponding features of these sub-models and different models are calculated. The results can be used as the training inputs of the ANNs. The training targets are determined as follows: the weighted approaching degree between each model and its own sub-models should be 1 and the value between a model and other model's sub-models can be calculated by decreasing the value from 1 to zero linearly, according to the difference of the actual tool wear value. After the training the constructed frame and associated weights of the ANNs can reflect the distinct importance of each individual feature for each model under specific cutting conditions. Consequently the future tool wear classification results can be reliable and accurate.

7. Tool wear states classification

In the practical tool condition monitoring process, the tool with unknown wear value is the object and it will be recognized as "new tool", "normal tool" or "worn tool". The approaching degrees between the corresponding features of the object and different models can be the inquiry input of the ANN. One of a pre-trained ANN is then chosen to calculate the weighted approaching degree between the object and a model under a specific cutting condition. The tool wear state should be classified to the model that has the highest weighted approaching degree with the tool being monitored. In a verifying experiment, fifteen tools with unknown flank wear value were used in milling operations under cutting condition1*. Figure 9 shows the classification results. It can be seen that all the tools were classified correctly with the confidence of higher than 80%. For other 60 experiments under 20 different cutting conditions the monitoring system provided similar classification results.

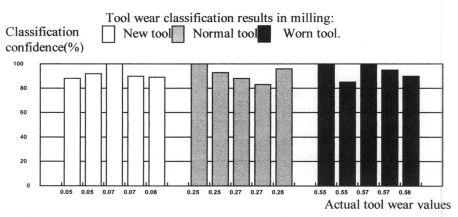

Fig. 9 Tool wear state classification results.

8. CONCLUSIONS

An intelligent multi-sensor tool condition monitoring system has been developed. Tool wear classification is realized by applying a fuzzy driven neural network. On the basis of this investigation, the following conclusions can be made.

(1) Power consumption, vibration, AE and cutting force sensors are applicable for monitoring tool wear in metal cutting process. The healthy signals picked up by these sensors and the signal features extracted describe tool condition comprehensively.

(2) The combination of ANNs and fuzzy logic techniques integrates the strong learning and classification ability of the former and the superb flexibility of the latter to express the distribution characteristics of signal features with vague boundaries and the fuzzy distances between them. This methodology indirectly solves the weight assignment problem of the conventional fuzzy pattern recognition system and let it have greater representative power and be more robust.

(3). Armed with the advanced pattern recognition methodology, the established intelligent tool condition monitoring system has the advantages of being suitable for different machining environments, robust to noise and tolerant to faults. Accurate tool wear classification can be achieved over a range of machining conditions.

* Cutting condition 1: cutting speed - 600 rev/min, feed rate - 1 mm/rev, cutting depth - 0.6 mm, workpiece material - EN1A, cutting inserts - Stellram SDHT1204 AE TN-42.

References

[1] M. A. Elbestawi, T. A. Papazafiriou and R. X. Du, "In-process Monitoring of Tool Wear in Milling Using Cutting Force Signature," Int. J. Mach. Tools Manufact. Vol. 31, No. 1, pp. 55-73, 1991.

[2] S. Yie, Y. Zhang and L. Pan, "On-line Tool Wear Monitoring for Turning," Research Paper of Nanging Aeronautical Institute, pp. 171-186 (in Chinese), 1992.

[3] Y. S. Liao, "Development of A Monitoring Technique for Tool Change Purpose in Turning Operations," Proc. 26th Int. Machine Tool Design and Research Conf., pp. 325-329, 1986.

[4] M. S. Lan and D. A. Dornfeld, "In-process Tool Fracture detection," J. Engng. Mater. Technol. Vol. 106, pp. 111-118, 1984.

[5] E. Kannatey-Asibu and D. A. Dornfeld, "Quantitative Relationships for Acoustic Emission from Orthogonal Metal Cutting," Trans. ASME, J. of Eng. Ind., Vol.103, pp. 330-340, 1981.

[6] I. Inasaki and S. Yonetsu, "In-process Detecting of Cutting Tool Damage by Acoustic Emission Measurement," 22nd Int. Mach. Tool Des. Res. Conf., pp. 261-268, 1981.

[7] G. Shteinhauz, S. Braun and E. Lenz, "Automated Vibration Based Tool Wear Monitoring: Application to Face Milling," Proc. of ASME Int. Computers in Engng. Conf., pp. 401-406, 1984.

[8] D. Grieshaber, S. Ramalingam and D. Frohrib, "On Real Time Fracture Monitoring in Milling," Proc. 15th North American Manufac. Research Conf. pp. 477-484, 1987.

[9] S. Rangwala and D. A. Dornfeld, "Integrated of Sensors via Neural Networks for Detection of Tool Wear States," Proc. Symposium on Integrated and Intelligent Manufac. Analysis and Synthesis, ASME, New York, pp. 109-120, 1987.

[10] G. S. Choi, Z. X. Wang, D. A. Dornfeld and K. Tsujino, "Development of An Intelligent On-line Tool Wear System for Turning Operations," Proc. Japan-USA Symposium on Flexible Automation, ISCIE, Kyoto, Japan, 1990.

[11] P. G. Li and S. M. Wu, "Monitoring Drilling Wear States by A Fuzzy Pattern Recognition Technique," Trans. ASME, J. of Eng. Ind., Vol.110, pp. 297, 1988.

Chapter 9

Feature Extraction by Self-Organized Fuzzy Templates with Applications

Eiji Uchino[1], Shigeru Nakashima[2] and Takeshi Yamakawa[3]

[1] Yamaguchi University

[2] Nippon Telegraph and Telephone Corporation

[3] Kyushu Institute of Technology

Abstract

This chapter proposes a feature extraction method by using a modified LVQ (learning vector quantization) and a fuzzy template matching. In this method, the feature of a pattern is captured efficiently by the modified LVQ, and it is reflected on the weight vectors assigned to the units on the competitive layers. The fuzzy templates are then constructed with use of these weight vectors. The classification of pattern is performed according to the matching grade of each pattern to these fuzzy templates.

The present method is actually applied to the discrimination problem between gas and water pipes by using time course patterns of heat conduction rate. The discrimination results are very promising for practical use.

Keywords : feature extraction, SOM(Self-Organizing Maps), LVQ (Learning Vector Quantization), modified LVQ, fuzzy template matching, feature of pattern, supervised learning, signal classification, winner weight vector, competitive layer, training phase, learning rate, learning rate for repulsion, matching grade, number density, heat conduction, heat conduction rate, cast iron pipe, gas pipe, water pipe, time course, training data, neighborhood area, discrimination between gas pipe and water pipe

9.1   Introduction

In cases of maintenance and replacement of the old gas and water pipes laid underground, we have to discriminate which is gas or water pipe. The problem is, in many cases, the gas and water pipes are laid underground almost at the same place, and what is worse, the same material of cast iron is used for them. Therefore it is very difficult to discriminate them just by looking at the external appearance, or just by touching them. If we make a mistake of discrimination, it may cause a serious accident.

There are some classical methods for discrimination of these pipes, for example, make a small hole on the pipe, or hit the pipe by a hammer and hear the sound. The former is straightforward but dangerous, and it needs to put it back to its former condition. The latter needs an expert skill, and sometimes lacks reliability. The method to use supersonic waves is also proposed, but is not practical nor suitable for the actual spot of construction.

In this chapter, we propose a new method for this problem, with simple measurement system, by utilizing the different property of heat conduction on the surface of each pipe. The time course pattern of the heat conduction rate is measured, the feature of which is captured by the modified LVQ onto its weight vectors, and then the fuzzy templates, constructed by these weight vectors, will be used to discriminate between gas and water pipes.

9.2   Feature Extraction by Modified LVQ and Fuzzy Template Matching

9.2.1   *Modified LVQ*

In this section, a LVQ proposed by Kohonen [1][2] is modified. The following is a supervised learning algorithm we propose here, which gives an efficient classification ability.

The modified LVQ is an efficient way to be used for pattern classification, when the class of the training data and the number of classes we want to discriminate are both known in advance.

Let $X^{c_v} \in R^s$ and $W_{ij}^{c_r} \in R^s$ be:

X^{c_v}: input vector belonging to class c_v $(v = 1, 2, \cdots, n)$,
$W_{ij}^{c_r}$: weight vector at unit (i, j) $(i = 1, 2, \cdots, l$ and $j = 1, 2, \cdots, m)$ on

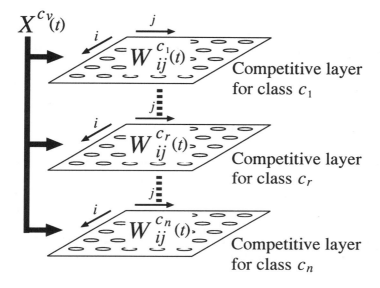

Fig. 9.1   Weight vectors and competitive layers.

the competitive layer prepared for classification of class c_v.

(1) Weight vectors $W_{ij}^{c_r}$ at each competitive layer in Fig. 9.1 are initialized randomly.
(2) Find winner weight vector $W_{i_r j_r}^{c_r}$ at each competitive layer ($r = 1, 2, \cdots, n$) which matches best to an input vector X^{c_v}, that belongs to class c_v. The winner weight vectors $W_{i_r j_r}^{c_r}$ are found at each layer r. The number of the winner weight vectors is n.
(3) Training phase: The winner weight vector $W_{i_v j_v}^{c_v}$ on the competitive layer for class c_v is renewed by:

$$W_{pq}^{c_v}(t+1) = W_{pq}^{c_v}(t) + \alpha(t)\{X^{c_v}(t) - W_{pq}^{c_v}(t)\}, \qquad (1)$$

where $\alpha(t)$ is a learning rate which decreases monotonously in learning time t, and $(p, q) \in D$, where D is a neighborhood of the best matching unit, which shrinks in the passage of learning time [3]. For winner weight vectors $W_{i_r j_r}^{c_r}$ ($r \neq v$), which are not on the competitive layer for class c_v, the following renewal procedure is taken:

$$W_{pq}^{c_r}(t+1) = W_{pq}^{c_r}(t) - \alpha(t)\beta(t)\{X^{c_v}(t) - W_{pq}^{c_r}(t)\}, \qquad (2)$$

where $\beta(t)$ is a learning rate for repulsion, which increases monotonously.

The updates of weights by Eq. (1) follow the conventional SOM (Self-Organizing Maps)learning algorithm. On the other hand, the function of Eq. (2) is as follows.

That is, at the beginning of learning, the updates of weights by Eq. (2) are small. As learning proceeds, $\beta(t)$ increases monotonously, and the weights begin to keep away from an input vector. In other words, by introducing $\beta(t)$, the present algorithm is similar to SOM at the beginning of learning, and as learning goes on, the contribution of $\beta(t)$ becomes greater and greater, and the present algorithm approaches to LVQ. We call this algorithm a modified LVQ, where SOM and LVQ are merged by $\beta(t)$.

The present modified LVQ has the following advantages.

- By introducing $\beta(t)$, the weight vectors of the same class of the input vector move towards the input vector, and for different class, they move away from the input vector. By this action, the discrimination rate of similar patterns, i.e., the patterns close to each other, is improved.
- The weight vectors of the conventional LVQ need to be initialized, by using, for example, SOM. However, concerning the present modified LVQ, the weight vectors can be initialized randomly. Therefore, there is no risk of local adaptation. Thus, the learning can be started without any preprocessing.

Originally, LVQ is good for discrimination of patterns and not for classification. For the purpose of discrimination of similar patterns that are very close, it is effective to merge SOM in LVQ. By using the modified LVQ, the more suitable template for discrimination and classification of unknown patterns can be constructed.

9.2.2   Fuzzy Template for Pattern Classification

Fuzzy template to discriminate pattern of class c_r is constructed by using the weight vectors $W_{ij}^{c_r}$ on the competitive layer of class c_r.

Let $F_{ij}^{c_v}$ be a local fuzzy template on unit (i,j) at the competitive layer of class c_v, that is given by:

$$F_{ij}^{c_v}(X) = \exp\{-\gamma\eta^{c_v}(X)(\|X - W_{ij}^{c_v}\|)^2\}, \tag{3}$$

where X is an input vector space, γ is a decay rate, and $\eta^{c_v}(X)$ is a function which controls the decay rate γ at X. The local fuzzy template $F_{ij}^{c_v}(X)$ has a center at $W_{ij}^{c_v}$, and decreases exponentially, following the decay rate $\gamma\eta^{c_v}(X)$.

The role of $\eta^{c_v}(X)$ is to change the basic decay rate γ at every point of X. The matching grade of the input vector to this local fuzzy template is calculated by $F_{ij}^{c_r}(X)$. This matching grade represents how the input vector is similar to the feature of the trained pattern. When the input vector completely matches to the trained pattern, $F_{ij}^{c_v}(X)$ equals to 1. When it doesn't, the matching grade to $F_{ij}^{c_v}(X)$ decreases exponentially according to its similarity.

$\eta^{c_v}(X)$ is calculated by the following procedure.

(1) Let $f_{ij}^{c_r}(X)$ be a function defined on each unit (i,j) at each competitive layer as follows:
For the layer $r = v$:

$$f_{ij}^{c_r}(X) = \exp\{-\gamma(\|X - W_{ij}^{c_r}\|)^2\} \tag{4}$$

and for the layer $r \neq v$:

$$f_{ij}^{c_r}(X) = -\exp\{-\gamma(\|X - W_{ij}^{c_r}\|)^2\}. \tag{5}$$

(2) $\eta^{c_v}(X)$ is given by:

$$\eta^{c_v}(X) = 1 - \frac{\sum_{i=1}^{l}\sum_{j=1}^{m}\sum_{r=1}^{n} f_{ij}^{c_r}(X)}{A} \tag{6}$$

with

$$A = \max_{X}\left(\sum_{i=1}^{l}\sum_{j=1}^{m}\sum_{r=1}^{n} f_{ij}^{c_r}(X)\right). \tag{7}$$

$\eta^{c_v}(X)$ is a function on vector space X, depending on class c_v, and it plays an important role to adjust γ locally on the vector space X. By introducing $\eta^{c_v}(X)$, fuzzy template which reflects the distribution of input vector is constructed. That is, $\eta^{c_v}(X)$ is constructed so that the higher is the number density of the weight vectors of class c_v, the higher is the matching grade. This is because the feature of pattern is condensed where the number density of the weight vectors is high. On the contrary, the matching grade is low where the number density is low. The matching grade is also low where the number density of the weight vectors is high, which don't belong to class c_v. This is an characteristic point of this present method.

$\eta^{c_v}(X)$ is not negative (i.e., $\eta^{c_v}(X) \geq 0$). The decrement of the fuzzy template $F_{ij}^{c_v}(X)$ becomes slower when $0 \leq \eta^{c_v}(X) < 1$, and the decrement becomes faster when $1 < \eta^{c_v}(X)$.

A fuzzy template with constant decrement rate is isotropic, meanwhile, the present fuzzy template $F_{ij}^{c_v}(X)$ becomes anisotropic because of $\eta^{c_v}(X)$. A fuzzy template belonging to class c_v has a small decrement near the weight vectors $W_{ij}^{c_v}(r = v)$ that belong to the same class, and has a large decrement near the weight vectors $W_{ij}^{c_r}(r \neq v)$ that belong to the different class from c_v. This makes it possible to discriminate close pattern, and contributes to an improvement of discrimination ability.

Now, summing up every fuzzy template at unit (i, j), $F_{ij}^{c_v}$, we get the following global (objective) fuzzy template $T^{c_v}(X)$ to be used for classification of class c_v:

$$T^{c_v}(X) = \sum_{i=1}^{l} \sum_{j=1}^{m} F_{ij}^{c_v}(X). \tag{8}$$

This fuzzy template is constructed for each competitive layer. By applying an unknown input vector $X^{c_r}(k)$ $(k = 1, 2, \cdots, N)$ to this global fuzzy template, the matching grade $T^{c_v}(X^{c_r}(k))$ is accumulated for $k = 1, 2, \cdots, N$. Then, the unknown input vector $X^{c_r}(k)$ is classified into class c_I with:

$$I = \arg\max_{v} \sum_{k=1}^{N} T^{c_v}(X^{c_r}(k)). \tag{9}$$

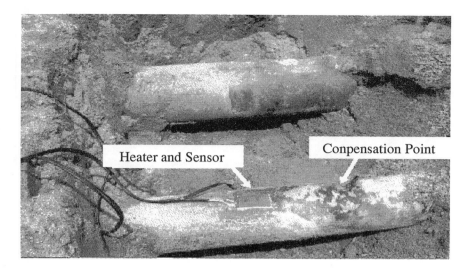

Fig. 9.2 Underground gas and water pipes made of cast iron.

9.3 Application to the Discrimination between Gas and Water Pipes

9.3.1 *Outline of Experiment*

The gas and water pipes underground are both made of cast iron, and they are laid almost at the same place as shown in Fig. 9.2. The diameters of pipes are 10, 15, 20, and 30 *cm*. It is almost impossible to discriminate them just by looking at the external appearance.

In this method, those pipes are efficiently discriminated by learning the different heat conduction properties of gas and water pipes[11]. That is, these properties are learned by the modified LVQ, and the weight vectors of W_{ij}^{gas} and W_{ij}^{water} at the competitive layer of each class are used to construct the fuzzy templates. By applying these fuzzy templates to the input vectors $X^{gas}(k)$ (time course of heat conduction rate of gas pipe) and $X^{water}(k)$ (that of water pipe), they are classified into gas or water pipe.

9.3.2 *Heater and Sensor Settings*

The surface of the objective pipe is heated by the special heater, and the surface temperature of the pipe is measured by the temperature sensors.

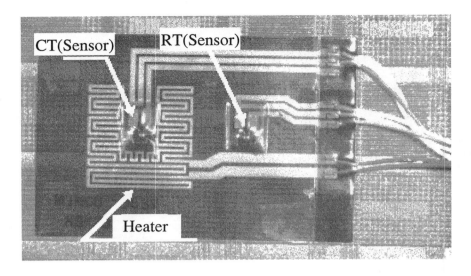

Fig. 9.3   Heater and sensor.

The heater and sensors used in the experiment are shown in Fig. 9.3.

They are protected by a thin and flexible polimide film, and it is stuck on the rough surface of the cast iron pipe by silicon rubber which has a good heat conductance. The polimide film has a strong tolerance to chemical reaction and corrosion. This realizes a measurement without any influence of the rust and/or the irregular condition of the surface of the pipe.

The heater and sensors are stuck on the pipe as shown in Fig. 9.4. CT, RT, and ST are temperature sensors. CT is located near the heater, and RT is located at 2 *cm* from CT. ST is a temperature compensation point, which is located far enough from CT.

9.3.3   *Measurements*

We employ the following heat conduction rate derived experimentally to grasp the feature of gas and water pipes:

$$R(k) = \frac{RT(k) - ST(k)}{CT(k) - ST(k)} \times 100 \quad (\%). \tag{10}$$

$RT(k)$, $ST(k)$, and $CT(k)$ are outputs of each temperature sensor. Sampling interval of measurement is 10 seconds. $R(k)$ is measured for 34 gas and 19 water pipes underground. Some of them are shown in Fig. 9.5 for reference.

9.3.4 *Experimental Results and Discussion*

As is apparent from Fig. 9.5, there are some differences on heat conduction rates of gas and water pipes, but some of them are partially overlapped. We try to grasp the feature of gas and water pipes by the modified LVQ. In this experiment, the structure of the modified LVQ consists of one input layer and two competitive layers as shown in Fig. 9.6. The feature of the gas pipe and that of the water pipe are grasped by each competitive layer respectively.

Typical time course of $R(k)$ of a gas pipe is chosen as a training data for the modified LVQ, and that of a water pipe is chosen as well. The rest is used for checking the discrimination ability of the present method.

In this experiment, $X^{c_r} \in R^2$ and $W_{ij}^{c_r} \in R^2$, and $r = 1, 2$ and $l = m = 5$. We employed $\alpha(t) = 0.5(1 - t/T)$ and $\beta(t) = (t/T)^2$ with $T = 1000$, and $\gamma = 0.01$.

As for the neighborhood area for learning, 24 connected neighbors for $1 \le t < 200$, 8 connected neighbors for $200 \le t < 600$, and no connected neighbors for $600 \le t \le 1000$, were taken.

Fig. 9.7(a) shows an example of local fuzzy template $F_{ij}^{c_r}$ constructed by the weight vectors $W_{ij}^{c_r}$. By incorporating η^{c_v}, the present fuzzy template

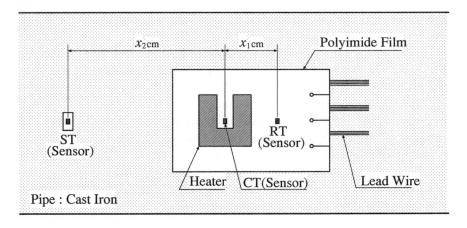

Fig. 9.4   Heater and sensor settings.

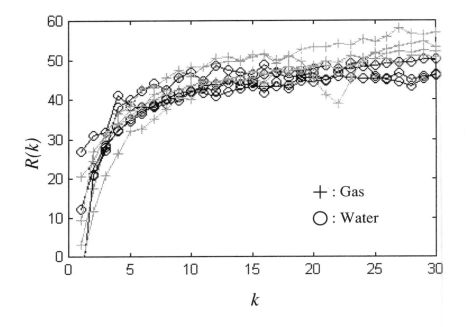

Fig. 9.5   Heat conduction rates for gas and water pipes.

becomes somewhat long along with the time axis (x_1) influenced by the other weight vectors. This makes it possible to discriminate between gas and water pipes by the time course of heat conduction rate in shorter period than isotropic fuzzy template shown in Fig. 9.7(b).

Fig. 9.8 shows the global fuzzy templates $T^{gas}(X)$ and $T^{water}(X)$. Fig. 9.9 shows $\sum_k T^{gas}(X(k))$ and $\sum_k T^{water}(X(k))$ for unknown 33 gas pipes and 18 water pipes.

The pipe is discriminated to be a gas pipe when $\sum_k T^{gas}(X(k))$ is greater than $\sum_k T^{water}(X(k))$, and vice versa. In this experiment, discrimination between gas and water pipes has been performed perfectly.

On the other hand, at the actual spot it is desirable to complete the discrimination in a small time. By the proposed method, from the start of measurement, the cumulative matching grade is calculated momentarily and we can do discrimination at every moment.

In order to provide with a user friendly interface, we employ the visualization technique to help the decision maker to discriminate visually.

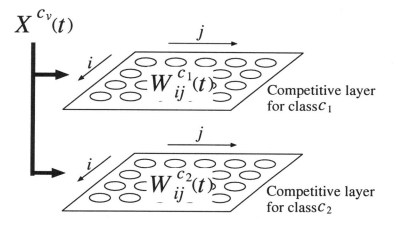

Fig. 9.6   Weight vector and competitive layer.

The cumulative matching grades until L steps, $\sum_{k=1}^{L} F_{ij}^{gas}(X(k))$ and $\sum_{k=1}^{L} F_{ij}^{water}(X(k))$, can be visualized as shown in Fig. 9.10.

The color (brightness) corresponding to each unit on the competitive layer changes with the passage of time. This helps the decision maker to recognize visually the belonging degree of an unknown pattern to the trained patterns by the modified LVQ. This can also provide more detailed information visually if we monitor these cumulative matching grades in real time, such as:

(1) Changing rate of color (brightness) is a good information which helps the decision maker to make a judgment of discrimination in a small time.

(2) In case of dark color (brightness) at every unit in the whole period of measurement, the troubles in the measurement system might be found in ease. For example, poor contact of the sensors to the pipe, or some other hardware troubles.

9.4   Comparisons on the Ability of Discrimination

In this section, we show the effectiveness of the modified LVQ for the learning of input pattern, and that of an anisotropic fuzzy template for discrimination of classes.

Here we perform the experiments on discrimination ability with use of SOM and LVQ for the learning of input pattern, and with use of the isotropic fuzzy template or anisotropic fuzzy template for discrimination of classes. The following experiments are performed combining each method.

(a) Modified LVQ, Anisotropic fuzzy template (Proposed method)
(b) Modified LVQ, Isotropic fuzzy template
(c) SOM, Anisotropic fuzzy template
(d) SOM, Isotropic fuzzy template
(e) SOM, LVQ, Anisotropic fuzzy template
(f) SOM, LVQ, Isotropic fuzzy template

Fig. 9.11 shows the experimental results of the above combination.

The ratio of cumulative matching grade in Fig. 9.11 means the ratio of the average one obtained at the class of input data to the one obtained at the different class from the input data. The larger is the ratio of cumulative matching grade, the easier becomes the discrimination.

Consider the combination of SOM and isotropic fuzzy template (Method (d)) as a standard. Usage of the modified LVQ will increase both the ratio of correct classification and the ratio of cumulative matching grade. The superiority of the anisotropic fuzzy template to the isotropic one can be seen.

It can be observed also that the modified LVQ is superior to SOM in grasping the feature of pattern, and the anisotropic fuzzy template is superior to the isotropic one in discrimination ability. Through these experiments, the proposed method, i.e., a combination of the modified LVQ and an anisotropic fuzzy template(Method(a)), is the best discrimination method among those.

It is also found by some experiments that LVQ is not suitable for mapping the pattern correctly, nor for constructing fuzzy template.

The LVQ employed here is trained after setting up the initial values of weight vectors by using SOM. The ratio of correct classification with this method is less than 50%, and the ratio of the cumulative matching grade is approximately 1. This means that the conventional LVQ can't be applied to this discrimination problem, and that the learning to leave the feature of the target pattern while keeping away from the other, which is realized by the modified LVQ, can't be realized by a simple combination of SOM and LVQ.

Next, the experiments are performed for comparisons on the ability of discrimination with short term measurement of the heat conduction rate. For a few minutes just after the start of measurement, the discrimination between gas pipe and water pipe is generally difficult, because there is little difference between them.

This discrimination experiment is performed for the inputs patterns where the pattern of each class is close. As the input data, the data until $L = 10$, $L = 20$, and $L = 30$ are used. The discrimination results of each method are shown in Fig. 9.12.

$L = 10$ corresponds to the measurement for 1 minute and 40 seconds. With these data, the ratio of correct classification by Method (a) is 78.4%, and the ratio of cumulative matching grade is 1.75, as is shown in Fig. 9.12(a). Comparing the results of the proposed method and those of the other methods, the proposed method is the best among them.

From these results, it can be said that the proposed method is also effective for pattern classification where each pattern is very close to each other. The visualized cumulative matching grades until $L = 10$ for a gas pipe calculated by each method are shown in Fig. 9.13.

As is described before, the visualization of the cumulative matching grade will help the decision maker to discriminate visually. The conditions that the decision maker makes a decision are a clear difference of the color (brightness) of each class and the size of area where the color (brightness) has changed. Even just after the start of measurement, once the decision maker recognizes a clear difference, he can discriminate at once.

Comparing Method (b) and Method (d) in Fig. 9.13, there are both some changes of color (brightness) on the competitive layer of a gas pipe, however, the changes of color (brightness) on the competitive layer of a water pipe of Method (b) are smaller than of Method (d). This also helps the decision maker to judge correctly with confidence.

Further comparing Method (a) and Method (b) in Fig. 9.13, the changes of color(brightness) are a little bit bigger for Method (a) than Method (b). This becomes more clear according as the passage of time.

9.5   Conclusions

In this chapter, pattern classification method by the modified LVQ and the fuzzy template matching was proposed. The feature of pattern has been captured efficiently by the modified LVQ. The fuzzy template, that was constructed by using the weight vectors of the modified LVQ, could well classify the input data.

The present method has been successfully applied to the actual gas/water pipe discrimination problem by using the time course patterns of heat conduction rate. In comparisons with the other methods, it has been shown that the proposed method is superior.

The future research is to make this system more compact in oder to be used at the actual spots of construction. The potential applications of this work are, e.g., person identification by speech and/or face, medical diagnosis based on EEG or ECG, application to fMRI data, and so on.

Acknowledgment

The authors would like to thank Saibu Gas company for the financial support of this research. Many thanks are also due to Mr. Y. Toyoda and Mr. K. Furukido for assistance of the experiment.

References

[1] T. Kohonen, "Self-Organization and Associative Memory," Springer-Verlag Berlin Heidelberg, 1984.

[2] T. Kohonen, "Self-Organizing Maps," Springer-Verlag Berlin Heidelberg, 1995.

[3] J. Dayhoff, "Neural Network Architectures: An Introduction," Van Nostrand Reinhold, 1990.

[4] R. Hecht-Nielsen, "Neurocomputing," Addison-Wesley Publishing Company, 1990.

[5] N. K. Pal, J. C. Bezdek and E. C.-K. Tsao, "Generalized Clustering Networks and Kohonen's Self-organizing Scheme," IEEE Trans. on Neural Networks, Vol.4, No.4, pp.549-557, 1993.

[6] K. Nakano, "An Introduction to Neurocomputing," Corona Publishing Co., Ltd., 1990.

[7] K. Kamei and T. Fukuoka, "Handwritten Character Recognition by Fuzzy Learning Vector Quantization," J. Japan Society for Fuzzy Theory and Systems, Vol.10, No.5, pp.899-906, 1998.

[8] S. Miyamoto, "Fuzzy c-means and Its Variations," J. Japan Society for Fuzzy Theory and Systems, Vol.8, No.3, pp.423-430, 1996.

[9] S. Murakami, "Image Processing Technology," Tokyo Denki University Publishing Department, 1996.

[10] T. Nakamizo, "Signal Analysis and System Identification," Corona Publishing Co., Ltd., 1988.

[11] J. Minkowycz, "Handbook of Numerical Heat Transfer," John Wiley, 1988.

[12] N. Issiki and N. Kitayama, "Heat Transfer Technology," Morikita Publishing Co., Ltd., 1984.

[13] K. Matsui, "Design and Manufacture for the Circuit with Sensors," CQ Publishing Co., Ltd., 1990.

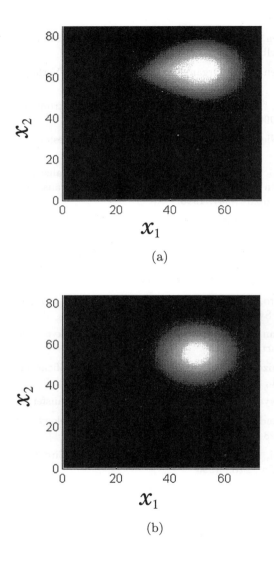

(a)

(b)

Fig. 9.7   (a) Proposed anisotropic fuzzy template, and (b) isotropic fuzzy template.

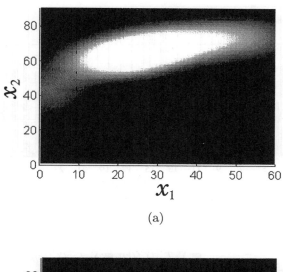

(a)

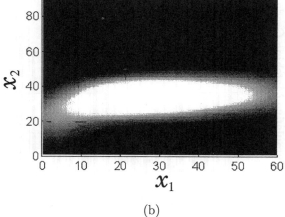

(b)

Fig. 9.8 Global fuzzy templates. (a) $T^{gas}(x_1, x_2)$, and (b) $T^{water}(x_1, x_2)$.

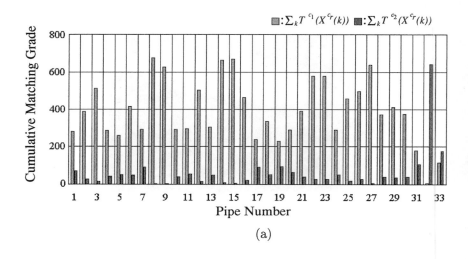

(a)

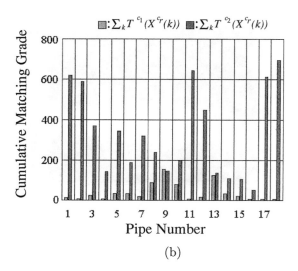

(b)

Fig. 9.9 $\sum_k T^{gas}(X(k))$ and $\sum_k T^{water}(X(k))$.   (a) Discrimination results for gas pipe data, and (b) discrimination results for water pipe data.

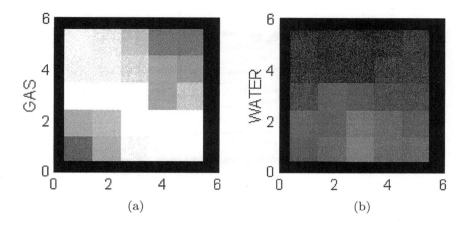

(a) (b)

Fig. 9.10 Cumulative matching grades to local fuzzy template at unit (i, j) until L steps. (a) $\sum_{k=1}^{L} F_{ij}^{gas}(X(k))$, and (b) $\sum_{k=1}^{L} F_{ij}^{water}(X(k))$.

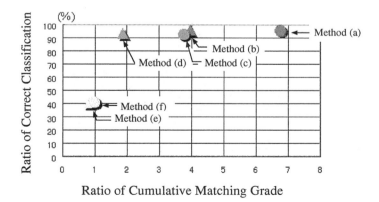

Fig. 9.11 Comparisons of the ability of discrimination.

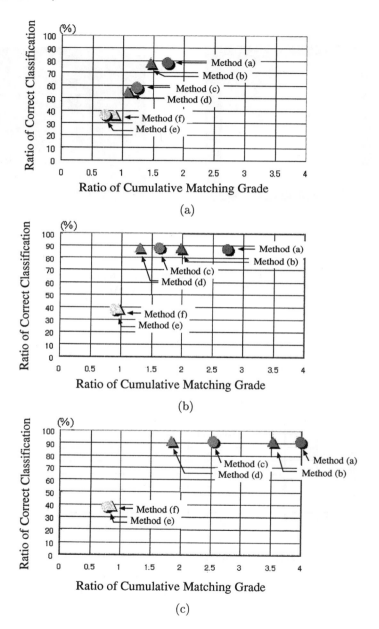

Fig. 9.12   Comparisons of the ability of discrimination with short term data. (a) $L = 10$, (b) $L = 20$, and (c) $L = 30$.

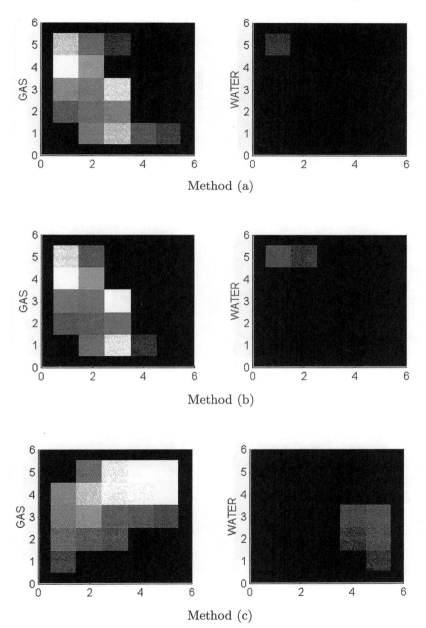

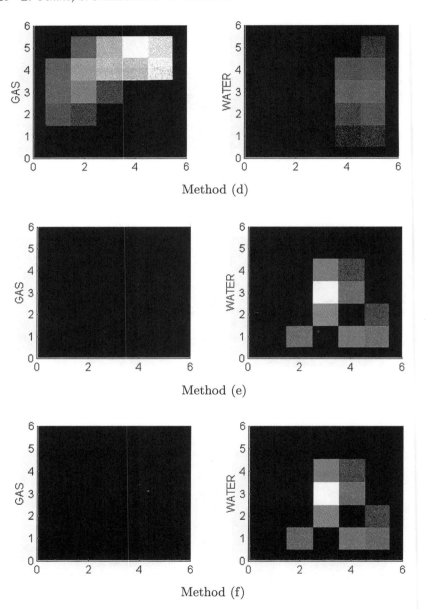

Fig. 9.13   Cumulative matching grades to local fuzzy template at unit (i, j) until $L = 10$ steps for a gas pipe.

Chapter 10

Inference of Self-Excited Vibration in High-Speed End-Milling Based on Fuzzy Neural Networks

Chuanxin Su, Junichi Hino and Toshio Yoshimura
The University of Tokushima, Japan

Abstract

This chapter introduces a new method for predicting chatter in milling process by a fuzzy neural network. Firstly, a milling experimental setup is built. And a set of the valuable experimental data is obtained under different tool wear states and cutting conditions. Secondly, since it is extremely difficult to construct an exact mathematical model for the setup, a fuzzy neural network model is proposed as a simplified one trained by using the experimental data. Thirdly, some simulation results are obtained based on the model. Finally, the further experiments are done to confirm the validity of predicting chatter in the model. The results show that chatter vibration in high-speed end milling could be exactly predicted via the model. Thus, the method described here is very effective to predict chatter in milling process.

Keywords: self-excited vibration, end milling, chatter prediction, fuzzy neural network.

10.1   Introduction

Chatter is one of the major limiting factors on the metal removal rate. Since it gives rise to poor surface finish and dimensional accuracy in the machined part, reduces tool life, and even damages machine tools, various kinds of researches concerning its prediction and avoidance have been carried out over the last several decades, particularly since the 1980s.

Tlusty(1981,1986) improved the past stability criterion of milling by considering the basic non-linearity and the varying directional orientation in machining, and investigated the effects of spindle speed on chatter and stability lobes and the effect of cutting speed on damping in high-speed milling. Tsai et al(1990) studied a cutting simulation system for estimating chatter in end milling by using a lumped-parameter model with two degrees of freedom. And a numerical simulation method and a simplified criterion were conducted to check the occurrence of chatter based on the model. Lee et al(1991) established a reliable stable region in end milling by exploiting the effects of work piece dynamics on the cutting process. Smith et al(1992) developed a system to eliminate chatter in milling by correctly adjusting the spindle speed. The major drawback of the system is that chatter must occur before it can be detected, which means that some portion of the work piece may be damaged before the stable speed is attained. Altintas et al(1992) used sound spectrum to detect milling chatter and subsequently suppressed it by spindle speed oscillation. The method requires a high-performance and high-torque-delivery spindle drive system, which seems difficult in practical milling. Minis etc.(1993) considered the structural dynamic compliance between the cutting tool and the work piece, and developed the milling equations to determine the limits of stability under various machining conditions. Altintas et al(1995) derived the dynamic milling model by considering the Fourier series expansion of the milling force coefficients, and the chatter-free axial depths of cut and spindle speeds were calculated directly from the proposed expressions. In order to suppress regenerative chatter vibration, Liao et al (1996) also proposed an on-line control method by adjusting spindle speed. The main disadvantage of the method is that the system is not brought to the stable state if a relatively large width of cut beyond the stability limit is employed.

Therefore, chatter in milling has not been predicted with satisfactory accuracy and reliability till now. Ehmann et al(1997) indicated that there were a number of unresolved or less understood issues in the modeling of the complex cutting processes. One of important research issues is the modeling of the tool wear effects on cutting forces. And, the dynamic characteristics of the spindle changes significantly at high spindle speeds. These effects should be incorporated in the dynamic model. Moreover, Smith (1997) pointed out that chatter avoidance in high-speed machining has become an important research topic. Therefore, it is necessary to propose new theoretical and experimental approaches for more exactly predicting chatter in high-speed milling.

The purpose of this paper is to introduce a new approach for predicting chatter in high-speed end milling by using a fuzzy neural network. Firstly, a milling experimental setup is built and a set of the valuable experimental data are acquired under different tool wear states and carefully selected cutting parameters. Secondly, the experimental system is simplified into a fuzzy neural network model which is trained in the experimental data. Thirdly, some simulation results are obtained on the basis of the trained model. Lastly, the calculated results are compared with the experimental ones in order to check the effectiveness of the method described here.

10.2　Milling Experimental System

The milling experiment is conducted on an NC jig grinding machine type JG35CPX (Waida Corporation, Japan) with a control device FANUC—11M which can alter cutting parameters. The machine tool has a DC 0.55kw spindle motor output power; its spindle revolution ranges over 3,000~45,000rpm and its table feed varies from 1 to 2,000 mm/min. The configuration is shown in Fig. 10.1.

Fig. 10.1   Configuration of NC jig grinding machine

The milling tool used in the experiment is a solid square type of end mill type TES2030(Hitachi Tool, Japan), and its parameters are listed in Table10. 1. The profile is shown in Fig. 10.2.

Table 10.1   Tool Parameters

Item	Unit	Value
Tool diameter	mm	3
Helical angle	degree	45
Number of teeth		2
Tool material		K10

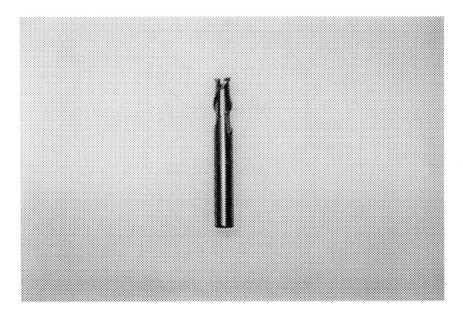

Fig. 10.2   Profile of end mill

Three types of different work piece materials(S50C, NAK80, and SKD11) shown in Table 10.2 are utilized to investigate the effect of different material hardness on milling chatter. The shape of all the work pieces is rectangular as shown in Fig. 10.3.

Table   10.2   Work piece materials

Material	Heat-treatment	Hardness(HRC)
SKD11	Oil hardening 1030°C, oil tempering 150°C.	59
NAK80		36
S50C		17

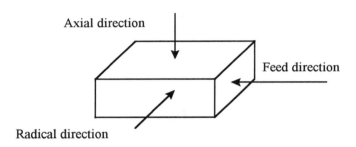

Fig. 10.3 Shape of work piece

Firstly, an experimental system is established, which is composed of an NC jig grinding machine with a control device, a force sensor, a charge amplifier and an FFT analyzer. The block diagram is shown in Fig. 10.4.

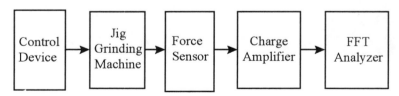

Fig. 10. 4   Block diagram of the experimental system

Then, in order to study the stability of high-speed milling process, the experimental data must be obtained with satisfactory condition. Therefore, the work pieces are cut by using several different cutting conditions in the experiment. The variation of the cutting conditions is realized by the control device in Fig. 10.4. The various cutting conditions are listed in Table 10.3.

Table 10.3   Cutting conditions

Item	Unit	Value
Spindle revolution	rpm	3009--13500
Table feed	mm/min	27--603
Radial depth of cut	mm	0.1,0.2,0.3
Axial depth of cut	mm	2.0--4.0
Type of milling		down milling
Coolant		dry

Thirdly, the cutting forces are measured by using a piezoelectric force sensor(Kistler 9257B, Kistler Instrument AG, Switzerland) during experiment and the measured force signal is transferred into the charge amplifier as the input. The amplified signal is analyzed by using the FFT analyzer(Rion SA74) to find whether the chatter has occurred under the given cutting condition or not.

Finally, the adequate experimental data under various cutting conditions are obtained and listed in Table 10.4.

Table 10.4   Experimental results

(1) Work piece material: S50C(Hardness: 17HRC)

No.	Tool wear state	Direction of cut (X or Y)	Radial depth of cut (mm)	Axial depth of cut (mm)	Spindle revolution (rpm)	Table feed (mm/min)	Chatter vibration
1	New	X	0.1	4	5400	100	No
2	New	Y	0.2	2	5014	300	Yes
3	New	Y	0.2	2	6003	240	Critical
5	New	Y	0.2	2	6997	419.8	No
6	New	Y	0.3	2	6997	419	No
7	New	Y	0.2	2	6997	279.8	No
8	New	Y	0.3	2	6997	279.8	No
9	New	Y	0.3	2	10019	601	No
10	Medium	Y	0.2	2	10019	400	No
11	Medium	Y	0.2	2	10019	200	No
12	Medium	Y	0.3	2	10019	200	No
13	Medium	Y	0.3	2	4012	240	Yes
14	Medium	Y	0.3	2	10050	603	Critical

(2) Work piece material: NAK80(Hardness: 36HRC)

No.	Tool wear state	Direction of cut (X or Y)	Radial depth of cut (mm)	Axial depth of cut (mm)	Spindle revolution (rpm)	Table feed (mm/min)	Chatter vibration
1	New	Y	0.1	2.5	13500	270	No
2	New	Y	0.1	2.5	5000	100	No
3	New	Y	0.2	2.5	5000	100	No
4	New	X	0.1	4	5400	100	No
5	New	X	0.1	4	7045	100	No
6	Medium	X	0.1	4	10310	200	No
7	Medium	X	0.1	4	4997	140	No
8	Medium	X	0.1	4	4997	200	No
9	Old	X	0.3	4	4997	52	Critical
10	Old	Y	0.1	2	4997	100	Yes
11	Old	Y	0.3	2	4997	27	Yes
12	Medium	Y	0.2	2	10000	600	No
13	Medium	Y	0.3	2	10000	420	No
14	Medium	Y	0.3	2	7000	420	No
15	Old	Y	0.3	2	5000	300	Yes
16	Old	Y	0.2	2	4005	240	Yes

(3) Work piece materials: SKD11(Hardness: 59HRC)

No.	Tool wear state	Direction of cut (X or Y)	Radial depth of cut (mm)	Axial depth of cut (mm)	Spindle revolution (rpm)	Table feed (mm/min)	Chatter vibration
1	New	Y	0.1	2.5	5000	100	No
2	New	Y	0.2	2	9971	598	No
3	New	Y	0.3	2	9971	598	No
4	New	Y	0.2	2	3009	180	Critical
5	Medium	Y	0.2	2	10050	603	No
6	Medium	Y	0.2	2	10050	402	No
7	Medium	Y	0.3	2	7025	421	No
8	Old	Y	0.1	2	7025	281	No
9	Old	Y	0.2	2	6019	361	No
10	Old	Y	0.1	2	6019	241	No
11	Old	Y	0.1	2	5005	200	No
12	Old	Y	0.2	2	4006	240	No
13	Old	Y	0.1	2	4006	160	Critical
14	Old	Y	0.2	2	3500	210	Critical

10.3　Chatter Prediction Model

10.3.1　*Experimental System Model*

It is known that the milling experimental system comprises a grinding machine, a milling tool, a jig, a work piece, and a control device. Whether chatter occurs during milling process or not is determined by the following factors:

(a) grinding machine: wear state and so on;

(b) jig: kinds;
(c)   milling tool: material, hardness, wear state, ratio of length and diameter, number of teeth, helical angle, and so on;
(d)   work piece: hardness, shape, material;
(e)   cutting conditions: spindle revolution, table feed, axial and radial depths of cut, direction of cut, type of milling(down or up), kind of coolant(dry, oil, et al).

However, since the most flexible part of typical milling systems is cutter-workpiece subsystem, the important factors affecting the stability of milling process, i.e., milling tool, work piece and cutting conditions, are only considered for the convenience of analysis. It considerably simplifies the milling process and does not restrict the applicability of the present analysis. Therefore, the experimental system is simplified into a model with multiple inputs and single output, as shown in Fig.10.5. Here, the inputs consists of tool wear state, material and hardness of work piece, and cutting conditions; and the output is whether or not chatter takes place during machining.

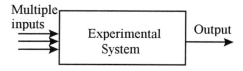

Fig. 10.5 Experimental system model

10.3.2   *Fuzzy Neural Network Model*

Since the milling experimental system has a nonlinear and complicated structure in the relation between input and output, it is difficult to construct the exact mathematical model.   Therefore, a fuzzy neural network model is proposed as a simplified one. Neural networks recognize ill-defined patterns without an explicit set of rules, while fuzzy systems estimate functions and control systems with partial descriptions of system behaviors. Neural networks may adaptively infer this heuristic knowledge from sample data. Thus, the experimental system is finally simplified into a fuzzy neural network model illustrated in Fig. 10.6.

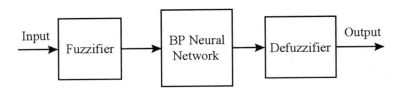

Fig. 10.6 Fuzzy neural network model

The input of the fuzzifier in Fig. 10.6 includes both numerical and linguistic variables, some of which are the fuzzy variables. According to the different characteristics of different input variables, the input variables are fuzzified, standardized or digitized. The input variable "Tool wear" is expressed as 3-dimensional row vectors: New=[1.0,0.0,0.0], Medium=[0.0,1.0,0.0], Old=[0.0,0.0,1.0]; "Directions of cut(X or Y)" are respectively represented by 0 and 1; "Radial depth of cut" and "Axial depth of cut" are divided by their maximum depths of cut and become in the range of 0.0 to 1.0; "Spindle revolution" and "Table feed" are standardized into from 0.0 to 1.0. Supposing that spindle revolution is x and table feed is y, their standardizing functions are:

$$f(x) = \frac{1}{1 + e^{\frac{-x+5000}{k}}}$$

if   x<=5000, k=200;   else, k=2000, and

$$f(y) = \frac{1}{1 + e^{\frac{-y+150}{k}}}$$

if   y<=150, k=10;   else, k=100, where f(x) and f(y) denote sigmoid functions.

The fuzzifier outputs standardized data from 0.0 to 1.0 as the input of the neural network. Various kinds of researches have been done on the development of neural networks and many different architectures have been proposed(Beale,1990). One of the neural networks widely utilized is the back-propagation neural network(BPNN), which was firstly proposed by Rumelhart etc (1986). The neural network shown in Fig. 10.6 uses the BPNN, in which the output of the neural network is a set of discrete values for a group of given inputs and must be defuzzified. Since the center of gravity method, one of defuzzification methods, is relatively reasonable and comprehensive, it is used for the defuzzification here. If the output of the BPNN is out[i] (i=0, 1, ..., n-1), the final output of the defuzzifier z is as follows:

$$z = (n - \frac{\sum\limits_{i=0}^{n-1} [out[i] \times (i+1)]}{\sum\limits_{i=0}^{n-1} out[i]}) \div (n-1) \times 100\%$$

Thus, the experimental system model shown in Fig. 10.5 has been simplified into the model with 10 input parameters and single output parameter, shown in Fig. 10.7. The number of the input, hidden and output layer nodes of the neural network is respectively 10, 30 and 3 in the figure.

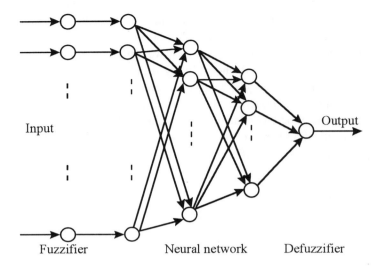

Fig. 10.7 Fuzzy neural networks

10.3.3   *Network Training*

On the basis of the fuzzy neural network model, a network training code is programmed. The block diagram of training algorithm is shown in Fig. 10.8. In programming, the initial training data are firstly inputted and the input data of the training data are fuzzified or standardized by membership functions and Sigmoid functions and so on. And then, these data are used as the inputs of the neural network. Using the BPNN method presented by Rumelhart et al(1986), the values of the weights and the biases can be adjusted. This process consists of the following two phases. In the first phase, the output is calculated for each unit in hidden and output layers and propagated forwards after the input is given. The output of each output layer unit is compared with the expected output, and the error signal is calculated. In the second phase, the error signal is passed through the network backwards and the weight is repeatedly modified until the error is less than the prescribed limit. Since the outputs from neural network are a set of discrete numerical values, the final output is attained as the weighted

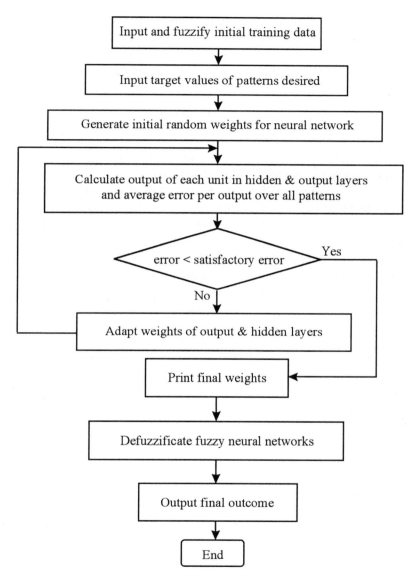

Fig. 10.8 Block diagram of training algorithm

average by using all the defuzzified outputs. In order to check whether the program is correct and the model is reasonable or not, the networks are trained with the experimental data of Section 2. In network training, sigmoid function is used as the threshold function of the BPNN method. In the sigmoid functions

$$f(u) = \frac{1}{1+e^{-ku}},$$

k's are selected to be respectively 3.5 and 1.2 in the hidden layer and the output layer by using trial-and-error method and doing a lot of calculations.

The results, shown in Table 10.5, are attained after 4567 iterations after carefully selecting the membership functions for the inputs and the standardized functions of the fuzzifier, and repeatedly adjusting the number of the hidden and output layer nodes of the neural network as well as the gain terms and momentum factors of BPNN method, where 0.0 means 'stable', 0.5 'critical' and 1.0 'unstable' in the desired outputs. And the average error per output unit over all patterns is less than 0.0001. It is concluded from Table 10.5 that the algorithm is correct and the model is reasonable.

Table 10.5 Results of network training

(1) Work piece material: S50C(Hardness:17HRC)

Pattern number	Desired output	Calculated results
1	0.0	0.000025
2	1.0	0.997375
3	0.0	0.005084
4	0.5	0.500639
5	0.0	0.000854
6	0.0	0.000956
7	0.0	0.001934
8	0.0	0.002708
9	0.0	0.000664
10	0.0	0.003082
11	0.0	0.000014
12	0.0	0.000037
13	1.0	0.994057
14	0.5	0.495474

(2) Work piece material: NAK80(Hardness: 36HRC)

Pattern number	Desired output	Calculated results
1	0.0	0.000026
2	0.0	0.000057
3	0.0	0.000109
4	0.0	0.000081
5	0.0	0.000042
6	0.0	0.000000
7	0.0	0.000200
8	0.0	0.000000
9	0.5	0.499733
10	1.0	0.995744
11	1.0	0.999270
12	0.0	0.000000
13	0.0	0.000002
14	0.0	0.000359
15	1.0	0.990863
16	1.0	0.998943

(3) Work piece material: SKD11(Hardness: 59HRC)

Pattern number	Desired output	Calculated results
1	0.0	0.001003
2	0.0	0.000146
3	0.0	0.000110
4	0.5	0.500923
5	0.0	0.000000
6	0.0	0.000000
7	0.0	0.000000
8	0.0	0.000050
9	0.0	0.000219
10	0.0	0.000017
11	0.0	0.000125
12	0.0	0.006617
13	0.5	0.502553
14	0.5	0.497481

10.4   Simulation Results

In order to use the proposed method to predict the chatter vibration in high-speed end milling process, the fuzzy neural network model for predicting chatter has been developed. The block diagram of prediction algorithm for chatter is shown in Fig. 10.9, and the effect of various input parameters on chatter vibration in high-speed milling is investigated.

Using the BPNN method, some simulation results were attained as shown in Table 10.6. On the part of "Chatter possibility" in the table, 0.00% means no chatter; 50.00% possible chatter; and 100.00% complete chatter.

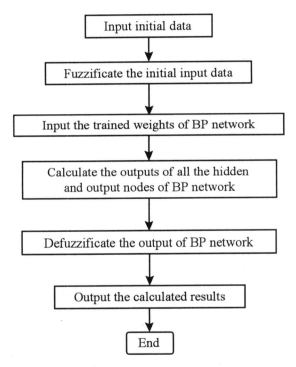

Fig. 10.9 Block diagram of prediction algorithm

Table 10.6   Simulation results

(1)   Work piece material: S50C(Hardness: 17HRC).

No.	Tool wear state	Direction of cut (X or Y)	Radial depth of cut (mm)	Axial depth of cut (mm)	Spindle revolution (rpm)	Table feed (mm/min)	Chatter possibi- lity(%)
1	New	X	0.1	4.0	5000	100	0.014
2	New	Y	0.3	2.0	6003	240	52.69
3	New	Y	0.2	2.0	10019	601	0.148
4	Medium	Y	0.2	2.0	4012	240	98.68

(2) Work piece material: NAK80(Hardness: 36HRC).

No.	Tool wear state	Direction of cut (X or Y)	Radial depth of cut (mm)	Axial depth of cut (mm)	Spindle revolution (rpm)	Table feed (mm/min)	Chatter possibi- lity(%)
1	Medium	X	0.1	4.0	6957	140	0.000
2	Old	Y	0.3	2.0	4997	52	99.21
3	New	Y	0.2	2.0	3000	180	96.83
4	Old	Y	0.3	2.0	6050	363	46.68

(3) Work piece material: SKD11(Hardness: 59HRC).

No.	Tool wear state	Direction of cut (X or Y)	Radial depth of cut (mm)	Axial depth of cut (mm)	Spindle revolution (rpm)	Table feed (mm/min)	Chatter possibi-lity(%)
1	Medium	Y	0.2	2.0	7025	421	0.000
2	New	Y	0.2	2.0	5005	300	0.013

10.5   Experimental Verification

Based on the same machining conditions and experimental setup in Section 2 further experiment is performed to validate the proposed method and the attained results are shown in Table 10.7, where "Yes", "No" and "Critical" respectively denote complete chatter, no chatter and possible chatter.

Table 10.7   Experimental verification

(1) Work piece material: S50C(Hardness: 17HRC)

No.	Tool wear state	Direction of cut (X or Y)	Radial depth of cut (mm)	Axial depth of cut (mm)	Spindle revolution (rpm)	Table feed (mm/min)	Chatter vibration
1	New	X	0.1	4	5000	100	No
2	New	Y	0.3	2	6003	240	Critical
3	New	Y	0.2	2	10019	601	No
4	Medium	Y	0.2	2	4012	240	Yes

(2) Work piece material: NAK80(Hardness: 36HRC).

No.	Tool wear state	Direction of cut (X or Y)	Radial depth of cut (mm)	Axial depth of cut (mm)	Spindle revolution (rpm)	Table feed (mm/min)	Chatter vibration
1	Medium	X	0.1	4	6957	140	No
2	Old	Y	0.3	2	4997	52	Critical
3	New	Y	0.2	2	3000	180	No
4	Old	Y	0.2	2	6050	363	Yes

(3)   Work piece material: SKD11(Hardness: 59HRC).

No.	Tool wear state	Direction of cut (X or Y)	Radial depth of cut (mm)	Axial depth of cut (mm)	Spindle revolution (rpm)	Table feed (mm/min)	Chatter vibration
1	Medium	X	0.2	2	7025	421	No
2	Old	Y	0.2	2	5005	300	No

Comparing the results shown Table 10.7 with those shown in Table 10.6, it is seen that the experimental results are quite consistent with the simulation results. Therefore, it is concluded that the proposed method is very effective to predict chatter.

10.6   Conclusions

This paper proposed a new approach for predicting chatter vibration in high-speed end milling operations by using a fuzzy neural network model. As the model proposed here is a comprehensive model, it can handle linguistic input parameters as well as numerical input ones. Some simulation results indicated that the simulation results entirely agreed with the experimental results. Therefore, it was seen that   milling chatter in practice was predicted. In further researches, other typical experiments should be conducted and more factors affecting milling chatter should be considered so that the system is more improved.

References

[1] Altintas, Y., and Chan, P.K,. "In-Process Detection and Suppress of Chatter in Milling", *Int. J. Mach. Tools Manufact.*, **32**, (3), pp.329-347, 1992.

[2] Altintas, Y., Budak, E., "Analytical Prediction of Stability Lobes in Milling", *Annals of the CIRP*, **44**, (1), pp.357-362, 1995.

[3] Beale, R., And Jackson, T., *Neural Computing: An Introduction*, Adam Hilger,1990.

[4] Ehmann, K. F., etc., "Machining Process Modeling: A Review", *Trans. ASME, J. Manufact. Sci. Eng.*, **119**, pp.655-663,1997.

[5] Kartalopoulos, S. V.,*Understanding Neural Networks and Fuzzy Logic: Basic Concepts and Applications*, IEEE Press, 1996.

[6] Lee, A. C., and Liu, C. S., "Analysis of Chatter Vibration in the End Milling Process", Int. J. Mach. Tools Manufact., **31**, (4), pp.471-479, 1991.

[7] Liao, Y.S., and Young, Y.C., "A New On-line Spindle Speed Regulation Strategy for Chatter Control", *Int. J. Mach. Tools Manufact.*, **36**, (5), pp. 651-660,1996.

[8] Minis, I., etc., "A New Theoretical Approach for the Prediction of Machine Tool Chatter in Milling", *Trans. ASME, J. Eng. Ind.*, **115**, pp. 1-8, 1993.

[9] Page, G. F., etc., *Application of Neural Networks to Modeling and Control*, Chapman & Hall,1993.

[10] Rumelhart, D. E., and McCleland, J. L., *Parallel Distributed Processing*, The MIT Press, 1986.

[11] Smith, S., and Tlusty, J., "Stabilizing Chatter by Automatic Spindle Speed Regulation", *Annals of the CIRP*, **41**,(1), pp. 433-436,1992.

[12] Smith, S., and Tlusty, J., "Current Trends in High-speed Machining", *Trans. ASME, J. Manufact. Sci. Eng.*,**119**, 664,1997.

[13] Tlusty, J., etc., "Basic Non-Linearity in Machining Chatter", *Annals of the CIRP*, **30**,(1), pp. 299-304,1981.

[14] Tlusty, J., "Dynamics of High-Speed Milling", *Trans. ASME, J. Eng. Ind.*, **108**, pp.59-67,1986.

[15] Tsai, M. D., "Prediction of Chatter Vibration by Means of a Model-Based Cutting Simulation System", *Annals of the CIRP*, **39**,(1), pp.447-450,1990.

Chapter 11

Fuzzy Logic and Neural Networks Approach – A Way to Improve Overall Performance of Integrated Heating Systems

Evgueniy Entchev

Canmet Energy Technology Centre

Abstract

The complexity of the novel integrated heating system's design requires a new control strategy that will not oppose the system functions while, at the same time, providing high efficiency, low emissions and optimal system performance. This paper will present a fuzzy logic control strategy that can be applied to integrated heating systems and a neural networks approach to hot water draw predictions. This approach differs from the conventional strategy since it takes into consideration a number of external and internal factors influencing the system's performance as well as the homeowner's distinct habits.

Keywords: heating systems, efficiency, controls, water draws, comfort

1.1 Introduction

The new and renovated buildings in Canada have half of the heating load in comparison to ten years ago. The low heating load is due to the advances in building technology such as low-emissivity/high efficiency windows, improved building envelope and high levels of insulation. This has challenged the heating industry to develop more efficient and sophisticated heating/cooling mechanical systems able to operate in an environment characterized by low heating loads, increased demand for improved indoor comfort and air quality, and high efficiency performance.

The recently developed novel heating system design integrates both space and water heating functions within a single energy generator (Fig. 1.1) sized to satisfy both space and water heating requirements.

Natural gas-fired high efficiency integrated systems can have seasonal efficiency over 90% while oil-fired systems perform in the range of 84-86%. Both systems could reduce hazardous emissions by more than 30% in relation to current conventional furnaces, heaters and boilers.

However, in practice, the realized efficiency is much less than expected. There are a number of reasons for reported low efficiency numbers and operational problems; these problems usually stem from flawed integration and a lack of adequate system control.

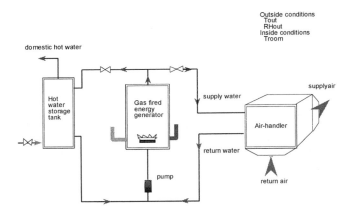

Fig. 1.1   Integrated Space/Water heating system.

1.2   Integrated Space and Water Heating Systems

Presently, most of the space and water heating requirements are met from separate pieces of equipment, each with their own energy generator. However, new homes are being built with increasingly low heating energy requirements so that the magnitudes of water and space heating loads are almost identical. This fact has opened a market for alternative approaches in supplying these two needs.

Integrated space and water heating systems (ISWHS) address these needs by combining the water and space heating supplies using one basic generator. The advantages include a lowering of overall capital cost, the elimination of multiple exhaust systems, an optimization of efficiency over a wide range of conditions, and a reduction of equipment footprint.

Integrated heating systems are appointed to satisfy two main requirements: a) to maintain an acceptable temperature level for hot tap water, and b) to supply the necessary space heating in accordance with varying outdoor conditions. The first requirement means that the temperature of supplied hot water should not drop below a certain minimum temperature during any part of the year. The second requirement postulates that, at all times, under any outdoor ambient conditions, the system must be able to deliver enough heat to compensate for all outside and internal influences on the building. Most of these influences could be compensated at the design stage while the rest should be corrected by the central and local control systems.

The main difference between heating systems and other energy systems' applications is that the heating system must perform in a stochastic environment defined by the changing weather conditions (outdoor temperature, wind velocity and direction, solar radiation, etc.), variable internal gains and occupants' distinct habits. On the other hand, the wide variety of factors influencing the constructional and thermal performance of the building shell introduce additional non-linearities and complications into the mathematical models.

1.3 Integrated system performance and control strategy

Most of the current integrated systems are equipped with powerful burners able to restore the system status in a very short time interval. Due to the new functions appointed to the ISWHS's energy generator, it tends to cycle more frequently with short on-time cycles; these cycles significantly decrease the overall system efficiency and produce unfriendly environmental pollutants. Presently, a large portion of the integrated heating/cooling appliances on the market are incorporating the old control strategy designed for single function generators. This strategy usually leads to keeping the storage-heating medium at an unnecessarily high temperature, causing increased stand-by heat losses. To avoid any complaints, the manufacturers usually oversize their equipment, which leads to frequent burner cycles that lower the efficiency and increase the pollutants. This design also fails to satisfy combined heating demands when they occur on cold winter days. The functional analysis showed that to improve the system efficiency and performance, a new innovative control strategy should be developed. The strategy should be able to control the system's modes of operation in conjunction with system heating capacity and external/internal conditions and influences. The system should be able to adjust its space heating output depending on the current status of room temperatures and ambient weather conditions. The domestic hot water availability should be a function of the homeowner usage pattern - both in magnitude and in time of day. The storage water-tank temperature settings should be continuously adjusted according to internal and external factors, so as to lower the stand-by heat losses, improve efficiencies and availability to satisfy all demands.

Recently, some of the manufacturers have introduced a priority control strategy that does not solve the above problems, but instead sacrifices one or more of the requirements. Existing controls usually apply one of the following strategies:

1. Start the burner if the tank water temperature drops below the tank aquastat deadband in order to restore the water temperature status in the tank, and to start the circulating water pump and blower motor when there is a demand for heat, as determined by the room thermostat. This type of control is cheap, simple and reliable, but may not always satisfy requirements.

2. Define a priority for hot water draw when both space heating and hot water draw demands occur at the same time.

The first type of control can lead to sub-optimal performance. It can cause the burner to operate more frequently as a separate device while its only function remains to maintain the water temperature in the generator at a level determined by the aquastat set point within the deadband. The operations of the circulation water pump and blower motor are similar, satisfying only the room thermostat setting.

The second strategy avoids some of the disadvantages of the first by giving priority to one demand. However, there can be a number of instances where a much longer-than-acceptable period without heating could occur, resulting in severe user dissatisfaction.

Advance warning or a prediction of upcoming energy usage patterns offers an opportunity to prepare the mechanical heating system to successfully meet the demands in an optimal structural and operational fashion. However, most of the existing systems have little or no anticipatory ability. Those larger commercial systems that do are based on a "black box approach" and are developed by simple or multiple regression. In most cases, the predictive models are steady-state linear approximations, dependent on a selected and limited number of variables. The results are a coarse approximation of the system performance, inaccurate predictions with less-than-optimal performance and higher emissions under many conditions.

The latest developments in Artificial Intelligence (AI) offer an opportunity for the development and commercialisation of applications involving Neural Networks and Fuzzy Logic techniques, which can yield better control, resulting in more efficient system performance with reduced greenhouse gas emissions.

1.4 Fuzzy Logic Control

A detailed examination of the design and operating environment shows that a new advanced control strategy should be able to explore the capabilities of new system devices such as modulating burners, variable speed blower motors, variable speed water pumps, etc. Such strategies should work towards improving the efficiency of energy use, reducing drafts and thermal stratification, while enhancing the thermal comfort and satisfying space and water heating demands throughout the house at all times.

The functional analysis for the new control strategy showed the following:

a) the system should be able to adjust its space heating output depending on the current status of room temperature and weather conditions;

b) the domestic hot water availability should be a function of the homeowner's usage patterns, both in magnitude and in time of day;

c) the tank aquastat setting should be capable of being continuously adjusted according to internal and external factors.

The developed fuzzy logic control strategy targets three of the heating systems' devices: the variable burner energy input rate, the air handler blower-motor operation and the water-storage tank aquastat settings.

The fuzzy logic burner strategy controls the energy input in conjunction with the current-storage-tank water temperature and room thermostat temperature differential. It minimizes the cycling and extends the operation length of each cycle and, as a result, increases the overall efficiency while dramatically lowering the emissions. The burner is a conventional two-stage burner and, despite the design limitations, the new control improves the burner efficiency, resulting in savings in the range of 3-5% and lowers the pollutant emissions by 10-15%.

The air-handler blower motor operation determines the heat utilization across the heating coil and the effectiveness of heat distribution around the house. The variable commutated programmable blower motor speed is controlled in relation with the outside temperature, room thermostat differential and mode of operation. By being aware of the status of the other system devices and the heating load, the optimal blower motor operation is set to enhance comfort while avoiding the overshooting and undershooting often seen with conventional control strategies. It is also reduces the temperature level required, and further increases efficiency.

Once the pattern of the house is established, the third loop manages the setting of the heat generator aquastat depending on the time of the day and the outside conditions. The variable aquastat settings improve the system performance by lowering the stand-by heat losses and adjusting the current water temperature according to the outdoor conditions and the occupants' usage pattern.

Subject to the environment and the occupant's habits, the developed overall fuzzy logic control strategy is able to set the system at optimal performance and efficiency mode, thus increasing its ability to satisfy the demands under a range of loads and requirements. The developed fuzzy logic approach to control the overall operation of the integrated heating system would result in improving system efficiency in the order of 8-10% and reduce pollutants for oil-fired systems by 25-30%.

1.5 Neural Networks for Predicting Building Usage Pattern

Knowledge of the upcoming hot water demands of the building offers the opportunity to prepare the heating /cooling system's mechanical systems in an optimal structural and operational manner in order to successfully meet the demand. Most of the current prediction techniques are based on the "black box" approach. In most cases, the predictive models are steady-state linear approximations, based on selected number of variables. The result is a coarse approximation of the system performance and can result in inaccurate predictions or less-than-optimal performance. Presently, predictive modelling is applied mainly to district heating systems. Predictive water supply temperature levels are based on weather files processing, compiled with the short-term predictive algorithms.

The applications of neural networks are, in general, possible in this part of the heating system where there is an established pattern for a certain period of time and the on-going processes have long-time constants. The prediction of the domestic hot water draw load would increase the comfort in the dwellings and would avoid the undesirable shortage of hot water during baths and/or other domestic activities. At the same time, it can optimize the mechanical system performance by preparing it in advance to meet the upcoming loads. Usually, every building has its own hot water draw schedule based on the occupants' water usage patterns. They vary, but could be differentiated by the type of the building (hotels, motels, hospitals, residential, commercial, etc.), time of day, day of the week and the season.

A neural net has been trained with hot water draw data files representing hot water draws of a three-bedroom house. The inputs were defined by month, day and hour. The output was the accumulative amount of hot water drawn every hour. The amount drawn has been presented as one following in the categories described by these linguistic terms: SDRAW - draw less than 15L, DRAW - draw between 16 - 40L and LDRAW - draw over 40L. The neural net was trained and, after 140 epochs, was able to repeat the test draw values with RMS error of 0.0012.

1.6 Conclusions

The proposed fuzzy logic strategy for controlling the operation of the integrated system with advance knowledge of the upcoming loads would enable optimal performance of the heating/cooling system's overall operation and would avoid the undesirable discomfort in the building while reducing the pollutant emissions. The neural network technique offers possibilities to prepare the system, in an optimal way, to meet the upcoming loads using historical data from the occupants' usage pattern and the building's thermal performance. The system is able to perform in a noisy, stochastic environment, recognizing the pattern in input data and producing the adequate outputs. The generated output values can be used as information parameters or as control signals to the heating system controller for further optimization of the heating system's operating conditions.

References

[1] Cox, E.; Integrating fuzzy Logic into Neural Nets, AI Expert, 1991.

[2] Cox E.; The Fuzzy Systems Handbook., Academic Press Ltd., London,1994.

[3] Entchev E.; Heating System Performance Predictions Using Neural Networks Approach., Combustion Canada, Ottawa,1996.

[4] Entchev, E., S. Hayden; Fuzzy Logic for Efficient Systems., Combustion Canada, Ottawa, 1996.

[5] Gheorghe, A.; Integrated Use of Neural Networks and Safety Assessment for Operational Safety, IAEA SM-321/38, Vienna, 1992.

[6] Grosberg, S.; Neural Networks and Natural Intelligence, MIT Press, Cambridge, MA, 1988.

[7] Holland, J.; Adaptation in Natural and Artificial Systems, MIT Press, Cambridge, MA, 1992.

[8] Jamshidi M.; at al., Fuzzy Logic and Control, Prentice Hall, Englewood Cliffs, NJ, 1993.

[9] Kosko B.; Neural Networks and Fuzzy Systems, a Dynamic Systems Approach to Machine Intelligence, Prentice Hall, Englewood Cliffs, NJ, 1992.

[10] Ogata K.; Modern Control Engineering, Prentice Hall, Englewood Cliffs, NJ, 1990.

[11] Roh, M. at al.; Power Prediction in Nuclear Power Plants Using a Backpropagation Learning Neural Network., Nuclear Technology 94,1991.

[12] Zadeh L.A., Fuzzy Sets and Applications: Selected Papers, John Wiley and Sons, New York, 1987.

Chapter 12

Application of Fuzzy Pattern Matching and Genetic Algorithms to Rotating Machinery Diagnosis

Jesús M. Fernández Salido[1] and Shuta Murakami[2]

[1] *Yaskawa Electric Corporation*
[2] *Kyushu Institute of Technology*

Abstract

This chapter shows how Fuzzy Pattern Matching techniques can be applied to the design of a knowledge-based system that can diagnose the most common faults of industrial rotating machinery through the evaluation of vibration data. The system is able to perform the tasks of Fault Detection, Fault Isolation and Fault Identification, and can handle the vagueness implicit in the diagnosis linguistic knowledge, as well as several sources for uncertainty that are generated during the vibration measurement process. Furthermore, a Genetic Algorithms-based module has also been included that, when enough fault data is available, has the ability to adapt some of the system's parameters in order to optimize its diagnosis performance.

Keywords : automatic diagnosis systems, knowledge-based systems, rotating machinery, predictive maintenance, vibration analysis, envelope analysis, power spectrum, cepstrum, unbalance, misalignment, outer race fault, inner race fault, ball fault, fuzzy decision making, weighted fuzzy pattern matching, genetic algorithms, fault detection, fault isolation, fault identification, fuzzy quantifiers, soft-AND operators, possibility measure, diagnosis sensibility, diagnosis robustness, symptom-fault sensibility.

12.1 Introduction

Unexpected failures of critical machinery can become an important economic burden for production in an industrial plant. This is the main reason why *Predictive Maintenance* programs have been widely implanted in industry during the last decades. With this approach, through continuous

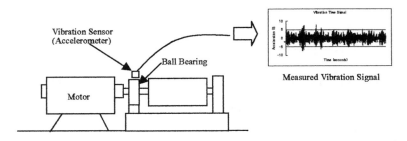

Fig. 12.1   Measurement of the Vibration Time Signal in a Motor's Ball Bearing

or periodic measurement and observation of certain properties of a machine during its normal operation mode, failures can be detected and diagnosed before they are fully developed, so that their correction can be planned ahead and carried out at the most convenient time.

Different Predictive Maintenance methods make use of oil analysis, infrared thermography, temperature and electric current control, as well as vibration and sound analysis. In the case of rotating machinery (such as industrial motors, pumps, fans or gearboxes), Vibration Analysis has become one of the the most widespread Predictive Maintenance techniques, as the vibration signals measured at critical points of a machine (for example, a ball bearing, as shown in Fig. 12.1) can produce a very rich information about the state of development of different possible faults [2; 22], like machine unbalance, axis misalignment, ball bearing and gear related faults, eccentricities or mechanical looseness. The measured vibration time signal will be submitted to an intensive signal processing in order to produce other signals (frequency spectrum, cepstrum, envelope spectrum) from which useful features for diagnosis can be obtained (Fig. 12.2 and Fig. 12.3). Due to the complexity and abundance of the features that can be extracted from these signals, it is still very difficult to implement a computational method that can automatically interpret the evolution of vibration data with a high degree of diagnosis accuracy.

The great development during the last years in different Artificial Intelligence techniques has resulted in an active research by several universities and specialized companies in their application to different industrial diagnosis methods. The traditional approach to technical diagnosis, Model-Based diagnosis, has been widely studied [6; 17] and can be implemented with

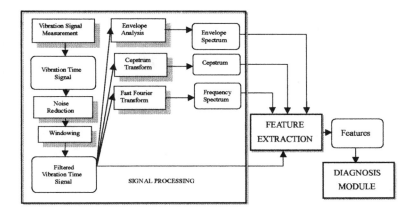

Fig. 12.2   Signal Processing and Feature Extraction of the Vibration Signal

good results when a mathematical model of the diagnosis object and its noise characteristics can be estimated. Lately, this type of analytical methods has been combined with Fuzzy Modeling [14], Fuzzy Inference and Possibility Matching [29] or Neuro-fuzzy Systems [1], which can be useful techniques in order to construct heuristic models. Modeling techniques, however, are not feasible for complex systems such as large industrial rotating machinery. In this case, their fault state can be determined from their vibration data, but it requires a considerable effort in human training. This has brought about an active research in the last years on the application of Expert Systems, Pattern Recognition using Neural Networks [16; 20], Fuzzy Clustering [15; 16], Rough Set theory [21] or Statistical Pattern Recognition for the automatic interpretation of vibration signals.

In a traditional expert system, a rules base is implemented containing the vibration analyst's basic knowledge about detection and isolation of the faults of interest. They can be effective for diagnosis of basic faults, but have limitations when machine-specific anomalies appear. Furthermore, the different sources for uncertainty and imprecision that the measurement and diagnosis process carries are not considered.

Neural Networks, and clustering techniques, on the other hand, are more tolerant towards imprecision, and can have the ability to detect fault patterns that are specific to a particular machine. However, for their implementation, a considerable amount of vibration data of the machine's

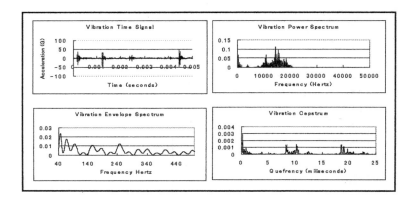

Fig. 12.3   Example of a Vibration Time Signal and Derived Signals

different fault states and non fault modes of operation is needed. Fault data is often scarce, specially of important and critical machinery, which is never let to function in an abnormal mode of operation.

In our case, *Fuzzy Pattern Matching* techniques [8; 23], with the necessary modifications, have been applied for diagnosis of five of the most usual faults that affect the industrial efficiency of general rotating machinery:

(1) Unbalance.
(2) Axis Misalignment.
(3) Fault in a ball bearing's outer race (ORF).
(4) Fault in a ball bearing's inner race (IRF).
(5) Fault in a ball bearing's rolling element (BF).

A Fuzzy Pattern Matching based approach has been adopted due to its effectiveness at dealing with several sources of uncertainty (due to noise and changes in the machine's load, rotating speed and measurement conditions) that are generated during the vibration signal measurement and feature extraction process. Furthermore, the Vibration Analysis expert's knowledge, often imprecise, can be easily implemented in the system using linguistic terms and in a flexible manner using fuzzy connectives.

The object of this research is the design of a Fuzzy Diagnosis method using Vibration Analysis data. Relevant features for diagnosis include different parameters estimated in the vibration time signal (kurtosis, skewness, crest factor ...), as well as peaks measured at certain frequencies in the signal's frequency spectrum, envelope spectrum or cepstrum. Among these frequencies of interest stand the rotating frequency and its harmonics, and certain frequencies (and its harmonics and side-bands) associated to the machine's ball bearing geometry (ORF frequency, IRF frequency and BF frequency).

This system should include general knowledge, implemented as linguistic rules patterns, about the development of the five faults under study in generic rotating machinery. It is intended to be used as a Decision Support Tool for the vibration expert, although it may be specially useful for the inexperienced technician.

The system's scope of application is extended to the most general kinds of rotating machinery and, being a knowledge-based system, previously measured fault data is not needed for its application to a particular machine. This advantage, however, also limits the system's diagnosis precision in comparison to other systems trained with fault data, like Neural Networks, that have the ability to detect specific fault patterns to a particular machine. For this reason, adaptation of the system's parameters in order to better reflect the fault characteristics of a certain machine has also been researched. In particular, the optimization power of Genetic Algorithms has been adopted for this purpose.

The results of this research are to be validated with a set of 24 samples of vibration acceleration signals measured in a test machine, that correspond to different fault and normal state cases.

12.2 Components of the Fuzzy Diagnosis System

In order to design an automatic diagnosis method, two important characteristics must be considered:

Sensibility : A sensible diagnosis system would be one that is able to detect very small faults.

Robustness : A diagnosis system is robust if it produces very few false alarms due to noise or changes in the measurement conditions.

Normally, it is difficult to design a very sensible and, at the same time, highly robust diagnosis system, and a compromise between both characteristics must be reached. This has been taken into consideration, while designing the three processes that a complete diagnosis system should be able to perform [17]:

(1) **Fault Detection:** noticing that something is wrong in the system.
(2) **Fault Isolation:** finding out the location of the fault.
(3) **Fault Identification:** measuring the size of the fault.

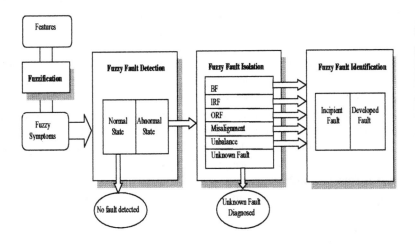

Fig. 12.4 Fuzzy Diagnosis Process

In Fig. 12.4, a sketch with the Fuzzy Diagnosis process proposed in this paper is shown. As it can be seen, in the first stage, crisp features extracted from the vibration time signal and derived signals, that have been previously been measured in the target machinery, are fuzzified (transformed into fuzzy symptoms), to take into account several factors for uncertainty produced in the measuring process. Through *Fuzzy Fault Detection*, it will be ascertained whether the machine has incurred into a fault state or is operating in normal conditions. If the machine is not working in its normal functioning state, the *Fuzzy Fault Isolation* process will try to establish the cause for abnormality. In case that the set of measured fuzzy symptoms match the pattern of one of the five kinds of faults that are being considered, *Fuzzy Fault Identification* has the task of evaluating whether the fault that has been detected is in an incipient or in a well developed state. The detection, isolation and identification processes have been designed using

Fuzzy Pattern Matching techniques. The following pages offer a detailed account of every one of these steps.

12.2.1 *Features Fuzzification*

Prior to diagnosis, every feature, F_j, measured in the vibration data, will be normalized, with respect to a reference value, F_{jref}:

$$S_j^* = \frac{F_j - F_{jref}}{F_{jref}} \tag{1}$$

F_{jref} can be obtained as the mean average of a set of samples of feature F_j, measured under nominal, no fault conditions. The resulting value, S_j^*, will be called a crisp symptom.

As an exception, some symptoms, like kurtosis or skewness, that are obtained as non-dimensional numbers will be interpreted better through their absolute values and do not need to be normalized.

In order to take into account the imprecision introduced in the measurement process, the crisp symptom S_j^* will be transformed into a fuzzy symptom S_j, defined by a triangular membership function, with height 1, and support $[S_j^* - a_j, S_j^* + a_j]$ (Fig. 12.5).

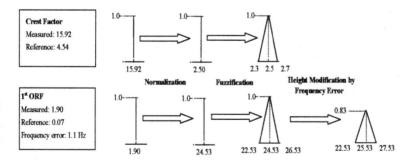

Fig. 12.5   Fuzzification of the Crest Factor and the 1st ORF Envelope Harmonic

a_j is a parameter that will normally be set by the expert for every symptom j. When enough experimental data is available, the value of a_j can also be defined in terms of the feature's standard deviation, σ_j, estimated under nominal, no fault conditions; for example, $a_j = \sigma_j/4$.

In this way, the parameter a_j is more sensibly defined to the specific characteristics of the target machinery.

For those features that consist of peak amplitudes measured at certain special frequencies (Rotating Frequency, ORF, IRF, BF, and its harmonics and side-bands) of the spectrum, cepstrum or envelope spectrum, another reason for uncertainty is introduced. Normally, due to changes in load and rotating speed and limitations in the spectrum resolution, the peak that is measured at the frequency of interest will not be found at the exact theoretical frequency, but at a nearby frequency . Therefore, an uncertainty is generated as to whether the peak being measured does really correspond to this frequency or has come up in the spectrum for another reason. In these cases, the absolute difference between the theoretic frequency at which a peak is expected to be found, and the real frequency at which it was found, shall be called *frequency error*. The uncertainty that the *frequency error* introduces shall be modeled as follows: for a spectral feature, if the *frequency error* is greater than a certain threshold, the height of the fuzzy symptom representing the feature shall be decreased proportionally. This effect is represented in Fig. 12.5 as well.

12.2.2 *Fuzzy Fault Detection*

The Fuzzy Fault Detection process will try to establish whether the system is working in an abnormal state. To reach this conclusion, the set of measured fuzzy symptoms will be compared with a linguistic pattern that describes how some of the symptoms are expected to behave when the machine is suffering some kind of anomaly. If the values of the measured set of symptoms agree with the requirements described in the pattern, a fault will be considered detected. Otherwise, the machine is judged to be functioning in good condition. Standard matching techniques have been applied to fault detection of rotating machinery as they were defined by D. Dubois and H. Prade [8].

12.2.2.1 *Basic Fuzzy Pattern Matching*

A pattern consists of a set of n_r requirements, that is, n_r assumptions expressed in linguistic terms that some of the symptoms should meet in order to consider a fault detected. The structure of the requirements used in the detection pattern can be written as:

Req. j : [NOT] $((S_k$ is $A_a)$ [OR $((S_l$ is $A_b)]$ [OR $((S_m$ is $A_c)] \ldots)$ (2)

Example: (*Vibration Level (5-40 KHz)* is *increased*) OR
(*Vibration Level (0-1 KHz)* is *increased*)

As it can be noted, every requirement j is a collection of several conditions of the form S_k is A_a, linked by fuzzy OR connectives, and modified by an optional NOT operator. Here, S_k represents a fuzzy symptom, while A_a stands for the fuzzy attribute that describes this symptom.

The composition of the detection pattern that was adopted for this research can be examined in Fig. 12.6.

Detection Pattern

Req. 1:   NOT (Kurtosis is *normal*)

Req. 2:   NOT (Frequency Mean is *normal*)

Req. 3:   (Vibration Level   (10 Hz - 5 KHz) is *increased*) OR
           (Vibration Level   (5KHz – 40 KHz) is *increased*)

Fig. 12.6   Detection Pattern

In Fig. 12.7, the possibility distributions of the basic set of fuzzy attributes that are used in the system are shown. These correspond to the *Normal, Slightly Increased, Quite Increased, Markedly Increased, Slightly Decreased, Quite Decreased* and *Markedly Decreased* attributes. Variations and combinations of these basic attributes bring about new ones, like *Increased, Normal* or *Slightly Changed*, or *At least Quite Increased* (Figs. 12.7 (b) (c) and (d)).

Once again, the parameters b_j, c_j, d_j, e_j, f_j, g_j, h_j, and i_j , that define these possibility distributions (Fig. 12.7), must be specified by the expert. Their values have a high dependency on the machine's type and rotating speed, and should be chosen carefully. Alternatively, if enough experimental data is available for the machine in nominal state of operation, these parameters can be defined in terms of σ_j (standard deviation of feature j

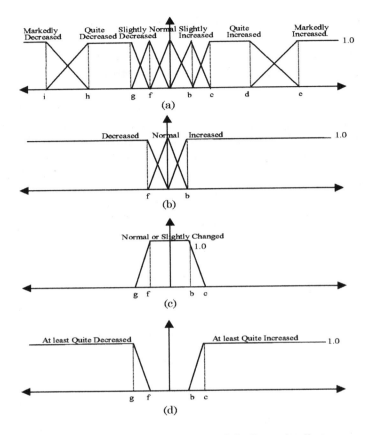

Fig. 12.7   Possibility Distribution of the Fuzzy Attributes

estimated under nominal conditions). For instance, they may be estimated as:

$$b_j = 2\sigma_j \qquad c_j = 4\sigma_j \qquad d_j = 8\sigma_j \qquad e_j = 15\sigma_j$$
$$f_j = -2\sigma_j \qquad g_j = -4\sigma_j \qquad h_j = -8\sigma_j \qquad i_j = -15\sigma_j \tag{3}$$

Let S_1', S_2',..., S_n', be the fuzzy symptoms measured from the vibration data. A matching index that indicates the degree of compatibility of the set of n measured symptoms with the detection conditions stated in the pattern's requirements can be obtained with the following procedure:

(i) For every condition, S_k is A_a, of each requirement j, the corresponding *measured* fuzzy symptom, S'_k, is matched with the possibility distribution of attribute A_a using a *possibility measure*, $\Pi(S'_k, A_a) = sup(S'_k \cap A_a)$. This matching index shall be represented as Π_k, and expresses the degree of compatibility of the measured value of symptom S'_k with the linguistic attribute A_a.

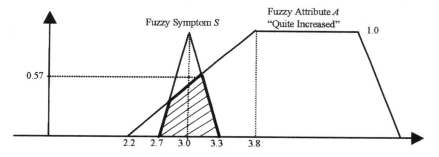

Fig. 12.8   Matching of Symptom S' and Attribute A using a Possibility Measure

In Fig. 12.8, matching of fuzzy symptom S' (taking, in this case, the value of fuzzy number $\hat{3}$) with the fuzzy attribute, A, "Quite Increased", is represented. Here, the fuzzy set $(S' \cap A)$ is the lined area in the graph. The matching index, $sup(S' \cap A)$, takes a value of 0.57.

In Fig. 12.9, a real case is presented. The peak corresponding to the 2nd harmonic of the ORF frequency obtained from the envelope spectrum (taking an approximate value, after normalization, of 1500), is matched with the Fuzzy Attribute "Markedly Increased". The resulting matching index is 1.

(ii) A matching index for every requirement j is calculated by aggregating the matching indexes of every condition, using fuzzy OR operators. For this purpose, the logical OR operator (maximum) has been chosen. Hence,

$$\Pi_{Req_j} = \Pi_k \vee \Pi_l \vee \Pi_m \vee \ldots \qquad (4)$$

Additionally, the indexes for negated requirements will be comple-

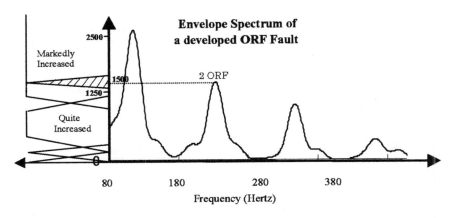

Fig. 12.9   Matching of the 2ⁿd ORF Envelope Harmonic with "Markedly Increased"

mented: $\Pi_{Req_j} = 1 - (\Pi_k \lor \Pi_l \lor \Pi_m \lor \ldots)$.

(iii) All the requirements' matching indexes should be combined as well, so as to obtain a global matching index for the detection pattern, Π_{Det}, that expresses the possibilty that a fault may have been detected, according to the measured symptoms. This is done by aggregating all the requirements' matching indexes using fuzzy AND operators,

$$\Pi_{Det} = \Pi_{Req\,1} \; AND \; \Pi_{Req\,2} \; AND \; \Pi_{Req\,n_r}, \tag{5}$$

where n_r stands for the number of requirements in the detection pattern. If the value calculated for Π_{Det} is greater than 0.5, a fault will be considered detected.

As the final value attained by the detection index will depend greatly on the nature of the AND operator, some considerations must be taken for its selection. The most simple choice would be the logical AND (minimum), that would result in a robust detection system, which would trigger few false detection alarms. The evident drawback of this selection is the decrease of sensibility, diminishing the diagnosis system's ability to detect small faults in which not all of the requirements may be fully met. For this reason, and as suggested by E. Sánchez [24], a Soft-AND operator, whose behaviour lies between a standard AND operator and an average operator, has been adopted. In particular, Salton's Soft-AND operator is the one to be applied:

$$x \text{ AND } y = 1 - \left[\frac{(1-x)^p + (1-y)^p}{2} \right]^{\frac{1}{p}} \quad (p \in [1, \infty)) \quad (6)$$

Although this operator is not associative, its formula can easily be extended for aggregating more than two indexes. It may be noted, as well, that high values of the p parameter approximate the output of this operator to those of the logical AND, and should be adopted when a robust detection strategy is preferred. Low values of p, on the other hand, make the operator closer to a mean operator ($x \text{ AND } y = (x+y)/2$), which is desirable for a sensible system.

12.2.3 *Fuzzy Fault Isolation*

If fault detection has been positive, fault isolation will try to establish which fault has triggered the detection alarm. In this step, as well, previously measured fuzzy symptoms will be matched with five patterns, one for each fault under study, that describe the expected behavior of the symptoms under the appearance of everyone of these faults. The fault pattern that attains the highest matching index will be considered the detected fault. If, on the other hand, the winning matching index is not higher than a certain threshold, an unknown fault will be diagnosed. At first sight, this pattern matching approach seems quite similar to Fuzzy Fault Detection. However, some innovations have been added to the process that need to be explained in detail. In particular, fuzzy quantified requirements have been incorporated, and weights that take into account the concept of symptom-fault sensibility have also been attached to these requirements. These innovations can be seen in the representative Fault Isolation Pattern shown in Fig. 12.10.

12.2.3.1 *Fuzzy Quantified Requirements*

In Fuzzy Fault Isolation, the symptoms that appear in the pattern that describes a fault will be those with the highest capacity to discriminate this

<table>
<tr><td colspan="2">Outer Race Fault Isolation Pattern</td></tr>
</table>

Req. 1:	(Kurtosis is *increased*)	**weight:** 0.8
Req. 2:	(Crest Factor is *at least quite increased*)	OR
	(K-Factor is *at least quite increased*)	**weight:** 0.7
Req. 3:	(Frequency Mean is *increased*)	**weight:** 0.7
Req. 4:	(*At least some* ORF Envelope Harmonics are *increased*)	**weight:** 1.0
Req. 5:	(*At least some* ORF Envelope Harmonics and Side-bands are *increased*)	**weight:** 0.8
Req. 6:	(*At least some* ORF Spectrum Harmonics are *increased*)	**weight:** 0.5
Req. 7:	(*At least some* ORF Spectrum Harmonics and Side-bands are *increased*)	**weight:** 0.5
Req. 8:	(*At least some* ORF Cepstrum Harmonics are *at least quite increased*)	**weight:** 0.4
Req. 9:	(Maximum Envelope Harmonic corresponds to ORF and is *increased*)	**weight:** 0.9

Fig. 12.10   ORF Fault Isolation Pattern

fault against the others. For instance, if a bearing related fault comes out, it will manifest itself very distinctly through peaks at certain frequencies and their harmonics and side-bands of the power spectrum, cepstrum or envelope spectrum.

Normally, it is not possible to know *a priori* which of the harmonics and side-bands may experiment the highest increases, so the Vibration Analysis expert may use diagnosis rules of thumb like "if many ORF envelope spectrum harmonics' peaks are markedly increased, then a ORF bearing fault has appeared", or "if some low frequency IRF power spectrum harmonics and side-bands are increased, we may have an incipient IRF fault". Including this kind of requirements in the patterns that describe these faults, requires the use of *Fuzzy Quantifiers* [33], that can handle, in a mathematical way, linguistic concepts that refer to a subjective quantity, such as *many, a few, at least some, a large fraction*, etc. Therefore, besides requirements with the same structure as those of Fuzzy Fault Detection (described by Eq. 2), Fault Isolation patterns may include requirements with quantified conditions, of the following type:

$$\textbf{Req. } j : [\text{NOT}] ((Q_k S_k \text{ are } A_a) [\text{OR} ((Q_l S_l \text{ are } A_b)] \ldots) \tag{7}$$

Example: (**At least some** *Rotating Frequency Harmonics (Spectrum)* are *markedly increased*)

In the research described in this chapter, only Fuzzy Quantifiers of the second kind, as specified by L.A. Zadeh [33], have been used. They refer to a relative count, and are expressed as fuzzy numbers defined in the interval (0,1). The Fuzzy Quantifiers that have been initially considered are *some*, *at least some*, *a few*, and *many*. Their membership functions are as shown in Fig.12.11 .

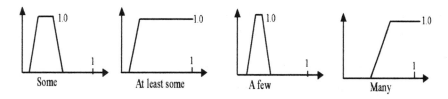

Fig. 12.11   Membership Functions of several Fuzzy Quantifiers

The matching process of a quantified condition can be explained using the example shown in Fig. 12.12. Here, the quantified proposition "**At least some** ORF envelope harmonics are markedly increased" is matched with the set of fuzzy symptoms that represent the ORF envelope harmonics that have been measured. In the example, the first 4 harmonics of the ORF frequency were obtained, giving normalized crisp values of 8, 5, 11 and 7.5. Each of the crisp symptoms is fuzzified and compared with the attribute *markedly increased*. The resulting matching indexes are 0.5, 0, 1 and 0.375. At this point, it is necessary to determine the relative count of ORF harmonics that are markedly increased, that is, the proportion of markedly increased ORF harmonics among all the measured ORF harmonics. To do this, the cardinality (number of elements) of a fuzzy set must be established. As Zadeh suggests [33], a simple way to extend the concept of cardinality to a fuzzy set **F** is to form the Σ-*count* (pronounced *sigma-count*), which is the arithmetic sum of the grades of membership in **F** :

$$\Sigma Count(F) = \sum_i u_i \quad i = 1, \ldots, n, \tag{8}$$

where u_i is the degree of membership of each element of **F**. Using this formula, the cardinality of the fuzzy set of markedly increased ORF harmonics in the example turns out to be 1.875. On the other hand, the cardinality of the crisp set of ORF harmonics for this case is, evidently, 4. Therefore, the proportion of markedly increased ORF harmonics is $1.875/4 = 0.46875$. As it is shown in the figure, if this result is matched, as a fuzzy singleton, against the fuzzy number *At least some*, a matching index, Π, for the condition is obtained. For this example, $\Pi=1$. Like in the case of not quantified requirements, the matching indexes of the quantified conditions are combined with other conditions of the requirements using logical OR operators, and may also be modified by an optional NOT operator. This result will be the requirement's matching index.

12.2.3.2   Weighted Requirements

Another important notion that is introduced in Fuzzy Fault Isolation is the concept of symptom-fault sensibility. If a numerical estimation of the size of both symptom k (S_k) and fault i (F_i) can be obtained, the sensibility (T_{ik}) of symptom k towards the appearance of fault i can be defined as De Miguel suggests [6; 7]:

$$T_{ik} = \frac{\Delta S_k}{\Delta F_i} \frac{F_i}{S_k} \tag{9}$$

This is a non-dimensional factor that expresses the degree in which symptom k increases in value, when fault i appears. Symptom-Fault sensibility values can be hard to estimate, as normally the fault's degree of development (F_i) cannot be measured directly. Moreover, they may adopt different values at different stages of fault development. For these reasons, representative values of symptom-fault sensibilities will normally be assigned by the expert.

If symptom k is very sensible towards fault i (high value for (T_{ik})), it will be a better discriminating indicator of the presence of fault i than a less sensible symptom. On the other hand, very low values of (T_{ik}) indicate that the symptom is highly insensible to the development of fault i. This can be useful in Fuzzy Fault Isolation, for determining which requirements of the Isolation pattern that describes fault i have more importance in order to distinct this fault from others.

For the pattern that describes fault i, every requirement j is usually designed so as to only include symptoms that have similar symptom-fault sensibilities for this fault. Hence, a sensibility value, T_{ik}, can be assigned to every requirement j, that could be either a representative value or the

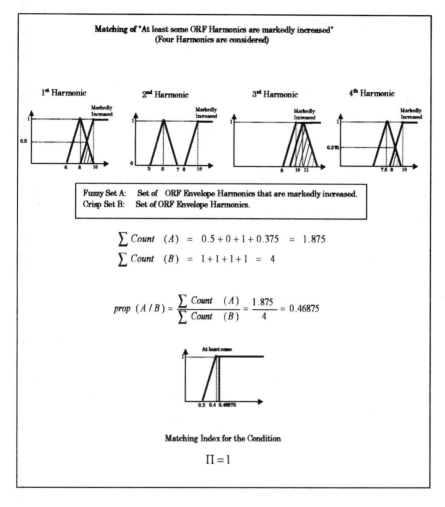

Fig. 12.12   Example of a quantified requirement matching

average of the sensibilities (for fault i) of the symptoms included in it. This requirement's sensibility value can be used to attach to every requirement j a weight, that expresses its importance for diagnosis of fault i, in the following way:

(1) For not negated requirements:

$$w_{ij} = \frac{T_{ij}}{\max T_{ij}} \qquad (10)$$

(2) For negated requirements (modified by a fuzzy NOT operator):

$$w_{ij} = 1 - \frac{T_{ij}}{\max T_{ij}} \qquad (11)$$

Here, $i = 1, \ldots, n_f$, and $j, l = 1, \ldots, n_r$. n_f represents the number of faults, while n_r stands for the number of requirements.

12.2.3.3 *Aggregation of Weighted Requirements' Indexes*

After the measured symptoms were matched with the requirements of the pattern that describes fault i, a set of n_r matching indexes were obtained. To every one of them, a weight w_{ij} is attached that expresses its importance for isolation of fault i:

$$
\begin{array}{cccc}
\Pi^i_{Req\,1} & \Pi^i_{Req\,2} & \cdots & \Pi^i_{Req\,n_r} \\
w_{i1} & w_{i2} & \cdots & w_{in_r}
\end{array}
\quad (w_{ij} \in (0,1)) \qquad (12)
$$

In order to obtain the matching index for the isolation of fault i, Π^i_{Iso}, the requirements' partial indexes must be ANDed, taking into account their respective weights.

The most simple approach to do this would be to apply Yager's general class of weighted AND operation [31]:

$$\Pi^i_{Iso} = (\Pi^i_{Req\,1} \text{ OR}(1 - w_{i1}) \text{ AND } \ldots (\Pi^i_{Req\,n_r} \text{ OR}(1 - w_{in_r}), \qquad (13)$$

where the most straightforward choice for the OR and AND operators, would be the maximum and minimum. Although this weighted AND operation is more sensible for fault isolation than the non weighted minimum, it will still not be able to isolate efficiently small faults in which sensible symptoms for that fault (and, consequently, with high weights) may not be fully developed. Taking this into account, the weighted version of Salton's Soft-AND operator [24] has been selected for aggregation of the requirements' matching indexes:

$$(x, w_x)\text{AND}(y, w_y) = 1 - \left[\frac{w_x^p(1-x)^p + w_y^p(1-y)^p}{(w_x^p + w_y^p)}\right]^{\frac{1}{p}} (p \in [1, \infty)), \quad (14)$$

where w_x stands for the weight associated to variable x, and w_y is variable y's weight.

As with the non-weighted case, the operator is not associative, but can be easily extended for more than two indexes. Here, as well, the value of parameter p will determine the nature of the operator. High values of p will enhance the diagnosis's robustness, while low values of this parameter will favor its sensibility.

12.2.4 *Fuzzy Fault Identification*

The objective of the Fuzzy Fault Identification process is to offer an estimation, in linguistic terms, of the size of the fault that has been detected and diagnosed. In this research, only two degrees of development for a fault have been considered: incipient faults and fully developed faults. For this reason, 10 patterns have been designed that describe the five faults under study in their incipient and fully developed states. However, only the patterns of the fault that has been diagnosed by the Fuzzy Fault Isolation process will be considered at the time of diagnosis. As there is no need to discriminate one fault against the others in this step, no weights have been attached to the Identification patterns' requirements. Therefore, the Identification patterns will have basically the same structure as the Detection patterns, although some fuzzy quantified requirements have also been included (Fig. 12.13). Once again, Salton's non weighted Soft-AND operator (Eq. 6) will be used to combine the identification requirements' matching indexes into a global index: Π_{Ide}^I, for the incipient fault pattern, or Π_{Ide}^D, for the developed fault pattern. The patron that obtained the highest matching index will be considered the fault's size.

12.3 Diagnosis Optimization using Genetic Algorithms

Genetic Algorithms (GA) are search algorithms based on the mechanics of natural selection, genetics and evolution. [18; 30] Since they were introduced by professor John Holland and his students in the mid 70's they have

---

ORF Fault Identification Pattern (Developed)

Req. 1:   (Kurtosis is *markedly increased*)

Req. 2:   (Maximum 10 peaks mean is *markedly increased*)

Req. 3:   (Clearance Factor is *markedly increased*)

Req. 4:   (*Many* ORF Envelope Harmonics are *markedly increased*)

Fig. 12.13   ORF Fault Identification Pattern (Developed)

found a wide field of application for optimization problems in areas such as image processing, systems optimization and control. They owe their success to their ability to optimize highly non-linear functions, and their *implicit parallel nature*, which rends them more efficient than other approaches at avoiding local optima. Genetic Algorithms can be very efficient tools for any problem in which the values of the parameters to be optimized can be codified in binary form, and an evaluation function can be established that measures the adequacy of these values in the problem. Although GA were already introduced by Toyota *et al* in the generation of new vibroacoustical symptoms through the arithmetic combination of basic symptoms [28], their application to Vibration Analysis remains a relatively unexplored field. In our case, GA have been applied for optimization of the Isolation Pattern weights. These weights have been set initially by the expert, considering the expected sensibilities of the symptoms in every requirement to the fault that they try to isolate. They reflect a part of the expert's general knowledge about the development of the faults under study in a certain type of rotating machine. As the results in Sec. 12.4 will prove, Fault Isolation using expert-set weights can give rather satisfactory Isolation results. However, as every machine functions under different types of load and operating conditions, the evolution of certain vibration symptoms in the presence of a fault may have different characteristics in two machines, even if they are of the same type. Therefore, as vibration data is being accumulated for a certain machine, and knowledge about the actual values of the different symptom-fault sensibilities for this machine is being gained, the diagnosis results can be improved by adjusting the weights' values for the isolation patterns.

Automatic tuning of these weights using standard mathematical optimization techniques can be quite difficult, specially when the number of available vibration samples is high. The reason for this is that the isolation matching indexes for every set of weights must be obtained computationally and, due to the application of fuzzy connectives, they have a non-linear nature. This is a situation in which good results can be obtained using the optimization power of Genetic Algorithms, without much programming effort.

Hence, if enough fault and non fault vibration data about the machine to be diagnosed is available, it is proposed that the search capabilities of Genetic Algorithms be used to adapt the different Isolation Patterns' sets of weights. This can be a very flexible approach. For a machine of which not enough case studies have been obtained, the isolation weights may initially be set by the expert. As different faults are being produced during the machine's operational life, this fault data may be used by the GA optimization algorithm to replace the original weights with others that better reflect the sensibilities of this specific machine.

12.3.1 *Implementation of the GA-based Optimization*

A canonical genetic algorithm has been applied for the optimization process, in which the only genetic operators considered were *reproduction, crossover*, and *mutation*, with no other special features. The resulting algorithm is used to adapt the weights of every isolation pattern independently, and has been provided with the following characteristics.

12.3.1.1 *GA General Parameters*

(1) n (population size): 1000 chromosomes.
(2) p_c (crossover probability): 0.6.
(3) p_m (mutation probability): 0.001
(4) G (Generation gap): 1.
(5) *Reproduction Operator*: Remainder Stochastic Sampling with Replacement.

12.3.1.2 *Pattern Weights Codification*

Every Isolation Pattern weight may attain a value included in the $[0, 1]$ interval. They are digitized in 10 bit string genes. Thus, each weight may have $2^{10} = 1024$ different values.

Every chromosome is the union of the genes representing every weight for the pattern. The size of every chromosome depends on the type of pattern being optimized: while the ORF, IRF and BF patterns, with 9 weights, are represented by chromosomes with 9 genes (90 bit strings), the unbalance pattern has 5 gene chromosomes (50 bit strings), and to the misalignment pattern corresponds with 6 gene chromosomes (60 bit strings).

12.3.1.3   *Evaluation Function*

Two types of evaluation functions have been considered for the optimization of every fault, i:

(i) Let's call N_i^F the number of vibration samples measured in the target machine, in which fault i has been diagnosed, while N_i^{NF} shall represent the number of samples that have been measured in this machine without fault i (samples corresponding to other faults and good condition state). As a whole, there are N_i samples, where $N_i = N_i^F + N_i^{NF}$.

Let's also represent by $N_i^{CC}(W_i)$, the number of samples that the diagnosis system correctly classifies from all of the N_i samples, using the set of weights W_i for the i isolation pattern. An obvious evaluation function to be maximized by the GA could be:

$$F_i^1(W_i) = \frac{N_i^{CC}(W_i)}{N_i} \tag{15}$$

That is, the ratio of correctly classified samples is to be maximized through optimization of the W_i set of weights. This can be interpreted as a "rough tuning" of the weights.

(ii) We may also want to make the matching indexes of samples in which fault i appears as high as possible, and those of non-fault cases, as low as possible. The following evaluation function may be maximized to do this "fine tuning":

$$F_i^2(W_i) = \frac{\sum_{k=1}^{N_i^F} \Pi_i^k(W_i) + \sum_{l=1}^{N_i^{NF}} (1 - \Pi_l^k(W_i))}{N_i} \tag{16}$$

Here, $\Pi_i^k(W_i)$ represents the matching index of the fuzzy symptoms extracted from sample k, with the the isolation pattern (using the weights set W_i) that represents fault i. This matching index is calculated by the fuzzy diagnosis system.

In practice, the best results are obtained by using a combination of both evaluation functions:

$$F_I = \alpha F_i^1 + (1 - \alpha)F_i^2 \qquad (17)$$

Heuristically, results improved with $\alpha > 0.5$. In particular, the results presented in this chapter have been obtained with α set to 0.8.

12.4   Application Results

The Fuzzy Diagnosis method proposed in this chapter has been tested with a set of 24 vibration samples provided by the German diagnosis company Prüftechnik A.G. The signal samples have been obtained in a test rotating machine, in which several faults have been provoked. The machine functions with cylindrical bearings of the type SKF 1204 EKTN9/C3. This sample set has been measured under different rotating speed modes. Therefore, satisfactory diagnosis results would prove the method's flexibility toward changes in the measurement conditions. The type of fault of every signal, and the test machine's rotating speed under which it was obtained are shown in Table 12.1.

Preliminary diagnosis results for this set of samples, in which the isolation weights are set by the expert, are presented in Table 12.2. For these results, the p parameter for Salton's aggregation operator has been set to 7 for the detection pattern; 10, for the isolation patterns; and 3 for the identification patterns. Also, in the Isolation step, the highest matching index must surpass a threshold of 0.3 in order to consider that fault isolated. If this requirement is not met, an unknown fault will be diagnosed.

Diagnosis results for this same data set, after the isolation weights were tuned by the GA, are those corresponding to Table 12.3. The p parameter is set with the same values as above, and the Genetic Algorithm's parameters are given the values that were set in Sec. 12.3.1.1. The algorithm converged after approximately 1600 generations.

As the results in Tables 12.2 and 12.3, and those of the comparative graph Fig. 12.4 prove, the GA optimization method has improved signifi-

Table 12.1   Sample Signals' type and Rotating Speed

#	FAULT TYPE	RPM	#	FAULT TYPE	RPM
1	Incipient ORF	750	13	Incipient IRF	750
2	Incipient ORF	750	14	Incipient IRF	750
3	Incipient ORF	1470	15	Incipient IRF	1470
4	Incipient ORF	1470	16	Incipient IRF	1470
5	Developed ORF	750	17	No Fault	1470
6	Developed ORF	750	18	No Fault	750
7	Developed ORF	1470	19	Developed Misalignment	3000
8	Developed ORF	1470	20	Developed Unbalance	1470
9	Developed IRF	1470	21	Dev. Misalignment & Unbal.	1050
10	Developed IRF	1470	22	Dev. Misalignment & Unbal.	1470
11	Developed IRF	750	23	Developed Misalignment	750
12	Developed IRF	750	24	Developed Unbalance	1470

cantly the diagnosis performance. Although the preliminary results (Table 12.2 were still quite satisfactory, the system had difficulty with the diagnosis of IRF Faults. This was due to the fact that some important symptoms for the diagnosis of this fault were assumed to evolve in a similar fashion as in the presence of ORF faults. The GA optimization procedure was able to correct this misconception.

A limitation in the diagnosis system seems to be in the inability to diagnose several faults that are present at the same time in the machine, as cases in # 21 and # 22. A more profound diagnosis study would require the construction of patterns that reflect several fault possibilities occurring at the same time.

12.5   Concluding Remarks

Fuzzy Pattern Matching, with the inclusion of quantified requirements and requirement weights that reflect symptom-fault sensibilities, can be a very appropriate approach to reproduce the Vibration Analysis expert's knowledge. The expert's know-how and experiences can be described in qualitative terms, resulting in a simple interface with the diagnosis system's user.

As the test application results prove, a diagnosis method using this technique can be applied with a good degree of reliability to general industrial

Table 12.2 Diagnosis Results (Isolation Weights set by the Expert)

#	Results / Fault Type	DETECTION			ISOLATION						IDENTIFICATION		
		Abnormal State	Normal State	R	ORF	IRF	BF	Unbal.	Misal.	R	Developed State	Incipient State	R
1	Incipient ORF	1.0	0.0	✔	0.602	0.126	0.008	0.001	0.0	✔	0.075	0.659	✔
2	Incipient ORF	1.0	0.0	✔	0.687	0.126	0.007	0.001	0.0	✔	0.090	0.885	✔
3	Incipient ORF	0.676	0.324	✔	0.578	0.107	0.007	0.001	0.054	✔	0.091	1.0	✔
4	Incipient ORF	0.545	0.455	✔	0.553	0.149	0.007	0.001	0.0	✔	0.0	0.370	✔
5	Developed ORF	1.0	0.0	✔	0.523	0.125	0.007	0.001	0.0	✔	0.695	0.188	✔
6	Developed ORF	1.0	0.0	✔	0.761	0.126	0.010	0.0	0.054	✔	1.0	0.091	✔
7	Developed ORF	1.0	0.0	✔	0.887	0.149	0.010	0.001	0.054	✔	1.0	0.091	✔
8	Developed ORF	1.0	0.0	✔	0.517	0.149	0.007	0.127	0.054	✔	1.0	0.091	✔
9	Developed IRF	1.0	0.0	✔	0.043	0.142	0.007	0.115	0.016	--	0.781	0.081	✔
10	Developed IRF	1.0	0.0	✔	0.105	0.243	0.007	0.001	0.054	--	0.0	1.0	✗
11	Developed IRF	1.0	0.0	✔	0.142	1.0	0.007	0.001	0.0	✔	1.0	0.0.	✔
12	Developed IRF	1.0	0.0	✔	0.142	0.243	0.007	0.0	0.054	--	1.0	0.0	✔
13	Incipient IRF	0.857	0.143	✔	0.010	0.189	0.007	0.001	0.0	--	0.104	0.677	✔
14	Incipient IRF	0.514	0.486	✔	0.010	0.570	0.010	0.001	0.054	✔	0.076	0.799	✔
15	Incipient IRF	1.0	0.0	✔	0.018	0.243	0.007	0.017	0.174	--	0.126	0.306	✔
16	Incipient IRF	1.0	0.0	✔	0.018	0.621	0.007	0.001	0.0	✔	0.126	0.399	✔
17	No Fault	0.410	0.590	✔									
18	No Fault	0.430	0.570	✔									
19	Developed Misalignment	0.978	0.022	✔	0.024	0.008	0.087	0.030	0.668	✔	1.0	0.0	✔
20	Developed Unbalance	1.0	0.0	✔	0.162	0.0	0.0	1.0	0.082	✔	1.0	0.0	✔
21	Developed Unb. & Mis.	1.0	0.0	✔	0.108	0.170	0.002	0.030	0.543	✔	1.0	0.0	✔
22	Developed Unb. & Mis.	1.0	0.0	✔	0.163	0.0	0.0	1.0	0.039	✔	1.0	0.0	✔
23	Developed Misalignment	1.0	0.0	✔	0.108	0.211	0.002	0.030	1.0	✔	1.0	0.0	✔
24	Developed Unbalance	1.0	0.0	✔	0.201	0.003	0.0	1.0	0.016	✔	1.0	0.0	✔

✔ : Correct Classification   ✗ : Incorrect Classification   — : Highest Matching Index is too low

Table 12.3   Diagnosis Results (Isolation Weights set by the Genetic Algorithm)

#	Results / Fault Type	DETECTION			ISOLATION						IDENTIFICATION		
		Abnormal State	Normal State	R	ORF	IRF	BF	Unbal.	Misal.	R	Developed State	Incipient State	R
1	Incipient ORF	1.0	0.0	✔	0.608	0.019	0.008	0.0	0.0	✔	0.075	0.659	✔
2	Incipient ORF	1.0	0.0	✔	0.695	0.019	0.007	0.0	0.0	✔	0.090	0.885	✔
3	Incipient ORF	0.676	0.324	✔	0.603	0.019	0.007	0.0	0.066	✔	0.091	1.0	✔
4	Incipient ORF	0.545	0.455	✔	0.598	0.02	0.007	0.0	0.0	✔	0.0	0.370	✔
5	Developed ORF	1.0	0.0	✔	0.530	0.019	0.007	0.0	0.0	✔	0.695	0.188	✔
6	Developed ORF	1.0	0.0	✔	0.765	0.019	0.01	0.0	0.0	✔	1.0	0.091	✔
7	Developed ORF	1.0	0.0	✔	0.889	0.020	0.010	0.001	0.054	✔	1.0	0.091	✔
8	Developed ORF	1.0	0.0	✔	1.0	0.020	0.007	0.130	0.0	✔	1.0	0.091	✔
9	Developed IRF	1.0	0.0	✔	0.145	0.020	0.007	0.115	0.016	✘	0.781	0.081	✔
10	Developed IRF	1.0	0.0	✔	0.060	0.994	0.007	0.0	0.066	✔	0.0	1.0	✘
11	Developed IRF	1.0	0.0	✔	0.060	1.0	0.007	0.0	0.0	✔	1.0	0.0 .	✔
12	Developed IRF	1.0	0.0	✔	0.060	1.0	0.007	0.0	0.0	✔	1.0	0.0	✔
13	Incipient IRF	0.857	0.143	✔	0.029	0.449	0.007	0.0	0.0	✔	0.104	0.677	✔
14	Incipient IRF	0.514	0.486	✔	0.029	1.0	0.010	0.0	0.0	✔	0.076	0.799	✔
15	Incipient IRF	1.0	0.0	✔	0.029	1.0	0.007	0.016	0.066	✔	0.126	0.306	✔
16	Incipient IRF	1.0	0.0	✔	0.029	1.0	0.007	0.0	0.0	✔	0.126	0.399	✔
17	No Fault	0.410	0.590	✔									
18	No Fault	0.430	0.570	✔									
19	Developed Misalignment	0.978	0.022	✔	0.073	0. 0	0.087	0.027	1.0	✔	1.0	0.0	✔
20	Developed Unbalance	1.0	0.0	✔	0.126	0.0	0.0	1.0	0.066	✔	1.0	0.0	✔
21	Developed Unb. & Mis.	1.0	0.0	✔	0.023	0.156	0.002	0.027	1.0	✔	1.0	0.0	✔
22	Developed Unb. & Mis.	1.0	0.0	✔	0.126	0.0	0.0	1.0	0.066	✔	1.0	0.0	✔
23	Developed Misalignment	1.0	0.0	✔	0.023	0.157	0.002	0.027	1.0	✔	1.0	0.0	✔
24	Developed Unbalance	1.0	0.0	✔	0.126	0.0	0.0	1.0	0.066	✔	1.0	0.0	✔

✔: Correct Classification   ✘ : Incorrect Classification   − : Highest Matching Index is too low

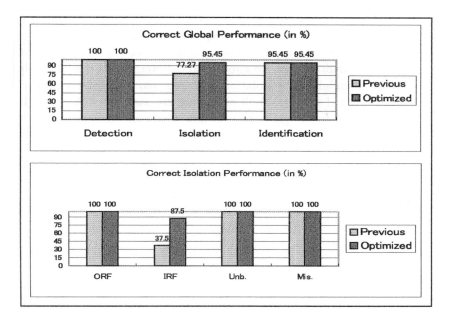

Fig. 12.14   Comparative Diagnosis Performance

rotating machinery. In addition, if enough vibration data for the fault states under study of a specific machine is available, it can be used to increase the system's diagnosis performance for this machine, with the use of Genetic Algorithms. With this, the diagnosis system can adapt its parameters to the special characteristics of a particular machine. As a consequence, the range of application of the proposed system becomes more flexible.

Finally, several future lines of investigation are also suggested:

(i) The diagnosis knowledge included in the current diagnosis patterns can be revised and extended in order to obtain more precise results. Moreover, new patterns may be included that describe other common rotating machinery faults, like eccentricities, mechanical looseness or resonance, not considered in the original scope of this research.

(ii) Failure situations in which several faults occur at the same time can also be described by new patterns.

(iii) Evolutionary symptoms may be added to the diagnosis patterns as well. This means that diagnosis would not only consider the state of a symptom at a certain moment, but also its past history.

(iv) GA based diagnosis performance optimization may not just be limited to adaptation of Isolation Patterns' weights. If the knowledge base containing the Isolation Patterns' requirements is properly codified and sufficient fault cases data are available, GA could also be applied to the generation of new requirements that better describe the faults of a specific machine.

Acknowledgements

The authors want to express their gratitude to Prüftechnik A. G., for providing the vibration data necessary for this research.

References

[1] M. Ayoubi and R. Isermann, "Neuro-Fuzzy Systems for Diagnosis", Fuzzy Sets and Systems, Vol. 89, p. 289, 1997.

[2] A. Barkov, N. Barkova and J. Mitchell, "Condition Assessment and Life Prediction of Rolling Element Bearings –Part 1", Sound & Vibration, June Issue, p. 10, 1995. (http://www.inteltek.com/ref.htm).

[3] A. Barkov, N. Barkova and J. Mitchell "Condition Assessment and Life Prediction of Rolling Element Bearings –Part 2", Sound & Vibration, September Issue, p. 10, 1995. (http://www.inteltek.com/ref.htm).

[4] D. Barschdorf, "Artificial Intelligence: Diagnostic Expert Systems, Fuzzy Logic and Neural Networks", Proceedings of the 8th International IMEKO Symposium on Technical Diagnostics, p. 46, Dresden, Germany, 1995.

[5] M. Y. Chow, Methodologies of Using Neural Networks and Fuzzy Logic for Motor Incipient Fault Detection, World Scientific, Singapore, 1997.

[6] L. J. De Miguel, Automatic Fault Diagnosis based on Parity Equations, Doctor Thesis, School of Industrial Engineers, University of Valladolid, Spain, 1994. (In Spanish).

[7] L. J. De Miguel, J. Fernández, and J. R. Perán, "Applying Fuzzy Logic to Rotating Machinery Diagnosis", Proceedings of the 4th International Conference on Soft Computing IIZUKA' 96, Iizuka, Japan, 1996.

[8] D. Dubois, H. Prade, and C. Testemale, "Fuzzy Weighted Pattern Matching", Fuzzy Sets and Systems, Vol 28, p. 313, 1988.

[9] J. Fernández, Predictive Maintenance System based on Vibrations Analysis, Graduation Thesis, School of Industrial Engineers, University of Valladolid, Spain, 1994. (In Spanish).

[10] J. Fernández, Design of a Diagnosis System for Rotating Machinery using Fuzzy Pattern Matching and Genetic Algorithms, Master Thesis, Kyushu Institute of Technology, Japan, 1988.

[11] J. Fernández and S. Murakami, "Fault Diagnosis of Rotating Machinery through Fuzzy Pattern Matching", Proceedings of the 3rd Asian Fuzzy Systems Symposyum AFSS'98, p. 203, Kyungnam, Korea, 1998.

[12] J. Fernández and S. Murakami, "Performance Optimization of a Fuzzy Diagnosis System for Rotating Machinery using Genetic Algorithms", Proceedings of the 5th International Conference on Soft Computing and Information/Intelligent Systems IIZUKA' 98, p. 259, Iizuka, Japan, 1998.

[13] P. M. Frank, "Application of Fuzzy Logic to Process Supervision and Plant Diagnosis", Proceedings of IFAC SafeProcess'94, p. 531, Espoo, Finland, 1994.

[14] P. M. Frank and T. Marcu "Fuzzy Techniques in Fault Detection, Isolation and Diagnosis", Fuzzy Logic Control -Advances in Applications, p. 135, edited by H. B. Verbruggen and R. Babuska, World Scientific, Singapore, 1999.

[15] B. Geropp, S. Schneider and A. Seeliger, "Automatic Diagnosis of Antifriction Bearings using Vibration Analysis and Fuzzy-Logic", Proceedings of COMADEM 97, Helsinki, Finland, 1997.

[16] B. Geropp, "Artificial Neural Networks and Fuzzy Logic used for Reliable Machine Diagnosis", Proceedings of Safeprocess 97, Hull, UK, 1997.

[17] J. Gertler, "Survey of Model-Based Failure Detection and Isolation in Complex Plants", IEEE Control Systems Magazine, December Issue, p. 3, 1988.

[18] H. Holland, Adaptation in Neural and Artificial Systems, University of Michigan Press, 1975.

[19] A. Kempkes, P. Burgwinkel, and B. Geropp, "Pattern Recognition with Fuzzy-Logic for Diagnosis of Antifriction Bearings", Proceedings of EU-FIT'95, Aachen, Germany, 1995.

[20] C. Kirkham and T. Harris, "A Hybrid Neural Network System for Generic Bearing Fault Detection", Proceedings of COMADEM 97, Helsinki, Finland, 1997.

[21] R. Nowicki, R. Slowinski and J. Stefanowski, "Evaluation of Vibroacoustic Diagnostic Symptoms by means of the Rough Set Theory", Computers in Industry, Vol. 20, p. 141, 1992.

[22] J. T. Renwick and P. E. Babson, "Vibration Analysis –A Proven Technique as a Predictive Maintenance Tool", IEEE Transactions on Industry Applications, Vol. 21, 2, p. 324, 1985.

[23] E. Sanchez, "Medical Applications with Fuzzy Sets", Fuzzy Sets Theory and Applications, p. 331, edited by A. Jones *et al*, D. Reidel Publishing Company, 1986.

[24] E. Sanchez, "Importance in Knowledge Systems", Information Systems, Vol. 14, p. 455, 1989.

[25] C. Stegmann, U. Suedmersen, A. Vortriede and W. Reimche, "Diagnostic Methods for Rotating Machinery", IMEKO Symposium on Technical Diagnostics, p. 299, Dresden, Germany, 1992.

[26] T. Toyota, Diagnosis Methods for Rotating Machinery, Japanese Society for Plant Maintenance, 1990. (In Japanese).

[27] T. Toyota, Signal Processing Methods for Rotating Machinery, Japanese Society for Plant Maintenance, 1996. (In Japanese).

[28] T. Toyota, P. Chen and M. Nasu, "Symptom Parameters of Self-Reorganization for Failure Diagnosis by Genetic Algorithms", Proceedings of the 4th International Conference on Soft Computing IIZUKA' 96, p. 502, Iizuka, Japan, 1996.

[29] M. Ulieru and R. Isermann, "Design of a Fuzzy-Logic based Diagnostic Model for Technical Processes", Fuzzy Sets and Systems, Vol. 58, p. 249, 1993.

[30] D. Whitley, A Genetic Algorithm Tutorial, Technical Report, Computers Science Department, Colorado State University, 1990. (http://landau.mines.edu/samizdat/ga_tutorial/).

[31] R. R. Yager, "A note on weighted queries in information retrieval systems", Journal of the American Society of Information Sciences, Vol. 38, p. 23, 1987.

[32] L. A. Zadeh "Fuzzy Sets as a Basis for a Theory of Possibility", Fuzzy Sets and Systems, Vol. 1, p. 3, 1978.

[33] L. A. Zadeh "A Computational Approach to Fuzzy Quantifiers in Natural Languages", Computers and Mathematics, Vol. 9, p. 149, 1983.

Chapter 13

Design and Tuning a Neurofuzzy Power System Stabiliser Using Genetic Algorithms

Ali Afzalian[1], and Derek A. Linkens[2]

[1] *Power and Water Institute of Technology, Iran*
[2] *University of Sheffield*

Abstract

The problem of selecting and tuning the parameters of a neurofuzzy Power System Stabiliser (PSS) using genetic algorithms is discussed in this paper. The neurofuzzy controller is implemented as a multilayer perceptron, in which the weights are fuzzy membership functions. The optimal values of the parameters of the if-part and the then-part membership functions have been found during the learning method by applying an appropriate fitness function based on the rotor speed deviations. The overall system has been tested on a simulation model in different operating conditions and improved responses have been achieved.

Keywords: Neurofuzzy Control, Fuzzy Logic, Genetic Algorithms, and Power System Stabiliser.

13.1 Introduction

Genetic algorithms (GA) are search methods rooted in the mechanisms of natural selection and natural genetics. They use a computationally simulated version of survival of the fittest and act on a set of strings (chromosomes). Genetic algorithms are iterative procedures that maintain populations of candidate solutions to optimise a fitness function. The fitness function, which is an evaluation function in a search problem, can be nonlinear and discontinuous. Genetic algorithms are not based on gradient descent search and they can avoid local minima problems. They search large spaces effectively without the need for derivative information of the objective function. They have been applied to several classes of optimisation and search problems, with impressive results. A survey on the applications of hybrid systems containing fuzzy logic, neural networks and genetic algorithms in control systems can be found in [1].

Fuzzy logic and evolutionary algorithms have been profitably combined and applied to real world problems. Karr [2] used a GA to vary some parameters of a fuzzy rule base which stabilised an inverted pendulum. Hashiyama [3] used a GA to determine some of the parameters of a fuzzy controller in a car suspension control system. They achieved about 8.15% improvement in the performance index by applying an improved GA which finds the best widths and centres of the triangular membership functions for the inputs and outputs of the fuzzy controller. The real power of the GAs lies in their ability to completely design controllers from scratch, when little is known about the nature of the controller.

Some efforts have been made in recent years to use a combined architecture of neural networks and fuzzy logic in a PSS. Sharaf and Lie [4] used a neural network in parallel with a conventional PSS and used a fuzzy logic gain scheduler to compare and to scale the output of neural networks and conventional PSS. The neural networks was trained using off-line for different disturbances and fault conditions. The fuzzy output scaling depict the possible relative sharing between the conventional and neural networks-based PSS. Another scheme for using both fuzzy logic and neural networks as a PSS was reported in [5]. To alleviate the dependence of the fuzzy control on the operating condition and the faults, the fuzzy logic system parameters were adjusted using a neural network A power system stabiliser based on an ANFIS model is reported in [6]. The ANFIS model was trained using a self-optimising pole shifting adaptive PSS as the training data set. In fact, the neurofuzzy model was trained to mimic the behaviour of an available working PSS. A neurofuzzy power system stabiliser based on a fuzzy perceptron was developed in [7, 8].

In many problems dealing with adjusting the parameters of a control system, a desired system output or a state trajectory is available, while the controller output rather than the plant output is needed for supervised learning processes in neural networks based controllers. In this study the desired PSS output is not available, but a performance index can be defined based on one of the system outputs, i.e. the changes in the rotor speed of the synchronous generator. This performance index is used in the GA to find the optimal values for the neurofuzzy controller.

The current paper presents the application of a GA to determine the optimal parameters for the neurofuzzy controller discussed in [7], and its applications as a power system stabiliser. The structure of a multilayer fuzzy perceptron which is used as the neurofuzzy controller is described in section 13.2, in section 13.3, GAs are used to find the parameters of the proposed neurofuzzy PSS.

13.2 Neurofuzzy Control Systems

A fuzzy controller can be combined with neural networks via various methods, to yield a neurofuzzy control system [9, 10]. The linguistic information can be used to identify the structure of a fuzzy controller and then the numerical information is used to adjust the neural network parameters such that the neurofuzzy controller can produce the desired action more accurately. A fuzzy logic system (FLS) can be implemented via a multilayer perceptron structure which is called a Fuzzy Perceptron (FP) [11]. In a FP, weights are modelled as fuzzy membership functions (fuzzy weights) and the neurones' activation functions are defined according to the t-norm and t-conorms functions used in the fuzzy inference system (Figure 1). The intention of this model is to interpret the neural network architecture in the form of linguistic rules and to use prior knowledge base about the system in the learning process, so that the learning does not have to start from scratch. The designers and operators of a system are interested in using all of their knowledge about the system to control it. The black-box behaviour of neural networks prevents us from knowing and understanding what is happening inside the network and what the physical meanings of the network parameters and their changes are. Employing FP as the controller is an attempt to tackle this problem. The parameters of the FP are actually the parameters of the if-part and then-part membership functions (MFs) and obviously are meaningful and have physical interpretations. After the learning process, the new parameters can be interpreted as physical knowledge about the system. They may confirm our previous knowledge about the system, or may even provide some new knowledge. In the latter case the learning procedure is acting as knowledge elicitation.

Figure 1: A multiplayer fuzzy perceptron with two inputs and one output.

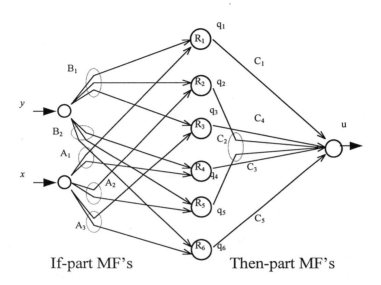

If-part MF's　　　　　　Then-part MF's

A hierarchical design and adjusting procedure for control systems using fuzzy perceptrons has been developed in this study. In the first design level, the experts' knowledge is used to predefine the rules and MFs. The second level starts with selecting the parameters of the fuzzy rules using a GA based on some desired objective functions. In the final level of the design procedure, the controller performance can be optimised by employing off-line supervised learning such as back propagation, using the parameters from the GA process as the initial weights. The resulting fuzzy rules can then be transferred to the system knowledge base. Using GAs to select the parameters of the neurofuzzy controller is discussed here and applying the neural network-based learning methods will be reported in future.

13.2.1. The Structure of a Multilayer Fuzzy Perceptron

A fuzzy perceptron has the architecture of a normal multilayer perceptron, but the weights are modelled as fuzzy sets and the activation and output functions are changed accordingly. A 3-layer fuzzy perceptron with two inputs: x and y, six hidden neurones, and one output u is shown in Figure 1. Each connection between the input layer and the hidden layer is labelled with a linguistic term. These fuzzy weights are the MFs of the if-part of the fuzzy inference system, i.e. $\mu_{A_1}(x)$, $\mu_{A_2}(x)$, $\mu_{A_3}(x)$, $\mu_{B_1}(y)$ and $\mu_{B_2}(y)$ with following descriptions:

$$\mu_{A_i}(x) = G(\eta_{A_i}, \sigma_{A_i}); \ i = 1, 2, 3$$
$$\mu_{B_j}(y) = G(\eta_{B_j}, \sigma_{B_j}); \ j = 1, 2 \tag{1}$$

where, $G(\eta, \sigma)$ is a Gaussian function with two parameters, η and σ;

$$G(\eta, \sigma) = e^{-(x-\eta)^2 / 2\sigma^2} \tag{2}$$

Each unit in the hidden layer is associated with one rule in the knowledge base. Each connection between the hidden units and the output unit is labelled with a linguistic term, C_k, $k=1, 2, ..., 5$, which has a Gaussian MF. They represent the MFs of the then-part of the fuzzy inference system.

$$\mu_{C_k}(u) = G(\eta_{C_k}, \sigma_{C_k}), \ k = 1, 2, ..., 5 \tag{3}$$

Connections coming from the same input and having identical labels bear the same fuzzy weight at all time. These connections are called *linked connections*. This condition guarantees identical fuzzy weights for identical linguistic terms during the learning process. Each hidden unit represents a fuzzy if-then rule. Considering the rules and using the Larsen's product inference method [12] for fuzzy implication, i.e. $\mu_{A \to B}(x_0, y) = \mu_A(x_0) \cdot \mu_B(y)$, and by interpreting "else" in the fuzzy rules as union ($\cup$), the consequence C' is defined as:

$$C' = (x \text{ and } y) \circ [(A_1 \text{ and } B_1 \rightarrow C_1) \cup \cdots \cup (A_2 \text{ and } B_3 \rightarrow C_5)] \tag{4}$$
$$= [(x \circ A_1 \rightarrow C_1) \cap (y \circ B_1 \rightarrow C_1)] \cup \cdots \cup [(x \circ A_2 \rightarrow C_5) \cap (y \circ B_3 \rightarrow C_5)]$$

where $\circ$ denotes max-product composition of fuzzy sets. When x and y are singletons x_0 and y_0 respectively, the consequence output, C' is given as:

$$\mu_{C'}(u) = [\mu_{A_1}(x_0) \cdot \mu_{B_1}(y_0) \cdot \mu_{C_1}(u)] \vee \cdots \vee [\mu_{A_3}(x_0) \cdot \mu_{B_2}(y_0) \cdot \mu_{C_5}(u)]. \tag{5}$$

The output of hidden units, $\mathbf{Q}$ is:

$$\mathbf{Q} = \mathbf{M}_A(x_0)\,\mathbf{M}_B(y_0), \tag{6}$$

where, $\mathbf{M}_A(x_0)$ and $\mathbf{M}_B(y_0)$ are vectors of fuzzy MFs over the fuzzy inputs x and y respectively, and $\mathbf{Q}$ is a vector of outputs of the hidden units:

$$\mathbf{M}_A(x_0) = [\mu_{A_1}\ \mu_{A_2}\ \mu_{A_3}\ \mu_{A_1}\ \mu_{A_2}\ \mu_{A_3}]'(x_0).$$
$$\mathbf{M}_B(y_0) = [\mu_{B_1}\ \mu_{B_1}\ \mu_{B_1}\ \mu_{B_2}\ \mu_{B_2}\ \mu_{B_2}](y_0) \tag{7}$$
$$\mathbf{Q} = [q_1\ q_2\ q_3\ q_4\ q_5\ q_6]'$$

Thus the membership function of the controller output is given in (8) by using the *max* operator as a *t-conorm*:

$$\mu_{C'}(u) = \max(q_1 \mu_{C_1}(u), q_2 \mu_{C_2}(u), q_3 \mu_{C_4}(u), q_4 \mu_{C_3}(u), q_5 \mu_{C_2}(u), q_6 \mu_{C_5}(u)) \tag{8}$$

Figure 2 illustrates the membership function of the fuzzy output of the neurofuzzy controller. The flow chart of the neurofuzzy controller and the way it generates its output is shown in Figure 3.

13.2.2 Defuzzification Approaches

To obtain a singleton u_0 which is a representative point for the resulting fuzzy set C', the centre of gravity method is used in the output unit. So the defuzzified controller output is:

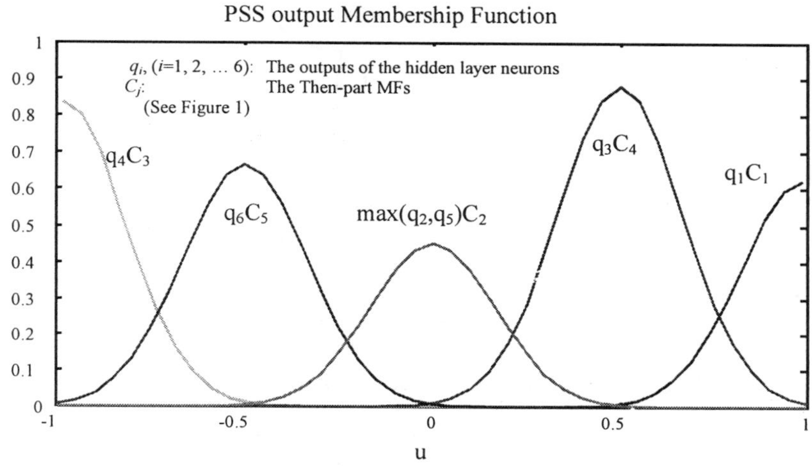

PSS output Membership Function

Figure 2: The neurofuzzy controller output membership function.

function elsewhere on the universe of discourse U. This approach is called *centre average defuzzifier* in the literature [13]. In that method the defuzzified output is given by (10) in discrete form.

$$u_0 = \frac{\sum\limits_{i,j} u_i q_j}{\sum\limits_{j} q_j} \qquad (10)$$

where, u_i is the centre of $\mu_{C_i}(u)$ and q_i is the output of ith neurone in the hidden layer. In equation (10), only one point of each then-part membership functions contributing in the output is used, and the other information in the MFs has no effect on the defuzzified output.

In this study a more accurate method is developed to evaluate (9). The output universe of discourse U, is divided into n equal intervals and the numerator and denominator integrands are written in discrete form over these intervals. As a result, more information in the output fuzzy set is used for the defuzzification process:

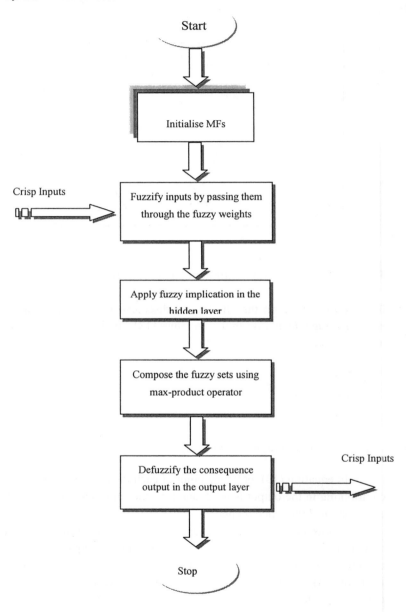

Figure 3: Flow chart of the neurofuzzy controller program.

$$u_0 = \frac{\sum_k u_k \mu_{C'}(u_k)}{\sum_k \mu_{C'}(u_k)}, \; k = 0, 1, 2, ..., n \qquad (11)$$

In equation (11), the number of intervals n, is a design parameter. As n increases, the defuzzification accuracy increases, as well as the computation burden. So, choosing n is a trade-off between getting a more accurate result and assuming more computation time. The widths and centres of the if-part and then-part MFs are the adjustable parameters which can be adapted using learning algorithms in neural networks or other search optimisation methods.

13.3 Genetic Algorithms for Adjusting the Neurofuzzy Controller

Figure 4 illustrates the block diagram of a control system with a GA adjusted neurofuzzy controller. The fuzzy perceptron has two inputs: x and y, six hidden neurones, and one output u. Each connection between an input layer and a hidden layer is labelled with a linguistic term. These fuzzy weights are the MFs of the if-part and then-part of the fuzzy inference. Each MF is introduced as a Gaussian function $G(\eta, \sigma)$ with two parameters; the centre of the function η, and its standard deviation σ which represents the width of the function. The changes in these parameters bring changes in the fuzzy sets of the controller inference engine and eventually change the performance of the behaviour of the control system. In this section a GA is used to find the optimal values of the MFs' parameters. There are three stages in optimising a neurofuzzy controller by GAs, including choosing the coding method, selecting and applying an appropriate fitness function, and processing the genetic operations.

13.3.1 Coding

The coding operation in genetic algorithms is a binary mapping or other format, which converts the fuzzy inference parameters into a row of binary values called a string or chromosome. The most commonly used representation in GAs is the binary coding although other representations can be used, e.g. integer, real valued etc. Since most problems in GAs are represented as a string of parameters, the solution can also be implemented as a fixed length vector. This vector is converted into a binary string by allocating each parameter a fixed number of bits, and concatenating the resulting binary numbers into one long string. The search process will operate on this encoding of the parameters rather than the parameters themselves. Each individual in a population contains the parameters of the MFs of the neurofuzzy controller and thus represents a hypothetical knowledge base for the fuzzy logic system. Grey coding is used here for encoding the controller's parameters. It is argued in the literature that genetic operations on grey codes will tend to be less disruptive as grey code values are more stable against the changing of a single bit [14, 15].

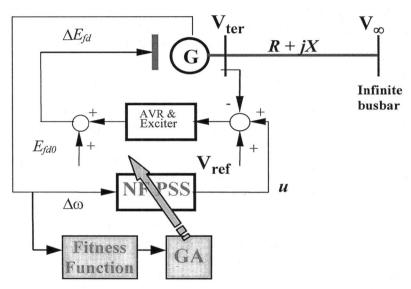

Figure 4: Genetic Algorithm for off-line learning of the parameters of a neurofuzzy PSS in a power system

13.3.2 Evaluation of Solutions

Each genotype in a population is a hypothetical knowledge-base of the neurofuzzy controller. The process of evaluating these knowledge-bases consists of applying each to a simulation model of the problem, and returning an assessment value according to an appropriate object function which is called the fitness function in GA literature. The object function is based on an output error of the controlled plant model. The sum of errors is then directly related to the individual fitness. This fitness is then used to generate new individuals in the next population through GA operators.

13.3.3 Population Size and Initialisation

The choice of an appropriate population size is an important decision to be taken in all GA implementations. When the population size is too small the GA will usually converge quickly and in many cases to a sub-optimal solution due to inadequate information in the population. On the other hand, too large populations will take a very long time to evaluate and in addition will result in slow progression toward the final solution. Therefore, when the GA computation is time consuming and computationally expensive, there is usually a need to trade off between the requirement for a large information capacity in the population and the desire to produce a solution within a limited amount of time. Typically, a population is composed of between 30 and 100 individuals. In the current study, population sizes between 30 and 40, with a string length of typically 180 bits have been used to find the optimal parameters of a neurofuzzy controller. An initial population is randomly created in the beginning of the GA process, considering the population size and the number of variables. Each variable is encoded by a 20 bit Grey code.

13.3.4 Applying GA Operators

After coding and initialising the population, the GA operators i.e. section, crossover and mutation can be applied to the individuals in the population. Selection is the process of determining the number of times, or trials, a particular individual is chosen for reproduction and, thus, the number of offspring that an individual will produce. The roulette wheel mechanism, which is a stochastic sampling method, is used to probabilistically select individuals based on some measure of their performance.

Crossover is the basic GA operator for producing new chromosomes. Like its counterpart in nature, crossover produces new individuals that have some of both parents' genetic material. Generally, crossover draws only on the information present in the solutions of the current population in generating new solutions for evaluation. The single-point crossover routine has been used in this study. It is performed with probability of 0.7 and the individuals in the population are ordered such that individuals in odd numbered positions are crossed with the individuals in the adjacent even numbered position. Mutation may now be applied to the reproduced offspring.

A *mutation* operator which arbitrarily alters one or more components of a selected structure, provides the means for introducing new information into the population. The presence of mutation ensures that the probability of reaching any point in the search space is never zero. In GAs, mutation is randomly applied with low probability, typically in the range of 0.001 and 0.01. Here this probability is $P_m=0.7/(N_{var}*Preci)=0.0039$, where, $N_{var}=9$ denotes the number of variables and $Preci=20$ is the number of bits in the Grey coded variable.

Once a new population has been produced through selection and recombination processes from the old population, the fitness of the individuals in the new population can be determined. If the number of individuals produced by recombination is less than the size of the original population, then the difference between the new and old population sizes is termed a generation gap. To maintain the size of the original population, the new individuals have to be inserted into the old population. A generation gap of 2 individuals has been used here. Therefore, the offspring must be reinserted into the current population. When selecting which members of the old population should be replaced, the obvious strategy is to replace the least fit members deterministically. Fitness-based reinsertion replaces the least fit members of the old population with the individuals resulting from the recombination process. The objective function values of the old population are thus required as inputs of reinsertion.

13.3.5 Termination of the Learning Process

Since GAs are stochastic search methods, it is difficult to formally specify convergence criteria. A common practice is to finish the GA after a prespecified number of generations and then test the quality of the best member of the population against the problem. If no acceptable solutions are found, the GA process may be restarted with different parameters. Here, the GA has been terminated after maximum number of generations, which is chosen to be between 150 and 200. Satisfactory values for the fuzzy MF have been achieved after the GA termination.

13.4 Adjusting the parameters of a Neurofuzzy Power System Stabiliser

This section demonstrates the application of GA to finding the optimal rules of a neurofuzzy power system stabiliser (NF PSS). The model of the power system consists of a single machine connected to an infinite bus bar through a transmission line. The nonlinear differential equations used for modelling the generator and the transfer functions of the governor, conventional PSS and the AVR & exciter block and also the systems parameters can be found in the Appendix.

13.4.1 Initialising the NFPSS

A 3-layer fuzzy perceptron with two inputs: x and y, six hidden neurones, and one output u has been used as a PSS in the electrical power system. The connections between input, hidden and output layers are labelled with linguistic terms. These fuzzy weights are the membership functions of the fuzzy inference engine. Figure 5 shows the table of the initial rules describing the function of the power system stabiliser. The controller inputs, x and y, are amplitude R and the angle θ respectively in the generator phase plane (Figure 6). By using a conversion from Cartesian co-ordination to polar co-ordination on the PSS inputs, we can reduce the number of required rules for describing the performance of the neurofuzzy PSS. Therefore, a knowledge base with 2 inputs and 6 rules has been employed that includes a total of 10 fuzzy MFs (including: 3, 2, and 5 MFs for the inputs R, θ and the output u respectively). The valid intervals of parameters for the MFs can be defined, using elementary knowledge about the system. The GA is then used to find the optimal values for these parameters for a given performance strategy.

Figure 5:Fuzzy rules for a power System Stabiliser

Figure 6: The phase plane of the synchronous generator

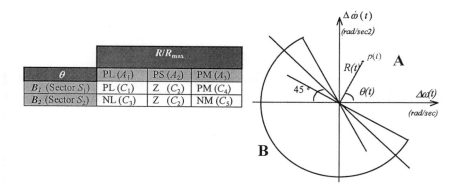

	R/R_{max}		
θ	PL (A_1)	PS (A_2)	PM (A_3)
B_1 (Sector S_1)	PL (C_1)	Z (C_2)	PM (C_4)
B_2 (Sector S_2)	NL (C_3)	Z (C_2)	NM (C_5)

13.4.2 Learning Phase

There are twenty adjustable parameters in the ten membership functions which are used in the if-part and the then-part of the fuzzy inference. Seven parameters have been chosen to be adjusted during the learning phase. The rest of the MFs' parameters are kept identical to adjusted parameters or are remained unchanged during the learning process to guarantee the symmetry of the control surface of the PSS. The GA has been run for a maximum of 150 generations with 30 individuals in each generation. A generation gap of 93.33% has been used that keeps the two best individuals from each generation in the next one. The output of the GA process after each generation is a set of parameter values for the neurofuzzy PSS. The first population has been generated randomly subject to the limitations on the real values of the parameters of the neurofuzzy PSS. These limitations guarantee to keep the parameters resulting from the GA process within reasonable intervals which are accessible by the physical system. The GA toolbox for Matlab was used for implementation of the GA process, while the power system and the neurofuzzy PSS models were simulated via the Simulink toolbox. The Simulink model is run for each generation to return the objective function and consequently the fitness function. When the generator is connected to a transmission line with impedance $Z_l = j0.4\ p.u.$ and delivering a power of $0.8 + j0.2\ p.u.$, a $0.2\ p.u.$ step change in the mechanical input power is applied at time $t=1$ sec. The training data are collected during the test and after 1.5 seconds an objective function based on changes in the rotor speed $\delta\omega$, is calculated and its value is passed to the GA block. Different criteria functions have been employed to evaluate the performance of each solution provided by GA in each generation. Integral of square timed errors is a popular performance index used in stability study of power systems [16]:

$$J = \int_0^t [t'\delta\omega(t')]^2 \, dt'. \tag{12}$$

After finishing the GA process, the optimal parameters of the NF PSS resulted from the genetic algorithm are available for applying to the power system model. The changes in the performance index J during the GA learning process are shown in Figure 7. The resultant neurofuzzy controller generates a control surface in the generator phase plane. The nonlinear surface guides the state of the generator to the equilibrium point, i.e. origin in the phase plane with an optimal performance. Here, optimal performance means reaching the equilibrium point in the shortest time and with minimum deviations. Figure 8 shows the control surface of the proposed neurofuzzy power system stabiliser. There is a small flat region near the origin which guarantees a stable system. This small flat region is surrounded by sharp slopes in all directions to provide

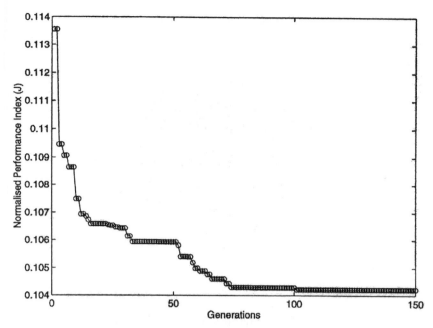

Figure 7: Change in the performance index of the neurofuzzy PSS during the GA generations.

a quick response by the controller to even small deviations in the speed or acceleration of the rotor. The membership functions for the rules resulting from the GA learning are shown in Figure 9. The simulation results of applying the controller to the study power system are given in the section.

13.4.3 Results of the Neurofuzzy PSS

A number of studies have been carried out with the GA-optimised neurofuzzy PSS and a nonlinear model of a single machine connected to an infinite bus-bar through a transmission line. The block diagram of the power system and the NF PSS is shown in Figure 4. Various disturbances and different operating conditions were considered in the simulation studies. The two major disturbances are:

❖ A three-phase to ground fault in the transmission line at t = 0.5 sec. This fault is cleared after 100 ms. The impedance of the line is reduced to half

Control Surface of the NF PSS

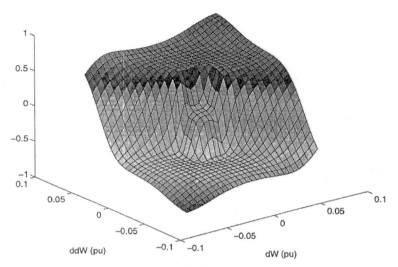

Figure 8: The control surface of the NF PSS trained by genetic algorithm.

of its steady state value during the fault and then returns to its previous value after clearing the fault.

❖ A step change in the mechanical input power to the generator. The amplitude of the disturbance has been chosen large enough to force the system to exhibit its nonlinear properties.

The disturbances are applied for different loads and different lead and lag power factors of the generator. The following are the test results for the neurofuzzy PSS adjusted by the GA:

❖ Light Load Test:

The power system is operating under a light load condition. The output power was 0.4 + j0.16 p.u. and a step change of 0.2 p.u. in the mechanical input power has applied at t = 0.5 sec.. The disturbance has removed after 4 seconds. Figure 10 shows the rotor angle, rotor speed deviations and the phase plane for conventional PSS, the NF PSS and the case with no PSS.

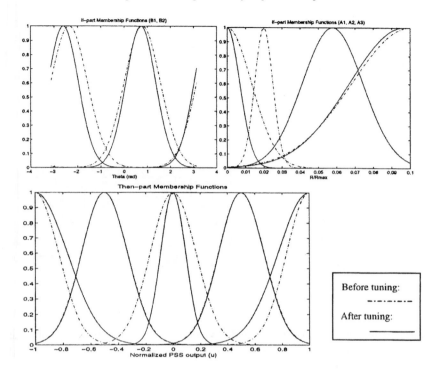

Figure 9: The if-part and the then-part membership functions after GA learning process.

The responses clearly demonstrate that the rotor oscillations have been damped faster with the GA-optimised NF PSS. The values of some normalised performance indexes are also included to provide a quantitative measure for comparing the NF PSS with conventional PSS. As shown in Figure 10 (d), all the performance indices were improved considerably, although ISTE index (J) was used in the GA to adjust the parameters of the NF PSS. The overall improvement in all the operating points can be considered as a consequence of the nonlinear fuzzy inference system.

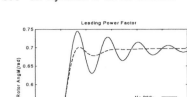

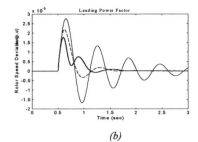

(a)   (b)

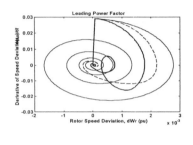

Perfor. Indexes	Different PSS's		
	No PSS	Conven.	Neurofuzzy
ISE	0.2179×10^{-5}	0.0783×10^{-5}	0.0464×10^{-5}
	100%	35.94%	21.28%
IAE	0.0017	0.0006	0.0005
	100%	34.51%	28.73%
ITSE	0.2032×10^{-5}	0.0515×10^{-5}	0.0313×10^{-5}
	100%	25.36%	15.41%
ISTE	0.2271×10^{-5}	0.0346×10^{-5}	0.0220×10^{-5}
	100%	15.23%	9.70%

(c)   (d)

Figure 10 Rotor angle (a), rotor speed deviation (b), the phase plane (c), and the normalised performance index (d) for the generator during a mechanical disturbance under a loading power factor test.

❖ Leading Power Factor Test:

It is sometimes necessary to operate the generator at a leading power factor to absorb the capacitive charging current in a large power system. When the generator is operating at a leading power factor condition, the stability margin is reduced and, thus, the PSS encounters a difficult situation. It is, therefore, necessary that the PSS be able to guarantee stable operation of the generator under leading power factor condition. When the generator output power was 0.7 - j0.15 p.u. a 0.2 p.u. step increase in the input mechanical power was applied at t = 0.5 sec. The results given in Figure 11 show that the rotor oscillations were damped quickly and illustrate the effectiveness of the neurofuzzy PSS in controlling the generator under leading power factor operating conditions.

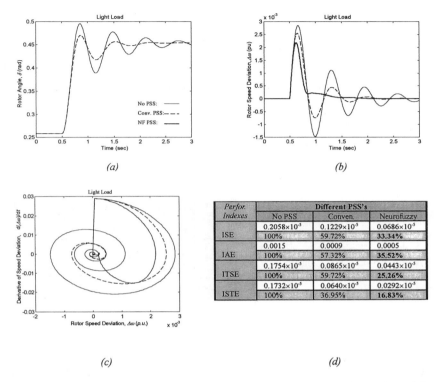

Figure 11 Rotor angle (a), rotor speed deviation (b), the phase plane (c), and the normalised performance index (d) for the generator during a mechanical disturbance under a light load.

❖ Short Circuit Test:

The performance of the GA adjusted neurofuzzy PSS was further verified by applying a three-phase to ground short circuit in the transmission lines. The fault occurred at t = 0.5 sec. and was cleared after 100 ms. The line impedance Z_1 changed from j0.4 p.u. to j0.2 p.u during the fault and then returned to the steady state value before fault occurrence. Figure 12 shows a very quick successful restoration to the steady state condition. The higher frequency oscillations in the speed derivatives $d(\delta\omega)/dt$ in Figure 12(d) are due to the short circuit and do not affect the PSS. The dominant performance of the PSSs actually started after finishing the higher frequency oscillations which took about 200 ms.

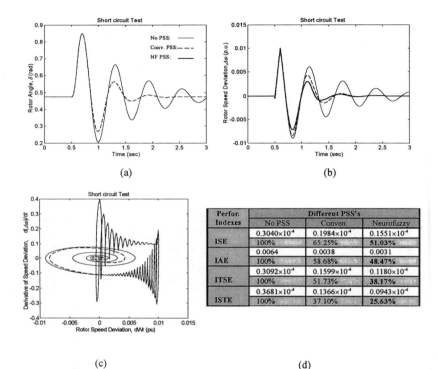

(c)   (d)

Figure 12 Rotor angle (a), rotor speed deviation (b), the phase plane (c), and the normalised performance index (d) for the generator in a three-phase to ground short circuit test.

❖ Stability Margin

The stability is the ability of a power system to remain in synchronism after the transient period until the system has settled down to the new steady state equilibrium. The stability margin is described by the maximum output power at which the system loses synchronism. A simulation study has been carried out, to demonstrate the effects of NF PSS on the stability margin. Under steady state operating conditions, with the output power at 0.94 p.u. and 0.9 power factor lag, the input power was increased gradually. Table 1 shows the stability margin for the system with conventional PSS, NF PSS and without PSS. The results indicate that the stability margin was increased by the NF PSS, and was higher than the conventional PSS which had been specially adjusted for this operating point.

Table 1: Stability margin for different PSSs.

Margins	Different PSSs		
	No PSS	Conventional	NF PSS
Max. Output Power (p.u.)	1.8	2.22	2.35
Max. Rotor Angel (rad)	1.21	1.97	2.03

13.5 Conclusions

Fuzzy logic allows the integration of expert knowledge into the control system very easily, but it is not easy to find the best controller rule base. A learning method based on genetic algorithms was developed to find the optimal values of the parameters of the fuzzy membership functions. When no learning signal is available, GAs are appropriate candidates for adjusting the parameters of a controller based on a performance index. The performance index has been translated into a fitness function which is employed to produce new generations of solutions in the GA selection process. Other GA operators, i.e. reproduction, crossover and mutation, have been tuned to provide an optimal solution in a reasonable number of generations. The developed GA-based neurofuzzy system has been applied in a case study to an electrical power system for damping the low frequency oscillations in the rotor of the synchronous generator. Well-damped and fast responses to different disturbances have been achieved for the GA-optimised neurofuzzy PSS.

13.6 Appendix

The synchronous generator model includes three damper windings, one along the d-axis, and the other two along the q-axis. The model also incorporates the stator transient via differential equations governing the variation in stator flux. In most of the power system stability studies, the turbo-alternator rotating mass is modelled as a single mass, whose dynamic is expressed through the following linear differential equations.

$$\dot{\delta} = \omega_b \cdot \omega$$

$$\dot{\omega} = (T_m - D_a \cdot (\omega + 1) - T_e)/M_g \qquad \text{(A-1)}$$

or

$$\dot{\omega} = (P_m - K_d \cdot (\omega + 1) - P_e)/2H$$

where $M_g = 2H/\omega_b$ and $K_d = D_a/\omega_b$. In Equation A-1, $M_g\dot{\omega}$, T_m and T_e are the accelerating torque, the mechanical input torque, and the electrical output torque, respectively all in per units. ω is the speed deviation in per unit, $\omega_b = 2\pi f$ is the base speed in rad/sec. The term $D_a(\omega + 1)$ represents the mechanical damping torque in per unit.

$$v_d = -r_a \cdot i_d + \frac{1}{\omega_b} \cdot \dot{\psi}_d - (\omega + 1) \cdot \psi_q$$

$$v_q = -r_a \cdot i_q + \frac{1}{\omega_b} \cdot \dot{\psi}_q + (\omega + 1) \cdot \psi_d$$

$$v_f = r_f \cdot i_f + \frac{1}{\omega_b} \cdot \dot{\psi}_f$$

$$0 = r_{D1} \cdot i_{D1} + \frac{1}{\omega_b} \cdot \dot{\psi}_{D1} \qquad \text{(A-2)}$$

$$0 = r_{Q1} \cdot i_{Q1} + \frac{1}{\omega_b} \cdot \dot{\psi}_{Q1}$$

$$0 = r_{Q2} \cdot i_{Q2} + \frac{1}{\omega_b} \cdot \dot{\psi}_{Q2}$$

where the field voltage E_{fd} is: $E_{fd} = (x_{md} / R_f) v_f$.

The model includes an AVR & Exciter and a Governor with the following transfer functions:

Input-output description of the AVR and Exciter block:

$$E_{fd}(s) = \frac{K_A}{1 + T_A s}[V_{ref}(s) - V_t(s) + U_{pss}(s)] \qquad \text{(A-3)}$$

The Governor transfer function:

$$\frac{G(s)}{\Omega(s)} = a + \frac{b}{1 + T_g s} \qquad \text{(A-4)}$$

The conventional PSS used for comparison studies has the following transfer function:

$$\frac{U_{PSS}(s)}{\Omega(s)} = K_{PSS} \frac{T_q s}{1 + T_q s} \frac{1 + T_1 s}{1 + T_2 s} \tag{A-5}$$

The values of parameters used in the simulation study are as follows. All time constants are in seconds and resistance and reactance are in p.u.:

$K_A = 200$ $\qquad$ $T_A = 0.01$

$A = -0.001238$ $\qquad$ $b = -0.17$ $\qquad$ $T_g = 0.25$

$K_d = 0.02714$ $\qquad$ $H = 3.46$ $\qquad$ $E_{fdmax} = 4.5$

$-0.15 < U_{PSS} < 0.15$

$r_a = 0.007$ $\qquad$ $r_f = 0.00089$ $\qquad$ $r_D = 0.023$

$r_{Q1} = 0$ $\qquad$ $r_{Q2} = 0.652$

$X_1 = 0.117$ $\qquad$ $X_f = 1.33$ $\qquad$ $X_D = 1.15$

$X_{Q1} = 0$ $\qquad$ $X_{Q2} = 0.652$ $\qquad$ $X_d = 1.15$

$K_{PSS} = 10$ $\quad$ $T_1 = 0.10$ $\quad$ $T_2 = 0.05$ $\quad$ $T_q = 2.5$

Bibliography

[1] D. A. Linkens and H. O. Nyongesa, "Learning Systems in Intelligent Control: An Appraisal of Fuzzy, Neural and Genetic Algorithm Control Applications," *IEE Proc. Pt. D, Control Theory and Applications*, vol. 143, pp. 367-386, 1996.

[2] C. L. Karr, "Design of an Adaptive Fuzzy Logic Controller Using a Genetic Algorithm," presented at Fourth International Conference on Genetic Algorithms, Sandiago, California, 1991.

[3] T. Hashiyama, T. Furuhashi, and Y. Uchikava, "A Creative Design of Fuzzy Logic Controller Using Genetic Algorithm," in *Genetic Algorithms and Fuzzy Logic systems: Soft Computing Perspectives*, E. Sanchez, Shibata, T, Zadeh, L. A., Ed.: World Scientific Publishing Co., 1997, pp. 37-48.

[4] A. M. Sharaf and T. T. Lie, "A Neuro-Fuzzy Hybrid Power-System Stabiliser," *Electric Power Systems Research*, vol. 30, pp. p.17-23, 1994.

[5] Y. Kawakita, Y. Ohsawa, and K. Arai, "Power-System Stabilising Control by SMES Using Fuzzy Techniques and Neural Networks," *Electrical Engineering In Japan*, vol. 114, pp. 9-17, 1994.

[6] A. Hariri and O. P. Malik, "A Fuzzy Logic Based Power System Stabilizer with

Learning Ability," *IEEE Trans. on Energy Conversion*, vol. 11, pp. 721-726, 1996.

[7]   A. Afzalian and D. A. Linkens, "Self-Organizing Fuzzy Perceptrons Applied to Power System Stability," presented at Annual Meeting of the North American Fuzzy Information Processing Society, NAFIPS'97, New York, U.S.A, 1997.

[8]   D. A. Linkens and A. Afzalian, "A Neuro-fuzzy Power System Stabiliser," presented at International Conference on Intelligent and Cognitive Systems, Tehran, Iran, 1996.

[9]   J. S. R. Jang and C. T. Sun, "Neuro-Fuzzy Modelling and Control," *Proceedings of the IEEE*, vol. 83, pp. 378-406, 1995.

[10]   J. Nie and D. A. Linkens, "Fast Self-Learning Multivariable Fuzzy Controllers Constructed from a Modified CPN Network", *International Journal of Control*, vol. 60, pp. 369-393, 1994.

[11]   D. Nauck and R. Kruse, "A Fuzzy Perceptron as a Generic Model for Neuro-fuzzy Approaches," presented at Fuzzy Systems' 94, 2nd GI workshop, Munich, Germany, 1994.

[12]   M. Mizumoto, "Fuzzy Control Under Various Fuzzy reasoning Methods," *Information Sciences*, vol. 45, pp. 129-151, 1988.

[13]   L. X. Wang, *Adaptive Fuzzy Systems - Design and Stability Analysis*. New Jersey: Prentice Hall, 1994.

[14]   R. A. Caruana and J. D. Schaffer, "Representation and Hidden Bias: Gray vs. Binary Coding," presented at 6th International Conference on Machine Learning, 1988.

[15]   R. B. Holstien, "Artificial Genetic Adaptation in Computer Control Systems," in *Department of Computer and Communication Sciences*. Ann Arbor: University of Michigan, 1971.

[16]   T. Hiyama, "Application of Rule-Based Stabilising Controller to Electrical Power System," *IEE Proc. Pt. C, Generation, Transmission and Distribution*, vol. 136, pp. 175-181, 1989.

Chapter 14
TECHNIQUES OF SOFT COMPUTING FOR EMERGENCY MANAGEMENT IN A MINERAL OILS DEPOSIT

Alessandro De Carli and Sonia Pisani.
Department of Computer and System Sciences, University of Rome "La Sapienza".

Abstract

In this paper, a different use of soft computing is shown. Commonly, genetic algorithms are used to solve problems that haven't an analytic formulation; neural networks are used like a black box able to model a system; fuzzy systems try to model human knowledge, transferring the action rules from the expert to a universal support based on fuzzy logic. In this work, instead, genetic algorithms are a way to solve a problem whose formulation doesn't allow to use another global optimization method; the result of the optimization process is used to train a neural network whose structure allows to describe the acquired knowledge in terms of linguistic variables. The efforts are to design an intelligent controller able to solve the problem and give knowledge about what the plant operators have to do, because actually they are unable to manage a good strategy in a risk situation.

Keywords : soft computing, genetic algorithm, fuzzy system, neural network, neuro fuzzy neutwork, heat transfer.

14.1   Introduction

The case of study is the management of a fire emergency in a complex system, in which the fires extinguish procedure is not well known because fire accidents never occurred. The aim of the paper is to design an intelligent procedure involving a soft computing approach. Due to the impossibility of direct tests and the lack of data related to similar events, the effects of a fire accident have been simulated by mans of a suitable model. This model has been used to work out an intelligent procedure for the fire extinction and to test its validity. The procedure has been designed by considering a fire condition particularly difficult to manage. All the methodologies developed in the soft computing framework have been applied to attain the result.

At first the modeling of the fire effects has been developed by taking into account the physical principles and plant structure. Genetic algorithms have been used to provide the training data for a neuro fuzzy controller. The set of the inference rules is very large due to complexity of both the system and the objective to achieve. The ability in the design is to work out an intelligent procedure, which should be clear and intuitive for the operator and should cover very general emergency situations. A neural method of rule compression and generalization for training the operators is thus proposed and discussed.

As far as common sense goes, an operator should spray to the maximum the neighbouring tanks, extinguishing the water resources in about 10 hours, while a tank could burn for days. The genetic solution (and consequently the neuro fuzzy one) offers a cooling strategy able to last two days. Observing the neuro fuzzy network structure, the operator can understand which rules he has to follow for cooling the selected part of the plant. Generalizing and compressing these rules, few criteria are offered to the operator to manage a more opportune cooling strategy.

On the current bibliography, no papers have been found on this specific topic. To produce this work, papers [2], [3], [5] were consulted to deduce the model for the heat transfer process. Information about laws and criteria as how to manage risk emergency in deposit of mineral oil has been obtained by paper [4]. Paper [6] has been used to be acquainted with genetic algorithm; papers [8], [9] with neural networks; papers [1], [9], [10] with the neuro fuzzy controller.

14.2   The case of study

The high-risk system is a deposit of mineral oils located in Northern Italy. The plant consists of 29 tanks of different heights and diameters, in which a different quality of petroleum is stocked.

On the average, the local weather conditions are:

temperature 12 °C;

relative humidity 77%;

typical wind speed 1.6 m/s.

The area is not seismic, it has not been struck by alluvial phenomena, and the average number of fulmination to earth during the year is equal to 2.5 per Km^2.

Since emergency have never occurred, the operators have no experience.

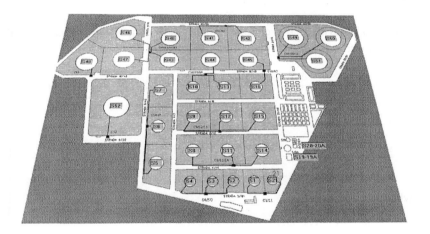

Fig 14.1   The map of deposit plant.

14.3   The actual fire extinction procedure

The actual fireproof system consists of two water tanks; each one has a capacity of 11800 m^3, an electro-pump and a diesel-pump providing a flow of 1600 m^3/h.

The critical situation is the management of the water resources during the fire of one tank. If this event should happen, the actual strategy suggested to the operators is: to leave the ignited tank to burn, to empty it by transferring the content in other tanks, to cool the walls of the neighbouring tanks by foaming the circular crowns. For the fire operators the best strategy is: "Spray to the maximum the surrounding tanks, wait for

the intervention of the Fire Brigade...".
Such an instinctive behaviour implies a relevant consumption of water
with possible damages if the fire is not totally extinguished before the
water has finished. An optimal strategy for cooling should suggest to the
operator the way as how to obtain a limited increase of the temperatures
on the wall of tanks closest to the ignited one by using the minimum
quantity of water, since its stored volume is limited. By minimizing the
water consumption, the time interval for fire extinction increases.

14.4   The model of the plant

In order to determine the change of the wall temperature of a tank, the
Fourier equation is used in its discrete form:

$$k \, (r \cdot \Delta \varphi \cdot \Delta z \, \frac{\Delta T_{+r} + \Delta T_{-r}}{\Delta r_i} + \Delta r_i \cdot \Delta z \, \frac{\Delta T_{+\varphi} + \Delta T_{-\varphi}}{r \Delta \varphi} +$$

$$+ r \cdot \Delta \varphi \cdot \Delta r_{i+1} \, \frac{\Delta T_{-z}}{\Delta z} + r \cdot \Delta \varphi \cdot \Delta r_{i-1} \, \frac{\Delta T_{+z}}{\Delta z}) + Q_i =$$

$$= c \cdot \rho \cdot r \cdot \Delta V \cdot \frac{\Delta T_{+\tau}}{\Delta z} = c \cdot \rho \cdot r \cdot \Delta \varphi \cdot \Delta r_i \cdot \Delta z \cdot \frac{\Delta T_{+\tau}}{\Delta z}$$

in which:

$$T = f(\tau, r, \varphi, z)$$

$$\Delta T_{\pm\gamma} = T(\alpha, .., \gamma \pm \Delta \gamma, ..\varsigma) - T(\alpha, .., \gamma, ..\varsigma)$$

$$Q = [h(T_{fluid} - T_{wall}) + a * J] * Area$$ for   the   surfaces

contacted with a fluid like air, water or oil, else $Q = 0$. $a = 0$ if the surface
is internal, a is a combination of water and tank absorption coefficients if
the surface is external; J [kWm^{-2}] is the radiation from the fire.
If the thermal exchange is due to convection, the h coefficient is worked
out by using the following equation:

$$h = Nu \frac{k}{L}$$

in which: Nu is the Nusselt number; L is the height of the exchange
area, k is the thermal conductivity.
The Forster and Zuber equation furnishes the thermal exchange

coefficient, when the wall temperature is higher than *100* °C and the water is boiling. It results:

$$h_{FZ} = \frac{.00122 \cdot \Delta T_{sat}^{.24} \cdot \Delta P_{sat}^{.75} \cdot c_{liq}^{.45} \cdot \rho_{liq}^{.49} \cdot k_{liq}^{.79}}{\sigma^{.5} \cdot H_{lg}^{.24} \cdot \mu_{liq}^{.29} \cdot \rho_{gas}^{.24}}$$

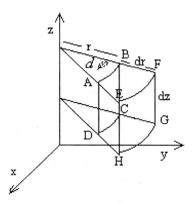

Fig 14.2   The cylindrical coordinates used to describe the thermal field of the tank.

where σ is the surface tension of the liquid, c_{liq} is the specific heat of the fluid, ρ_{liq} is the density of the liquid, k_{liq} is the thermal conductivity of the water, H_{lg} is the enthalpy of evaporation, μ_{lg} is the dynamic viscosity of the fluid, ρ_{gas} is the steam density.

When the water is boiling, the forced convection should then be considered. The Steiner and Taborek equation gives the thermal exchange coefficient, which results:

$$h_{ST} = (h_B^3 + h_{FC}^3)^{1/3}$$

The amount of evaporated water and the temperature of the remaining water change dynamically according to the following equation:

$$Q_{H_2O} = a_{H_2O} \cdot J + h_{air\_H_2O} \cdot (T_{H_2O_i} - T_{air}) + h_{H_2O\_wall} \cdot (T_{H_2O_i} - T_{wall})$$
$$= Q_{evap} + Q_{absor}$$

$$Q_{evap} = M_{evap} \cdot \lambda; Q_{abssr} = [(M - M_{evap}) \cdot c_{liq} + M_{evap} \cdot c_{vap}] \cdot (T_{H_2O_f} - T_{H_2Oi_i})$$

$$M_{evap} = \frac{Kx}{\lambda}(X' - X)\frac{PM_{H_2O}}{PM_{air}} Area$$

$$K_x = \frac{h}{cLe}$$

where L_{H_2O} is the water temperature at time τ, $T_{H_2O_{if}}$ is the water temperature at time $\tau + \Delta\tau$, Le is Lewis number, λ is the latent heat of evaporation, M_{evap} is the evaporated water mass, c_{vap} is the specific heat of the steam, c is the specific heat of the moist air, X is the absolute humidity of the original air, X' is the steam pressure, PM is the molecular weight, a_{H_2O} is the water absorption coefficient, J is the heat produced by the fire.

The velocity of the cooling film, flowing down the external wall of the tank, can be obtained by applying the following equation:

$$\overline{u} = \frac{\Gamma}{\delta \cdot \rho_{liq}}$$

$$\delta = \left\{ \frac{3 \cdot \mu_{liq} \cdot \Gamma}{{}^2_{liq} \cdot g} \right\}^{1/3}$$

in which: Γ is the flow rate of film mass per unit of wall periphery, δ is the local thickness of the film.

With this information, the Reynolds number is worked out so as the estimated amount of water dropping to the lower plate. The amount of the radiant energy has been obtained by a dedicated simulation program, developed by a mineral oil agency for the fire risk evaluation in mineral oils deposits.

The set of the above deduced equations form the model applied to work out the proposed procedure.

14.5   The genetic approach

The model describes how the temperature changes during the fire and the cooling period. In order not to break the tank wall, its temperature has to be less than an established one. So the model is a constraint for the problem; but this function isn't linear or such to permit the use of a standard global optimization method. Genetic algorithms were used because it doesn't require any particular hypothesis on the formulation of the functions to be optimized.

Due to the complexity of both the whole system's model and the optimization method by using genetic algorithms, the optimal forcing inputs are worked out for the emergency management of a subsystem of the plant. This latter has been chosen so as to take into account the general characteristic in the position of the tanks.

Following this criterion, it has been recognized that the burning of the petrol tank number S47 has the desired characteristics. When it burns, according to the actual procedure, the plant operators open the water cooling to the maximum, but this solution is not the best, as it is shown in Fig. 4.5. If the temperature of a tank should exceed *300°C*, the wall could fissure and the stocked oil could flow out supplying the fire. That is why it is convenient to keep them below the safety temperature of 270°C.

14.6   Problem analysis

The fire extinction of the S47 tank is the case study. An optimal cooling strategy for the first hour of fire is the task. The targets are: cooling the neighbouring tanks; minimizing the water consumption; respecting the constrains of capacity and holding the temperature of the tank below *270°C*

In order to avoid the thermal stress of the tank wall, a limit on the temperature variation has been considered.

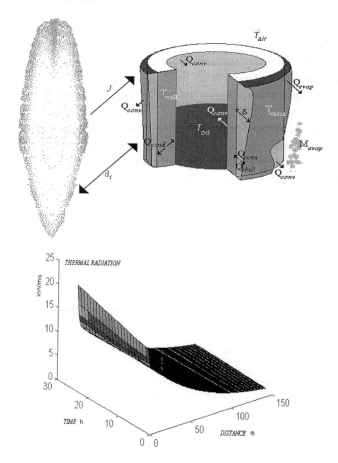

Fig 14.3   The most important physical phenomena taken into account inside the model.

The objective function, to be minimized, is

$$z = \left[\begin{array}{c} \displaystyle\int_0^D \sum_{j=1}^5 u_j(t)dt \\ \dfrac{\partial T_j}{\partial t} t \in [t_{\gamma_j}, D] \end{array} \right]$$

in which D is the time interval in which the cooling action is operating,

t_{r_j} is the starting time of the cooling action.

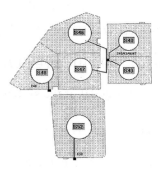

Fig 14.4   Subsystem involved in the critical emergency.

	Diameter	Height	Distance from S47
S48	79.62 m	17.09 m	65.3 m
S46	79.62 m	17.08 m	44.72 m
S40	70 m	17 m	133.38 m
S43	64 m	16.45 m	126.14 m
S52	88.494 m	19.6 m	125.9 m

Table 14.1: Geometrical characteristics.

The constrains are:

$$\int_0^{t_2} \sum_{j=1}^{5} u_j(t)\, dt \leq 11800\,[m^3]$$

(limited water resources)

$$\sum_{j=1}^{5} u_j(t) \leq 1600 \left[\frac{m^3}{h} \right]$$

(constraint over the pump dynamics)

$$T_j(p,t) \le 270°C \ \forall p \in J_j \ j = 1..5 \ \forall t \in [0,D]$$

(safe operating conditions)

$$T_j(p,t) = f(T_j(t-1), u_j(t-1), Irr_j, T_{air}, T_{liq}, P_{atm}, P_{liq}, r\_d, l_j)$$

$$u_j(t) = q_j(t) * area_j * 60 * 10^{-3} \ \forall t \in [0,D] \ j = 1..5$$

(model of the system)

where J_j is the jth tank, $area_j$ is its surface, $q_{t,j}$ results: $\dfrac{l}{min \cdot m^2}$, Irr_j is the power heating the tank, T_{air} is the air temperature, T_{liq} is the oil temperature, P_{atm} is the atmospheric pressure, P_{liq} is the oil pressure, r_d is the relative damp, l_j is the filling degree of the tank.

14.7   The genetic solution

In order to solve the above formulated problem by using a genetic algorithm, each individual of the solver population is an array. Its dimension is the number of tanks to cool. By this way, every gene indicates the flow rate to supply the associated tank in a definite time interval.

To improve the algorithm convergence, a variant of the classic genetic algorithm has been implemented: i.e. the "steady state genetic algorithm".

At time instant t, for each population, the number of generated sons is fixed and is lower than the number of the population individuals. In creating the son population, the crossover and mutation is applied on the new partial population, selected from the old one using the operator "roulette wheel" that selects genes according to their own relative fitness function. The best new chromosomes substitute the worst ones in their parent population only if one is better then one of its parents.

By this variant, the population consists of few individuals. After few generations, the population loose its diversity implying a premature convergence of the algorithm, since when a chromosome increases a lot its fitness, it tends to attract the whole population. Furthermore, to avoid local minima, it is advisable to use an appropriate tuned mutation probability, in order to avoid the convergence of the population to a local minimum.

To realize this algorithm, a population of 20 individuals generating 10 sons has been chosen. The stop rule is: verify that the population converges to a single chromosome; after the processing of at least 300 iterations, verify if the best result in the current population isn't different from the one in last generations one.

The fitness function is tied to the problem formulation in the following way: if constraints are not fulfilled the penalty on the fitness function is set very large and consequently the chromosome has high probability to be eliminated in the next generation.

14.8   The genetic result

By taking into account the following situation: S47 & S52 tanks are 40% fulfilled; S48 & S46 tanks are empty; S40 & S43 tanks are completely fulfilled; the genetic solution is shown in Fig. 14.6.

The solution by the genetic algorithm indicate a water consumption of 29.6050 m^3 during the first hour, instead of 1600 m^3 suggested by the actual strategy.

By using genetic solutions to train a neuro-fuzzy controller a set of rules will be produced which is objectively valid, being the inference generated by an optimization process.

14.9   The neuro fuzzy controller

There are two ways of training a neuro fuzzy controller. The first one consists of using the rules to determine the connections in the knowledge base of the controller. The genetic trajectories are therefore used to optimize the network behaviour. In the second way, in which even an unsupervised learning is used during the training period, the trajectories are only given to the neuro fuzzy controller so as it is possible to predict the rules from the optimal trajectories themselves. This second possibility requires more steps during the learning process, but it is the only one able to bypass the rule acquisition from the operator, not available in this case.

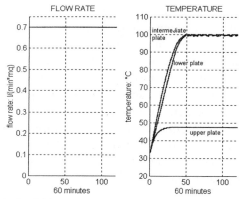

Fig 14.5   The result for S46 tank obtained by applying the actual procedure.

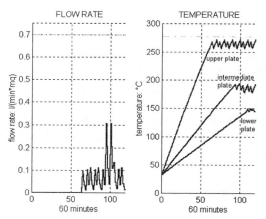

Fig 14.6   The solution obtained by applying the genetic algorithm for S46 tank.

The network training is performed by using classic algorithms. The four main steps are:

  collection of training data (Genetic algorithms);

  off line network set up (Kohonen Feature Map);

  off line rule determination (Instar Learning);

  off line error minimization (Back propagation).

The fuzzy system realized by using a neural network has a multi-layer feedforward structure, as shown in Fig.14.8. The inputs of the first layer are the input linguistic variables of the controller, instead the fifth layer is the output layer. The neurones belonging to the second and forth layers act like membership function and represent the linguistic values of each variable. The third layer is the rule base one and each neurone is a rule for the fuzzy system.

Fig 14.7 The step used to train the network.

The inferential engine consists of the links between the third and forth layers. In fact, the third layer outputs are the preconditions for each rule, while the forth outputs are the relative consequences. According to this description, it is possible to have one or zero link between a neuron belonging to the third layer and another belonging to the forth one.

Every neuron has a function f used to combine the input information, and an output activation function a. So if u_i^k is the ith input for the kth layer, w_i^k is the weight of the link between the ith layer and the kth one, and p is the input connection number for a kth layer neuron i. Then its output is: $o_i^k = a(f)$ in which $f = f(u_1^k, u_2^k, ..., u_p^k, w_1^k, w_2^k, ..., w_p^k)$.

The first layer neurons have $f = u_i^1$ and $a = f$; the link weight is fixed: $w_i^1 = 1$.

The second layer neurons represents the membership function, their shape is like a bell, so they have $f = -\dfrac{(u_i^2 - m_{ij})^2}{\sigma_{ij}^2}$ and $a = e^f$ in which m_{ij} is the function mean value and σ_{ij}^2 is the variance. The coefficient m_{ij} is the weight of the second layer link, so $w_{ij}^2 = m_{ij}$.

The third layer neuron outputs are the antecedents of the associated rules.

So this layer neurons acts as the fuzzy intersection operator, i.e.
$f = \min(u_1^3, u_2^3, .., u_p^3)$, $a = f$ and $w_i^3 = 1$.

The forth layer neuron acts in two different ways: from right to left and
from left to right. If the network is working, the information goes from left

to right and the neurons realize the fuzzy OR operator; so $f = \sum_{i=1}^{p} u_i^4$,

$a = \min(1, f)$ and $w_i^3 = 1$. When the broadcast is from right to left, the

network is in training. In this case neurons and links acts like the second

layer ones.

Two kinds of neurons belong to the fifth layer: the first ones are used

during the training step, they receive the information from right and

broadcast to left without changing the input signals; so $f = y_i$ and

$a = f$. The second type of neurons is used when the network is working

and it is used to defuzzify. If m_{ij}^4 and $(\sigma_{ij}^2)^4$ assume respectively the mean

value and variance of the output membership functions. If centroid method

is   used   to   defuzzify,   fifth   layer   neurones   result

$$f = \sum_i w_{ij}^5 u_i^5 = \sum_i m_{ij}^4 \sigma_{ij}^4 u_i^5 , \quad a = \frac{f}{\sum_i \sigma_{ij}^4 u_i^5} , \quad \text{and } w_{ij}^5 = m_{ij}^4 \sigma_{ij}^4 .$$

In order to train the described network, the two steps learning algorithm,
proposed by Lin and Lee, has been applied.
In the first step the rules are determined, while in the second one the
parameters optimization is effected.
In the first step the membership function are fixed. The ith rule node
output (from right to left) is $o_i^3(t)$ whereas $o_j^4(t)$ is the forth layer j^{th}
node output (from left to right). In order to determine which term
matches a rule consequent, instar learning algorithm is used to update

the generic weight w_{ij} :

$$dw_{ij} = lr \cdot o_j^4(-w_{ij} + o_i^3)$$

$$w_{ij} = w_{ij} + dw_{ij},$$

in which lr is the learning step.

When w_{ij} coefficients are worked out, the forth layer links having weights less than the maximum, are eliminated, because each rule must have just a consequent. If all the link weights between a rule node and a consequent are small, these links are eliminated because they don't have a great influence upon the output. If a rule isn't connected to a consequent, it's eliminated since it doesn't influence the output.

The number of rules can then be reduced. A rule set could become a single rule if:

  all the rules have the same consequent;

  the rules of the set have preconditions in common;

  the other preconditions union is the universe for one or more variables in the rule antecedent.

If a rule set satisfies the described conditions, it can be substituted with a single neuron, whose inputs are the common preconditions.

When the fuzzy rule are found, the network weights are calculated using the backpropagation learning algorithm.

Now the target is to minimize the error function $E = \dfrac{1}{2}[y(t) - \hat{y}(t)]^2$ where

$\hat{y}(t)$ is the desired output and $y(t)$ is the current one.

For each training data set, the outputs for each network node are computed. Starting from output nodes and coming back, $\dfrac{\partial E}{\partial y}$ is worked out for every hidden node. If w is the parameter to modify, the learning rule is:

$$dw \propto -\frac{\partial E}{\partial w} = -\frac{\partial E}{\partial f}\frac{\partial f}{\partial w} = -\frac{\partial E}{\partial a}\frac{\partial a}{\partial f}\frac{\partial f}{\partial w}$$

$$w(t+1) = w(t) + \eta \cdot dw,$$

in which η is the learning rate.

In order to determinate m_i for the fifth layer nodes, it's used:

$$m_i(t+1) = m_i(t) + \eta[y(t) - \hat{y}(t)]\frac{\sigma_i u_i}{\sum_i \sigma_i u_i}$$

To calculate σ_i it's used:

$$\sigma_i(t+1) = \sigma_i(t) + \eta[y(t) - \hat{y}(t)]\frac{m_i u_i(\sum \sigma_i u_i) - (\sum m_i \sigma_i u_i)u_i}{(\sum_i \sigma_i u_i)^2}.$$

The error $\delta^5 = -\dfrac{\partial E}{\partial \hat{y}} = y(t) - \hat{y}(t)$ has to be propagated to the precedent layer.

Since none parameter has to be updated in the forth layer, the error signal to propagate is:

$$\delta_i^4 = [y(t) - \hat{y}(t)]\frac{m_i\sigma_i(\sum \sigma_i u_i) - (\sum m_i\sigma_i u_i)\sigma_i}{(\sum_i \sigma_i u_i)^2}.$$

As far as the forth layer is concerned, it's necessary to calculate just the error signal for the third layer neurons: $\delta_i^3 = \delta_i^4$.

The relationships for nodes of the second layer are:

$$m_{ij}(t+1) = m_{ij}(t) - \eta\frac{\partial E}{\partial a_i}e^{f_i}\frac{2(u_i - m_{ij}(t))}{\sigma_{ij}(t)},$$

$$\sigma_{ij}(t+1) = \sigma_{ij}(t) - \eta\frac{\partial E}{\partial a_i}e^{f_i}\frac{2(u_i - m_{ij}(t))^2}{\sigma_{ij}(t)}.$$

The implemented network was trained to produce the strategy to follow the first hour of the emergency. Its inputs are the filling level for the six tanks. The terms that describe the linguistic variable "level" are: "high", "medium", "low". For each minute the network produces five outputs, that are the flow rate needed to cool the five tanks close to the burning one. The output linguistic variable "flow rate" is described by eight terms:

"near to null", "very low", "low", "medium low", "medium high", "high", "very high", "maximum".

The network has six inputs; each one has three membership functions. At the beginning, the rules in the network are $3^6 = 729$ for each tank to cool and for each control range. After the first learning phase, the rule number can be reduced to 183.

The stem measuring devices have an essential role even in the transfer of experience from the evaluative support to the neuro-fuzzy one.

The input variables to the neuro-fuzzy controller are only a subset of those ones used by the genetic algorithm to produce the optimal solution. Specifically, due to the lack of many sensors in the plant, the temperature could not be measured by the neuro-fuzzy controller. Dealing with the implemented neuro-fuzzy controller, the inputs are only the filling degrees of the tanks belonging to the considered sub plant; these inputs do not change when the controller is operating, while the rule base is time variant.

Suppose that the fired tank is 80% fulfilled; the S48 tank is 10% fulfilled; the S46 tank is empty; the S52 tank is 47% fulfilled and the other ones are full. In the Fig. 4.9 and Fig. 4.10, the strategy proposed by the genetic algorithm and the neuro-fuzzy controller to cool the S46 tank are illustrated.

It is worthwhile mentioning that the neuro-fuzzy network is able to overcome the lack of numerical information about many not measurable variables characterizing the subsystem.

The realised neuro-fuzzy controller is specific to the ignited tank and to the individual event of fire.

A set of 183 rules for each control time instant and for each tank to spray is obtained. Due to the large amount of rules and their local validity, a generalization and compression method is required to transfer the knowledge contained in these rules to the operators.

14.10   Rule generalization and compression

The rules, deduced for the above mentioned situation, overlay general principles describing the behaviour of the whole system.

A relationship, between the antecedents of the obtained rules and many general attributes characterizing the system, is investigated. The procedure can be divided into three main steps:

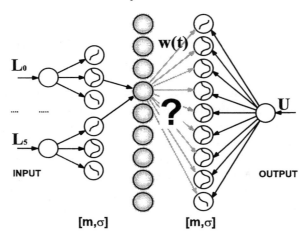

Fig 14.8   The genetic training of network for determining the inference.

14.10.1 *Rule for the localization of general parameters*

The measurable parameters, that could put together to form the input space
of a generalized and compressed controller of the system, are:

L_0: oil level of the burning tank

t: control time

l_i : oil level of the tank

$$A_{S_i} = \frac{A_i}{\max_{j=1..5}(A_j)}, \quad H_i = \frac{H_2O_i}{\max_{j=1..5}(H_2O_j)}$$: uncovered lateral surface of the

tank and cooling water used up to the current instant, related to the

other flows, respectively

d_i: distance of the tank from the ignited one.

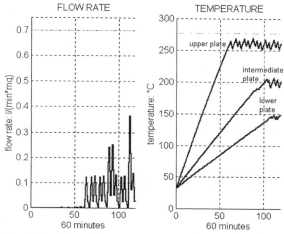

Figure 14.9: Result obtained for S46 tank, according to the strategy proposed by the network

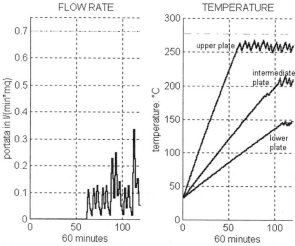

Figure 14.10: Result obtained for S46 tank, according to the strategy proposed by the genetic algorithm.

14.10.2 *Building up a rule analyzer network*

The rule analyzer network receives the rules antecedents, relates them to temporal and structural information about the plant, and produces the antecedents expressed in the new generalized linguistic input space. The old antecedent is reconstructed and substituted in the new space of parameters.

A rule decomposition tree, whose leaves form the new antecedent is then built up.

14.10.3 *Rule clustering and learning*

Each local rule is a data used for the training of a neural structure, composed of the series of the tree and one single layer perceptron.

The training set for the input of the perceptron is provided by the rule analyser outputs, while the training set for the output is composed of the consequent of each old local rule previously found. The perceptron is then trained, and the generalised rules are deduced by the connections of the perceptron, at the end of the learning period.

In this way, the maximum number of attainable rules is equal to the number of the perceptron outputs, that is equal to the number of the membership functions associated to the linguistic output variable inside the neuro-fuzzy controller shown in Fig. 14.11.

Using the described method, three main rules are obtained:

$$t_\downarrow or \cdot H_{i\uparrow} \cdot then \cdot q_{\downarrow\downarrow};$$

$$((t_\uparrow and \cdot H_{i\downarrow})and(d_{i\uparrow}or \cdot d_{i\downarrow}and(l_{i\uparrow}or(A_{S_i\uparrow}and \cdot L_{0\downarrow}))))then \cdot q_\downarrow;$$

$$t_\uparrow and \cdot L_0 and \cdot H_{i\downarrow}and \cdot d_{i\downarrow}and \cdot l_{i\downarrow}then \cdot q_\uparrow.$$

The observation of these relations allows to deduce a general criterion for a rational management of the water resources. First of all, it can be observed that two temporal phases exist: They can be expressed in linguistic words, according to the deduced rules:

Starting period: a time interval for organizing the strategy is available because it is not necessary to spray at the beginning of the fire.

During the fire: if the water consumed to spray is elevated, then it is possible to decrease partially or totally the flow rate supplying; on the contrary, if the tank is distant or it is full and near, this tank should be sprayed with an intermediary flow rate.

If the fire has modest relevance and the uncovered area of the lateral surface is great, this tank should be sprayed with an intermediary flow rate. If the fire is great, and the burning tank is close to the flame, and it doesn't have an elevated filling degree, and the water supplying is little, then the flow rate should be increased to bring it to a high value.

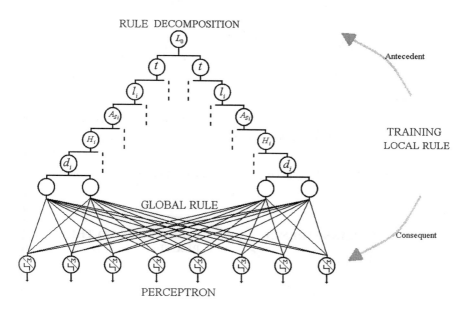

Figure 14.11: The rule generalizer and compressor neural network.

14.11   Conclusions

In this paper the usefulness of fuzzy controllers for very complex plants has been investigated.

In general, since the precision and significance have mutually excluding characteristics when the complexity of the system increases, the application of fuzzy systems approach is very convenient.

The specific application, which is really complex, has shown that the granularity of the rules, which should be included in the neuro-fuzzy controller could increase too much, and consequently the neuro-fuzzy system loose its transparency and become a neural network.

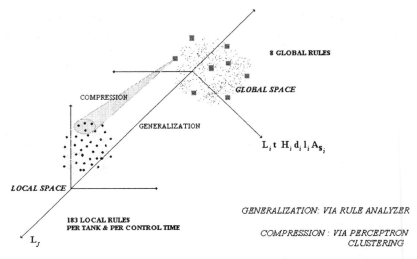

Figure 14.12: The procedure of generalization and compression.

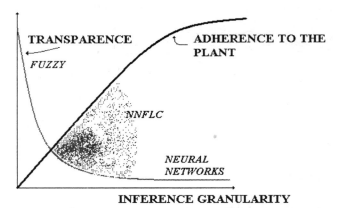

Figure 14.13: Conflict between transparency and adherence to the plant for a neuro fuzzy controller.

A method of rule compression and generalization is then needed to translate the acquired knowledge to the operators.

References

[1] De Carli A., Arcangeli L., Cerrini A., Caso A., "Translating human and artificial experience into knowledge based control systems. A systematic approach using white box neural networks". *Eufit'97* (vol.2)

[2] Kern D. Q., "Process Heat Transfer", *McGraw-Hill International Edition* (1986).

[3] Necati Özisik M., "Heat Transfer", *McGraw-Hill International Edition* (1990).

[4] Cannalire C., "Analisi delle conseguenze degli eventi incidentali; aspetti rilevanti di modellazione di fenomeni complessi ai fini dell'utilizzo nelle analisi di sicurezza.", I*stituto Superiore Antincendi, Corso per Analisti di Rischio* (18 Aprile 1996).

[5] Thomas H., "The Size of Flame From Natural Fires", 9th *Int. Combustion Symposium* (1963).

[6] Goldberg D. E., "Genetic Algorithm in Search, Optimization and Machine Learning", .*Addison-Wesley Publishing Company* (1989).

[7] Schaffer J. D., "Multi objective optimization with vector evaluated Genetic Algorithms", *Proceedings of an International Conference on Genetic Algorithms and their applications*, 74-79 (1985).

[8] Cohen M.A.:, Grossberg S., "Absolute Stability of Global Pattern Formation and Parallel Memory Storage By Competitive Neural Networks", *IEEE Trans. Syst. Man Cybernet.*, SMC 13,815-26 (1983)

[9] Yager R.R.,. Zadeh L. A, "Fuzzy Sets, Neural Networks, and Soft Computing", *VNR, New York* (1994).

[10] Lin C. T., Lee C. S. G.,"Neural-network-based fuzzy logic control and decision system", *IEEE Trans. Computers* C-40(12) 1320-1336 (1991)

References

Chapter 15

An Application of Logic Programs with Soft Computing Aspects to Fault Diagnosis in Digital Circuits

Hiroshi Sakai   Atsushi Imamoto   Akimichi Okuma

Kyushu Institute of Technology

Abstract

We are now touching a problem how we add soft computing aspects to logic programming and we have been discussing a new framework for handling incomplete attribute values on logic programs. For handling incomplete information, we depend upon the concept 'Rule of Thumb' and we syntactically introduce a functor *set* into logic programs. This functor *set* causes some soft computing aspects to logic programs. In this chapter we first show our new framework, then we apply our realized theorem prover to simulation and diagnosis in digital circuits. We have also realized an user interface for managing a theorem prover, a program translator and a knowledge base with several rules, so every user does not have to know the logic programs and he can easily operate our system.

Keywords : application, logic programs with functor set, soft computing, fault diagnosis, digital circuit, null attribute value, unknown real value, modality, single fault assumption, may-system, sure-system, accuracy, implementation, theorem prover, query interpreter, hypothetical reasoning, program in prolog, knowledge-based system, diagnostic system, simulation, model for fault, diagnostic knowledge, user interface

15.1   Introduction

It is very important problem that how we handle the incompleteness and the uncertainty in problem solving, information systems and knowledge based systems. There are several approaches for this problem, for example, hypothetical reasoning[1], abduction[2], default reasoning[3], non-monotonic reasoning[4], disjunctive logic program[5], near-horn prolog[6], fprolog[7], fuzzy prolog[8], Prolog-ELF[9], null value[10], incomplete relational database[11], deductive databases with null values[12], etc. We are now touching a problem how we add soft computing aspects to logic programs and we have been discussing a new framework for handling null attribute values on logic programs[13,14,15,16,17]. We introduce a functor *set* into logic programs for handling null attribute value '*'. The functor *set* has a list $LIST$ as an argument and a compound term $set(LIST)$ implies there is a truth element in the $LIST$. Namely, we positively use the rule of thumb for null value *. We show examples.

(1) If we know that Tom's affiliation is either s1 or s2 section, then we positively express it as $affiliation(tom, set([s1, s2]))$ instead of $affiliation(tom, *)$.

(2) For incomplete information such that the criminal wore either black, navy or gray jacket, we express it as $\forall X(criminal(X) \leftarrow color\_of\_jacket(X, set([black, navy, gray])))$ instead of $\forall X(criminal(X) \leftarrow color\_of\_jacket(X, *))$.

In (1) and (2), there exists an *unknown real value* in $[s1, s2]$ and $[black, navy, gray]$. In (1), we see $affiliation(tom, s1) \lor affiliation(tom, s2)$ holds and we see $affiliation(tom, s1)$ may hold. In (2), we see there is a real formula in the following three definite formulas,

$\forall X(criminal(X) \leftarrow color\_of\_jacket(X, black))$,
$\forall X(criminal(X) \leftarrow color\_of\_jacket(X, navy))$,
$\forall X(criminal(X) \leftarrow color\_of\_jacket(X, gray))$.

If we know John wore black jacket, then we conclude $criminal(john)$ may hold. In the above examples, we need to discuss modalities like certainty and possibility related to unknown real value. Furthermore, the typical prolog identifies the formula in (1) as Tom belongs to named $set([s1, s2])$ section, which is different from our interpretation. Namely, we also need a theorem prover which can recognize the meaning of the functor *set*. The introduction of the functor *set* causes such new problems related to soft computing aspects on logic programs.

Now we go to the application of our theorem prover. We apply our prover to simulation and diagnosis in digital circuits. As for simulation in a circuit, we can easily get all possible pairs of input and output values for specified gates. For example, if we use $gate(a, set([andg, org, xorg]))$ which implies gate a may be one of AND-gate, OR-gate or XOR-gate, then our prover responds all output values depending upon each gate. The prover can also assign gate a to one of AND-gate, OR-gate or XOR-gate by specifying some input and output values. As for diagnosis, we know some famous works[18,19,20]. However in our system depending upon functor *set* seems to be more suitable for expressing the digital circuits with broken gates, especially for handling *single fault assumption*[18]. We can easily express it as $broken(circuit\_name, set([gate_1, \cdots, gate_n]))$, which implies there is a broken gate in $gate_1, \cdots, gate_n$. We have only to change the argument in the *set* for handling other cases and we do not have to touch any other program. Of course, we can get all possible input and output values depending upon every broken gate.

In this chapter, we first propose a framework for logic programs with functor *set*, then we show semantics of programs and a theorem prover depending upon this semantics. Furthermore, we apply our framework to the diagnostic system for digital circuits and we discuss the details of this system.

15.2 Purpose and Aim in Logic Programs with Functor Set

We propose a way for dealing with unknown real attribute values, i.e., we use a set where the real attribute value exists. We call this set *upper approximation* for the unknown real attribute value. We may call this strategy *rule of thumb* for the unknown real attribute value. We positively use this upper approximation. Namely, if there exists a program clause $\forall X(p(X) \leftarrow q(X, *))$ where $*$ implies a null attribute value and we know the upper approximation $[a, b, c]$ for this $*$, then we use a clause $\forall X(p(X) \leftarrow q(X, set([a, b, c])))$. According to functor *set*, we get the following merits.

Merit 1: Even though we do not know the distinct attribute values, we can manage to express knowledge in program clauses.

Merit 2: We can sequentially get real attribute values through question-answering.

Merit 3: We can apply this framework to optimal assignment problem and decision support under uncertain information.

These merits are applicable to all cases with incomplete and uncertain information. Of course, the diagnosis in digital circuits is also depending upon these merits. We think that the addition of such merits to logic programs will be to add soft computing aspects to logic programs.

15.3   Logic Programs with Functor Set

Now in this section, we discuss the syntax and semantics for logic programs with functor *set*.

15.3.1   *Syntax for logic programs with functor set*

We introduce new functor *set* to logic programs. The functors *set* is a special symbol, which takes the roll of handling indefinite values. We mainly depend upon [21] for some basic definitions.

Definition 3.1   For constants $c_1, \cdots, c_n (n \geq 2)$, we call $set([c_1, \cdots, c_n])$ *set-term*.

Definition 3.2   For $m(\geq 2)$-ary predicate p, terms $t_1, \cdots, t_{m-1}, set(LIST)$, we call $p(t_1, \cdots, t_{m-1}, set(LIST))$ *set-atom*.

Definition 3.3   Suppose every p, q_1, $\cdots$, $q_n (n \geq 0)$ is either an atom or an *set*-atom. Then, we call a formula $p \leftarrow q_1, \cdots, q_n (n \geq 0)$ *programs clause(with functor set)*. A *logic program with functor set* is a finite set of program clauses.

If a program clause F contains free variables $X_1, \cdots, X_m$ then we see that every free variable is universally quantified. Namely, we see this formula $\forall X_1, \cdots, X_m F$.

15.3.2   *An example of programs*

In this subsection, we show a simple example. We use this example to clarify our framework.

Example 3.1[14] There are three persons Mike, Susan and John. As for their blood types, we know $blood(mike, a)$, $blood(susan, o)$ and $blood(john, set([a, o]))$. We also know the two rules of transfusion, i.e., transfusion between the same type persons and transfusion from type o person to everyone. In this case, can we transfuse whose blood into whom? The answers are as follows:

(1) We can surely do Susan's blood into Mike and John by the latter rule.
(2) Since John's type may be a, we may do Mike's blood into John by the former rule.
(3) Since John's type may be o, we may do John's blood into Susan by the

former rule.

(4) We can surely do John's blood into Mike. Because if John's type is *a* then we can do by the former rule and if John's type is *o* then we can also do by the latter rule.

In this example, we showed the incomplete information by using *set* and discussed the inferences under uncertainty. We can see modalities *may* and *sure* appear in the conclusion. John's blood type has uncertainty, but we can conclude the above answer (4) which is not effected by the uncertainty. The following is the program $P_{3.1}$.

```
(1)  transfuse(X,Y):-type(X,Blood_X),type(Y,Blood_X),X/==Y.
(2)  transfuse(X,Y):-type(X,o),type(Y,_),X/==Y.
(3)  type(mike,a).
(4)  type(susan,o).
(5)  type(john,set([a,o])).
(6)  headpred([type(X,Y)]).
```

(1) to (5) deal with knowledge and (6) is necessary for query processing.

15.3.3 *Semantics for logic programs with functor set*

Now in this section, we clarify the semantics of programs.

Definition 3.4 The follows are definitions of every *extension*.

(1) For every term *set(LIST)*, we call every element in the *LIST* an *extension* of *set(LIST)*.

(2) In every *set*-atom, if we replace the *set(LIST)* with its extension then we get an atom without *set*, which we call an *extension* of *set*-atom. The extension for every atom which does not have functor *set* is atom itself.

(3) For a program clause $\psi \leftarrow \phi_1 \wedge \cdots \wedge \phi_m$, if we replace every *set*-atom with its extension then we get a clause without *set*, which we call an *extension* of the program clause.

(4) For a program P, if we replace every program clause with its extension then we get a logic program without functor *set*, which we call an *extension* of the program P. We express the set of all extensions of P as $EXT(P)$.

By (2), *set*-atom $height(a, set([5.6, 5.7]))$ has two extensions $height(a, 5.6)$ and $height(a, 5.7)$. In (4), we know that there exists a real program in

$EXT(P)$, but we do not know which is the real program. However every element in $EXT(P)$ is a typical logic program, so the typical semantics holds and we can use SLD-resolution[21]. We also know definitions that a formula F is a logical consequence of $Q(\in EXT(P))$ and the follows;

$M(Q)(least\ model\ of\ Q)$
$= \bigcap_I \{I \subset B_Q(Herbrand\ base\ of\ Q)|I\ is\ an\ Herbrand\ model\ of\ Q\}.$
$= \{F \in B_Q|F\ is\ a\ logical\ consequence\ of\ Q\}.$
$= lfp(T_Q)(least\ fixed\ point\ of\ closure\ operator\ T_Q) = T_Q \uparrow \omega$
$= \{F \in B_Q|There\ exists\ SLD\text{-}refutation\ of\ \{\leftarrow F\} \cup Q\}.$

Definition 3.5 Let P be a program. A formula F is a *may*-consequence of P, if F is a logical consequence of some $Q \in EXT(P)$. A formula F is a *sure*-consequence of P, if F is a logical consequence of all $Q \in EXT(P)$. Furthermore, we set $B_P = \cup_{Q \in EXT(P)} B_Q$, $MAY(P) = \{F \in B_P|F$ is a may-consequence of $P\}$ and $SURE(P) = \{F \in B_P|F$ is a sure-consequence of $P\}$.

From now we call two evaluation systems *May-system* and *Sure-system*, respectively. The May-system characterizes atoms which may hold in unknown real program and the Sure-system does atoms which surely holds in unknown real program. We can easily get the following theorem related to two consequences.

Theorem 3.1 *Let P be a program and $M(Q)$ be a least model of $Q \in EXT(P)$. Then we get (1) and (2).*
(1) $MAY(P) = \bigcup_{Q \in EXT(P)} M(Q)$.
(2) $SURE(P) = \bigcap_{Q \in EXT(P)} M(Q)$.

Definition 3.6 Let P be a program, F be a conjunction of ground atoms and $|A|$ be the number of elements in a set A. Furthermore, suppose $POS(P, F) = \{Q \in EXT(P)|F$ is a logical consequence of $Q\}$. The accuracy of F in P is a ratio $|POS(P, F)|/|EXT(P)|$.

The accuracy is a value between 0 to 1, which shows the degree to sure-consequence. Of course, F is a sure-consequence of P is equivalent to accuracy of F in P is 1. Now we apply the above theory to Example 3.1.

In this program $P_{3.1}$ we have a functor $set([a, o])$ in $type(john, set([a, o]))$, so there are two extensions of this program. We suppose them Q_1 and Q_2, namely $EXT(P) = \{Q_1, Q_2\}$. we also suppose $type(john, a) \in Q_1$ and $type(john, o) \in Q_2$. In this case,

$M(Q_1) = \{type(mike, a), type(susan, o), type(john, a),$
$\qquad transfuse(mike, john), transfuse(susan, mike),$
$\qquad transfuse(susan, john), transfuse(john, mike)\}.$

$M(Q_2) = \{type(mike, a), type(susan, o), type(john, o),$
$\qquad transfuse(susan, mike), transfuse(susan, john),$
$\qquad transfuse(john, mike), transfuse(john, susan)\}.$

$MAY(P_{3.1}) = M(Q_1) \bigcup M(Q_2).$

$SURE(P_{3.1}) = M(Q_1) \bigcap M(Q_2) = \{type(mike, a), type(susan, o),$
$\qquad transfuse(susan, mike), transfuse(susan, john),$
$\qquad transfuse(john, mike)\}.$

The above $MAY(P_{3.1})$ and $SURE(P_{3.1})$ agree the discussion in Example 3.1. In the subsequent sections, we show how we realize a theorem prover which can handle such logical consequences.

15.4 An Implementation of Theorem Prover for Logic Programs with Functor Set

Now in this section we discuss the overview of theorem prover. Our theorem prover mainly consists of the following three programs.

- *Program translator*
- *Query interpreter*
- *User interface*

We first initialize every program by program translator, then we use query interpreter. To execute a query $\leftarrow G(G$ is a conjunction of atoms) in every system, we do a query like $\leftarrow mayall(G)$, $\leftarrow sure(G)$ and $\leftarrow accuracy(G)$. The May-system responds not only the solutions but also extensions of clauses which cause every solution. We can also evaluate every query through the user interface.

15.4.1 *Program translator in the theorem prover*

Here, we show the internal expression of programs with functor *set*, program translator and the algorithm for it.

We need to specify clauses with *set*, so we use an atom *headpred(LIST)*. In *headpred(LIST)*, every element in the *LIST* is a predicate which is a head of clause with *set*. The program translator picks up the first element from *headpred(LIST)*, then it sequentially translates every clause with this head and finally makes a set of the following atoms.

- hypo(num,extension_of_clause)
- ic([num1,num2])

Here, every clause whose head is not in *headpred(LIST)* is not translated and it is still remained. On the other hand, even though a clause *head* ← *body* does not have *set*, if *head* is in *headpred(LIST)* then it is translated to *hypo(num, head* ← *body)*. In *hypo(num, extension_ of_clause)*, *num* is a sequential number of *extension_of_clause* related to *set*. The *ic([num1, num2])* implies that every extension of clause whose number is between *num1* and *num2* comes from the same clause.

Definition 4.1 Let P be a program. We express a set of translated atoms as $TRANS(P)$. We also do a set of clauses whose head is not in *headpred(LIST)* as $NOTRANS(P)$. We call the union of these two sets an *internal expression* of a program P, and we express it as $INT(P)$.

Overview of algorithm for translation

Input: A program P and *headpred(LIST)*.
Output: An internal expression $INT(P)$.

(1) Assert *hyponumber*(1), which is a counter for numbering extensions of clauses.

(2) If $LIST = []$ in *headpred(LIST)* then clear garbages and end else pick up predicate h from *headpred([h|LIST])*, assert *current(h)* and revise *headpred([h|LIST])* to *headpred(LIST)*.

(3) For *current(h)*, if we can pick up clause *head'* ← *body* where h and *head'* is unifiable then go to the following steps else retract *current(h)* and go to 2.

    (a) For $body(= q_1 \wedge \cdots \wedge q_n)$, pick up every q_i. If *set* is in q_i then make a list $[q_i^1, \cdots, q_i^{m_i}]$ whose elements are extensions of q_i else make a list $[q_i]$. Then make cartesian products of n lists and make a list $listbody = [[q_1^1, \cdots, q_n^1], \cdots, [q_1^{m_1}, \cdots, q_n^{m_n}]]$. If $body = \emptyset$ then $listbody = []$.

    (b) For *head'*, if *set* is in *head'* then make a list *listhead* =

$[head'_1, \cdots, head'_l]$ whose elements are extensions of $head'$ else make a list $listhead = [head']$.

(c) Pick up $hyponumber(num)$ and set $num^* = num$. Then, continue the next procedure for finishing all cases.

    i. Pick up $hyponumber(num)$.

    ii. Pick up elements $head1 \in listhead$ and $body1 \in listbody$, and assert a clause $hypo(num, (head1 \leftarrow body1))$.

    iii. Revise $hyponumber(num)$ to $hyponumber(num + 1)$.

(d) Pick up $hyponumber(num)$. If $num^* < num - 1$ then assert $ic([num^*, num - 1])$.

(e) Retract a clause $head' \leftarrow body$ and go to 3.

15.4.2   *Query interpreter in the theorem prover*

In this subsection, we discuss the query interpreter for programs. We first show the resolution in the internal expression of programs and sequentially show every proof procedure.

Here, we need a procedure to check a formula F is a logical consequence of $Q \in EXT(P)$. The easy way is to check sequentially the refutation of $\{\leftarrow F\} \cup Q$ for $Q \in EXT(P)$. This seems to be easy, but there seems to be much loads for every user in using theorem prover. Because, every user has to repeat the same procedure for every $Q \in EXT(P)$. Therefore, we use the hypothetical reasoning strategy[1] for realization. In hypothetical reasoning, we have two groups of knowledge, i.e., $GROUP1$ which is a set of knowledge without uncertainty and $GROUP2$ which is a set of knowledge with uncertainty. For a query, we try to solve the query by knowledge in $GROUP1$, and if we can not get a solution then we use subset of $GROUP2$ to solve the query. In our framework, $NOTRANS(P)$ corresponds to $GROUP1$ and $TRANS(P)$ does $GROUP2$. Furthermore in this case, we have to remark the next constraint: *For every $ic([num1, num2])$, we can not use different extensions $ext1$ and $ext2$ such that $hypo(n1, ext1)$, $hypo(n2, ext2)$, $num1 \leq n1 \leq num2$ and $num1 \leq n2 \leq num2$ at the same time.* We can easily simulate the above procedure in prolog and our theorem prover is depending upon the above procedure. The following is the basic program in prolog. To solve a goal $GOAL$ we execute $\leftarrow solve(GOAL, [], ANS)$. We have extended this basic program for query interpreter in May-system and SURE-system.

Basic Program in Prolog

```
solve(GOAL,CUR,ANS):-functor(GOAL,FUN,_),FUN/==(,),!,
    solve1(GOAL,CUR,ANS).
solve(GOAL,CUR,ANS):-arg(1,GOAL,GOAL1),solve1(GOAL1,CUR,ANS1),
    arg(2,GOAL,GOAL2),solve(GOAL2,ANS1,ANS).
solve1(GOAL,CUR,ANS):-clause(GOAL,true),!,ANS=CUR.
solve1(GOAL,CUR,ANS):-clause(GOAL,BODY),!,solve(BODY,CUR,ANS).
solve1(GOAL,CUR,ANS):-hypo(NUM,GOAL),check(NUM,CUR),!,
    (member(NUM,CUR)->ANS=CUR;ANS=[NUM|CUR]).
solve1(GOAL,CUR,ANS):-hypo(NUM1,(GOAL:-BODY)),check(NUM,CUR),
    (member(NUM,CUR)->solve(BODY,CUR,ANS);
    solve(BODY,[NUM|CUR],ANS)).
```

15.4.2.1   *Realization of May-system*

Now we go to the realization of May-system. We first reconfirm that a formula F is a may-consequence of a program P if F is a logical consequence of some $Q \in EXT(P)$. The following shows the relation between procedure *solve* and may-consequences[14,15,16].

Proposition 4.1 *Let P be a program. The (1) and (2) are equivalent.*
(1) *There is a refutation of $\{\leftarrow solve(GOAL, [], ANS)\} \cup INT(P)$.*
(2) *There is an SLD-refutation of $\{\leftarrow GOAL\} \cup Q$ for some $Q \in EXT(P)$.*

Theorem 4.2   *Let P be a program. If there is a refutation for $\{\leftarrow solve(GOAL, [], ANS)\} \cup INT(P)$ with substitution θ, then $(GOAL)\theta$ is a may-consequence of P.*

Theorem 4.3 *Let P be a program and $(GOAL)\theta$ be a may-consequence of P. Then, there is a refutation for $\{\leftarrow solve((GOAL)\theta, [], ANS)\} \cup INT(P)$.*

According to the above theorem, it is enough to find refutations for $\{\leftarrow solve(GOAL, [], ANS)\} \cup INT(P)$ to get may-consequences of program P. The simple definition of predicate *mayall* is

```
mayall(GOAL):-solve(GOAL,[],ANS),display(ANS),fail.
mayall(GOAL).
```

In realized theorem prover, we extended this simple definition to powerful definitions.

15.4.2.2 *Side effects in May-system*

Now we go to the side effects in May-system, which is deeply related to diagnosis procedure. After finding a refutation for $\{\leftarrow solve(GOAL, [], ANS)\} \cup$ $INT(P)$ the ANS has a set of numbers, where every number has been assigned to extension of clause used in the refutation. According to this ANS, we can know that there is an SLD-refutation in which extension of program $Q \in EXT(P)$. We call it an *side effect* in May-system. We can get useful information by such side effects. In diagnosis of digital circuits, we specify a pair of input and output values and we execute the resolution. After getting a refutation, we can get the broken gate which satisfies the pair of input and output values as an side effect.

15.4.2.3 *Realization of SURE-system*

In this subsection, we discuss the Sure-system. Let P be a program and $GOAL$ be conjunctions of atoms. Suppose there are n refutations for $\{\leftarrow solve(GOAL, [], ANS)\} \cup INT(P)$ and we get refutations for $(GOAL)\theta_1$ with $ANS_1, \cdots, (GOAL)\theta_n$ with ANS_n. For every $(GOAL)\theta_i(1 \le i \le n)$, we can check there is an SLD-refutation in every $Q \in EXT(P)$ or not by $ANS_1, \cdots, ANS_n$. The following is the overview of proof procedure for Sure-system.

Overview of proof procedure in Sure-system

Input: A query $\leftarrow sure(GOAL)$, where $GOAL$ is a conjunction of atoms.
Output: All sure-consequences $(GOAL)\theta$ of program P.

(1) Assert $exlist((GOAL)\theta_i, ANS_i)$ for every refutation of $\{\leftarrow solve$ $(GOAL, [], ANS)\} \cup INT(P)$.

(2) If there is no asserted $exlist((GOAL)\theta_i, ANS_i)$ then end else pick up $(GOAL)\theta_i$ and $ANS_i(= [a_1^i, \cdots, a_n^i])$ from $exlist((GOAL)\theta_i, ANS_i)$, and set $current\_goal = (GOAL)\theta_i$ and $A_i = \{a_1^i, \cdots, a_n^i\}$. Assert $ans(A_i)$, retract $exlist((GOAL)\theta_i, ANS_i)$ and continue the following procedure.

    (a) Pick up every $(GOAL)\theta_j$ which are the same as $current\_goal$. Then, assert $ans(A_j)$ and retract $exlist((GOAL)\theta_j, ANS_j)$. We suppose $ans(A_1'), \cdots, ans(A_n')$ are asserted.

(b) Mark $ic(LIST_k)$ such that $LIST_k \cap A_i' \neq \emptyset$ for some $ans(A_i')$.

(c) For the marked $ic(LIST_k)(1 \leq k \leq m)$, make the cartesian products of $LIST_k$, which we express as $IND(P, current\_goal)$.

(d) For every $ind_j \in IND(P, current\_goal)$, check there is an $ans(A_i')$ such that A_i' is a subset of ind_j. If so, *current_goal* is a sure-consequence of P. Otherwise, *current_goal* is not so.

(e) Clear $ans(A_1'), \cdots, ans(A_n')$ and other garbages and go to 2.

15.4.2.4 *Realization of accuracy for query*

We revise the step 2-(d) in proof procedure in Sure-system for calculating accuracy ratio.

2-(d) Count the number of $ind_j \in IND(P, current\_goal)$ such that A_i' is a subset of ind_j for some $ans(A_i')$, and suppose we get the number num. Then calculate a ration $num/|IND(P, current\_goal)|$.

The every element in $SURE(P)$ surely holds and it does not depend upon the *set*. On the contrary, every element in $MAY(P)$ depends upon the *set*. The accuracy can assign a degree$(0 < \text{degree} \leq 1)$ to every may-consequence. Namely, the accuracy will be a factor which recovers the gap between may-consequences and sure-consequences.

Now we show the real execution of Example 3.1.

```
?-may(transfuse(X,Y)).
[1]Answer=transfuse(mike,john)
Hypo 3=type(john,a)
[2]Answer=transfuse(susan,john)
Hypo 4=type(john,o)
     :        :        :
[9]Answer=transfuse(john,susan)
Hypo 4=type(john,o)
EXEC_time=0.09440898895(sec)
X=X,
Y=Y
?-sure(transfuse(X,Y)).
[1]SLD-Refutation found in Sure-system
Answer=transfuse(susan,mike)
[2]Refutation found in Sure-System
```

```
Answer=transfuse(susan,john)
[3]Refutation found in Sure-System
Answer=transfuse(john,mike)
EXEC_time=0.02825701237(sec)
X=X,
Y=Y
?-accuracy(transfuse(X,Y)).
[1]SLD-Refutation found in Sure-system
Answer=transfuse(susan,mike)
[2]Answer=transfuse(mike,john):accuracy=1/2
[3]Answer=transfuse(susan,john):accuracy=2/2
[4]Answer=transfuse(john,mike):accuracy=2/2
[5]Answer=transfuse(john,susan):accuracy=1/2
EXEC_time=0.06015694141(sec)
X=X,
Y=Y
```

15.5 Logic Programming and Soft Computing

In the previous sections, we showed the overview of logic programs with functor *set*, which is an attempt to add soft computing aspects to logic programs. We can also see such new attempts[22], which show perspectives on how to combine soft computing's tolerance of imprecision with logic programming's power and semantics to provide a way forward for the implementation of intelligent knowledge-based systems. We think that logic programs with soft computing aspects will be very important issue for artificial intelligence and knowledge engineering.

15.6 Overview of the Diagnostic System for Digital Circuits

From now on we discuss the diagnostic system for digital circuits as an application of logic programs with functor *set*[23]. We first discuss the representation of circuits in logic programs. Then we introduce some definitions for faults in every gate. The followings are basic factors.

Circuit: Digital circuits with AND, OR, NOT, XOR-gates, where AND, OR and XOR-gate have two input values and one output value,

NOT-gate has one input value and one output value.

Faults: Single fault assumption.

Causes of faults: Faults in every gate and disconnection of line between two gates.

Diagnostic procedure: Procedure by May and Sure-systems.

User's roll: To specify a circuit definition file, a cause of fault and some pairs of input and output values.

Response from system: Every name of gate or every place of disconnection in line which causes pairs of input and output values.

We can easily apply our theorem prover for detecting fault in gates. We have also realized an user interface which manages a theorem prover, a program translator and a knowledge base with several rules. In the subsequent sections, we will show details of the diagnostic system.

15.7   Representation of Digital Circuits in Logic Programs

In this section, we discuss how we express the digital circuits according to [18], where the following items are necessary.

(C1) Name of the circuit like `circuit(f,4,3)` which implies a circuit named f has four input and three output values.

(C2) Name and the sort of the gate like `gate(a1,andg)` which implies a gate named $a1$ is an AND-gate.

(C3) Connection between every gate like `conn(o(1,a1),i(2,a2))` which implies the output of gate $a1$ is the second input of the gate $a2$.

(T1) Transaction of a value between two gates which is
`v(X,Y):-conn(Z,X),v(Z,Y).`

(T2) Transaction of input and output in every gate like
`v(o(1,X),1):-gate(X,andg),v(i(1,X),1),v(i(2,X),1).`

We call a program and a file which consist of items from $(C1)$ to $(C3)$ a *circuit definition program* and a *circuit definition file*, respectively. We also call a program and a file which consist of items from $(T1)$ to $(T2)$ a *transaction program* and a *transaction file*, respectively.

Now, we show a real example for digital circuits $cir1$ in Figure 15.1, which we usually call adder. The $cir1$ has four input values $i(1, cir1)$, $i(2, cir1)$, $i(3, cir1)$, $i(4, cir1)$ and three output values $o(1, cir1)$, $o(2, cir1)$, $o(3, cir1)$. Every input and output value is either 0(low) or 1(high), and the value $o(1, cir1) * 4 + o(2, cir1) * 2 + o(3, cir1)$ in decimal is the sum of input values.

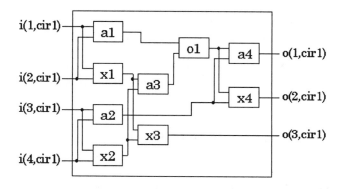

a1,a2,a3,a4:AND gate, o1:OR gate, x1,x2,x3,x4:XOR gate

Fig. 15.1   A Circuit cir1

The followings are the circuit definition program for *cir*1 and the transaction program for every circuit, which we use through the subsequent sections.

Circuit definition program for cir1
```
circuit(cir1,4,3).
gate(a1,andg),gate(a2,andg),gate(a3,andg),gate(a4,andg),gate(o1,org),
gate(x1,xorg),gate(x2,xorg),gate(x3,xorg),gate(x4,xorg).
conn(i(1,cir1),i(1,a1)),conn(i(2,cir1),i(2,a1)),conn(i(1,cir1),i(1,x1)),
conn(i(2,cir1),i(2,x1)),conn(i(3,cir1),i(1,a2)),conn(i(4,cir1),i(2,a2)),
conn(i(3,cir1),i(1,x2)),conn(i(4,cir1),i(2,x2)),conn(o(1,x1),i(1,a3)),
conn(o(1,x2),i(2,a3)),conn(o(1,x1),i(1,x3)),conn(o(1,x2),i(2,x3)),
conn(o(1,a1),i(1,o1)),conn(o(1,a3),i(2,o1)),conn(o(1,o1),i(1,a4)),
conn(o(1,a2),i(2,a4)),conn(o(1,o1),i(1,x4)),conn(o(1,a2),i(2,x4)),
conn(o(1,a4),o(1,cir1)),conn(o(1,x4),o(2,cir1)),conn(o(1,x3),o(3,cir1)).
```

Transaction program for circuits
```
v(X,Y):-conn(Z,X),v(Z,Y).
v(o(1,X),1):-gate(X,andg),v(i(1,X),1),v(i(2,X),1).
v(o(1,X),0):-gate(X,andg),((v(i(1,X),0),v(i(2,X),_));(v(i(1,X),_),v(i(2,X),0))).
```

```
v(o(1,X),1):-gate(X,org),((v(i(1,X),1),v(i(2,X),_));(v(i(1,X),_),v(i(2,X),1))).
v(o(1,X),0):-gate(X,org),v(i(1,X),0),v(i(2,X),0).
v(o(1,X),1):-gate(X,notg),v(i(1,X),0).
v(o(1,X),0):-gate(X,notg),v(i(1,X),1).
v(o(1,X),1):-gate(X,xorg),v(i(1,X),I1),v(i(2,X),I2),I1/==I2.
v(o(1,X),0):-gate(X,xorg),v(i(1,X),I1),v(i(2,X),I2),I1==I2.
```

We revise the above circuit definition program and transaction program for handling circuits with either a fault or a disconnection line.

15.8   Simulation in Circuits with Functor Set

We can easily run the above program in prolog and we can simulate the input and output transaction in every circuit. However, if we use functor *set* then we can get more useful information in circuits. For example, if we replace *gate(a1, andg)* with *gate(a1, set([andg, org, xorg]))*, then our prover responds output values depending upon three cases. The following is the real execution for input values (1,1,0,0).

```
    ?-mayall((v(o(1,cir1),X),v(o(2,cir1),Y),v(o(3,cir1),Z))).
    [1]Answer=v(o(1,cir1),0),v(o(2,cir1),1),v(o(3,cir1),0)
    Hp 1:0=gate(a1,andg)
    [2]Answer=v(o(1,cir1),0),v(o(2,cir1),1),v(o(3,cir1),0)
    Hp 2:0=gate(a1,org)
    [3]Answer=v(o(1,cir1),0),v(o(2,cir1),0),v(o(3,cir1),0)
    Hp 3:0=gate(a1,xorg)
    EXEC_time=2.014023066(sec)
    X = X,
    Y = Y,
    Z = Z
```

In this execution, we are calculating the output values depending upon three cases. Namely, we can get all possible output values by using *set([andg, org, xorg])* instead of *andg*, which will be helpful information. Then, we execute the next query in Sure-system, which implies 'Is the output value of *o(1, cir1)* depending upon the selection from *andg*, *org* and *xorg* ?'

```
    ?-sure(v(o(1,cir1),X)).
    [1]Refutation found in Sure-System
    Answer=v(o(1,cir1),0)
    EXEC_time=0.7502919436(sec)
```

X = X

This execution shows the value of $o(1, cir1)$ is always 0, which does not depend upon the selection from *andg*, *org* and *xorg*.

15.9 Fault Diagnosis in Circuits

Now we go to the diagnosis in circuits. The purpose is to detect the broken gate or the disconnection of line in every circuit. This problem is reduced to find the extension of program by specified pairs of input and output values. Namely, every user specifies a circuit definition program and he adds some pairs of input and output values to the system. The system responds the broken gates or the disconnection of line which satisfy the pairs of input and output values.

15.9.1 *Models for faults*

There are several factors which make troubles in a circuit and we suppose the following four models of faults and single faults assumption.

(Model-1) The output value is opposite for the truth value in a gate.
(Model-2) The output value is always unique in a gate.
(Model-3) The output value is the same value as an input value in a gate.
(Model-4) There is a disconnection of line between gates.

To cope with circuits with a broken gate, we add the following three special formulas to circuit definition program.

(C4) broken(circuit_name,set([gate$_1$,$\cdots$,gate$_n$])) for a circuit.
(C5) state(gate,set([ok,broken])) for every gate.
(C6) headpred([broken(_,_),state(_,_)]) for a circuit.

The first formula (C4) shows that there is a broken gate in $gate_1, \cdots, gate_n$ for (Model-1) to (Model-3) and it also shows that there is a disconnection of output line from a gate in $gate_1, \cdots, gate_n$ for (Model-4). Namely, this first formula (C4) causes single fault assumption in a circuit. We usually specify all gates in the second argument of predicate *broken*, however if we know either one of AND-gates is broken then we can positively remove other gates from there. For example in the circuit *cir1*, if we know either one of AND-gates is broken then we should use $broken(cir1, set([a1, a2, a3, a4]))$.

The second formula (C5) implies every gate is either *ok* or *broken*. The third formula (C6) shows heads of program clause with functor *set*, which is necessary for program translation.

15.9.2   May-system and diagnosis in circuits

Now we show how we apply our theorem prover for logic programs with functor *set* to diagnosis in circuits. Every circuit definition program consists of (C1) to (C6). In (C4) and (C5), there are functors *set* which causes the $EXT(P)$. Every extension $Q \in EXT(P)$ is a possible case from program P. Therefore, to detect a fault in a circuit is reduced to find the extension of program Q by specified pairs of input and output values. In this way, we can apply our theorem prover to diagnosis for digital circuits.

15.9.3   Diagnostic knowledge in circuits based on Model-1

Now we pick up the (Model-1) and briefly show the diagnosis in a circuit $cir1$. In (Model-1), we deal with a fault such that *the output value in a gate is opposite for the real value, i.e., the output value is 0 and 1 for the real value 1 and 0, respectively.* Here, we need to revise transaction program (T2) according to (Model-1). The following is a case of AND-gate.

```
v(o(1,X),1):-gate(X,andg),state(X,broken),broken(CIR,X),andgate0(X).
v(o(1,X),1):-gate(X,andg),state(X,ok),andgate1(X).
v(o(1,X),0):-gate(X,andg),state(X,broken),broken(CIR,X),andgate1(X).
v(o(1,X),0):-gate(X,andg),state(X,ok),andgate0(X).
andgate1(X):-v(i(1,X),1),v(i(2,X),1).
andgate0(X):-(v(i(1,X),_),v(i(2,X),0));(v(i(1,X),0),v(i(2,X),_)).
```

As for transaction rules in other gates, we need to revise by using predicates *state* and *broken*. In circuit definition program, if we knows an AND-gate is broken then we can positively specify $broken(cir1, set([a1, a2, a3, a4]))$ and $state(o1, ok)$, $state(x1, ok)$, $\cdots$, $state(x4, ok)$. It is enough for every user to change the elements of $LIST$ in $broken(cir1, LIST)$ for handling other cases. In the above program, if $broken(cir1, X)$ is once selected, then prover fails to solve $broken(cir1, Y)(X \neq Y)$. The predicate *state* is necessary, because prover sometimes uses both '*gate is broken*' and '*gate is not broken*' in a resolution, which makes contradiction. To escape this contradiction, we introduced predicate *state*.

15.9.4 *Diagnostic knowledge in circuits based on Model-2*

Now we pick up the (Model-2). In (Model-2), we deal with a fault such that *the output value in a gate is unique for every input value, i.e., the output value is uniquely 0 or 1 for every input value.* Here, we need to revise transaction program (T2) according to (Model-2). The following is a case of OR-gate.

```
v(o(1,X),set([0,1])):-gate(X,org),state(X,broken),broken(CIR,X),
    v(i(1,X),_),v(i(2,X),_).
v(o(1,X),1):-gate(X,org),state(X,ok),orgate1(X).
v(o(1,X),0):-gate(X,org),state(X,ok),orgate0(X).
orgate1(X):-(v(i(1,X),1),v(i(2,X),_));(v(i(1,X),_),v(i(2,X),1)).
orgate0(X):-v(i(1,X),0),v(i(2,X),0).
```

As for transaction rules in other gates, we need to revise by using predicates *state* and *broken*. The first rule implies output values $o(1, X)$ is either 0 or 1 which does not depend upon input values. This clause is internally translated to the following three formulas

```
hypo(num1,(v(o(1,X),0):-gate(X,org),state(X,broken),broken(CIR,X),
    v(i(1,X),_),v(i(2,X),_))).
hypo(num2,(v(o(1,X),1):-gate(X,org),state(X,broken),broken(CIR,X),
    v(i(1,X),_),v(i(2,X),_))).
ic([num1,num2]).
```

According to the $ic([num1, num2])$ the prover can use either one of hypothesis, which causes the condition in (Model-2). In this transaction program, we use functor *set* in the predicate $v(\_,\_)$, so we need to revise the (C6) as follows:

```
(C6') headpred([broken(_,_),state(_,_),v(_,_)]).
```

As we have shown, the $broken(cir1, X)$ holds only one time, so the first rule also holds one time. The $broken(cir1, X)$ keeps the single fault assumption.

15.9.5 *Diagnostic knowledge in circuits based on Model-3*

Now we pick up the (Model-3). In (Model-3), we deal with a fault such that *the output value in a gate is the same value as an input value.* Here, we need to revise transaction program (T2) according to (Model-3). The following is a case of XOR-gate.

```
v(o(1,X),set([V1,V2])):-gate(X,xorg),state(X,broken),broken(CIR,X),
```

```
    v(i(1,X),V1),v(i(2,X),V2).
v(o(1,X),1):-gate(X,xorg),state(X,ok),xorgate1(X).
v(o(1,X),0):-gate(X,xorg),state(X,ok),xorgate0(X).
xorgate1(X):-(v(i(1,X),1),v(i(2,X),0));(v(i(1,X),0),v(i(2,X),1)).
xorgate0(X):-(v(i(1,X),1),v(i(2,X),1));(v(i(1,X),0),v(i(2,X),0)).
```
The first rule implies output values $o(1, X)$ is either $V1$ or $V2$. It is automatically translated to the following three formulas
```
hypo(num1,(v(o(1,X),V1):-gate(X,xorg),state(X,broken),broken(CIR,X),
     v(i(1,X),V1),v(i(2,X),V2))).
hypo(num2,(v(o(1,X),V2):-gate(X,xorg),state(X,broken),broken(CIR,X),
     v(i(1,X),V1),v(i(2,X),V2))).
ic([num1,num2]).
```
According to the $ic([num1, num2])$ the prover can use either one of hypothesis, which causes the condition in (Model-3). As for transaction rules in other gates, we need to revise by using predicates *state* and *broken*. In (Model-3), we need to revise (C6) like (Model-2).

15.9.6   *Diagnostic knowledge in circuits based on Model-4*

Now we pick up the (Model-4). In (Model-4), we deal with a disconnection of line between gates and we see the disconnection as follows: *The disconnection from gate A to gate B implies that the input signal from gate A to B is 0(low).* We have expressed the possible broken gate by $broken(circuit, set([gate_1, \cdots, gate_n]))$. Here in (Model-4), we have to pay attention. If the output line from the broken gate is unique then there is no problem. For example, $conn(o(1, a3), i(2, o1))$ holds in $cir1$, so $a3$ is broken implies line from $a3$ to $o1$ is disconnected. However, if the lines from the broken gate are not unique then we can not see which line is not connected. For example, $conn(o(1, x1), i(1, a3))$ and $conn(o(1, x1), i(1, x3))$ hold in $cir1$, so $x1$ is broken implies either line from $x1$ to $a3$ or $x1$ to $x3$ is disconnected. To escape this problem, we added the extra knowledge for program translation. It handles $broken(circuit, LIST)$, $conn(FROM, TO)$ and $state(gate, set([ok, broken]))$, and remake the following formulas from (C4) and (C5):

(C4') broken(circuit_name,set([con(gate$_1$,gate$_1$'),$\cdots$,con(gate$_n$, gate$_n$')])) for a circuit, where $gate_i \in LIST$ for $broken(circuit, LIST)$ and $conn(o(1, gate_i), i(\_, gate'_i))$ hold.

(C5') `state(con(gate`$_i$`,gate`$_i$`'),set([ok,broken]))` for all connected gates $gate_i$ and $gate'_i$.

The translated (C4') and (C5') from (C4) and (C5) have no ambiguity for connection. Our prover calls this preprocessing before the program translation, namely (C4') and (C5') are automatically realized from (C4) and (C5). We show the overview for this preprocess.

Preprocess before program translation in (Model-4)

(1) Suppose $broken(circuit, set([gate_1, \cdots, gate_n])), conn(FROM, TO)$ and $state(gate, set([ok, broken]))$.

(2) Pick up $gate_i(1 \leq i \leq n)$ and continue the following process.

    (2-1) Find $conn(o(1, gate_i), i(\_, gate'_i))$, then assert $state(con(gate_i, gate'_i), set([ok, broken]))$ and $con(gate_i, gate'_i)$.

    (2-2) Retract $state(gate_i, set([ok, broken]))$.

(3) For asserted $con(gate_i, gate'_i)$, make list $LIST^* = [con(gate_1, gate'_1), \cdots, con(gate_n, gate'_n)]$. Then, assert $broken(circuit, LIST^*)$ and retract $broken(circuit, set([gate_1, \cdots, gate_n]))$.

Here, we revise transaction program (T1) according to (Model-4).

```
v(i(Q,Q1),0):-conn(o(P,P1),i(Q,Q1)),state(con(P1,Q1),broken),
    broken(CIR,con(P1,Q1)),v(o(P,P1),Y).
v(i(Q,Q1),Y):-conn(o(P,P1),i(Q,Q1)),state(P1,ok),v(o(P,P1),Y).
v(i(Q,Q1),Y):-conn(i(P,P1),i(Q,Q1)),v(i(P,P1),Y).
v(o(Q,Q1),Y):-conn(o(P,P1),o(Q,Q1)),v(o(P,P1),Y).
```

The first rule implies that if the line from gate $P1$ to gate $Q1$ is disconnected then the signal is always 0. The real signal Y in $v(o(P, P1), Y)$ is not sent to $Q1$. We can replace 0 with 1 in the first rule, if the signal of disconnection is 1(high).

15.9.7 *Overview of diagnostic operations*

Now we go to the overview of diagnostic procedures and operations. The following is the overview.

(Step1) Prepare the circuit definition program `circuit.pl` according to (C1) to (C6).

(Step2) Call the theorem prover `prover.pl` depending upon prolog interpreter.

(Step3) Execute `go` subcommand, where we specify the file name `circuit.pl` and a cause of fault from (Model-1) to (Model-4). After specification, every program is automatically translated to the internal expression.

(Step4) Initialize the question answering by `allclear` subcommand.

(Step5) Set a pair of input and output values by `condition` subcommand.

(Step6) Execute the search by `mayall` subcommand, then prover shows the possible solutions. To reduce solutions, we try (Step5) and we use `intersection` subcommand. To clear the possible solutions, we go back to (Step4).

We have realized an user interface which can manage the above procedures and operations.

15.9.8   *Real execution in cir1*

Now we show the real execution in *cir*1. We inputted the underlined part.

```
?-go.
Circuit Definition File:'circuit.pl'.
Selection of Model
1:   Model-1
2:   Model-2
3:   Model-3
4:   Model-4
:   4.
Executing...
Initialization complete!!
EXEC_time=0.03868198395(sec)
Diagnostic Mode OK
yes
```

In the above execution, we specified circuit definition file and (Model-4), then the prover automatically translates a program to internal expression. After this procedure, we can use *condition*, *intersection* and *allclear* subcommands.

```
?-condition.
Specify Input digital signals for Circuit
```

```
VALUE 1 = 1.
VALUE 2 = 0.
VALUE 3 = 1.
VALUE 4 = 0.
Specify Output digital signals for Circuit
VALUE 1 = 0.
VALUE 2 = 0.
VALUE 3 = 0.
[1]Answer=v(o(1,cir1),0),v(o(2,cir1),0),v(o(3,cir1),0)
Hp 10:0=broken(cir1,con(o1,x4))
[2]Answer=v(o(1,cir1),0),v(o(2,cir1),0),v(o(3,cir1),0)
Hp 4:0=broken(cir1,con(a3,o1))
[3]Answer=v(o(1,cir1),0),v(o(2,cir1),0),v(o(3,cir1),0)
Hp 7:0=broken(cir1,con(x2,a3))
[4]Answer=v(o(1,cir1),0),v(o(2,cir1),0),v(o(3,cir1),0)
Hp 5:0=broken(cir1,con(x1,a3))
EXEC_time=4.907007933(sec)
yes
```

We called *condition* subcommand and specified input and output values according to the prompt. There are four answers. The last answer shows line from $x1$ to $a3$ is not connected. To reduce the solutions, we execute the *condition* subcommand again.

```
?-condition.
Specify Input digital signals for Circuit
VALUE 1 = 1.
VALUE 2 = 1.
VALUE 3 = 0.
VALUE 4 = 0.
Specify Output digital signals for Circuit
VALUE 1 = 0.
VALUE 2 = 0.
VALUE 3 = 0.
[1]Answer=v(o(1,cir1),0),v(o(2,cir1),0),v(o(3,cir1),0)
Hp 10:0=broken(cir1,con(o1,x4))
[2]Answer=v(o(1,cir1),0),v(o(2,cir1),0),v(o(3,cir1),0)
Hp 1:0=broken(cir1,con(a1,o1))
EXEC_time=4.117717028(sec)
yes
```

```
?-intersection.
[1]Hp 10:0=broken(cir1,con(o1,x4))
EXEC_time=0.0342849493(sec)
yes
```

We called *condition* subcommand again and get other solutions. To reduce the solution, we called the *intersection* subcommand and we found unique solution $broken(cir1, con(o1, x4))$, namely output line from $o1$ to $x4$ is not connected.

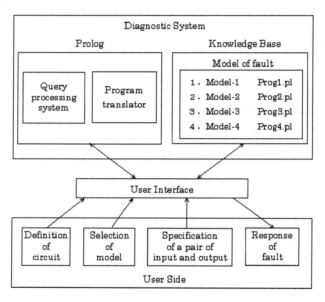

Fig. 15.2   Structure of Diagnostic System

15.10   Structure of Diagnostic System

Now we go to the structure of diagnostic system. We show the overview in Figure 15.2. Every subsystem except user interface is implemented by prolog. There are query processing subsystem, program translation subsystem and knowledge bases dealing with faults in circuits. As for user interface, it is implemented by TCL/TK library and it connects every subsystem and user inputs.

15.11 Diagnosis through User Interface

Now we show the user interface in Figure 15.3. It consists of the following three parts.

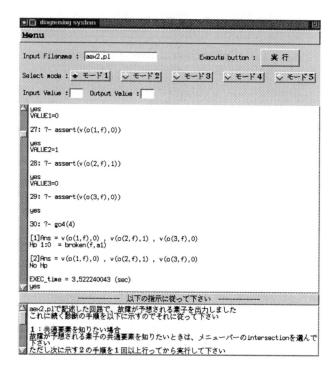

Fig. 15.3 Execution of Diagnosis through User Interface

(1) The *user operation part* is the upper area of the user interface, where we input the name of circuit definition file, we select the model of fault and finally we specify a pair of input and output values.

(2) The *monitor part* is the middle area, where we can see called sub-commands in prolog and the trace of processing.

(3) The *user support part* is the lower area, where we can see some useful knowledge for using this system.

Gates	Model-1	Model-2	Model-3	Model-4
3	0.14	0.47	0.25	0.11
7	0.71	6.34	1.71	0.76
12	9.34	158.96	19.75	11.21
16	27.25	455.46	83.53	31.92
20	68.82	1694.87	172.02	70.10

Table 15.1   Comparison of Execution Time (Sec)

In Figure 15.3, we are handling a circuit named f, which is the same as $cir1$. We selected (Model-1) for fault and we specified input values $(0, 1, 0, 1)$ and output value $(0, 1, 0)$. We can see that every value is internally asserted as either $v(o(1, f), 0)$ or $v(o(1, f), 1)$. Then, subcommand $mayall((v(o(1, f), 0), v(o(2, f), 1), v(o(3, f), 0)))$ is internally executed, which is the procedure to detect faults. There are two responses. The first response implies the gate $a1$ is broken. The second one does there is no broken gate, because $(0, 1, 0)$ is the correct output values for input values. As for query, we can also use variables instead of 0 or 1. In this case the system finds value 0 or 1 for variables which satisfy the query. Therefore, if we input variables for every output values then we can get all possible output values. However, we have to remark that we need to specify all input and output values. Otherwise, the search path may not reach some broken gates, which makes the system fail to detect the broken gates.

15.12   Evaluation of Execution Time

Now we discuss the execution time for diagnosis, which may be a negative result. The user interface will be useful for every user, but it may cause much execution time as well as search time for detecting broken gate. The query processing subsystem basically depends upon hypothetical reasoning, whose computational complexity is NP-complete[24]. Therefore, we experimentally examined the execution time for diagnosis. We prepared ten circuits, which consist of minimally three gates and maximally twenty gates. We show the result in Table 1. The left column shows the number of gates in circuits and the top line shows models of faults, i.e., (Model-1) to (Model-4). Every execution time is the time to find all possible solutions which satisfy a pair of input and output values. To summarize the result, we can really use this system for circuits with twenty gates in (Model-1), (Model-3) and (Model-4). We can also do circuits with about ten gates in (Model-2).

15.13 Concluding Remarks

We have been proposing logic programs with functors *set* for handling incomplete attribute values and we applied our prover to diagnosis of digital circuits, which has the following properties:

(1) We have enough to specify programs for circuits. We do not need any knowledge of prolog.
(2) As for simulation, we can get all possible cases according to a formula like $gate(gate\_name, set(LIST))$.
(3) As for diagnosis, to change a formula $broken(circuit, set(LIST))$ is enough for various cases.
(4) We can easily detect a broken gate by some pairs of input and output values.
(5) There exists a friendly graphical user interface.

We think the notation depending upon functor *set* seems to be suitable for expressing single fault assumption and so on.

As for $set(LIST)$, we saw there exists an unknown real value in the $LIST$. This unknown real value causes modal concepts, which we have included in logic programs. However, we can see it implies the possibility of selection, where is no unknown real value. If we take this interpretation then we will apply our framework to the planning or decision support under some constraints. We distinguish such two information and we express them as $setu(LIST)$ and $sets(LIST)$. The $setu(LIST)$ implies a set with unknown real value and $sets(LIST)$ does a set with selective values. We are also touching new framework by $setu$ and $sets$[17].

In this paper, we showed a developed theorem prover handling functor *set* and the possibility for applying it to diagnosis of circuits. We will add such soft computing aspects to logic programs from now on.

References

[1] D.Poole, R.Goebel and R.Aleliunas, "Theorist: A Logical Reasoning System for Defaults and Diagnosis", The Knowledge Frontier: Essays in the Representation of Knowledge, Springer-Verlag, pp.331-352, 1987.

[2] R.Kowalski, "Problems and Promises of Computational Logic", Computational Logic(ed. J.W. Lloyd), Springer-Verlag, pp.1-34, 1990.

[3] R.Reiter, "A Logic for Default Reasoning", Artificial Intelligence, 13, pp.81-132, 1980.

[4] D.McDermott and J.Doyle, "Non-Monotonic Logic 1", Artificial Intelligence, 13, pp.41-72, 1980.

[5] J.Lobo, J.Minker and A.Rajasekar, Foundations of Disjunctive Logic Programming, MIT press, 1992.

[6] D.Loveland, "Near-Horn Prolog", Proc. 4th Int'l. Conf. on Logic Programming, pp.456-469, 1987.

[7] T.Matrin, J.Baldwin and B.Pilsworth, "The Implementation of FPROLOG", Fuzzy Sets and Systems, 23, pp.119-129, 1987.

[8] M.Mukaidono, Z.Shen and L.Ding, "Fuzzy Prolog", Proc. 2nd IFSA Congress, pp.844-847, 1987.

[9] N.Kanai and M.Ishizuka, "Prolog-ELF Incorporating Fuzzy Logic", Transaction of Information Processing Society, 27, pp.411-416, 1986.

[10] E.F.Codd, "A Relational Model of Data for Large Shared Data Banks", Communication of ACM, 13, pp.377-387, 1970.

[11] W.Lipski, "On Semantic Issues Connected with Incomplete Information Databases", ACM Transaction on Data Base Systems, 4, pp.262-296, 1979.

[12] L.Lakshmanan, "Evolution of Intelligent Database Systems: A Personal Perspective", Incompleteness and Uncertainty in Information Systems, Springer-Verlag, pp.189-208, 1993.

[13] H.Sakai, "On a Framework for Logic Programming with Incomplete Information", Fundamenta Informaticae, 19, pp.223-234, 1993.

[14] H.Sakai, "Some Proof Procedures and Their Application for Realizing Another Fuzzy Prolog", Proc. 7th Australian Joint Conf. on AI, World Scientific Publisher, pp.283-290, 1994.

[15] H.Sakai, "On Semantics for Logic Programming with Incomplete Information", Transaction of Information Processing Society of Japan, 35-5, pp.706-713, 1994.

[16] H.Sakai and A.Okuma, "Applications of Logic Programs with Functor Set to Automated Problem Solving under Uncertainty", Proc. 9th Int'l. Conf. on IEA/AIE, Gordon and Breach Science Publisher, pp.377-382, 1996.

[17] H.Sakai, "On Logic Programs with Functors Setu and Sets Related to Concept Rule of Thumb", Proc. 10th Australian Joint Conf. on AI, pp.173-178, 1997.

[18] M.Genesereth and N.Nillson, Logical Foundations of Artificial Intelligence, Morgan Kaufmann Publisher, 1987.

[19] R.Davis, "Diagnostic Reasoning based on Structure and Behavior", Artificial Intelligence, 24, pp.347-410, 1984.

[20] J.deKleer and B.Williams, "Diagnosing Multiple Faults", Artificial Intelligence, 32, pp.97-139, 1987.

[21] J.Lloyd, Foundations of Logic Programming, Springer-Verlag, 1984.

[22] T.Martin and F.Arcellifontana, Logic Programming and Soft Computing, Research Studies Press, 1998.

[23] H.Sakai, A.Imamoto and A.Okuma, "On A Diagnostic System for Digital Circuits", Proc. IIZUKA98, World Scientific Publisher, pp.255-258, 1998.

[24] H.Kautz and B.Selman, "Hard Problems for Simple Default Logics", Proc. 1st. Int'l. Conf. on Principles of Knowledge Representation and Reasoning, 1989.

Chapter 16

Determination of the Motion Parameters from the Perspective Projection of a Triangle

Myint Myint Sein and Hiromitsu Hama

Osaka City University

Abstract

We present an estimation method of the motion parameters of a camera moving in static environment. The approach is based on the perspective projection of a triangle constructed from any three points in a 3D scene. The motion parameters are estimated from the image of the triangle related to the each camera lens center. Unlike most methods, our method does not restrict the intrinsic parameters of the camera as focal length, zoom and so on. And accurate position is selected by the surface normal vector and viewing direction vector of the triangle in many possible positions. The possible application of this approach is the determination of the required motion of the camera for any work from the image frames to reach the goal position. Experimental results with real images are illustrated, and the effectiveness of our method is confirmed through them.

Keywords : perspective projection, nodal points, motion parameters, camera center coordinate system, nonlinear system, projected image of a triangle, normal vector of a surface, viewing direction vector, camera motion model, structure estimation, photogrammetry

16. 1 Introduction

To reach the accurate desire position is an important task for a lot of camera control works as movie work, autonomous flight work, automatic landing of a helicopter, robotic control and so on. In these works, the accurate estimation of the required angle and movement of the camera is essentially needed to catch the desire posture of an object from the present one. The motion parameters of the camera are detected from the relative positions of the object to the camera which moves from one place to others. To determine the structure of an object, the set of nonlinear equations is established by using the nodal points of a triangle created by any three points in a 3D scene and their corresponding projected image points. According to Haralick [1], the works relating with the three points perspective pose estimation problem, early were done by Grunet (1841), Finster Walder (1903), Merritt (1949), Linnainmaa *et al.* (1988), Fishels and Bolles (1981) and Grafarend (1989). Their approach are also based on a triangle and derived the set of nonlinear equations from the trigonometric relation of the edges and angles. Haralick *et al.* discussed about the difference of their approaches and solutions. They summarized that there were more than four solutions by solving the system of nonlinear equations, some of which were singular. Haralick [2] derived a system of equations to determine the camera look angle parameters from perspective projection of a rectangle. Liu and Huang [3] proposed a method to determine the camera location from 2-D to 3-D straight line or point correspondences. Zhang [4] proposed an algorithm for determining the 3D motion and structure from the *n* correspondences of line segments between two perspective images by using a calibrated camera with unit focal length. The algorithm is based on the epipolar constraint and he solved the motion problem by maximizing the overlap of the line segments.

Our objective is to estimate the motion parameters of a moving camera and to obtain the position and orientation of the camera. Unlike other camera calibration methods [1]-[4] from known measurement of an object, the impeccable pose of the object relative to the camera can be determined from the orientation of the object. The method proposed here can uniquely estimate the relative position parameters of the three points to the camera by detection the normal vector of a triangle surface. It is based on the normal vector of the surface of a triangle which is constructed from any three lines which have common vertexes each other, or any three points in a 3-D scene. As a result it becomes possible to get the three dimensional information about the scene through stereography.

We investigate the camera motion parameters from the normal vector of the triangle surface related to the camera motion. The six extrinsic parameters of a camera, that is, three position parameters and three orientation parameters are also computed from only one image of the triangle whose edges are known. The right angle triangle is more convenience than others to use. It is reasonable to get the known right angle triangle from the image of the scene in our environment. For example, some rigid object as book, table, desk and machine, room corner, building and road in outdoor and indoor scene contain the right angle corner and some things is possible to know the length of their sides. The system of nonlinear equations are derived in any directional component of the triangle by using the nodal points of the triangle and their corresponding projected image points to determine the structure of the object. We compute the viewing direction vector and normal vector on the surface of the triangle to estimate the camera look angle parameters from the images. Images are taken from different positions and orientations by manually moving a camera at time $t_i (i = 1,2,..)$. In Section 16.2, the changes of the direction of the surface of the triangle due to the camera motion are detected for the accurate position of the object. The 3-D scene is projected into a 2-D picture through the process of optical imaging. The camera center coordinate system is defined and derived the system of linear equations and nonlinear equations. In Section 16.3, we derive the system of nonlinear equations in terms of the rotation and translation parameters using the surface normal vectors. Some mathematical techniques are used for solving these linear equations and nonlinear equations. Parameter estimation algorithm is discussed in Section 16.4. Section 16.5 presents the experimental results for the algorithm with real images. Finally, in Section 16.6, this approach has been summarized.

16.2   Model and Notations

16.2.1   *Notations of the Image Plane*

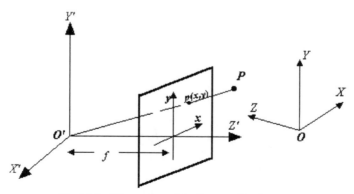

Fig.16.1   Illustration of the Perspective Geometry.

Let $P'(X',Y',Z')$ denote the Cartesian coordinates of a 3-D scene point with respect to the camera, and let $p(x, y)$ denote the corresponding coordinates in the image plane. Pinhole camera model is used (see Fig.16.1). For the camera center coordinate system, the image plane is located at the focal length f and the relation between the 3-D point and 2-D point is expressed by:

$$x = f\frac{X'}{Z'},$$

$$y = f\frac{Y'}{Z'}.$$

(1)

16.2.2 *Structure Estimation*

The system of nonlinear equations is derived for the estimation of the structure of the object by using the edges of a triangle in a 3-D scene. The triangle is created by using the three control points which are projected from a planar surface in the 3-D scene. The imaging geometry is illustrated in Fig. 16.2, where O_1 is the first camera position, n_1 is the normal vector of the triangular surface S and there are the nodal points $P_i (i = 1,2,..)$ and the corresponding projected triangle s_1 with the nodal points $p_i (i = 1,2,..)$ on the image plane. We denote the nodal points of three vertices of S as $P_1(X_1,Y_1,Z_1)$, $P_2(X_2,Y_2,Z_2)$, $P_3(X_3,Y_3,Z_3)$ and the corresponding projected nodal points in the image plane as $p_1(x_1,y_1,-f)$, $p_2(x_2,y_2,-f)$, $p_3(x_3,y_3,-f)$.

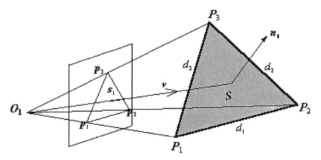

Fig.16.2   Imaging Geometry of a Triangle in a 3D Space.

The lengths of each edge of the triangle d_1, d_2 and d_3 can be expressed by the three nodal vectors P_1, P_2 and P_3 as

$$|P_1 - P_2| = d_1,$$
$$|P_2 - P_3| = d_2,$$
$$|P_3 - P_1| = d_3. \tag{2}$$

Using the Eq. (1) and (2) we get the quadratic polynomials in Z,

$$aZ_1^2 + bZ_2^2 - 2eZ_1Z_2 = d_1^2,$$
$$bZ_2^2 + cZ_3^2 - 2gZ_2Z_3 = d_2^2, \tag{3}$$
$$cZ_3^2 + aZ_1^2 - 2hZ_3Z_1 = d_3^2,$$

where

$$a = \frac{1}{f^2}(x_1^2 + y_1^2 + f^2), e = \frac{2}{f^2}(x_1x_2 + y_1y_2 + f^2),$$

$$b = \frac{1}{f^2}(x_2^2 + y_2^2 + f^2), g = \frac{2}{f^2}(x_2x_3 + y_2y_3 + f^2),$$

$$c = \frac{1}{f^2}(x_3^2 + y_3^2 + f^2), h = \frac{2}{f^2}(x_3x_1 + y_3y_1 + f^2).$$

Let $Z_2 = kZ_1$ and $Z_3 = rZ_1$, then they can be rewritten as

$$Z_1^2 = \frac{d_1^2}{a + bk^2 - 2ek} = \frac{d_2^2}{bk^2 + cr^2 - 2gkr} = \frac{d_3^2}{a + cr^2 - 2hr}, \tag{4}$$

$$a + bk^2 - 2ek = d_{12}^2(bk^2 + cr^2 - 2gkr), \tag{5}$$

$$a + cr^2 - 2hr = d_{32}^2(bk^2 + cr^2 - 2gkr). \tag{6}$$

The value of k^2 can be obtained in terms of k and r from Eq. (5);

$$k^2 = \frac{a - 2ek + d_{12}^2 r(2gk - cr)}{b(d_{12}^2 - 1)}.$$

Then, the value of k can be obtained in terms of r as follows:

$$k = \frac{(d_2^2 - d_3^2 - d_1^2)cr^2 + 2(d_1^2 - d_2^2)hr + a(d_2^2 + d_3^2 - d_1^2)}{2d_3^2(e - gr)}, \tag{7}$$

where $d_{ij}^2 = \dfrac{d_i^2}{d_j^2}$ $(1 \le i \le j \le 3)$. The Eq. (5) can be rewritten as the fourth

order polynomial in r.

$$R_4 r^4 + R_3 r^3 + R_2 r^2 + R_1 r + R_0 = 0, \tag{8}$$

where

$$R_4 = c(d_1^2 - d_2^2 + d_3^2)\{4g^2 d_1^2 d_3^2 + cb(d_1^2 - d_2^2)\} - 4cg^2 d_1^2 d_3^4,$$

$$\begin{aligned}R_3 &= 4c(d_1^2 - d_2^2 + d_3^2)\{bh(d_1^2 - d_2^2)^2 - ged_3^2(d_1^2 + d_2^2)\} \\ &\quad + 8gd_1^2 d_3^2 \{ecd_3^2 - gh(d_1^2 - d_2^2)\},\end{aligned}$$

$$\begin{aligned}R_2 &= 2(d_1^2 - d_2^2)\{abcd_3^4 - abc(d_1^2 - d_2^2)^2 + 4eghd_3^2(d_1^2 + d_2^2) - 2bh^2(d_1^2 - d_2^2)\} \\ &\quad + 4d_2^2 d_3^2 \{ag^2 d_3^2 - ce^2(d_2^2 - d_1^2 - d_3^2)\} \\ &\quad - 4d_1^2 d_3^2 \{ce^2 d_3^2 + ag^2(d_2^2 - d_1^2 + d_3^2)\},\end{aligned}$$

$$\begin{aligned}R_1 &= 4a(d_2^2 - d_1^2 + d_3^2)\{ged_3^2(d_1^2 + d_2^2) - bh(d_1^2 - d_2^2)^2\} \\ &\quad - 8ed_2^2 d_3^2 \{agd_3^2 - eh(d_1^2 - d_2^2)\},\end{aligned}$$

$$R_0 = a(d_1^2 - d_2^2)\{4e^2 d_2^2 d_3^2 - ab(d_2^2 - d_1^2 + d_3^2)^2\}.$$

At least four real roots of r are obtained from this polynomial. After obtaining the value of r by solving it, the values of k are computed for each r by Eq. (7). Then the nodal point $Z_i (i = 1,2,..)$ can be easily obtained from Eq. (4). The points (x_i, y_i), (x_j, y_j), $(1 \le i \le j \le 3)$ are observed from the image of the known triangle. It is sufficient to determine the positions, which is described of the vertices of the triangle in the 3-D scene on the camera center coordinate system, from only one perspective image of the triangle. We can obtain the position parameters of the triangle.

16.3   Surface Normal Vector of a Triangle

In this section, the surface normal vector of the triangle is detected to determine the accurate position of a triangle to the camera. For convenience, the coordinate system centered at the camera is called the camera centered coordinate system and abbreviated as CCS, and the surface normal vector is abbreviated as SNV. If without any notice, the coordinate system means the world coordinate system. The SNV n of the triangle surface S can be determined using its three position vectors P_1, P_2 and P_3, as

$$n = \frac{(P_2 - P_1)(P_3 - P_1)}{|(P_2 - P_1)(P_3 - P_1)|} \ . \tag{9}$$

By using Eq. (1), we can rewrite the SNV n with the parameters of the image points as

$$n = \frac{(\lambda, \mu, \nu)}{|(\lambda, \mu, \nu)|} , \tag{10}$$

where,

$$\lambda = \frac{1}{f}\{Z_1 Z_2 (y_1 - y_2) + Z_2 Z_3 (y_2 - y_3) + Z_3 Z_1 (y_3 - y_1)\} ,$$

$$\mu = \frac{1}{f}\{Z_1 Z_2 (x_2 - x_1) + Z_2 Z_3 (x_3 - x_2) + Z_3 Z_1 (x_1 - x_3)\} ,$$

$$\nu = \frac{1}{f^2}\{Z_1 Z_2 (x_1 y_2 - x_2 y_1) + Z_2 Z_3 (x_2 y_3 - x_3 y_2) + Z_3 Z_1 (x_3 y_1 - x_1 y_3)\} .$$

The image points (x_1, y_1), (x_2, y_2) and (x_3, y_3) are collected from the image of the object. Then, the SNV n depends only on the depth measurements Z_1, Z_2 and Z_3. According to the camera position, the direction of the surface normal and viewing direction will be changed. We consider the motion of the moving camera with respect to a triangle in the scene. The camera is at the first position, and next moves from the first position to the second position and so on. So there are many CCS's, for example, the first camera CCS, the second camera CCS and so on. Such a system is illustrated in Fig. 16.3. When the camera is at the initial time instant and initial position $O_1(A_1, B_1, C_1)$, we denote the SNV on the 1st camera CCS by n_1. The camera reaches the second position $O_2(A_2, B_2, C_2)$ and the SNV is observed in second image frame by n_2 on the 2nd camera CCS after moving. The camera moves to the kth position $O_k(A_k, B_k, C_k)$ and the surface normal vector n_k ($k = 1, 2, ..$) is observed from the image frames of the triangle taken from the different camera positions. Due to the camera motion, the orientation of the SNV n changes depending on the camera CCS therefore we can expresses

$$n = T_1 \circ n_1 = T_2 \circ n_2 = \ .... = T_k \circ n_k , \tag{11}$$

$$n_2 = T_{12} \circ n_1 , \quad n_3 = T_{23} \circ n_2 , \quad ...... , \quad n_k = T_{(k-1)k} \circ n_{(k-1)} ,$$

where

n = the SNV of the triangle on the world coordinate system,

n_1 = the SNV of the 1st camera CCS (the initial position),

n_2 = the SNV of the 2nd camera CCS,

...　...　.　....　.　....　.　....　.　...　......

n_k = the SNV of the kth camera CCS ,

and T_k 's are the transformation from the kth camera CCS to the world coordinate system. $T_{(k-1)k}$'s are the transformations from the $(k\text{-}1)^{th}$ camera CCS to k^{th} one.

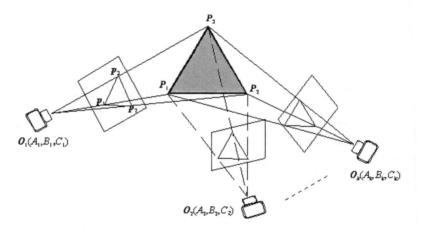

Fig. 16.3　Camera Motion Model.

The transformation T has two components, that is, a rotation R and a translation D. We can express as

$$T = RD .\tag{12}$$

Similarly, the unit vector v_k along the viewing direction of the kth camera CCS can be represent by the direction $v_{(k-1)}$ of the $(k\text{-}1)^{th}$ camera CCS.

$$v_2 = T_{12} \circ v_1 , \quad v_3 = T_{23} \circ v_2 , \quad ....., \quad v_k = T_{(k-1)k} \circ v_{(k-1)}\tag{13}$$

$$v_k = \frac{O_k - P_C}{\|O_k - P_C\|},$$

where P_C is the center of the triangle and O_k is the camera center (ie. camera position).

16.4 Parameter Estimation

According to the Eq. (11) and (13), the coordinate transformation from the world coordinate system to the camera CCS can be represent in a homogeneous form as,

$$P' = TP,\tag{14}$$

$$P' = RDP,$$

where the coordinate $P = (X, Y, Z, 1)^T$ in the 1st camera CCS system is observed as $P' = (X', Y', Z', 1)^T$ in the next camera CCS. The rotational transformation between the camera coordinate system and world coordinate one is represented by the angles α, β and γ which denote the angle between Z' and X axis, Z' and Y axis and Z' and Z axis, respectively. And $\cos \alpha = \cos \phi \cos \gamma$ and $\cos^2 \alpha + \cos^2 \beta + \cos^2 \gamma = 1$. The rotation matrix R can be expressed in a homogeneous form as,

$$R = \begin{pmatrix} C_1 C_2 & S_1 C_2 & -S_2 & 0 \\ -S_1 & C_1 & 0 & 0 \\ C_1 S_2 & S_1 S_2 & C_2 & 0 \\ 0 & 0 & 0 & 1 \end{pmatrix},\tag{15}$$

where $C_1 = \cos\phi$, $C_2 = \cos\gamma$, $S_1 = \sin\phi$ and $S_2 = \sin\gamma$. Translation of the origin of the world coordinate system to the camera CCS is accomplished by the 4×4 translation matrix D.

$$D = \begin{pmatrix} 1 & 0 & 0 & -A \\ 0 & 1 & 0 & -B \\ 0 & 0 & 1 & -C \\ 0 & 0 & 0 & 1 \end{pmatrix}.\tag{16}$$

Eq. (14) can be rewritten as

$$
\begin{pmatrix} X' \\ Y' \\ Z' \\ 1 \end{pmatrix} = \begin{pmatrix} C_1C_2 & S_1C_2 & S_2 & -AC_1C_2 - BS_1C_2 + CS_2 \\ -S_1 & C_1 & 0 & -AS_1 - BC_1 \\ C_1S_2 & S_1S_2 & C_2 & -AC_1S_2 - BS_1S_2 + CS_2 \\ 0 & 0 & 0 & 1 \end{pmatrix} \begin{pmatrix} X \\ Y \\ Z \\ 1 \end{pmatrix}. \tag{17}
$$

The three vertex points of the triangle give us the nine equations with in the five independent parameters. By solving this system of equations, we get

$$
\phi = \tan^{-1} \frac{Y_1'(Y_2 - Y_3) + Y_2'(Y_3 - Y_1) + Y_3'(Y_1 - Y_2)}{Y_1'(X_2 - X_3) + Y_2'(X_3 - X_1) + Y_3'(X_1 - X_2)},
$$

$$
\gamma = \tan^{-1} \frac{\varepsilon(X_1' - Y_1') - \zeta(X_2' - X_3')}{X_1'(Z_2 - Z_3) + X_2'(Z_3 - Z_1) + X_3'(Z_1 - Z_2)},
$$

$$
\alpha = \tan^{-1} \frac{\sqrt{1 - \cos^2 \phi \sin^2 \gamma}}{\cos \phi \sin \gamma}, \tag{18}
$$

$$
A = X_1 - X_1'C_1C_2 + Y_1'S_1 - Z_1'C_1S_2,
$$

$$
B = Y_1 - X_1'S_1C_2 + Y_1'C_1 - Z_1'S_1S_2,
$$

$$
C = Z_1 - X_1'S_2 - Z_1'C_1,
$$

where

$$
\varepsilon = (X_3 - X_2)C_1 + (Y_2 - Y_3)S_1,
$$

$$
\zeta = (X_1 - X_2)C_1 + (Y_1 - Y_2)S_1.
$$

By using this system of equations (18), we compute the position and orientation parameters of the camera relative to a triangle. And we estimate the rotation and translation parameters of the camera between four frames.

16.5   Experimental Results

The four image frames of a model of a house are used in our experiments (see in Fig. 16.4). Images are taken from different positions and orientations using the MINOLTA 3CCD digital camera (RD-175). The image contains 1528 × 1146 pixels. First, we extract the any three-vertex points, which are projected from a planer surface of an object in the 3-D scene, in the first frame and their corresponding points in the other's frames. Initialization data for the length of a triangle's edges and camera focal lengths are shown in Table 16.1. The actual data of the camera calibration in a 3D scene are measured by the 3SPACE FASTRAK.

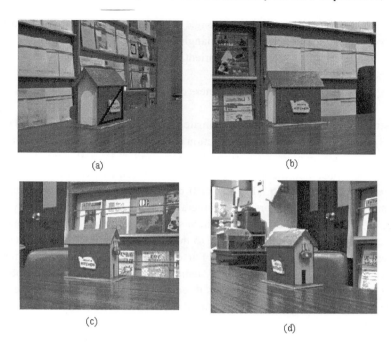

(a)

(b)

(c)

(d)

Fig. 16.4 Experiment with Real Image: (a), (b), (c), (d) are the images of a house taken from the different positions and angles. One triangle used here is shown in image (a).

Table 16.1   Given Measurements for Edges of the Triangle and Camera Focal Lengths.

$d_1 = 12.05$cm	$d_2 = 14.354$cm	$d_3 = 7.95$cm
$f = 24$mm $f''' = 35$mm	$f' = 28$mm	$f'' = 25$mm

The procedure for the estimation is as follows:

(1)   Preprocessing (Trace of the contour and noise reduction and so on.)

(2)   Detection of the any three correspondence feature points which are projected from the planar surface of an object from image frames

(3)   Estimation of the structure of the object relative to the camera.

(4) Detection of the camera look angle direction using the surface normal vector and position vector of a triangle to the camera.
(5) Calculation of the position and orientation parameters for the each camera position.
(6) Estimation of the motion parameters of the camera.

The structure of the object can be estimated by using the system of Eq. (4), (7) and (8). We calculate the normal direction and viewing direction of the triangle surface for each camera CCS from Eq. (10) and (13), and next detect the camera locations. The translation parameters between two coordinate systems can be computed from Eq. (16) and (18) using some mathematical technique. The six extrinsic parameters of a camera are also computed from only one image of the right- angled triangle which sides are known. Relative errors are caused in the experimental results due to the noises in the input image data and the resolution of the digital camera. For each image, the camera parameters relative to the object are computed by using the several triangles in an object. Table 16.2 shows the coordinates of three points of the triangle in the first image frame and ones of their correspondent points in other frames. Table 16.3 expresses the actual data and computational results for the camera motion parameters. Fig. 16.5 and Fig. 16.6 illustrate the relative errors of the computational results.

Table 16.2   Observation Data from the Four Image Frames.

	Frame 1	Frame 2	Frame 3	Frame 4
x_1	26.79	21.78	17.21	18.30
y_1	32.18	31.31	30.42	30.12
x_2	35.02	36.16	31.00	26.67
y_2	30.04	30.50	31.10	31.62
x_3	35.02	36.05	30.61	26.48
y_3	19.79	20.20	20.86	20.80

Table 16.3   Computational Results.

	1ˢᵗ to 2ⁿᵈ		2ⁿᵈ to 3ʳ		3ʳᵈ to 4ᵗʰ	
	True	Computed	True	Computed	True	Computed
A	31.65 cm	32.5597	62.05 cm	63.2020	27.65 cm	28.6705
B	-1.9	-2.0382	0.0	1.2011	0.5	1.0394
C	8.7	9.0836	3.0	3.3602	3.47	3.5601
Dist	32.8789 cm	33.8644	62.1225	63.3027	27.8714	28.9094
α	35°	36.83°	45.43°	47.13°	24.07°	26.61°
β	-1.43°	1.7°	3.0°	4.8°	-3.22°	-1.02°
γ	-32.65°	- 31.94°	11.2°	12.2°	30°	31.3°

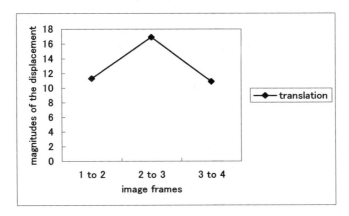

Fig. 16.5   The magnitudes (in millimeters) of the translation error vectors.

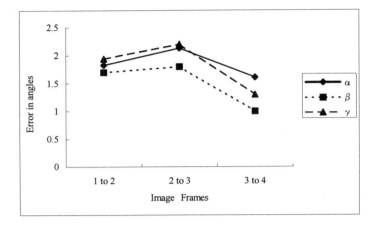

Fig. 16.6   Errors in the computation of the rotation angles.

16.6   Conclusion

In this study, the estimation method of the motion parameters of a moving camera in static scenes is proposed and the effectiveness is demonstrated for the real images. From the image frames, we extract the vertices of a triangle constructed by using any three points of an object whose distances are known, from the image frames. Then the structure of the object relative to the camera CCS can be obtained. By processing these images, the rotation and translation parameters of the camera are determined. The effectiveness of our proposed method is confirmed from the experimental results.

Our approach can be applied in variety of the control works as robot control and navigation problem, autonomous flight control work, movie work and so on. Nowadays, motion control cameras are occupied with the essential roll in movie world. They use motion control cameras for improvising the artificial posture of scene to create the great movie. The accurate camera parameter is important to catch the goal posture. In the next step, we should take into consideration the reconstruction of a 3-D scene from 2-D images based on this approach.

Appendix A.

Position Estimation

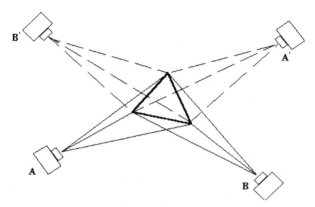

Fig. A.1   Illustration of the Possible Camera Positions.

At least four real roots can be obtained by the fourth order polynomial as shown in Fig.A.1. There may be at least two possible positions for a camera in front of the triangle and two corresponding solutions whose points are behind the triangle. We find the motion parameters of a camera from the images of the rigid object in the same scene. Therefore, two possible positions behind the surface of the triangle can be neglect without lose of generality. The unique solution for the triangle, which gives the accurate camera position, is determined from two possible positions in front of the triangle. As we discussed in Section 1.3, the direction of the surface normal of the triangle would be changed due to the camera motion (see Fig. A.2).

Fig. A. 2 Surface Normal Vector of the Triangle.

The accurate triangle position relative to the camera coordinate system can be determined by detection of the normal direction and viewing direction vector of the triangle surface from Eq.(10), (11) and (13).

References

[1] Haralick, R. M., Lee, C. N, Ottenberg, K. and Nölle, M., "Review and Analysis of Solutions of the Three Point Perspective Pose Estimation Problem," *International Journal of Computer Vision*, Vol. **13**, pp. 331-356, 1994.

[2] Haralick, R. M., " Determining Camera Parameters from the Perspective Projection of a Rectangle", *Pattern Recognition*, Vol. **22**, pp. 225-230, 1989.

[3] Liu, Y. C. and Huang, T. S., " Determination of the Camera Location from 2--D to 3--D Line and Point Correspondences", *IEEE Trans. Pattern Analysis and Machine Intelligence*, Vol.**12** (1), pp. 28-37, Jan., 1990.

[4] Zhang, Z., " Estimating Motion and Structure from Correspondences of Line Segments between Two Perspective Images", *IEEE Trans. Pattern Analysis and Machine Intelligence*, Vol.**17** (12), pp. 1129-1139, Dec., 1995.

[5] Adiv, G., " Determining Three Dimensional Motion and Structure from Optimal Flow Generated by Several Moving Objects", *IEEE Trans. Pattern Analysis and Machine Intelligence*, Vol. **7** (4), pp. 384-401, July., 1985.

[6] Hong, Z. Q., and Yang, J-Y, " An Algorithm for Camera Calibration using a Three- dimensional Reference Point", *Pattern Recognition*, Vol. **26** (12), pp. 1655-1660, 1993.

[7] Burger, W., and Bhanu, B., "Estimating 3-D Egomotion from Perspective Image Sequences", *IEEE Trans. Pattern Analysis and Machine Intelligence*, Vol.**12** (11), pp. 1040-1058, Nov., 1990.

[8] Tsai, R. Y., "A versatile camera calibration technique for high-accuracy 3D machine vision metrology using off-the sheft camears and lenses", *IEEE journal of Robotics and Automation*, RA-**3** (4), pp. 323-344, Aug., 1987.

[9] Holt, R.J. and Netravali, A. N., "Number of the Solutions for the Motion and Structure from the Multiple Frame Correspondence," *International Journal of Computer Vision*, Vol. **23** (1), pp. 5-15, Dec., 1997.

[10]Fu, K.b S., Gonzalez, R. C. and Lee, C. S. G., " ROBOTICS: Control, Sensing, Vision and Intelligence," *McGraw-Hill Inc.*, 1987.

[11]Sein, M. M. and Hama, H., "Determination of the Motion Parameters of a Moving Camera from the Perspective Projection of a Triangle" *Proc. of the 5th Int. Conf. on the Soft Computing and Information/ Intelligent Systems*, pp. 983-986, IIZUKA'98 , Fukuoka, Japan , 1998.

[12]Andrews, H. C., "Computer Techniques in Image Processing," Academic Press, New York, 1970.

[13]Rosenfeld, A and Kak, A. C., "Picture Processing by Computer," New York, 1969.

[14]Rosenfeld, A., "Digital Picture Processing," Second Edition , Vol. **2**, Academic Press INC., San Diego, California, 1982.

About the Authors

Ali Afzalian
BSc (Eng), MSc, PhD, MIEEE

Department of Electrical Engineering
Power & Water Institute of Technology
P.O. Box 16765-1719, Tehran, Iran

E-mail address: afzalian@excite.com
Tel.: +98 (021) 733 9441
Fax: +98 (021) 733 9425
URL: http://www.acse.shef.ac.uk/~afzalian/

Ali A Afzalian received his BSc and MSc in Electrical Engineering from the University of Tehran, Iran in 1988 and 1991 respectively and his PhD from Department of Automatic Control and Systems Engineering, University of Sheffield in 1998. He has been a lecturer in the Department of Control Systems at the Power and Water Institute of Technology (PWIT), Tehran since 1990. His research interests include fuzzy logic, neural networks, neurofuzzy systems, genetic algorithms, and power systems control.

386

De Carli Alessandro

Department of Computer and System Science
University of Rome, La Sapienza
Via Eudossiana 18 - 00184 Roma, Italy

E-mail : adecarli@dis.uniroma1.it
Phone : ++39 6 44585357
Fax : ++39 6 44585367

De Carli Alessandro, born in Rome, Italy, 1937.
1961 Degree in Electrical Engineering at "La Sapienza" University of Rome.
1967 Assistant Professor of Automatic Control at "La Sapienza" University of Rome.
1969 Associate Professor of Automatic Control at "La Sapienza" University of Rome.
1975 Full Professor of Automatic Control at University of Pisa.
1984 Full Professor of Control System Technology at "La Sapienza" University of Rome.
Co-ordinator of the IFAC Working Group on "Motion Control".
Chairman of the NOC in IFAC Symposium on "Low Cost Automation".
Chairman of the IPC in IFAC Workshop on "Motion Control for Intelligent Automation", 1992.
Associate Editor of Control Engineering Practice IFAC Journal.
Author of more than 80 papers, the majority on International Journals or Proceedings.
Fields of Interest: Advanced Control Strategy design for Power Electronics, Motion Control for Industrial Applications and Intelligent Control for Industrial Plants.

Zeungnam Bien

Department of Electrical Engineering
Faculty of Control Engineering
Korea Advanced Institute of Science & Technology
373-1 Kusong-dong, Yusong-gu, Taejon 373-1, Korea

E-mail : zbien@ee.kaist.ac.kr
Phone : +82-42-869-3419
Fax   : +82-42-869-8751
URL   : http://ctrgate.kaist.ac.kr/~zbien/

Zeungnam Bien received the B.S. degree in electronics engineering from Seoul National University, Seoul, Korea, in 1969 and the M.S. and Ph.D. degrees in electrical engineering from the University of Iowa, Iowa City, Iowa, U.S.A., in 1972 and 1975, respectively.

During 1976-1977 academic year, he taught as assistant professor at the Department of Electrical Engineering, University of Iowa. Then Dr. Bien joined Korea Advanced Institute of Science and Technology, Summer, 1977, and is now Professor of Control Engineering at the Department of Electrical Engineering, KAIST. He also worked as a visiting faculty at the University of Iowa during his 1981-1982 sabbatical year, as a visiting researcher at CASE Center of Syracuse University, New York for 6 months since September, 1987, and as a visiting professor at Department of Control Engineering, Tokyo Institute of Technology in Spring, 1988. Dr. Bien was the president of the Korea Fuzzy Logic and Intelligent Systems Society during 1990-1995 and the general chair of IFSA World Congress 1993. He serves as Vice President for IFSA, and General Chair for FUZZ-IEEE99.

His current research interests include intelligent control methods with emphasis on fuzzy logic systems, service robotics and large-scale industrial control systems.

388

Sung-Bae Cho

Department of Computer Science
Yonsei University
134 Shinchon-dong, Sudaemoon-ku
Seoul 120-749, Korea

E-mail : sbcho@csai.yonsei.ac.kr
Phone : +82-2-2123-2720
Fax : +82-2-365-2579
URL : http://sclab.yonsei.ac.kr/

Sung-Bae Cho received the B.S. degree in computer science from Yonsei University, Seoul, Korea, in 1988 and the M.S. and Ph.D. degrees in computer science from KAIST (Korea Advanced Institute of Science and Technology), Taejeon, Korea, in 1990 and 1993, respectively.

He worked as a Member of the Research Staff at the Center for Artificial Intelligence Research at KAIST from 1991 to 1993. He was an Invited Researcher of Human Information Processing Research Laboratories at ATR (Advanced Telecommunications Research) Institute, Kyoto, Japan from 1993 to 1995, and a Visiting Scholar at University of New South Wales, Canberra, Australia in 1998. Since 1995, he has been an Associate Professor in the Department of Computer Science, Yonsei University. His research interests include neural networks, pattern recognition, intelligent man-machine interfaces, evolutionary computation, and artificial life.

Dr. Cho was awarded outstanding paper prizes from the IEEE Korea Section in 1989 and 1992, and another one from the Korea Information Science Society in 1990. He was also the recipient of the Richard E. Merwin prize from the IEEE Computer Society in 1993. He was listed in Who's Who in Pattern Recognition from the International Association for Pattern Recognition in 1994, and received the best paper awards at International Conference on Soft Computing in 1996 and 1998. Also, he received the best paper award at World Automation Congress in 1998, and listed in Marquis Who's Who in Science and Engineering in 2000. He is a Member of the Korea Information Science Society, INNS, the IEEE Computer Society, and the IEEE Systems, Man, and Cybernetics Society.

Hee Tae Chung

Department of Electronic Engineering
Pusan University of Foreign Studies
55-1 Uam-dong, Nam-ku, Pusan, 608-738
South Korea

E-mail   : htchung@taejo.pufs.ac.kr
Phone   : +82-51-640-3425
Fax   : +82-51-645-4525
URL   : http://www.pufs.ac.kr/

Hee Tae Chung received the B.S., M.S., and Ph. D. degrees all in electronic engineering from the Kyungpook National University, Taegu, Korea, in 1986, 1988, and 1996, respectively. Between 1996 and 1997, he worked as a Patent Examiner at the Korean Industrial Property Office. Currently, he is an Assistant Professor at the Department of Electronic Engineering, Pusan University of Foreign Studies, Pusan, Korea since 1997.

His current research interests include the application of intelligent control to robot systems, adaptive control and neural networks.

390

Agustinus Drijarkara

School of Electrical, Computer
and Telecommunications Engineering,
University of Wollongong,
Northfields Ave.,
Wollongong,
NSW 2522,
Australia

E-mail : Propbeau@rocketmail.com
Phone : +61 2 42213411
Fax : +61 2 42213236
URL: http://www.elec.uow.edu.au/people/postgraduate/apd04

Agustinus Drijarkara was born in Indonesia, 7 December 1971. Hefinished his primary and secondary education in Indonesia, then studied for a Bachelor of Engineering in the University of Wollongong, Australia. He graduated in 1995 with Honours. In 1997, he commenced an Honours Master of Engineering at the same university with a thesis about fuzzy detection of microcalcifications in mammograms. Currently he is a staff member at the Laboratory of Dimensional Metrology in the Indonesian Institute of Sciences. His research interest is in image processing and dimensional metrology.

Evgueniy Entchev

Advanced Combustion Technologies Laboratory
CANMET Energy Technology Centre
Natural Resources Canada
1 Haanel Dr., Nepean, K1A 1M1 Canada

E-mail : eentchev@nrcan.gc.ca
Phone : +613-992-2516
Fax : +613-9992-9335
URL : http://nrcan.gc.ca/

Evgueniy Entchev received his B. Eng. degree in thermal and nuclear engineering (1977) and his M. Sc. Degree in applied mathematics (1979) from the Technical University of Sofia, Bulgaria. In 1983, the same institution awarded him with a Ph.D. degree for his studies on stochastic analysis, modeling and optimization of the processes of large energy systems.

From 1983 to 1986, he worked as a Research Scientist in Sofia's Problem Research Laboratory on the " New utilization technologies for low-calorific value fuels". Between 1986 and 1989, Dr. Entchev was employed as a Research Scientist with the Thermal and Nuclear Energy Laboratory. From 1983 to 1989 he also worked as a part-time Assistant Professor and Lecturer in the Faculty of Energy. In 1990, Dr. Entchev joined the Thermal and Nuclear Energy Department of the Technical University of Sofia and received a full professorship." As of 1992, he has been employed by the Energy Research Laboratory and later the Canmet Energy Technology Centre as a Research Scientist. Dr. Entchev is also certified by the International Atomic Energy Agency as a specialist in Probabilistic Safety Assessment of Nuclear Power Plant Operation. His main research interests lie in the implementation of fuzzy logic and neural networks in energy systems and in the employment of different techniques to optimize performance of conventional and nuclear energy systems in order to lower the greenhouse gas emissions and increase efficiency. Furthermore, Dr. Entchev has been involved in the risk and probabilistic safety assessment of several nuclear power plants operating with WWER and BWR reactors. His most recent research deals with the development of a solid-oxide fuel cell stationary co-generation energy system.

In his spare time, Dr. Entchev enjoys playing tennis, skiing and swimming; however, he is also fond of art, classical music and, naturally, science fiction literature.

Pan Fu

Systems Engineering Faculty
Southampton Institute
East Park Terrace
Southampton SO14 OYN
U.K.

E-mail: Pan_fu@hotmail.com
Phone: +44 1703 319943

Pan Fu received the B. Eng. degree in mechanical engineering in 1982 and M. Eng. degree in instrumentation in 1987 from Chongqing University in China. He is now studying for his Ph.D. degree in Southampton Institute in U.K.
Pan Fu worked as a design engineer in a big plant for 2 years. He was a lecture in Chongqing university for 8 years. He had successfully accomplished over 10 research projects and published over 20 papers.
His main research interest lies on signal collecting and processing, precision measurement techniques, pattern recognition and artificial intelligence.

Takeshi Furuhashi

Department of Information & Electronics
Nagoya University
Furo-cho Chikusa-ku Nagoya 464-8603, Japan

E-mail : furuhashi@nuee.nagoya-u.ac.jp
Phone : +81-52-789-2792
Fax : +81-52-789-3166
URL : http://www.bioele.nuee.nagoya-u.ac.jp/member/furuhashi/

Takeshi Furuhashi received the BE, ME and Ph.D. degrees in Electrical Engineering from Nagoya University, Japan, in 1980, 1982 and 1985, respectively.

He was with Toshiba Corporation from 1985-1988. From 1988-1990, he was with the Department of Electrical Engineering of Nagoya University as an Assistant Professor.

From 1990-1994, he was with the Department of Electronic-Mechanical Engineering of Nagoya University as an Associate Professor. Since June 1994, he has been An Associate Professor of the department of Information & Electronics of Nagoya University. His current research interests are in soft computing.

Hiromitsu Hama

Department of Information & Communication Engineering
Faculty of Engineering
Osaka City University
3-3-138 Sugimoto, Sumiyosi-ku, Osaka 558-8585, Japan.

E-mail : hama@info.eng.osaka-cu.ac.jp
Phone : +81-6-6605-2772
Fax : +81-6-6605-2772
URL : http://www.info.eng.osaka-cu.ac.jp

Hiromitsu Hama received the B.E., M.E and Dr. Eng. degrees in Electrical Engineering from Osaka University, Japan, in 1968, 1970 and 1983, respectively. He was with Department of Electrical Engineering, Osaka City University in 1971. He is currently professor of Department of Information and Communication Engineering at Osaka City University. His research interests are in the areas of picture processing and understanding, reconstruction of 3-dimensional scene, computer vision, cognitive science, medical image processing, pattern recognition, learning algorithm and so on. He is a member of IEEE (Institute of Electrical and Electronics Engineers, Inc.), SPIE (Society of Photo-Optical Instrumentation Engineers), IEICE (Institute of Electronics, Information and Communication Engineers), IIITE (Institute of Image Information and Television Engineers) and IPSJ (Image Processing Society of Japan) and so on.

Junichi Hino

Department of Mechanical Engineering
Faculty of Engineering
The University of Tokushima
Minami-josanjima 2-1, Tokushima 770-8506
Japan

E-mail :   hino@me.tokushima-u.ac.jp
Pnone :   +81-88-656-7384
Fax   :   +81-88-656-9082

Junichi Hino was born in Tokushima, Japan, in 1959. He received MS degree in mechanical engineering from the University of Tokushima and Ph.D. in mechanical engineering from Tokyo Institute of Technology in 1984 and 1988, respectively. In 1984, he joined the University of Tokushima. From 1984 to 1989 he was a research assistant and from 1989 to 1994 he was a lecturer in the Department of Mechanical Engineering. His current interests are intelligent control, multi-body dynamics and expert system for end milling.

Atsushi Imamoto

Department of Computer Engineering
Faculty of Engineering
Kyushu Institute of Technology
Tobata, Kitakyushu, Fukuoka, Japan

E-mail : aimamoto@math.comp.kyutech.ac.jp
Phone : +81-93-884-3258
Fax   : +81-93-884-3258

Atsushi Imamoto graduated in the Department of Information and Computer Sciences at Kumamoto National College of Technology in 1996 and then he joined the Department of Computer Engineering, Faculty of Engineering, Kyushu Institute of Technology, Tobata, Japan. He received the B. Eng. degree from this department in 1998. He is now a graduate student in this department.

He is interested in logic programming and uncertain information. He is trying to add soft computing aspects to logic programs. He is also trying to apply this new framework to the diagnosis problems.

Jun Oh Jang

Department of Computer Control Engineering
Uiduk University
Kyungju, Kyungpook, 780-713
South Korea

E-mail   : jojang@mail.uiduk.ac.kr
Phone   : +82-0561-760-1624
Fax   : +82-0561-760-1506
URL   : http://www.uiduk.ac.kr/

Jun Oh Jang received the B.S., M.S., and Ph. D. degrees all in electronic engineering from the Kyungpook National University, Taegu, Korea, in 1988, 1992, and 1998, respectively. He is currently a faculty at Department of Computer Control Engineering, Uiduk University, Kyungju, Korea.

His current research interests include intelligent control using neural networks, fuzzy logic, and genetic algorithm, and applications of these tools to real systems.

Hiroaki Kobayashi

Hokkaido Refinery
Idemitsu Kosan Co., Ltd.
25-1, Masago-cho Tomakomai, Hokkaido, Japan

E-mail : kobahiro@sie.idemitsu.co.jp
Phone : +81-144--0122
Fax   : +81-144-0127
URL   : http://www.idemitsu.co.jp/

Since 1974, Hiroaki Kobayashi has worked for Idemitsu Kosan Co., Ltd., Japan, is now a system engineering staff of Refining Section in Idemitsu Hokkaido Refinery. He worked in the plant operation section, and in the plant construction and coordination section.

He has three years of development experience of advanced automation systems using fuzzy logic, and his current research interests includes applications of expert system, neural networks and fuzzy logic of a petroleum field.

Derek A. Linkens
BSc, MSc, PhD, DSc, FIEE, FInstMC

Department of Automatic Control and
Systems Engineering,
University of Sheffield,
Mappin Street, Sheffield S1 3JD, UK

E-mail address: d.linkens@shef.ac.uk
Tel.: +44 (0114) 2225133
Fax : +44 (0114) 2225614
URL: http://www.shef.ac.uk/~acse/staff/d.a.linkens/

Derek Arthur Linkens received a BSc (Eng.) degree in Electrical Engineering from Imperial College, London, MSc in Systems Engineering from the University of Surrey, PhD from the University of Sheffield and DSc from the University of London.

After working in underwater weapon and aerospace technology he joined the University of Sheffield in 1969. He has been Head of the Department of Automatic Control and Systems Engineering, and Dean of the Faculty of Engineering. He is currently Research Professor in the area of intelligent system engineering relating to both biomedical and industrial engineering problems. He is also the Director of the Institute for Microstructural and Mechanical Process Engineering: The University of Sheffield (IMMPETUS).

He has published over 300 refereed papers and has been Author and Editor of 7 books. He is a Fellow of the IEE and the Inst. MC of which he was president in 1993.

400

Shuta Murakami

Department of Computer Science
Faculty of Engineering
Kyushu Institute of Technology
1-1 Sensui-cho, Tobata-ku
Kitakyushu-shi, Japan 804

E-mail   : murakami@comp.kyutech.ac.jp
Phone   : +81-3-884-3244
Fax   : +81-3-884-3244

Shuta Murakami received the B.E. degree in Control Engineering from Kyushu Institute of Technology, Kitakyushu, in 1964, and the M.E. (1966) and Dr. of Engineering (1969) in Control Engineering from Tokyo Institute of Technology, Tokyo, Japan. He joined the Department of Control Engineering at KIT in 1969 as a Lecturer in Control, and has been in the Computer Engineering course since 1984 as a Professor in Control Systems. His research work has been focused on Fuzzy Control, Fuzzy Modeling and Fuzzy Decision-Making. He is a current member of the SICE, the Operations Research Society of Japan, and the International Fuzzy Systems Association.

Fazel Naghdy

School of Electrical, Computer
and Telecommunications Engineering,
University of Wollongong,
Northfields Ave.,
Wollongong,
NSW 2522,
Australia

E-mail : f.naghdy@uow.edu.au
Phone : +61 2 42213398
Fax : +61 2 42213236
URL : http://www.elec.uow.edu.au/people/

Fazel Naghdy received his first degree from Tehran University in 1976. He then received an MSc from the Postgraduate School of Control Engineering, University of Bradford, England, in 1980 and received his PhD from the same University in 1982. Currently he is an Associate Professor at the University of Wollongong, School of Electrical, Computer & Telecommunication Engineering.

Fazel Naghdy has been heavily involved in professional activities. He is on the Editorial Board of the Journal of Control Engineering Practice published by International Federation of Automatic Control (IFAC), a member of International Computer Science Conventions (ICSC) Academic Advisory Board, and has served on a large number of International scientific committee of various international conferences. He is also a member of IEE Regional Committee for NSW.

402

Golshah Naghdy

School of Electrical, Computer
and Telecommunications Engineering,
University of Wollongong,
Northfields Ave.,
Wollongong,
NSW 2522,
Australia

E-mail : g.naghdy@uow.edu.au
Phone : +61 2 42213411
Fax : +61 2 42213236
URL : http://www.elec.uow.edu.au/people/

Golshah Naghdy is a Senior Lecturer at the Department of Electrical and Computer Engineering, University of Wollongong, Australia. She was born in Iran and received B.Sc. degree in Electrical and Electronic Engineering from Aryamehr University of Technology in Tehran in 1977. She received MPhil in Control Engineering from Bradford University and PhD in Electronic Engineering from Portsmouth University, England, in 1982 and 1986, respectively. She was a Senior Lecturer at Portsmouth University before emigrating to Australia in 1989. Her major research interest is in biological and machine vision and medical image processing.

Since 1989 Golshah has been researching in the area of biological and machine vision in particular a generic vision system for natural texture classification. One of the major application of such system would be in medical image processing. In this context, she has worked in three areas of medical image processing; lossless image coding for tele-medicine or archiving, medical image enhancement, and mammogram image analysis for clinical decision support systems.

Shigeru Nakashima

Department of Control Engineering & Science
Faculty of Computer Science & Systems Engineering
Kyushu Institute of Technology
680-4 Kawazu, Iizuka, Fukuoka 820-8502, Japan

E-mail : shige@tsuge98.ces.kyutech.ac.jp
Phone   : +81-948-29-7712
Fax   : +81-948-29-7742
URL   : http://tsugenoki.ces.kyutech.ac.jp/

Shigeru Nakashima received the B.E. and M.E. degrees in control engineering and science from Kyushu Institute of Technology in 1997 and 1999, respectively. He presently works at Nippon Telegraph and Telephone Corporation. His current research interests include signal processing and pattern recognition.

404

Akimichi Okuma

Department of Computer Engineering
Faculty of Engineering
Kyushu Institute of technology
Tobata, Kitakyushu, Fukuoka, Japan

E-mail : okuma@comp.kyutech.ac.jp
Phone : +81-93-884-3252
Fax   : +81-93-884-3252

Akimichi Okuma received the B. Sci. degree in mathematics in 1964 from Kyushu University, Fukuoka, Japan and the M. Sci. degree in mathematics in 1966 from Kyushu University. He received the Ph.D. in mathematics for his studies on statistical decision theories in 1975 from Kyushu University.

From 1966 to 1975, he was an Assistant at department of mathematics, Kyushu University. In April 1975 he was an Assistant Professor at Kyushu Institute of Technology (KIT), Tobata, Japan and was an Associate Professor in December 1975. He received a full professorship in January 1983. He is now a professor of Department of Computer Engineering in KIT, Tobata.

His main research interest lies on mathematical statistics based on incomplete data, theoretical analysis of dichotomous data sequences, and incomplete information system.

James F. Peters

Department of Electrical & Computer Engineering
University of Manitoba
ENGR 504, Winnipeg, MB R3T5V6 Canada

E-mail   : jfpeters@ee.umanitoba.ca
Phone   : +1-204-474-7419
Fax   : +1-204-261-4639

James F. Peters received the M.Sc. degree in 1967 and the Ph.D. degree in 1991. He is an Associate Professor (Computer Engineering) in the Department of Electrical and Computer Engineering, University of Manitoba, Winnipeg, Canada. He has published numerous papers on computational intelligence, intelligent system modeling, granular computing, and applications of CI in control systems and in software engineering. He serves as Associate Editor of Control Engineering Practice, special issue Editor the International Journal of Intelligent Systems and Fundamenta Informatica. He is also an IEEE Distinguished Lecturer in Formal Methods in System Design. His current research interest is in system identification and intelligent system modeling using granular computing techniques.

Petar B. Petrović

Department for Production Engineering and
Computer Integrated Manufacturing
Faculty of Mechanical Engineering
Belgrade University
27 marta 80, 11000 Belgrade, Yugoslavia

E-mail : petar@cent.mas.bg.ac.yu
Phone : 381-11-3370-341
Fax : 381-11-3370-364

Petar B. Petrović was born in Belgrade, Yugoslavia, in 1958. He graduated with the degree of B. Eng. in Mechanical Engineering in 1982 at the University of Belgrade and received the M. Eng. degree in Mechanical Engineering in 1989 at the University of Belgrade. He was honored Ph.D. in Mechanical Engineering, with thesis "Adaptive control of redundant manipulating robots in part mating process" in 1996 at the University of Belgrade.

During 1982-1984, as a young engineer, he worked for the firm "Ivo Lola Ribar", and was involved in production of numerically controlled machine tools and industrial robots. After two years of working in a design department, he became a Research Assistant at the University of Belgrade and was involved in the development of flexible assembly systems and industrial robots. During the period of 1984-1994 he was involved in many projects supported by the industry and the government. At the same time, he was lecturing in the subject of Flexible automation at the Faculty of Mechanical Engineering, University of Belgrade. In 1994 he was involved in the long-term project "Intelligent Manufacturing Systems" which covered the field of AI approaches and Soft Computing in designing flexible production systems. From 1998 he became an Associate Professor at the University of Belgrade, lecturing in the subject of Cybernetics and Designing Manufacturing Systems. In 1999 he was elected as corresponding member of CIRP - International Institution for Production Engineering Research, (Paris).

His main research interest is in a design of Flexible Assembly Systems, design and control of Industrial Robots and Fuzzy Dynamic Formal Structures and its application in control of nonlinear dynamical systems.

He likes carpentry and artwork in a wood. He plays a piano and a guitar. He is married and has to sons. His wife is a doctor in Medicine and is of a great help to him to understand the basic principles of bio-systems and human intelligence.

Sheela Ramanna

Department of Electrical & Computer Engineering
University of Manitoba
ENGR 504, Winnipeg, MB R3T5V6 Canada

E-mail   : ramanna@ee.umanitoba.ca
Phone   : +1-204-474-7419
Fax   : +1-204-261-4639

Sheela Ramanna received the M.Sc. degree in 1983 and the Ph.D. degree in 1991. She is an Associate Professor   (Computer Science) and Head of Department of Business Computing, University of Winnipeg, Manitoba, Canada, and an Adjunct Professor (Computer Engineering) in the Department of Electrical and Computer Engineering, University of Manitoba, Winnipeg, Canada. She has published numerous papers on intelligent system modeling, granular computing, multicriteria decision-making, application of fuzzy integration, real-time systems, integrity of databases, and software engineering. Her current research interest is in the theory and applications of rough and fuzzy sets in software engineering and control systems.

408

Jesús M. Fernández Salido

Yaskawa Electric Corporation
Development Section
Inverter Plan
2-13-1 Nishimiyaichi, Yukuhashi City
Fukuoka 824-8511 Japan

E-mail : fernan@yaskawa.co.jp
Phone : +81-9302-3-4800
Fax   : +81-9302-3-3010

Jesús M. Fernández Salido was born in 1969 in Jerez de la Frontera (Spain). In 1994, he received the degree of Industrial Engineer at the University of Valladolid, taking the specialization on Control Engineering and Electronics. In 1995 he came to Japan with a scholarship from the Japanese Ministry of Education and received the Master of Engineering degree in 1998 from Kyushu Institute of Technology. Currently, he is enrolled at the Inverter Development Section of Yaskawa Electric Corporation, while at the same time working towards his Ph. D. degree at Kyushu Institute of Technology. His research interests include Fuzzy Systems, Automatic Diagnosis Systems and Power Electronics.

Hiroshi Sakai

Department of Computer Engineering
Faculty of Engineering
Kyushu Institute of Technology
Tobata, Kitakyushu, Fukuoka, Japan

E-mail : sakai@comp.kyutech.ac.jp
Phone : +81-93-884-3258
Fax   : +81-93-884-3258
URL   : http://math.comp.kyutech.ac.jp/~sakai

Hiroshi Sakai is an Associate Professor at Department of Computer Engineering, Fuculty of Engineering, Kyushu Institute of Technology, Tobata, Japan. He received his B.Sci., M.Sci. and Dr.Sci. in the field of applied mathematics and computer science from Kyushu University, Japan in 1982, 1984 and 1988, respectively.

From 1987 to 1989, he served as a Research Assistant in Information Science Center at Kyushu Institute of Technology. He joined the Faculty of Engineering as an Assistant Professor in April 1989. In 1990, he studied at Duke University in USA for 10 months as a Visiting Researcher supported by the Japanese Ministry of Education. From 1994, he has been an Associate Professor.

He is interested in incomplete information system, logic programming, knowledge-based system and rough sets theory.

Myint Myint Sein

Department of Information & Communication Engineering
Faculty of Engineering
Osaka City University
3-3-138 Sugimoto, Sumiyosi-ku, Osaka 558-8585, Japan.

E-mail   : sein@sys.info.eng.osaka-cu.ac.jp
Phone   : +81-6-6605-2773
Fax   : +81-6-6605-2773
URL   : http://www.sys.info.eng.osaka-cu.ac.jp

Myint Myint Sein received the B.Sc and M.Sc degree in Applied Mathematics from Yangon University, Myanmar, in 1980 and 1983, respectively. From 1983 to 1995 she joined Yangon University, Myanmar as a Lecturer. She is presently working for her doctoral degree in electrical engineering in the Graduate School of Science, Osaka City University, Japan. Her research interests are in the areas of motion analysis, image processing, reconstruction of 3-dimensional scene and computer vision. She is a member of IEEE (Institute of Electrical and Electronics Engineers, Inc.) and IEICE (Institute of Electronics, Information and Communication Engineers).

Seung C. Shin

Department of Electrical Engineering
Faculty of Control Engineering
Korea Advanced Institute of Science & Technology
373-1 Kusong-dong, Yusong-gu, Taejon 373-1, Korea

E-mail   : ssc@ctrsys.kaist.ac.kr
Phone   : +82-42-869-5419
Fax   : +82-42-869-8751
URL   : http://ctrgate.kaist.ac.kr/~ssc/

Seung C. Shin received the B.S. degree in electronics engineering from Kyung-Pook National University, Taegu, Korea, in 1992 and the M.S. degree in electrical engineering from Korea Advanced Institute of Science & Technology (KAIST), Teajon, Korea, in 1995. He is currently a doctoral candidate in the Department of Electrical Engineering at the KAIST, Teajon, Korea.

His current research interests include adaptive and learning systems, neural networks and their application to predictive control problems.

412

Pisani Sonia

Department of Computer Sciences Engineering at
University of Rome "La Sapienza",
Via Eudossiana 18, 00184 Rome, Italy

E-mail : aspisani@tin.it ; Sonia.Pisani@Formula.it
Phone : ++39 6 44585357
Fax : ++39 6 44585367

Pisani Sonia, Born in Rome, Italy, 1972.
1997 Degree in Computer Sciences Engineering at "La Sapienza" University of Rome.

Chuanxin   Su

Room 416, Mechanical Dynamics Lab
Department of Mechanical Engineering
Faculty of Engineering
The University of Tokushima
Minami-josanjima 2-1, Tokushima 770-8506
Japan

E-mail :   resk360@me.tokushima-u.ac.jp
Phone :   +81-88-656-7384, 7385
Fax   :   +81-88-656-9082

Chuanxin   Su graduated from Department of Precision Instrumentation, Harbin Institute of Technology, China in 1982, and received M. Eng. from the same institute in 1985. And in January,1996, he was admitted into Department of Mechanical Engineering, The University of Tokushima, Japan as a research student, and is a doctoral student in the same department since October, 1996. His current main research fields are stability of milling process, and the design of active suspension systems of ground vehicles.

414

Tetsuji Tani

System Technology Department Center
Manufacturing Dept.
Idemitsu Kosan Co., Ltd.
26 Anesaki-kaigan, Ichihara, Chiba 299-0107, Japan

E-mail : ttani@sie.idemitsu.co.jp
Phone : +81-436-61-7895
Fax : +81-436-61-7836
URL : http://www.idemitsu.co.jp/

Tetsuji Tani received the B.S. degree in 1974, the M.S. degree in 1976 in Industrial Engineering from Hiroshima University.

He received the Licensed Consulting Engineer (PE) in Information Technology in 1993 from Science and Technology Agency (STA) and the Dr. of Engineering degree in 1995 in System Engineering from Osaka University, Japan.

He has worked for Idemitsu Kosan Co., Ltd. since 1976 and is now a chief consulting engineer of System Technology Development Center, Manufacturing Department. His research interests include applications of soft computing to petroleum plants, especially nonlinear control systems.

Eiji Uchino

Department of Physics, Biology, and Informatics
Faculty of Science
Yamaguchi University
1677-1 Yoshida, Yamaguchi 753-8512, Japan

E-mail : uchino@sci.yamaguchi-u.ac.jp
Phone   : +81-83-933-5699
Fax   : +81-83-933-5768
URL   : http://gw.ic.sci.yamaguchi-u.ac.jp/

Eiji Uchino received the Dr. Eng. degree in systems engineering from Hiroshima University in 1988. He is presently a Professor of the Department of Physics, Biology, and Informatics at Yamaguchi University. He was a Visiting Professor at the Aachen Institute of Technology, Germany, 1994, and the University of Bristol, UK, 1996. His research interests include adaptive system modeling, intelligent signal and image processing, human brain based information processing system. Professor Uchino is the author of more than 120 published papers.

416

Takeshi Yamakawa

Department of Control Engineering & Science
Faculty of Computer Science & Systems Engineering
Kyushu Institute of Technology
680-4 Kawazu, Iizuka, Fukuoka 820-8502, Japan

E-mail : yamakawa@ces.kyutech.ac.jp
Phone : +81-948-29-7712
Fax   : +81-948-29-7742
URL   : http://tsugenoki.ces.kyutech.ac.jp/

Takeshi Yamakawa received his Dr. Eng. degree in electrochemistry from Tohoku University. He is a Professor of the Department of Control Engineering and Science, Kyushu Institute of Technology. He is also the Chairman of a Japanese foundation, Fuzzy Logic Systems Institute (FLSI), which was established by him for aiming at international collaboration on soft computing. He received Grigore Moisil Gold Medal in 1994 for his contribution to Engineering Application of Fuzzy Systems. He acted as Organizing/Program Committee members for over 60 international conferences and serves as associate editors of over 10 international journals in the field of soft computing.

Toshio   Yoshimura

Department of Mechanical Engineering
Faculty of Engineering
The University of Tokushima
Minami-josanjima 2-1, Tokushima 770-8506
Japan

E-mail :   yosimura@me.tokushima-u.ac.jp
Phone :   +81-88-656-7382
Fax   :   +81-88-656-9082

Toshio   Yoshimura graduated from Department of Mechanical Engineering, The University of Tokushima in 1963, and received Ph.D. from Kyoto University in 1974. He became Assistant Professor, Associate Professor and Professor of Department of Mechanical Engineering, The University of Tokushima in 1970, 1973 and 1982, respectively. He received Award for outstanding achievements of his technical papers from Japan Society of Engineers in 1973. Now he is interested in the design of active suspension systems of ground vehicles, and the application of fuzzy and sliding mode control theories to mechanical systems.

Keyword Index